REDISCOVERING THE WISDOM OF THE CORINTHIANS

Rediscovering the Wisdom of the Corinthians

Paul, Stoicism, and Spiritual Hierarchy

Timothy A. Brookins

William B. Eerdmans Publishing Company
Grand Rapids, Michigan

Wm. B. Eerdmans Publishing Co.
4035 Park East Court SE, Grand Rapids, Michigan 49546
www.eerdmans.com

© 2024 Timothy A. Brookins
All rights reserved
Published 2024

Book design by Lydia Hall

Printed in the United States of America

30 29 28 27 26 25 24   1 2 3 4 5 6 7

ISBN 978-0-8028-8323-0

Library of Congress Cataloging-in-Publication Data

A catalog record for this book is available from the Library of Congress.

To Bruce Longenecker,
Doktorvater and exemplar

Contents

Acknowledgments   ix

List of Abbreviations   xi

I   Rediscovering the Wisdom of the Corinthians

1. 1 Corinthians 1–4 in Modern Scholarship   3
2. The Problems of Definition and Comparison   27

II   Reading 1 Corinthians 1–4

3. 1 Corinthians 1:17b–31: One λόγος against Another   51
4. 1 Corinthians 2:1–5: Proclaiming Christ Crucified   83
5. 1 Corinthians 2:6–16: A Spiritual σοφία   104
6. 1 Corinthians 3:1–4:5: The Apostles and the σοφία of God   130
7. 1 Corinthians 4:6–13: The Apostles and the Corinthian σοφοί   162
8. 1 Corinthians 4:14–21: Paul as Founder and Teacher   189
9. The Sub-Stoic Wisdom of the Corinthians   206

III Reconstructing the Occasion

10. 1 Corinthians 1:10–17a:
    The Paul Faction as Philosophical School   239
11. Philosophy in the Roman Empire and Roman Corinth   271
12. Church Prosopography and the Sub-Stoic School in Corinth   290

Conclusion   307

Bibliography   313

Index of Authors   333

Index of Subjects   337

Index of Scripture and Other Ancient Sources   341

Acknowledgments

I have been thinking seriously about the "wisdom of the Corinthians" in 1 Corinthians 1–4 since my graduate studies at Baylor University in the spring of 2009. The present book is a sequel to my dissertation written for Baylor's doctoral program, published with Cambridge University Press in 2014 as *Corinthian Wisdom, Stoic Philosophy, and the Ancient Economy*. My thinking has changed on some points and I here interpret some passages differently. Above all this book offers a much more technical, focused, and fully elaborated thesis about the Corinthians' wisdom and the nature of the divisions that occupy Paul's discussion in these chapters. But the description of the Corinthians' wisdom remains essentially the same.

The list of people who contributed in some way to this finished product would be too long to include, for this project is in some ways the culmination of a course of life that began long before I knew where it was headed. Providence brought together in graduate school my love of the Bible and my love of classics, both of which began in my youth. Countless people have influenced me along the way, and I believe I have been sustained along this long path, as the apostle Paul says, "by the prayers of many."

A good portion of this book was written in the spring of 2021 during my sabbatical at Houston Christian University, for which I am grateful. I benefited much in dialoguing with students about 1 Corinthians 1–4 in my Greek exegetical course in spring 2022, as I have also with my colleagues Ben Blackwell, Chris Kugler, Jason Maston, and Paul Sloan at HCU. I owe special thanks to several people who read portions of the proposal or manuscript and offered helpful feedback, including Joseph Dodson, Mark Reasoner, Kyle Sher-

ACKNOWLEDGMENTS

ling, and several who offered critical feedback on important chapters and helped sharpen my argument considerably—namely, Richard Fellows, Max Lee, James Ware, and Richard Wright. I've been encouraged by my friends in Houston who don't really know what I "do" but know that I've been writing a book and think that that's great. As always, my wife and kids deserve my deepest thanks for making possible, in ways both big and small, the kind of work that it takes to complete a project of this kind. I also thank James Ernest and Trevor Thompson at Eerdmans for agreeing to take on this project, along with Jenny Hoffman, Amy Kent, and the editorial staff, who read the manuscript with careful attention to detail and meticulously checked formatting and references. For completion of the ancient sources index, I thank Laura Trotta, who always does excellent work.

Finally, I would like to thank two of the last half century's most eminent biblical scholars, each of whom has helped me in different ways. First, I am grateful to the late Abraham Malherbe, who greatly encouraged me with a surprise email during my time at Baylor, expressing his approval of many aspects of my developing thesis on 1 Corinthians and disclosing that, in so many words, had he been younger, this is a book he would have written. And second, I thank my Doktorvater, Bruce Longenecker. His work in "social" aspects of the Greco-Roman world has helped direct my own research interests both through his influence and through the opportunities he has given me to participate with him. Apart from his scholarship, Bruce has also influenced me immensely as, truly, a model teacher and mentor. I dedicate this book to Bruce.

Abbreviations

ACC	Ancient Christian Commentary on Scripture
AE	*L'Année épigraphique.* Edited by René Cagnat et al. Paris: Presses universitaires de France, 1888–
AnBib	Analecta Biblica
ANRW	*Aufstieg und Niedergang der römischen Welt: Geschichte und Kultur Roms im Spiegel der neueren Forschung.* Part 2, *Principat.* Edited by Hildegard Temporini and Wolfgang Haase. Berlin: de Gruyter, 1972–
AYBC	Anchor Yale Bible Commentaries
BCH	*Bulletin de correspondance hellénique*
BDAG	Danker, Frederick W., Walter Bauer, William F. Arndt, and F. Wilbur Gingrich. *Greek-English Lexicon of the New Testament and Other Early Christian Literature.* 3rd ed. Chicago: University of Chicago Press, 2000
BDF	Blass, Friedrich, Albert Debrunner, and Robert W. Funk. *A Greek Grammar of the New Testament and Other Early Christian Literature.* Chicago: University of Chicago Press, 1961
BETL	Bibliotheca Ephemeridum Theologicarum Lovaniensium
BHT	Beiträge zur historischen Theologie
Bib	*Biblica*
BibInt	*Biblical Interpretation*
BJRL	*Bulletin of the John Rylands University Library of Manchester*
BSac	*Bibliotheca Sacra*
BT	*The Bible Translator*

ABBREVIATIONS

BZ	*Biblische Zeitschrift*
BZNW	Beihefte zur Zeitschrift für die neutestamentliche Wissenschaft
CBQ	*Catholic Biblical Quarterly*
CIL	*Corpus Inscriptionum Latinarum*. Berlin, 1862–
CLE	*Carmina Latina Epigraphica*. Edited by Franz Buecheler. Leipzig: Teubner, 1895–1897
CTL	Cambridge Textbooks in Linguistics
CurBR	*Currents in Biblical Research*
CWS	Classics of Western Spirituality: A Library of the Great Spiritual Masters. Mahwah, NJ: Paulist, 1978–
DSS	Dead Sea Scrolls
EKKNT	Evangelisch-katholischer Kommentar zum Neuen Testament
Ephesos	McCabe, Donald F. *Ephesos Inscriptions. Texts and List*. The Princeton Project on the Inscriptions of Anatolia. Princeton: The Institute for Advanced Study, Princeton, 1991
HbibS	Herder's Biblical Studies
HTR	*Harvard Theological Review*
HTS	Harvard Theological Studies
IBM	*The Collection of Ancient Greek Inscriptions in the British Museum*. Edited by C. T. Newton. Oxford: Clarendon, 1864–1916
ICC	International Critical Commentary
IDidyma	*Didyma. II. Die Inschriften*. Edited by R. Rehm. Berlin, 1958
IG	*Inscriptiones Graecae. Editio Minor*. Berlin: de Gruyter, 1924–
IGUR	*Inscriptiones graecae urbis Romae*. Edited by Luigi Moretti. 4 vols. in 5 parts. Rome, 1968–1990
IKorinthKent	Kent, John Harvey. *The Inscriptions 1926–1950*. Vol. 8.3 of *Corinth: Results of Excavations*. Cambridge, MA: Harvard University Press, 1966
Int	*Interpretation*
IOlympia	Dittenberg, W., and K. Purgold. *Die Inschriften von Olympia*. Berlin, 1896
IPrusaOlymp	Corsten, T., ed. *Die Inschriften von Prusa ad Olympum*. Vol. 1. Bonn, 1991
ISardBR	Buckler, W. H., and D. M. Robinson. *Sardis*. Vol. 7, *Greek and Latin Inscriptions*, Part 1. Leiden: Brill, 1932
JBL	*Journal of Biblical Literature*
JRH	*Journal of Religious History*
JSNT	*Journal for the Study of the New Testament*
JSNTSup	Journal for the Study of the New Testament Supplement Series

Abbreviations

JTS	*Journal of Theological Studies*
Kaibel	Kaibel, Georg. *Epigrammata graeca ex lapidibus conlecta*. Berlin 1878. Reprint: Hildesheim 1965
LCL	Loeb Classical Library
LGPN	*A Lexicon of Greek Personal Names*. 8 vols. Oxford: Oxford University Press, 1987–. https://www.lgpn.ox.ac.uk/home
LNTS	Library of New Testament Studies
LS	Long, A. A., and D. N. Sedley. *The Hellenistic Philosophers*. 2 vols. London: Cambridge University Press, 1987–
LSJ	Liddell, Henry George, Robert Scott, Henry Stuart Jones. *A Greek-English Lexicon*. 9th ed. with revised supplement. Oxford: Clarendon, 1996
NA[28]	*Novum Testamentum Graece*, Nestle-Aland, 28th ed.
Neot	*Neotestamentica*
NICNT	New International Commentary on the New Testament
NIGTC	New International Greek Testament Commentary
NovT	*Novum Testamentum*
NovTSup	Supplements to Novum Testamentum
NPNF[1]	*The Nicene and Post-Nicene Fathers*, Series 1. Edited by Philip Schaff. 1886–1880. 14 vols. Reprint, Peabody, MA: Hendrickson, 1994
NTS	*New Testament Studies*
OGIS	*Orientis Graeci Inscriptiones Selectae*. Edited by Wilhelm Dittenberger. 2 vols. Leipzig: Hirzel, 1903–1905
PNTC	The Pillar New Testament Commentary
RB	*Revue biblique*
RE	*Real-Encyklopädie für protestantische Theologie und Kirche*
RQ	*Restoration Quarterly*
SBLDS	Society of Biblical Literature Dissertation Series
SEG	Supplementum epigraphicum graecum
SIG	*Sylloge Inscriptionum Graecarum*. Edited by Wilhelm Dittenberger. 4 vols. 3rd ed. Leipzig: Hirzel, 1915–1924
SNTSMS	Society of New Testament Studies Monograph Series
SP	Sacra Pagina
SVF	*Stoicorum Veterum Fragmenta*. Hans Friedrich August von Arnim. 4 vols. Leipzig: Teubner, 1903–1924
TAM II	*Tituli Asiae Minoris, II. Tituli Lyciae linguis Graeca et Latina conscripti*, ed. Ernst Kalinka. 3 fasc. Vienna, 1920–1944
TAM III	*Tituli Asiae Minoris, III. Tituli Pisidiae linguis Graeca et Latina*

	conscripti. 1. *Tituli Termessi et agri Termessensis.* Edited by R. Heberdey. Vienna, 1941
TDNT	*Theological Dictionary of the New Testament.* Edited by Gerhard Kittel and Gerhard Friedrich. Translated by Geoffrey W. Bromiley. 10 vols. Grand Rapids: Eerdmans, 1964–1976
TynBul	*Tyndale Bulletin*
UBS[5]	*The Greek New Testament*, United Bible Societies, 5th ed.
WUNT	Wissenschaftliche Untersuchungen zum Neuen Testament
ZNW	*Zeitschrift für die neutestamentliche Wissenschaft und die Kunde der älteren Kirche*

PART I

*Rediscovering the Wisdom
of the Corinthians*

———

1

1 Corinthians 1–4
in Modern Scholarship

Perhaps no section in the Pauline corpus has inspired a more diverse range of historical reconstructions than 1 Cor 1–4. Only the general picture is clear. The newly founded church has broken into factions of some sort. "Each" of them says, "'I am of Paul,' and 'I am of Apollos,' and 'I am of Cephas,' and 'I am of Christ'" (1:12).[1] The remainder of these chapters appears to identify the cause, or at least the most important one. Whether it was only a faction or it was a majority of the church, some of the Corinthians conducted themselves according to what Paul calls "the wisdom of the world" (1:20; 3:19). They considered themselves "wise" (3:18; 6:5). They boasted in someone or something (1:29, 31; 3:21; 4:6, 18, 19) and were preoccupied with status in the eyes of their peers (4:6–8; cf. 1:26–30). Some considered themselves "spiritual" (2:15).

Modern scholarship's diversity of interpretation on these chapters is owed largely to limitations of data, partly to the fancies of imagination, and not a little to the changing trends of scholarship. Exactly what constituted this "wisdom" espoused by the Corinthians has been a subject of disagreement and ever-changing opinion. Over the last forty years, scholarship has taken a sharp turn away from interpretations of preceding generations. While no consistent picture of the church's conflict has emerged, a basic consensus has been reached on certain essential points in question. It is my view, however, that recent consensus is, on many of these points, wrong. The purpose of this book will be to reconsider the "wisdom of the Corinthians."

---

1. Bible translations are my own unless otherwise indicated.

1 Corinthians 1–4 in Modern Scholarship

Thematic Concerns

On several matters interpreters generally agree. First Corinthians 1–4 constitutes a discrete and integrated unit; it forms a part of the original integrity of 1 Corinthians;[2] it serves as an introduction to chapters 5–16;[3] and the intertwining themes of "wisdom" and factionalism constitute the main subject. The subsections in this unit fall under two main headings. Some take up the topic of "wisdom," or σοφία, explicitly (1:17b–3:3; 3:18–23), and others the dynamics of unity and factionalism (1:10–17a; 3:4–4:5). The final portion furnishes a conclusion to the discussion (4:6–21). Interpreters almost universally agree that the themes of both σοφία and factionalism reflect ad hoc concerns and that chapters 1–4 identify σοφία itself as the main contributor to the factions.[4] In terms of verse count, σοφία thematically occupies more attention than factionalism; and interpreters overall have given greater weight to this theme than to its complement.[5] Still, interpreters remain intent on the question of how these themes relate.

---

2. Johannes Weiss's compilation theory (1:1–6:11 constituting Letter B) never won a consensus. Weiss, *Der erste Korintherbrief* (Göttingen: Vandenhoeck & Ruprecht, 1910), xxxix–xliii. A table summarizing older partition theories can be found in J. C. Hurd, *The Origin of 1 Corinthians* (New York: Seabury, 1965), 45. More recent proponents who view chs. 1–4 as a separate letter include Gerhard Sellin, "Das 'Geheimnis' der Weisheit und das Rätsel der 'Christuspartei' (au 1 Kor 1–4)," *ZNW* 73 (1982): 69–96, esp. 72–73; and Frank W. Hughes and Robert Jewett, *The Corinthian Correspondence: Redaction, Rhetoric, and History* (Minneapolis: Fortress Academic; Lanham, MD: Lexington Books, 2021). Margaret M. Mitchell has made a conclusive case for the letter's integrity based on the coherence of Paul's rhetorical strategy throughout the sixteen chapters of the letter. Mitchell, *Paul and the Rhetoric of Reconciliation* (Louisville: Westminster John Knox, 1993).

3. For the argument that chs. 1–4 announce the letter's main themes, see for example Paul W. Barnett, *The Corinthian Question: Why Did the Church Oppose Paul?* (Nottingham: Apollos, 2011), 84–85; Harm-Jan Inkelaar, *Conflict over Wisdom: The Theme of 1 Corinthians 1–4 Rooted in Scripture* (Leuven: Peeters, 2011), 67. Anthony C. Thiselton argues that the letter's integrity centers around its response to "realized eschatology." Thiselton, "Realized Eschatology at Corinth," *NTS* 24 (1978): 510–26, esp. 526.

4. M. V. P. Branick appears to stand alone in finding no connection between σοφία and the divisions. Branick, "Source and Redaction Analysis of 1 Corinthians 1–3," *JBL* 101 (1982): 251–69.

5. For the argument that σοφία is the main focus, see, e.g., Weiss, *Der erste Korintherbrief*, 23; A. T. Robertson and A. Plummer, *A Critical and Exegetical Commentary on the First Epistle of St. Paul to the Corinthians*, ICC (Edinburgh: T&T Clark, 1914), 15; Hurd, *Origin of*

Complicating matters are an abundance of subordinate themes, which the interpreter must also relate to the situation. Among the most commonly cited are status, boasting, and the Spirit.[6] Whether "baptism" ties in with these themes (1:13–16) is more seriously debated.[7] This plurality of themes has led many interpreters to conclude that Paul identifies factionalism as being caused not by σοφία alone, but by an assortment of factors not interrelated.[8]

Corinthian σοφία

Overview

Until recent decades, reconstructions of the church's conflict focused more or less exclusively on the *content* of the Corinthians' σοφία. The proposed

---

1 Corinthians, 76, 77; Robert Funk, "Word and Word in 1 Cor 2:6–16," in *Language, Hermeneutic, and Word of God* (New York: Harper & Row, 1966), 275–303, esp. 277; C. K. Barrett, *A Commentary on the First Epistle to the Corinthians* (London: Adam and Charles Black, 1971), 275–76; James A. Davis, *Wisdom and Spirit: An Investigation of 1 Cor 1:18–3:20 against the Background of Jewish Sapiential Traditions in the Greco-Roman Period* (Lanham, MD: University Press of America, 1984), 132; Gordon Fee, *First Epistle to the Corinthians*, NICNT (Grand Rapids: Eerdmans, 1987), 64; Fee, *First Epistle to the Corinthians*, 2nd ed. (Grand Rapids: Eerdmans, 2014), 67; S. M. Pogoloff, *Logos and Sophia: The Rhetorical Situation of 1 Corinthians*, SBLDS 134 (Atlanta: Scholars Press, 1992), 105; Inkelaar, *Conflict over Wisdom*, 7, 2, 106; and many others. Others find the focus in a "pneumatic" theme, as opposed to "wisdom": Branick, "Source and Redaction Analysis," 268. Others view the focus as factionalism: D. W. Kuck, *Judgment and Community Conflict: Paul's Use of Apocalyptic Judgment Language in 1 Corinthians 3:5–4:5*, NovTSup 66 (Leiden: Brill, 1992), 154. Others see the focus as partisan loyalty to leaders: William Baird, "'One against the Other': Intra-Church Conflict in 1 Corinthians," in *The Conversation Continues: Studies in Paul and John in Honor of J. Louis Martyn*, ed. Robert T. Fortna and Beverly R. Gaventa (Nashville: Abingdon, 1990), 116–36, esp. 131; or as leadership: Barnett, *Corinthian Question*, 84.

6. Cf. Baird, "One against the Other,'" 131; Pogoloff, *Logos and Sophia*, 105; Kuck, *Judgment and Community Conflict*, 155; Bruce W. Winter, *Philo and Paul among the Sophists: Alexandrian and Corinthian Responses to a Julio-Claudian Movement*, 2nd ed. (Grand Rapids: Eerdmans, 2002), 180; Branick, "Source and Redaction Analysis," 268.

7. For one proponent of the view that baptism was a major issue, see Stephen J. Patterson, "The Baptists of Corinth: Paul, the Partisans of Apollos, and the History of Baptism in Nascent Christianity," in *Stones, Bones and the Sacred: Essays on Material Culture and Religion in Honor of Dennis E. Smith*, ed. Alan H. Cadwallader, Early Christianity and Its Literature 21 (Atlanta: SBL Press, 2016), 315–27.

8. Hans Conzelmann, *1 Corinthians: A Commentary on the First Epistle to the Corinthians*, Hermeneia (Philadelphia: Fortress, 1975), 6, 8; Baird, "'One against the Other,'" 130. For Davis (*Wisdom and Spirit*, 132), wisdom predominates among the causes.

reconstructions changed dramatically across that stretch.[9] One can trace a basic evolution of perspectives, though not in any definite line. Early theses viewed Corinthian σοφία in relation to Jewish/Petrine Christianity (connected with the "Cephas party").[10] Across the early and mid-twentieth century, interpreters identified σοφία (as γνῶσις) with Gnosticism (connected with the "Christ party").[11] In the second half of the twentieth century, the gnostic view, with its emphasis on special "knowledge" and spiritual discernment, morphed into a "spiritual enthusiasm" (*Enthusiasmus*) view.[12] The latter view in turn came to be articulated as "(over)realized eschatology."[13] Interpreters at this point generally abandoned the premise that the Corinthians' σοφία derived from specific cultural influences, favoring the view that it reflected the influence of a generic Hellenistic religiosity.[14] Some emphasized that the Corinthians' eschatology resulted from their own innovations and

---

9. For two fairly recent histories of scholarship, see Edward Adams and David G. Horrell, eds., *Christianity at Corinth: The Quest for the Pauline Church* (Louisville: Westminster John Knox, 2004), 13–40; spanning from F. C. Baur (1831) through Richard Horsley's commentary (1997) and covering scholarship through the first decade of the twenty-first century is Oh-Young Kwon, "A Critical Review of Recent Scholarship on the Pauline Opposition and the Nature of Its Wisdom (σοφία) in 1 Corinthians 1–4," *CurBR* 8 (2010): 386–427.

10. J. E. C. Schmidt, *Bibliothek für Kritik und Exegese des Neuen Testaments und älteste Christengeschicthe*, vol. 2.3 (n.p.: Hadamar, 1801); F. C. Baur,"Die Christusparti in der korinthischen Gemeinde, der Gegensatz des paulinischen und petrinischen Christentums in der altesten Kirche, der Apostel Petrus in Rom," *Tübinger Zeitschrift für Theologie* 4 (1831): 61–206; but much more recently, M. D. Goulder, "Σοφία in Corinthians," *NTS* 37 (1991): 516–34.

11. W. Lütgert, *Freiheitspredigt und Schwarmgeister in Korinth* (Göttingen: C. Bertelsman, 1908); followed by a few others, and then later Ulrich Wilckens, *Weisheit und Torheit*, BHT 26 (Tübingen: Mohr, 1959); and finally revived by W. Schmithals, *Die Gnosis in Korinth: Eine Untersuchung zu den Korintherbriefen* (Göttingen: Vandenhoeck & Ruprecht, 1969); ET: *Gnosticism in Corinth: An Investigation of the Letters to the Corinthians* (Nashville: Abingdon, 1971). Much more recently, Todd E. Klutz has argued for continuities with the brand of Gnosticism represented by the author of the Gospel of Philip. Klutz, "Re-reading 1 Corinthians after Rethinking 'Gnosticism,'" *JSNT* 26 (2003): 193–216.

12. For example, "Spirit people" in Jerome Murphy-O'Connor, *Paul: A Critical Life* (Oxford: Oxford University Press, 1996), 275–84.

13. Traced throughout 1 Corinthians in Thiselton, "Realized Eschatology at Corinth." Kuck (*Judgment and Community Conflict*, 16–25) reviews the history of scholarship and characterizes this thesis as the "consensus view in NT scholarship" as he writes (16).

14. Conzelmann, *1 Corinthians*, 14–16; Richard A. Horsley, in a series of articles between 1976 and 1978, the first of which was "Pneumatikos vs. Psychikos: Distinctions of Spiritual Status among the Corinthians," *HTR* 69 (1976): 269–88; Davis, *Wisdom and Spirit*, 82–83; Davis identifies a main influence in Hellenistic Judaism.

distortion of Paul's teaching.[15] Yet, through the final third of the twentieth century and beyond, some have continued to argue for more specific influences, including the influence of Hellenistic Judaism or popular philosophy, even Stoicism, Cynicism, or Epicureanism specifically.[16] Those who advocate for particular influences have tended to argue that the Corinthians had not an *over-realized* eschatology, but rather *no* eschatology.[17]

Despite a discernible chronological trajectory in this story—or rather series of trajectories—there is no definite line of descent from beginning to end, and the genealogical connections are complicated. Thus, instead of taking a linear approach, one might arrange the views by situating them on a series of conceptual axes which partially correlate: (1) Explanations of the conflict vary in their emphasis on either the Spirit or wisdom. (2) These emphases generally correlate respectively with the features of over-realized eschatology and no eschatology. (3) The dualities of axis 2 generally correlate with an emphasis on spiritual enthusiasm / spiritual gifts, on the one hand, and Greek wisdom / Greek philosophy on the other. (4) Interpreters variably place the Corinthians' influences on either the Jewish or the Greek side. (5) One sees a general chronological movement from theses that emphasize single or specific "history-of-religions" influences to theses that emphasize multiple influences or general Hellenistic influence. (6) One also finds vari-

---

15. Hurd, *Origin of 1 Corinthians*. Thiselton ("Realized Eschatology at Corinth," 512) viewed the Corinthians' realized eschatology as a distortion of Paul's teaching.

16. Hellenistic Judaism: B. A. Pearson, *Pneumatikos-Psychikos Terminology in 1 Corinthians* (Missoula: Society of Biblical Literature for the Nag Hammadi Seminar, 1973); Davis, *Wisdom and Spirit*. Popular philosophy: Dale B. Martin, *Corinthian Body* (New Haven: Yale University Press, 1995), 71–73; Richard B. Hays, "Conversion of the Imagination," *NTS* 45 (1999): 391–412, esp. 409. Epicurean philosophy: Norman Wentworth De Witt, *St. Paul and Epicurus* (Minneapolis: University of Minnesota Press, 1954); Graham Tomlin, "Christians and Epicureans in 1 Corinthians," *JSNT* 68 (1997): 51–72. Cynic philosophy: F. Gerald Downing, *Cynics, Paul, and the Pauline Churches* (London: Routledge, 1998). Stoic philosophy: Robert M. Grant, "The Wisdom of the Corinthians," in *The Joy of Study*, ed. S. E. Johnson (New York: Macmillan, 1951), 51–55; Terrence Paige, "Stoicism, *Eleutheria*, and Community at Corinth," in *Worship, Theology and Ministry in the Early Church*, ed. Michael J. Wilkins and Terrence Paige (Sheffield: JSOT Press, 1992), 180–93; Timothy A. Brookins, *Corinthian Wisdom, Stoic Philosophy, and the Ancient Economy*, SNTSMS 159 (Cambridge: Cambridge University Press, 2014). Note also the connection with the mystery cults proposed by Stephen J. Chester, *Conversion at Corinth: Perspectives on Conversion in Paul's Theology and the Corinthian Church*, Studies of the New Testament and Its World (London: T&T Clark, 2003).

17. Kuck, *Judgment and Community Conflict*, 63.

ation in respect to the weight interpreters attribute to cultural influences versus Corinthian innovations.

Recent Trends

Since the late 1970s, a radical shift of perspective has taken place as scholarship has considered the role of "social" or "secular" factors in precipitating the church's disunity. While studies have tended to view the causes now as being more complex,[18] most studies identify a single social institution or complex of social conventions as the leading or "primary" cause. Factors commonly cited include socioeconomic stratification, secular conceptions of leadership, the conventions of benefaction and patronage, political factionalism, values related to the honor/shame complex, elite ideology, elite education, and especially the influence of the Greco-Roman rhetorical culture.[19]

---

18. In addition to studies cited below, see David G. Horrell, *The Social Ethos of the Corinthian Correspondence: Interests and Ideology from 1 Corinthians to 1 Clement*, Studies of the New Testament and Its World (Edinburgh: T&T Clark, 1996); Craig Steven de Vos, *Church and Community Conflicts: The Relationships of the Thessalonian, Corinthian, and Philippian Churches with Their Wider Civic Communities*, SBLDS 168 (Atlanta: Scholars, 1999), 179–232; Bruce W. Winter, *After Paul Left Corinth: The Influence of Secular Ethics and Social Change* (Grand Rapids: Eerdmans, 2001).

19. Social stratification: Gerd Theissen, *The Social Setting of Pauline Christianity* (Philadelphia: Fortress, 1982), esp. 96–98; Wayne Meeks, *The First Urban Christians* (New Haven: Yale University Press, 1983), 118–19. Secular conceptions of leadership: Andrew D. Clarke, *Secular and Christian Leadership in Corinth: A Socio-historical and Exegetical Study of 1 Corinthians 1–6* (Leiden: Brill, 1993), esp. 41. The conventions of benefaction and patronage: Ronald F. Hock, *The Social Context of Paul's Ministry: Tentmaking and Apostleship* (Philadelphia: Fortress, 1980), 52–65; Peter Marshall, *Enmity in Corinth: Social Conventions in Paul's Relations with the Corinthians*, WUNT 2/23 (Tübingen: Mohr Siebeck, 1987), esp. xii; John K. Chow, *Patronage and Power*, JSNTSup 75 (Sheffield: JSOT Press, 1992), esp. 12. Political factionalism: L. L. Welborn, *Politics and Rhetoric in the Corinthian Epistles* (Macon, GA: Mercer University Press, 1997), esp. 16–28; cf. Bradley J. Bitner, *Paul's Political Strategy in 1 Corinthians 1–4: Constitution and Covenant*, SNTSMS 163 (Cambridge: Cambridge University Press, 2015). Values related to the honor/shame complex: Mark T. Finney, *Honour and Conflict in the Ancient World: 1 Corinthians in Its Greco-Roman Social Setting*, LNTS 460 (London: T&T Clark, 2011), esp. 2. Elite ideology: Martin, *Corinthian Body*, esp. xiv–xv; John M. G. Barclay, "Crucifixion as Wisdom: Exploring the Ideology of a Disreputable Social Movement," in *The Wisdom and Foolishness of God: First Corinthians 1–4 in Theological Exploration*, ed. Christophe Chalamet and Hans-Christoph Askani (Minneapolis: Fortress, 2017), 1–20, esp. 2. Elite education: Robert S. Dutch, *The Educated Elite in 1 Corinthians: Education and Community Conflict in Graeco-Roman Context*, JSNTSup 271 (New York: T&T Clark, 2005), esp. 29–42. Greco-Roman rhetorical culture: Pogoloff, *Logos and Sophia*;

Studies vary in their degree of emphasis on σοφία specifically. At times σοφία fades into a broad symbol of elite values that might be subsumed under the heading of paideia—educational achievement symbolizing high status and aristocratic values. More often it is identified specifically with the "wisdom" of rhetoric. Even studies that emphasize the primary importance of other social factors almost invariably include rhetoric among the critical factors thought to have determined the church's divided loyalties between ministers; and usually rhetoric figures in an integral way in the interpreter's overall reconstruction.

The "rhetorical thesis" has found expression in two primary variants, though elements of both can be found in most recent treatments of 1 Corinthians. (1) One variant sees Paul rejecting the value of rhetoric as a tool of persuasion in proclamation of the gospel and emphasizing that success in preaching owes exclusively to the power of the Spirit.[20] (2) The other sees Paul rejecting society's (and the Corinthians') high estimation of rhetorical ability as a measure of status.[21] Interpreters' association of σοφία with rhetoric marks a categorical shift of definition in the history of scholarship, as it redefines σοφία in terms of form of speech, against most earlier conceptions of σοφία in terms of religious or philosophical content.

The Corinthian Parties

Explanations of the church's "parties" vary to an equal degree. The nature of the connection between σοφία and the party allegiances is only one piece of the puzzle. While the party slogans in 1:12 imply the existence of four parties ("of Paul," "of Apollos," "of Cephas," "of Christ"), interpreters debate whether distinct parties existed as such, and, if so, whether there were more, or perhaps fewer, than four, and whether some of these were more central to the controversy than others.

As with the matter of σοφία, one theory about the parties has emerged over the last several decades as the prevailing one. According to this theory,

---

Duane Litfin, *St. Paul's Theology of Proclamation: 1 Corinthians 1–4 and Greco-Roman Rhetoric*, SNTSMS 79 (Cambridge: Cambridge University Press, 1994); Bruce Winter, "Philo and Paul among the Sophists: A Hellenistic Jewish and a Christian Response" (PhD diss., Macquarie University, 1988).

20. Litfin, *St. Paul's Theology*, esp. 246–62.

21. Pogoloff, *Logos and Sophia*, esp. 119. Winter's thesis ("Philo and Paul among the Sophists," 180–202) fits on this side, though he would agree (esp. 159) with Litfin on the latter's main point.

the conflict in chapters 1–4 concerned chiefly the "Paul party" and the "Apollos party." This theory in turn subdivides around interpreters' explanations for why the partisans of Apollos favored him. Three explanations are common: it was (a) because of the *content* of Apollos's wisdom (identified with Hellenistic Judaism in the stream of Philo of Alexandria); or (b) because of the *form* of his wisdom (his rhetorical abilities); or (c) because, unlike Paul, he was willing to enter into a patron-client relationship with influential members of the church.[22]

Evaluating the History of Scholarship

I have offered perhaps a more protracted opening summary of the history of scholarship than is customary. I have done so for an important reason. My own evaluation of the secondary literature has led me to some observations that suggest to me it is time for a critical review of trajectories in the study of 1 Cor 1–4. I do not just mean a critical review of recent *readings* of 1 Cor 1–4. I mean also a critical consideration of *vectors* in scholarship's movement and of the logic used to legitimate these vectors. In other words, evaluating the state of the question requires some critical consideration of how we got here.

---

22. Hellenistic Judaism: Pearson, *Pneumatikos-Psychikos Terminology*, 8, 46, 59; Davis, *Wisdom and Spirit*, 132–33; Horsley, "Wisdom of Word," 224–39, esp. 231–32; Niels Hyldahl, "Paul and Hellenistic Judaism in Corinth," in *The New Testament and Hellenistic Judaism*, ed. Peder Borgen and Soren Giversen (Peabody, MA: Hendrickson, 1995), 204–16, esp. 211–15. On rhetoric, see Pogoloff, *Logos and Sophia*, 178–83; Winter, *Philo and Paul among the Sophists*, 178; Litfin, *St. Paul's Theology*, 153–62, 228–33; Bullmore, *St. Paul's Theology of Rhetorical Style: An Examination of 1 Corinthians 2:1–5 in the Light of First-Century Rhetorical Criticism* (San Francisco: International Scholars Publications, 1995), 207; L. L. Welborn, "Μωρὸς γενέσθω: Paul's Appropriation of the Role of the Fool in 1 Corinthians 1–4," *BibInt* 10 (2002): 420–35, esp. 432; Corin Mihaila, *The Paul-Apollos Relationship and Paul's Stance toward Greco-Roman Rhetoric*, LNTS 402 (London: T&T Clark, 2009), 1; Finney, *Honour and Conflict*, 85–87; Maria Pascuzzi, "Baptism-Based Allegiance and the Divisions in Corinth: A Reexamination of 1 Corinthians 1:13–17," *CBQ* 71 (2009): 813–29; among others. See also a lengthy treatment in Donald P. Ker, "Paul and Apollos—Colleagues or Rivals?," *JSNT* 77 (2000): 75–97. Cf. Joop F. M. Smit, "'What Is Apollos? What Is Paul?' In Search for the Coherence of First Corinthians 1:10–4:21," *NovT* 44 (2002): 231–51. Smit puts the emphasis on Paul's "rational argumentation" in distinction from rhetoric (244–47). On patronage, see Marshall, *Enmity in Corinth*, 173–258; also Hock, *Social Context*, 52–65; Chow, *Patronage and Power*, 103–12.

From Specific to General Influences

Through the 1970s, reconstructions of 1 Cor 1–4 and evaluation of Corinthian σοφία were based to a substantial degree upon the identification of ideological "parallels" between Corinthian σοφία and other cultural ideologies roughly contemporary. Beginning with extra-biblical literary sources, interpreters identified common vocabulary and ideas apparently shared between Paul's Corinthian "opponents" and some or another of the various philosophical or religious systems roughly contemporary with them and based on these parallels identified the one "wisdom" with the other. At its worst, this approach had several shortcomings.[23] (1) Scholarship explained parallels in terms of direct *genealogical* relationship between the Christian material and their sources of influence. (2) Abstracted from a concrete context, parallel language could be, and was, explained in relation to a wide variety of philosophical or religious systems. (3) Conceived as containers of "ideas," verbal parallels could be, and sometimes were, detached from their historical setting and thus applied to the Corinthian setting anachronistically.

Widespread recognition of these shortcomings in the final decades of the twentieth century prompted three important developments in scholarship. (1) Interpreters increasingly refrained from the language of influence, derivation, or genealogical connection. (2) Interpreters increasingly rejected the view that any *specific* history-of-religions influences stood behind the Corinthians' views. (3) Interpreters increasingly pushed the question of ideological influences to the side, either (a) favoring historically rooted social practices as factors in the divisions or (b) turning from backgrounds to rhetorical- or audience-oriented readings of the text.[24]

These developments are reasonable responses to the kinds of problems that many have noted in earlier scholarship. These developments, however, are also "reactions" of a sort, stimulated both by the inadequacies of the

---

23. For criticisms, see especially Samuel Sandmel, "Parallelomania," *JBL* 81 (1962): 1–13; and L. Michael White and John T. Fitzgerald, "*Quod est comparandum*: The Problem of Parallels," in *Early Christianity and Classical Culture*, ed. J. T. Fitzgerald, T. H. Olbricht, and L. M. White (Leiden: Brill, 2003), 13–39.

24. For (b) see especially Mitchell, *Paul and the Rhetoric of Reconciliation*. See also L. L. Welborn, *Paul, the Fool of Christ: 1 Cor 1–4 in the Comic-Philosophic Tradition* (London: T&T Clark, 2005); Devin L. White, *Teacher of the Nations: Ancient Educational Traditions and Paul's Argument in 1 Corinthians 1–4*, BZNW 227 (Berlin: de Gruyter, 2017); Anna C. Miller, "Not with Eloquent Wisdom: Democratic *Ekklēsia* Discourse in 1 Corinthians 1–4," *JSNT* 35 (2013): 323–54.

parallels approach at its worst and by the frustrations of the reconstructive task. One must consider that simply because it can be difficult to prove genealogical derivation does not mean that genealogical derivation does not happen in history. And the simple fact that it is sometimes possible to construe language in relation to a variety of discursive domains due to our limited access to context need not mean that the relevant language, in context, does not function in relation to some more specific domain. Moreover, just because verbal parallels can be used anachronistically does not mean that comparing verbal similarities is an anachronistic enterprise by its nature. In terms of the Corinthian conflict, the possibility of direct influence from a specific religious or philosophical system, I believe, must be regarded as an open possibility, however much interpreters have been frustrated by the attempt to locate one.

From "Religious" to "Sociological" Explanations

The more robustly sociological approach that has prevailed in recent decades represents a definite methodological advance,[25] and it has led to genuine new insights on the text. Yet, in critical retrospect one finds that the sea change of opinion on 1 Cor 1–4 depends in part upon some questionable leaps and omissions. Once made, these leaps serve to construct a narrative that "confirms" the legitimacy of the movement by virtue of what it has omitted. In this regard the narrative reflects a partly *proleptic* account of the supersession of newer interpretations over older ones, an account that is then used as ex post facto justification for abandoning readings that have actually not as yet been sufficiently refuted. Thus, the narrative writes the "history of scholarship," rather than the actual history of scholarship writing the narrative.

One notable defect in attempts to justify this trajectory has been a failure to justify the abandonment of older conclusions simultaneously with the abandonment of the imperfect methods used to reach them. As noted, the move from a more philological or parallels or genealogical or history-of-religions approach to a robust sociological approach has corresponded with a move from "religious" explanations (like Gnosticism, Hellenistic Judaism)

---

25. Marking the beginning of this phase were: E. A. Judge, *The Social Pattern of Christian Groups in the First Century* (London: Tyndale, 1960); Theissen, *Social Setting*; Abraham J. Malherbe, *Social Aspects of Early Christianity* (Philadelphia: Fortress, 1983); Meeks, *First Urban Christians*.

1 Corinthians 1–4 in Modern Scholarship

to "social" explanations focused on cultural practices (like the conventions of benefaction and patronage). It requires little reflection, however, to recognize that a sociological approach need not rule out all religious explanations—as if religions were not a feature of the social world. Yet, many interpreters in the newer era have explicitly pitted the "religious" and "social" options against each other, often speaking in mutually exclusive terms, for instance asserting that "the problems in Corinth were not theological but social," and things of that sort.[26] In other cases, interpreters' "social" explanations rule out the alternatives implicitly, as where they offer nonreligious explanations for the very passages that were once interpreted in religious terms. We witness this not only in the absolute reinterpretation of σοφία as a synonym for social refinement, paideia, and often more specifically rhetoric, but also in more recent treatments of texts like 4:6–8 as centering around practices of patronage and benefaction.[27] In many cases the new explanations do not supplement the older ones; if correct, they supplant them.

Replacement of older views is not a problem in principle. What we are missing is justification for *preferring* the newer options. Several tendencies expose this lacuna. Even through the 1970s and '80s, when studies in the "social" line did address the comparative value of their explanations, they invariably mentioned only the oldest, and most widely rejected, thesis—that of Gnosticism—at a time when the Hellenistic-Judaism and over-realized-eschatology theses were already in their heyday.[28] For instance, Marshall's *En-*

---

26. Cf. Pogoloff, *Logos and Sophia,* 104; Welborn, *Politics and Rhetoric,* 7; Witherington, *Conflict and Community,* 74n9; Clarke, *Secular and Christian Leadership,* xiii; J. D. G. Dunn, "Reconstructions of Corinthian Christianity," in Adams and Horrell, *Christianity at Corinth,* 303; Bengt Holmberg, "Methods of Historical Reconstruction," in Adams and Horrell, *Christianity at Corinth,* 261; Roy Ciampa and Brian Rosner, *The First Letter to the Corinthians,* PNTC (Grand Rapids: Eerdmans, 2010), 4. On the other hand, many clarify that they intend only to supplement the insights of earlier studies: e.g., Theissen, "Social Integration and Sacramental Activity: An Analysis of 1 Cor. 11:17–34," in *Social Setting of Pauline Christianity,* 145–74, esp. 123; Malherbe, *Social Aspects,* 84; Chow, *Patronage and Power,* 12; John Hiigel, *Leadership in 1 Corinthians: A Case Study in Paul's Ecclesiology,* Studies in the Bible and Early Christianity 57 (Lewiston, NY: E. Mellen, 2003), 2; Chester, *Conversion at Corinth,* 220–21.

27. E.g., Marshall, *Enmity in Corinth,* 165–258. Finney, rightly, recognizes that Paul's description of the Corinthians in 4:8 (and also 1:26) refers to "spiritual values" (*Honour and Conflict,* 95–98), though Finney gives little indication how the Corinthians' spiritual pretensions relate to the fact that their "wisdom" concerns, as Finney says, rhetoric or eloquence.

28. Note the comments on the inferiority of the gnostic thesis in Pearson, *Pneumatikos-Psychikos Terminology,* 4; Horsley, "Pneumatikos vs. Psychikos," esp. 270; Marshall, *Enmity*

mity in Corinth (1987) declines to interact with the over-realized-eschatology thesis at all despite concentrating on the text that became the very linchpin for that thesis, namely 1 Cor 4:8.[29] Klutz argues that even the gnostic thesis has never been evaluated at the level of critical engagement with gnostic sources or demonstrated to be wrong absolutely.[30]

Relatedly, we find a perplexing tendency of studies to overlook, or even "scrub," the σοφία-as-philosophy option from the history of scholarship. Several studies characterize the rhetorical thesis as "the view of older scholars," despite the fact that the scholars they mention identify σοφία with both rhetoric *and* philosophy and sometimes with philosophy more specifically than rhetoric.[31] Moreover, I have found in quite a number of places summaries of the history of research that leave the philosophy option out entirely, including an article called "A Critical Review of Recent Scholarship" by Oh-Young Kwon.[32]

These problems are not universal, and scholarship in the newer line has by no means lacked robust argumentation for its views. However, when one pauses to critically evaluate the overall movement of scholarship, it appears in view of the tendencies described that, to some degree, the movement happened before the argument, that the resulting trajectory then crystallized into a narrative, and that the narrative then legitimated the movement.

---

in Corinth, x, 218, 404; Winter, "Philo and Paul among the Sophists," later published as *Philo and Paul among the Sophists*, where he deletes his interaction with Gnosticism.

29. And Winter (*After Paul Left Corinth*, 26) mentions Gnosticism, incipient Gnosticism, and over-realized eschatology in one paragraph and dismisses the last option in one sentence, alleging misinterpretation of "4:6ff."

30. Klutz, "Re-reading 1 Corinthians," 201–6. Klutz argues for continuities with the brand of Gnosticism represented by the author of the Gospel of Philip.

31. For such characterizations, see Litfin, *St. Paul's Theology of Proclamation*, 3, 8; Mihaila, *Paul-Apollos Relationship*, 82; L. L. Welborn, "On the Discord in Corinth: 1 Corinthians 1–4 and Ancient Politics," *JBL* 106 (1987): 85–111, esp. 102. But see the actual language in Wilckens, "Σοφία, σοφός, σοφίζω," *TDNT* 7:522; Johannes Munck, "Menigheden uden Partier," *Dansk Teologisk Tidsskrift* 15 (1952): 215–33; ET: "The Church without Factions: Studies in 1 Corinthians 1–4," in *Paul and the Salvation of Mankind* (London: SCM, 1959), 135–67; George Kennedy, *Classical Rhetoric and Its Christian and Secular Tradition from Ancient to Modern Times*, 2nd ed. (Chapel Hill: University of North Carolina Press, 1999), 131–32. See also on philosophy: Weiss, *Der erste Korintherbrief*, 23, 158–59.

32. Litfin, *St. Paul's Theology of Proclamation*, 3–4; Bullmore, *St. Paul's Theology of Rhetorical Style*, 5; Winter, *After Paul Left Corinth*, 26; Mihaila, *Paul-Apollos Relationship*, 6, 70–94. Kwon even omits it from "Critical Review."

From Text to Social Backgrounds

An astonishing feature of several important studies in the newer line is just how much space is given to "social background" and how little to exegesis. One finds this pattern in studies on both the rhetorical and the patronage side. I note for instance Marshall's 130 pages dedicated to friendship conventions; Litfin's 114 pages on the history of Greco-Roman rhetoric; and Bullmore's expatiation on Greco-Roman rhetoric that occupies almost the entirety of his book, with just a short final chapter on 1 Cor 2:1–5.[33] Such studies offer, I want to suggest, a "*background* of the text" rather than a "background of the *text*." With the imbalance of attention between background and text, the reconstruction becomes little more than a "sketch," which focuses on themes and shared vocabulary but is not subjected to extensive testing exegetically. As I seek to demonstrate in the following chapters, these sketches often fit uncomfortably with the text when scrutinized.

The Fragmentation of Insights

Another noticeable feature of the recent era of scholarship is a tendency toward greater "fragmentation of insights." Scholarship has increasingly emphasized that the problems contributing to the church's divisions were many and cannot be reduced to any single cause (like a religious system). While this is undoubtedly correct, this openness has gradually built a rather unintegrated picture of the situation. According to recent studies, the divisions in Corinth were caused by socioeconomic stratification, the quest for honor, varying leadership preferences, enmity and friendship over patronage relationships, hard feelings toward Paul because he had not returned, and, perhaps above all, criticism of Paul's rhetorical abilities (and praise of Apollos's). The complexity of the situation is only compounded for those who admit that "theological" factors still played a role.[34] Interpreters generally make a case for one factor in particular while also assuming that several, if not all,

---

33. Marshall, *Enmity in Corinth*, 1–130; Litfin, *St. Paul's Theology of Proclamation*, 21–134; Bullmore, *St. Paul's Theology of Rhetorical Style*, 205–22.

34. Note the mix of factors affirmed in Hiigel, *Leadership in 1 Corinthians*; Horrell, *Social Ethos*. Advocates of the rhetorical thesis sometimes remark in passing that the Hellenistic-Judaism thesis may help explain some aspects of the problem, without explaining how these aspects of wisdom integrate: e.g., Marshall, *Enmity in Corinth*, viii; Timothy Lim, "Not in Persuasive Words of Wisdom, but in the Demonstration of the

of these factors were in play. Yet, interpreters often fail to explain how these factors integrate into a fully coherent picture. Consequently the reader struggles to understand how the interpreter sees the picture in lucid detail.

Reconsidering the Wisdom of the Corinthians

The purpose of this book will be to undertake a full reconsideration of the Corinthians' σοφία and the situation behind 1 Cor 1–4. Our specific thesis will take us away from recent explanations oriented around Greco-Roman rhetoric and patronage practices toward an explanation oriented around Greek philosophy, and more specifically, Stoicism.[35] In my view, it is not scholarship itself that has ruled out the philosophical option. It is the story that has been told about the history of scholarship. We have been *told* that the problems in Corinth were "not theological," not *shown* that they were not. As noted, history-of-research summaries representing the accepted narrative have frequently and inexplicably omitted, entirely, studies that relate the Corinthians' σοφία to Greek philosophy, or to its more specific varieties, like Stoicism.[36] Apart from a few earlier studies, the Stoic thesis in particular has not yet received the consideration that, I hope to show, is merited by the evidence. We shall pursue a new version of this thesis here, though with more elaborate development of the connecting themes and, as never before, a detailed reconstruction of the social situation in which Corinthian σοφία was implicated.

Spirit and Power (1 Cor 2:4)," *NovT* 29 (1987): 137–49, 145–46; Litfin, *St. Paul's Theology of Proclamation*, 253; Kwon, "Critical Review," 405.

35. We seem to be witnessing an upsurge of attention to the philosophical landscape of the first century and its relevance to early Christianity. Troels Engberg-Pedersen has been prolific: *Paul and the Stoics* (Louisville: Westminster John Knox, 2000); *Cosmology and Self in the Apostle Paul: The Material Spirit* (Oxford: Oxford University Press, 2010); *John and Philosophy: A New Reading of the Fourth Gospel* (Oxford: Oxford University Press, 2017). See also a plethora of articles and collections of essays, including the essays in Joseph R. Dodson and David E. Briones, eds., *Paul and Seneca in Dialogue*, Ancient Philosophy and Religion 2 (Leiden: Brill, 2017); Joseph R. Dodson and Andrew W. Pitts, eds., *Paul and the Greco-Roman Philosophical Tradition*, LNTS 527 (London: T&T Clark, 2017). Most recent is Max Lee's voluminous *Moral Transformation in Greco-Roman Philosophy of Mind*, WUNT 2/515 (Tübingen: Mohr Siebeck, 2020), which is the first installment of two volumes to be published on moral transformation in philosophy, ultimately as related to Paul.

36. See n. 32 above.

A Sociohistorical Approach

Guiding Principles of Reconstruction

I want to lay out five guiding principles that will govern my approach to reconstruction of the conflict in 1 Cor 1–4.

(1) *Exegesis takes "priority" over backgrounds.* There is no denying that text and background are mutually interpreting. The text of 1 Corinthians, however, must take priority over backgrounds in one sense of the term *priority*—specifically, in that we have access to *this* situation only through this particular letter. Interpretation must begin with exegesis for we must "first" have something to interpret. We would know something about the Corinthian conflict if we had only the letter but little understanding of the world external to it. We would know nothing about the conflict without the letter. This observation may seem rather obvious. Yet, it will be my contention that recent trends in the interpretation of 1 Corinthians have succeeded largely due to a lack of attention to the text at a focused exegetical level.[37] To repeat, studies have offered a "*background* of the text" rather than a "background of the *text*." Renewed attention to exegesis will be necessary both to test the validity of newer lines of interpretation and to make a legitimate case for the argument that shall be offered here.

(2) *Generic significations do not rule out specific significations.* This "specificity" principle is grounded firmly in the principles of sociolinguistics.[38] It may be true that the Corinthians' language or views, at a level of abstraction, find parallels in multiple cultural discourses, not just the ones proposed in this or that study as specific influences.[39] Likewise, there is analytic legitimacy in the notion of cultural "commonplaces." One must not, however, confuse a plurality of "semiotic *potential*" with the "significant *situational* value" of language in context.[40] This is to acknowledge the category of "register," or "a variety [of language] associated with a particular situation of

---

37. Studies that acknowledge the importance of exegesis often lament that their focus on cultural themes precludes attention to the former: e.g., Clarke, *Secular and Christian Leadership*, 132.

38. Bitner (*Paul's Political Strategy*, 110) also approaches his study through sociolinguistics.

39. So Martin, *Corinthian Body*, 71–72.

40. This distinction is from M. A. K. Halliday and Ruqaiya Hasan, *Language, Context, and Text: Aspects of Language in a Social-Semiotic Perspective* (Oxford: Oxford University Press, 1989), 100.

use."[41] With respect to the linguistic features, my approach here will not be simply to note similarities in vocabulary and thought but also to consider these similarities from the perspective of form analysis. More importantly, I shall need to demonstrate similarity between the Corinthian σοφία and the doctrines of Stoicism at a level of technicality and some systematicity. We shall also have to consider the Corinthians' immediate environment. If it can be demonstrated from a convergence of contextual factors—that is, demonstrated on sociolinguistic grounds—that the Corinthians' views can be associated distinctly with Stoicism, then our more particular claims will be justified.

(3) *The more historically probable explanation is the best.* I point out the obvious only because the "historicity" principle has definitively ruled out only one widely prevalent view in the history of scholarship: the gnostic thesis associated classically with Lütgert, Schlatter, Wilckens, and Schmithals. Among the more plausible options, the best will be the one that establishes plausibility in relation not just to the general Greco-Roman milieu, but to the milieu of first-century Greece, even Corinth itself, and in relation to the profile of the Corinthian church in particular, even its specific members, as much as can be known about them.

The external evidence necessary for this kind of inquiry includes both (a) sociocultural evidence and (b) linguistic evidence. (a') On the sociocultural side, I shall draw heavily from literary sources for a description of Stoic philosophy while drawing primarily from inscriptional evidence for investigation of contemporary philosophical culture and the environment of first-century Corinth. (b') Linguistic evidence largely concerns shared vocabulary and ideas along with literary "parallels" shared between the text of 1 Corinthians and Stoic discourse. Part of my purpose here will be to demonstrate the historical and sociolinguistic probability of ties between the Corinthians' σοφία and the discourse of Stoic philosophy.

(4) *"Social" causes blend with "theological" ones.* As noted, scholarship has largely discarded older (theological) explanations along with the imperfect (philological) methods used to reach them. A "sociological" approach, however, does not rule out "theological" explanations. For on the one hand, a "theological" explanation need not preclude the influence of "social" factors on "theology";[42] and on the other hand, "social" problems can surely

---

41. D. Biber and S. Conrad, *Register, Genre, and Style*, CTL (Cambridge: Cambridge University Press, 2009), 4–6.

42. Through Gerd Theissen's seminal work on the Corinthian letters, the terms *theolog-*

be grounded in a "theological" rationale. In this regard, religious and philosophical explanations for the Corinthians' σοφία are not, by nature, "disembodied from social contexts" (even if the original gnostic explanation was).[43] Stoicism was a social phenomenon. It was a philosophical system advocated first by a philosopher named Zeno, who founded a school that consisted of students who followed his teachings. By the first century CE, there were Stoic schools everywhere, and thousands of people who sought to live on some level according to Zeno's traditional teachings. The Stoic thesis therefore does not rely merely upon finding overlap of abstract "ideas." It relies rather on demonstrating Stoic connections at some level of sociolinguistic specificity while at the same time making a historically situated case that Stoicism was present and likely influential on the kinds of people that belonged to the Corinthian church. On the other hand, to connect the Corinthians' σοφία primarily with Stoicism is not necessarily to reduce the Corinthians' conflict *only* to Stoic influence. We must consider what kinds of people might have found Stoicism more attractive and what factors, external to the Stoic system itself, might have attracted them to it.

(5) *Coherence is the best test of validity.* This principle could be considered our preeminent criterion of validity. The "criterion of coherence" concerns the coherence of a reading at a "global" level. Put in terms of sociolinguistics, global coherence entails coherence at three levels of meaning. The need for coherence applies, in the first place, (a) to the *internal* coherence of our reading of the text. The interpreter is obligated to test and to demonstrate coherence through careful consideration of the text at the exegetical—not just the thematic—level. Without thorough exegesis, a theory cannot be fully tested, and hence cannot be proven. (b) The principle of coherence also applies to our reconstruction of the *external* situation. Articulating a coherent reconstruction requires arrangement of all the "facts" into a coherent picture. As this relates to 1 Cor 1–4, these facts include at the broadest level that the church is divided, that the divisions have largely to do with σοφία, and that those who deem themselves σοφοί are boasting in someone or something. At a finer level, we shall have to answer such questions as, Were there distinct

---

ical and *social* have become a standard pair in related discussions: Theissen, *Social Setting*, 146. Theissen's purpose was to explore the sociological dimensions of problems that he believed also had theological basis. See, for example, Theissen, "Social Integration," 123. So also Malherbe, *Social Aspects*, 84.

43. This is Pogoloff's (*Logos and Sophia*, 161) language in reference to Schmithals' consideration of "Judaism." But note the more nuanced conception of Gnosticism found in Theissen, *Social Setting*, 132–40.

parties in the church or was there only general dissension? How many parties were there—two, three, four, or more? Was it one party that championed what Paul calls the "wisdom of the world"? Who was boasting, and in whom? How were the Corinthians' orientations toward σοφία interrelated with their loyalties to respective ministers? If the Corinthians decided loyalties based on the social conventions of friendship or patronage, what connection might this have had with the matter of σοφία? (c) Finally, the coherency principle applies to the *match* between (b′) our external reconstruction and (a′) the internal details of the text.

A coherence-based approach might be distinguished from two other approaches common in studies on 1 Corinthians. The differences of approach are partly a matter of aspectual focus and partly a matter of scope. (1) One approach takes as its objective a demonstration of a particular *background*—like the background of sophistry (Winter) or the background of patronage (Marshall). (2) A second approach elaborates on a particular *theme* in the text—as for example the theme of honor seeking (Finney). Such approaches can be fruitful. Their limitation is that their argumentative strategy deprioritizes, and to some extent even neglects, exegesis. The result may be a "coherent" thesis, but not a "globally coherent" one, all evidence considered. My contention is that some of the most influential recent studies on 1 Cor 1–4 fail in coherence when one presses the details and how they hold together.

Reconstructing the Corinthian Habitus

I have gestured toward the point that I am not just concerned with the Corinthians' views in the sense of their "ideas." Since ideas and social practices are mutually reinforcing, I shall prefer to describe the Corinthian disposition in terms of what has been called *habitus*.[44] The concept of *habitus* describes perceptions of the world as inseparable from practice, so that "body"—or how we "are" in the world—becomes a "constitutive ingredient of how we perceive, order, and practice reality itself."[45]

Our reconstruction of the Corinthians' *habitus* will depend upon the following kinds of evidence.

(1) *What Paul says in 1 Corinthians.* (a) This kind of evidence includes, first, Paul's topical coverage in the letter. At a minimum we can gather from 1 Cor

---

44. A term that is becoming more and more prevalent in biblical scholarship; see, for example, Engberg-Pedersen, *Cosmology and Self*, 141–42; John M. G. Barclay, *Paul and the Gift* (Grand Rapids: Eerdmans, 2015), 506–7.

45. Barclay, *Paul and the Gift*, 507.

1–4 that the church was divided, apparently into parties centering around different ministers (and possibly Christ), that these divisions were caused in large part by the Corinthians' conception(s) of σοφία, and that for some reason they were boasting. (b) Paul of course leaves certain facts of the situation undeclared since the facts are antecedently known to the participants. Filling in this antecedent space requires some degree of "mirror-reading," or working back indirectly to the situation from what Paul says about it.[46] (c) Finally, we may conjecture, on grounds of basic relevance theory, a connection between Paul's rhetoric or the linguistic domains appropriated, on the one hand, and the mindset and preferred parlance of his audience, on the other.

(2) *Corinthian language embedded in 1 Corinthians.* As interpreters have long agreed, a number of "catchwords" and "slogans" originating with the Corinthians are embedded in Paul's discourse at points throughout the letter.[47] Identifying this language is crucial to our understanding of the Corinthians' conception of wisdom and the general *habitus* that contributed to their conflict.

(a) Corinthian language in chapters 1–4 consists mostly in individual terms or pairs of terms. We can scarcely doubt that certain individuals considered themselves σοφοί ("wise," esp. 3:18; 6:5) and to have possessed σοφία ("wisdom").[48] These individuals apparently also considered themselves πνευματικοί ("spiritual"), while considering others ψυχικοί ("unspiritual"; 2:14–15; cf. 14:12, 37); and considered themselves τέλειοι ("perfect"), but others νήπιοι ("immature," 2:6; 3:1; cf. 13:10–11; 14:20).[49] Related are several terms that

---

46. *Mirror-reading* has become a loaded term, often used to discredit another's interpretation as unjustified speculation; note George Lyons's definition in his fierce attack on the practice. Lyons, *Pauline Autobiography*, SBLDS 73 (Atlanta: Scholars, 1985), 79–120, esp. 96. John M. G. Barclay, however, has laid out a more responsible approach to the practice in "Mirror-Reading a Polemical Letter: Galatians as a Test Case," *JSNT* 31 (1987): 73–93.

47. For a lengthier discussion of Corinthian language, see Brookins, *Corinthian Wisdom*, 82–101.

48. As Inkelaar points out, not only do a vast majority of occurrences of the σοφός/σοφία terminology in Paul's letters occur in 1 Corinthians (twenty-eight times in 1 Corinthians of only thirty-four instances in the Pauline corpus), his citations of the OT in 1 Cor 1–4 almost always include or allude to the σοφός, language that is rare in the books cited (*Conflict over Wisdom*, 165–67). Few have been convinced by the view that chapters 1–4 contain a pre-Pauline homily rather than an ad hoc response to the Corinthian situation; for the homily view, see Wilhelm Wuellner, "Haggadic Homily Genre in 1 Corinthians 1–3," *JSNT* 89 (1970): 199–204; Branick, "Source and Redaction Analysis."

49. Schmithals, *Gnosticism in Corinth*, 151; Pearson, *Pneumatikos-Psychikos Terminology*, 27. But this is not just the view of older interpreters. More recent representatives include Fee, *First Epistle to the Corinthians*, 99–100 (2nd ed., 106); John M. G. Barclay, "Thessalonica and Corinth: Social Contrasts in Pauline Christianity," *JSNT* 47 (1992): 61–62;

Paul directly predicates of the Corinthians: some of them were "powerful [δυνατοί]" and "well born [εὐγενεῖς]" (1:26); some were "rich [ἐπλουτήσατε]" and "kings [ἐβασιλεύσατε]" (4:8), "prudent [φρόνιμοι]," "strong [ἰσχυροί]," and "honored [ἔνδοξοι]" (4:10). Judging from its prevalence in these chapters, δύναμις (1:18, 24; 2:4, 5; 4:19, 20) may also have been a Corinthian term.

(b) The so-called Corinthian slogans seem to be concentrated in chapters 6–8 (cf. 10:23). By interpreters' virtually unanimous agreement, Paul cites slogans in 6:12a, c (repeated in 10:23), 13a; 7:1a–b; 8:1a, 4, 5–6, 8.[50] Recent arguments add support to the already considerable group of interpreters who have detected a slogan in 6:18b.[51] Paul cites the Corinthians through indirect discourse in 15:12. Many interpreters find Corinthian terminology in the statements of 2:14, 15, including not only the πνευματικός-ψυχικός pair (identified above), but also the term ἀνακρίνεται; some interpreters identify 2:14, 15 itself as a slogan.[52] A running theme in the ideology of the slogans is an attitude of indifference toward the body and how one uses it (6:12 // 10:23; 6:13, 18; 8:8; 15:12). Related to this theme is the Corinthians' emphasis on "knowledge" and the priority of the intellectual or spiritual faculties as a criterion for ethical judgments or personal evaluation (6:18; 8:1, 4, 5–6).

The methods used to identify this language need not detain us,[53] for the conclusions are widely accepted, and we must—I have urged—get on more

---

Christian Wolff, *Der erste Brief des Paulus an die Korinther* (Leipzig: Evangelische Verlagsanstalt, 1996), 63; Richard A. Horsley, *1 Corinthians* (Nashville: Abingdon, 1998), 57–61; Anthony C. Thiselton, *First Epistle to the Corinthians*, NIGTC (Grand Rapids: Eerdmans, 2000), 225; Joseph Fitzmyer, *First Corinthians*, AYBC 32 (New Haven: Yale University Press, 2008), 183; Wolfgang Schrage, *Der erste Brief an die Korinther*, 4 vols., EKKNT 7 (Zürich: Benziger Verlag, 1991–2001), 1:240–41; Jacob Kremer, *Der erste Brief* (Regensburg: Pustet, 1997), 57–62, 67; Finney, *Honour and Conflict*, 100; and many others. Chester (*Conversion at Corinth*, 283) notes "widespread agreement among commentators" that the πνευματικοί-ψυχικοί pair reflects Corinthian terminology (saying in a footnote that "nearly all accept the pair of terms as Corinthian," 283n60).

50. See the tabulation of commentators' views in Brookins, *Corinthian Wisdom*, 92.

51. Andrew David Naselli, "Is Every Sin outside the Body except Immoral Sex? Weighing Whether 1 Corinthians 6:18b Is Paul's Statement or a Corinthian Slogan," *JBL* 136 (2017): 969–87.

52. Affirmed in Funk, "Word and Word," 299; Horsley, *1 Corinthians*, 61; Charles H. Talbert, *Reading Corinthians: A Literary and Theological Commentary* (Macon, GA: Smyth & Helwys, 2002), 18; Antoinette Clark Wire, *The Corinthian Women Prophets: A Reconstruction through Paul's Rhetoric* (Philadelphia: Fortress, 1990), 54; Thiselton, *First Epistle to the Corinthians*, 271–72.

53. For some methodological discussions, see for example: David R. Hall, *The Unity of the Corinthian Correspondence*, JSNTSup 251 (London: T&T Clark, 2003), 201–4; Jay E. Smith, "Slogans in 1 Corinthians," *BSac* 167 (2010): 74–86; Edward W. Watson and Martin M.

seriously with the task of exegesis. As a starting point, I will assume that this language, if not all derived from the Corinthians, is at least reflective of the Corinthian self-understanding.

(3) *The cultural milieu.* External evidence drawn from the cultural environment illuminates not only intellectual currents of the day but also the interrelated behaviors and relational patterns that prevailed to establish the social institutions in which the denizens of that world participated. In this regard, I rely here primarily on literary and epigraphical evidence, with some appeal to archeological evidence. Naturally, this evidence puts constraints on what interpretations of the letter can be considered likely or even possible.

The Stoic Thesis

The present study is not the first to argue for affinities between the Corinthian *habitus* and the doctrines of Stoicism. However, this study represents one in a very short list of book-length treatments of this comparison. The most recent contribution is my own 2014 monograph, *Corinthian Wisdom, Stoic Philosophy, and the Ancient Economy*.[54] I summarize the contributions of that volume below. I then address the differences between that study and the present one. Finally, I offer an overview of the present project.

Brookins (2014)

A sudden flood of publications in the 1990s succeeded in moving the general opinion of scholarship to the view that the σοφία of the Corinthians concerned Greco-Roman rhetoric. By the time *Corinthian Wisdom* was published in 2014, this background was no longer argued; it was generally assumed. My purposes then were twofold. First, I pushed firmly against the consensus regarding the rhetorical background of 1 Cor 1–4. Second, I proposed that σοφία should be read instead against the background of Stoic philosophy.

My positive contributions were primarily semantic and thematic. I demonstrated from the ancient evidence that σοφ- language is more fittingly under-

---

Culy, *Quoting Corinthians: Identifying Slogans and Quotations in 1 Corinthians* (Eugene, OR: Pickwick, 2018). For a broader look at identifying "Paul's opponents," see Jerry Sumney, *Identifying Paul's Opponents: The Question of Method in 2 Corinthians* (Sheffield: JSOT Press, 1990), 76–113.

54. Brookins, *Corinthian Wisdom*. Otherwise, I note only Albert V. Garcilazo, *The Corinthian Dissenters and the Stoics* (New York: Peter Lang, 2007). For a couple of articles, see n. 16 above.

stood in connection with philosophy than with rhetoric: seeing that σοφία was well established as a technical term for "philosophy," just as σοφός was for the "philosopher"; that these meanings are offered by every lexicon; that this vocabulary occurs in literary sources far more prevalently in connection with philosophy than with rhetoric; and that although biblical scholarship that has advocated for the rhetorical interpretation connects σοφία with rhetoric at the thematic level of argument, embedded in the same discussions is a somewhat hidden acknowledgement that this language pairs with philosophy semantically, as shown by interpreters' usage of terms.[55] Moreover, based on what most interpreters presume to be "Corinthian terminology" or "Corinthian slogans" (as noted above) and the recurrence of certain themes across the letter, I was able to establish several thematic connections between the views of the Corinthians and the doctrines of Stoicism. Chief among these themes were the self-conception of some church members as σοφοί, understood in terms of the philosophical "wise man"; a distinction in intellectual status between the σοφοί as τέλειοι and "knowledgeable" (cf. γνῶσις) on the one hand, and others as νήπιοι and ἀσθενής on the other; a strong emphasis on "freedom"; and an orientation of "indifference" toward matters related to the body.[56]

Thesis and Overview of the Present Work

Building on my earlier observations, I aim here to advance the Stoic thesis further in four ways. First, given my overarching purposes in *Corinthian Wisdom*, I was not able to engage extensively with the text of 1 Corinthians *exegetically*. It will be one of the main burdens of this book to test the theories of recent scholarship through close analysis of the text while demonstrating the cogency of the Stoic thesis on the same terms. Second, I seek to demonstrate a similarity between the Corinthian σοφία and the doctrines of Stoicism at a level of technicality and some systematicity. My third contribution is sociohistorical. While I offered arguments in *Corinthian Wisdom* that some of the Corinthians were of such a status as made some level of formal philosophical training a reasonable possibility, I shall pursue an extended examination of philosophical activity in Roman culture and in first-century Corinth specifically to determine the likelihood of local influence. Fourth,

---

55. Brookins, *Corinthian Wisdom*, 30–44. Regarding usage, note that Pogoloff's title, *Logos and Sophia*, correlates the former term with rhetoric and the latter with philosophy. The coordination of terms in these senses occurs passim in Litfin, *Paul's Theology of Proclamation*.

56. Brookins, *Corinthian Wisdom*, 153–200.

I attempt to offer a full *reconstruction* of the conflict behind chapters 1–4, one that includes not only a thesis about the Corinthians' σοφία and how it came to them but also a theory about the sequence of events that led to the formation of the parties, about the Corinthians' conceptions of the parties, and about how the parties related to the problem of σοφία.

Regarding my understanding of Corinthian σοφία, my specific thesis is this. The σοφοί in the church adopted—probably directly and probably consciously—a theological framework that was in content and structure analogous to a fairly complex network of ideas endemic to Stoic philosophy. Constituting this framework was a similar configuration of systemically related parts located, specifically, at a cross-section where Stoic physics and anthropology intersected with Stoic ethics. I argue that, drawing from "tonic" distinctions articulated in Stoic physics, the σοφοί in Corinth distinguished between higher- and lower-level believers, whose respective statuses varied according to the strength of their union with connate Spirit. They themselves were "wise" (and "spiritual"); the others were "immature" (and "unspiritual"). On the side of ethics, the σοφοί viewed the immanent Spirit as a peculiar property of themselves as human beings, resulting in the possibility of αὐτάρκεια, or human self-sufficiency, and a right to boast in what was "their own." The σοφοί made local modifications to this Stoic complex through the substitution of a structurally compatible "replacement part"; specifically, adapting the Stoic view of "indifferents," they replaced Stoic virtue with Spirit, thus elevating spiritual faculties above bodily behavior and making the spiritual faculties the sole criterion of personal evaluation. What resulted was a substitution of the Stoic ethical classification good, bad, and indifferent with the parallel classification spiritual, unspiritual, and indifferent.

One of our tasks will be to decide how best to characterize the overall balance between "Stoic" and "Christian" elements. I will suggest that the resulting Corinthian system was not purely Stoic, but "sub-Stoic"—or a "sub-(ordinated) Stoicism," akin to Stoicism but nevertheless "subordinate" to the Christ-faith declared by the subjects.

As to my reconstruction of the situation, I summarize as follows. A few members of the church, by virtue of their social location, had some direct acquaintance with the doctrines of Stoicism. Although they professed faith in Christ, they reflectively integrated Paul's teaching into a Stoic framework. These—the self-proclaimed σοφοί—constituted none other than the core constituents of the Paul faction (1:12). Having begun their instruction under Paul within the walls of a household in Corinth, they viewed Paul as their teacher and (despite their affinities for Stoicism) as founder, as it were, of a new philosophical school. Their commitment to Paul was analogous to the kind of philosophical allegiance demonstrated in philosophical sects of the day. Other parties formed in the church in reaction.

I have arranged the study in three parts. Together with the present introduction, part 1 includes a chapter on methodological approaches (chapter 2) that considers the problems of definition (how to define Stoicism or the Corinthians' σοφία) and of comparison (genealogical vs. illustrative comparison). In light of recent discussions about how ancient people interacted with the doctrines of philosophy or with rival philosophies, I here propose *sub-Stoicism* as an appropriate label for the Corinthians' σοφία. Consisting of seven chapters (chapters 3–9), part 2 runs consecutively through 1 Cor 1:17b–4:21 (chapters 3–8) and seeks to accomplish several goals: (a) It offers a critical examination of recent scholarship as we move through the text. (b) It illustrates the extensive linguistic, conceptual, and structural parallels evident between the *habitus* of the Corinthian σοφοί and the discourse of Stoicism. (c) It demonstrates how the proposed thesis, including our comprehensive reconstruction of the situation, works at the fine exegetical level. In this part of the book, attention to detail is sometimes meticulous, and the reader will benefit greatly by following the arguments in the original Greek text. I emphasize that *the cogency of these arguments cannot be evaluated apart from the reader's critical interaction with the exegesis involved.* Conversely, the reader is advised not to judge the Stoic thesis based on the exegetical chapters alone (chapters 3–8). In the final chapter of part 2 (chapter 9), I lay out the comparison between the Corinthian σοφία and the relevant Stoic doctrines in detail.

The third and final part of the book circles back to the opening section of the letter, where Paul first introduces the matter of the divisions (1:10–17a). Thus, rather than forming a hypothesis about the nature of the divisions that is then carried forward into 1:17b–4:21, I evaluate the divisions in light of our prior examination of its causes as discussed in the latter section. I argue in this part for an analogy between the attitude of the Paul party and the stance of philosophical allegiance exhibited by students in the philosophical schools of the day (chapter 10). Finally, I examine the evidence for philosophical activity within the Corinthians' contemporary and immediate environment (chapter 11) and evaluate the possibility of direct contact with Stoic philosophy among the people in the Corinthian church (chapter 12). The conclusion summarizes these analyses.

2

The Problems of Definition and Comparison

In coming to 1 Cor 1–4, one cannot say that the Corinthians' σοφία "was the wisdom of Torah," or that it "was Hellenistic Judaism," or that it "was Stoicism" or "Epicureanism" or "Gnosticism" without raising a host of methodological questions. In this chapter we shall deal with two vital problems that any comparative thesis faces. First is the problem of definition. Is it possible to isolate a stable, or "essentialist," definition of any religious or philosophical system? Closely related is the problem of comparison. To what extent can one say that the Corinthians' σοφία was like, much less identical with, any other ancient system? And to the extent that the Corinthians made their own modifications, to what extent is it legitimate to insist upon nominal identity? Addressing these questions requires some theoretical discussion about criteria for defining concepts in sociological analysis. It also requires that we address methodological considerations related to the nature of comparison in such analysis.

Hence, in the present chapter, we discuss, first, the history of ancient Stoicism and the question of how to define Stoicism and the Stoic. In the second part, we relate the problem of defining Stoicism and the Stoic to the issue of defining the Corinthians' σοφία by exploring the dynamics of philosophical exchange among ancient philosophical schools.

A Brief History of Stoicism

The Stoic School in Athens

Around 300 BCE a philosopher named Zeno (335–263 BCE) founded a school on the "portico" (Στοά) in Athens. At first known as "Zenonians" (Ζηνώνειοι),[1] Zeno's students soon came to be known as "those from the Stoa" (οἱ ἀπὸ τῆς Στοᾶς), or simply as "Stoics" (Στωικοί), after the location of the school. Upon Zeno's death, the school passed to the leadership of Cleanthes (331–232 BCE), and after his death to Chrysippus (280–207 BCE), and thereafter to others, in a clear line of succession that went on for over a century.

In one sense, a "Stoic" during the early period was simple to define: it was a student who went devotedly to the school under the portico (Στοά) in Athens under the instruction of Zeno or one in the line of scholarchs who followed him. This was the empirical school of the Stoics. In another sense, the definition of a Stoic is more nebulous. Zeno himself had been a student of the Cynic Crates (ca. 368/365–288/285 BCE), who had himself learned under the instruction of philosophers before him (Crates learned from Diogenes the Cynic). Zeno and his successors drew from Aristotle and (especially in the later phases of the school) from Plato, as well as some of the less influential teachers.[2] During Zeno's lifetime, the "Stoic" school exhibited little institutional uniformity and had no established orthodoxy.[3]

As a dogmatic system, Stoicism owed more to Zeno's later successor Chrysippus (280–207 BCE). Following Zeno's threefold division of philosophy into the "physical," "logical," and "ethical" parts,[4] Chrysippus integrated these areas into a single coherent system. None of Chrysippus's writings survive in full,[5] but the chief doctrines associated with Stoicism for ages to come all

---

1. Diogenes Laertius, *Vit. phil.* 7.5.
2. On earlier philosophical influences on Stoicism, see, e.g., D. N. Sedley, "The School, from Zeno to Arius Didymus," in *Cambridge Companion to the Stoics*, ed. Brad Inwood (Cambridge: Cambridge University Press, 2002), 7–32, esp. 10; D. N. Sedley, introduction to *The Cambridge Companion to Greek and Roman Philosophy* (Cambridge: Cambridge University Press, 2003), 1–19; B. Inwood and L. P. Gerson, eds., *The Stoics Reader: Selected Writings and Testimonia* (Indianapolis: Hackett, 2008), x–xv; and A. G. Long, *Plato and the Stoics* (Cambridge: Cambridge University Press, 2013).
3. Sedley, introduction, 13–18.
4. *SVF* 2:35–40, esp. 2:37. For the subdivisions, see Seneca, *Ep.* 89; Cicero, *Tusc.* 5.23.69–72.
5. The books constituting his voluminous oeuvre are catalogued in full in Diogenes Laertius, *Vit. phil.* 7.189–202.

trace to his codifications: that the universe is constituted by two principles, matter (the elements) and causation (divine Reason); that Cause/Reason, as Spirit, infuses and is mixed with all things, and hence that the universe and all it contains is One; that the world will end by conflagration, and that end will be succeeded by beginning, and that the cycle of cosmic destruction and rebirth will continue in perpetuity; that the soul is bodily and not uniquely immortal, though it may survive beyond death for a time; that all things, including the cosmic cycle and the fortunes of individuals, happen according to an unbreakable concatenation of causes and effects governed by Providence; that Nature constitutes a Law by which all citizens of the world(-city) should abide; that virtue is the highest good, to be sought for its own sake, and that all things external and bodily should be regarded as indifferent; that the virtuous life consists in shunning the passions and following the dictates of reason; and that the highest human end is to become a σοφός ("wise man") by living consistently in conformity with nature.[6] In these doctrines are integrated all three of the parts of philosophy: Nature provides the paradigm for ethics (= physics + ethics); reason provides the means of distinguishing between what is good, bad, and indifferent (= logic + ethics); and reason is rooted in nature (= logic + physics).

With the achievements of Chrysippus, "Stoicism," or "the Stoic philosophy" (ἡ στωϊκὴ φιλοσοφία),[7] was now a complete and more or less consistent doctrinal "system." The Stoic school had become a distinctive *hairesis*, or "sect," sharply defined by its doctrinal commitments and allegiance to the scholarchs who formulated them. While Chrysippus's synthesis became the canon against which to measure, retrospectively, the orthodoxy of figures from the period of Zeno himself,[8] as the school's founder Zeno remained the ultimate authority.[9] Thus, "Stoic" was synonymous with "one who maintains allegiance to Zeno and his teachings."

---

6. The views of Chrysippus have been collected in Hans von Arnim, *Stoicorum Veterum Fragmenta*, vols. 2–3 (Leipzig: Teubner, 1903–1924; repr. 1964); logic and physics: vol. 2; ethics: vol. 3.

7. ἡ στωϊκὴ φιλοσοφία in *SVF* 2:75,14.

8. Long and Sedley remark that Chrysippus developed "all aspects of Stoic theory with such flair, precision and comprehensiveness that 'early Stoicism' means for us, in effect, the philosophy of Chrysippus." A. A. Long and D. N. Sedley, *The Hellenistic Philosophers* (Cambridge: Cambridge University Press, 1987), 2:3. Evidence in Epictetus (*Diatribai*), Plutarch (*On Stoic Self-Contradictions*), and Galen (*On the Doctrines of Hippocrates and Plato*) reveals that Chrysippus's writings continued to be recognized as the canon for Stoic dogma.

9. Sedley, introduction, 17.

Inevitably, Stoicism evolved, not only in response to perceived discrepancies in the system but also for purposes of innovation, needed to answer the exigencies of social and intellectual circumstances. Several distinct phases in the school's history can be delineated.[10] The phase reaching from Zeno to Chrysippus, or the "early" phase (313–207 BCE), set Stoicism apart as a new philosophy in its own right. The Athenian scholarchs Diogenes of Babylon (240–152 BCE) and Antipater (second century BCE) maintained the legacy of the early phase. Subsequently, innovations inspired by Platonism and Aristotelianism under the leadership of Panaetius (Stoic scholarch 129–109 BCE) and Posidonius (lived 135–51 BCE) ushered in a "middle" phase.[11] Until Panaetius, maintenance of a basically Chrysippean orthodoxy was ensured through the school's centralization in Athens and its leadership under a single head, in a line of legitimate succession, up to its sixth head. But these institutional checks were soon undone by catastrophe. In 86 BCE, Rome struck Athens, and the philosophers scattered, henceforth unseating Athens as the headquarters of the major philosophical schools.[12]

The Stoic Dispersion

Taking leave of the Portico, the Stoics resettled in various locations, including Rome, Alexandria, Rhodes, and Tarsus. With this dispersion began the "late," or "Roman," period of Stoicism. Stoic schools now existed in various cities, and in individual households, each having their own teachers.[13] Evidence suggests that these teachers sometimes regarded each other as rivals. A second-century CE source makes mention of rival Stoic clubs known under the names *Diogenists*, *Antipatrists*, and *Panaetiasts*, perhaps reflecting a split of loyalties between the last three heads of the school before the empirical school in Athens disbanded.[14] Thus, while Stoics of the late period remained loyal to the teachings of the earlier scholarchs, they could no longer appeal

---

10. Jacques Brunschwig and David Sedley ("Hellenistic Philosophy," in *The Cambridge Companion to Greek and Roman Philosophy*, 151–83) divide the school's history into the phases "early," "middle," and "imperial" or "Roman" Stoicism (165). Sedley ("School, from Zeno to Arius Didymus," 7) notes that this is the usual way of dividing Stoicism's history, although he himself divides it into five periods.

11. Sedley, "School, from Zeno to Arius Didymus," 22.

12. For a brief sketch of the events, see Sedley, "School, from Zeno to Arius Didymus," 24–25.

13. For attestations of Stoics in the Roman Empire, see chapter 11.

14. Sedley ("School, from Zeno to Arius Didymus," 29) raises this point of speculation.

to a living scholarch as an arbitrator of doctrinal disputes, and it was left to the discretion of teachers to discern what were legitimate applications of their founders' teachings.

The Problem of Definition

Diversity in Stoicism

Despite the meticulously systematic nature of the Stoic system and the stalwart allegiance of self-proclaimed Stoics to the teachings of Zeno and Chrysippus, it would be incorrect to say that Stoicism was an entirely stable and consistent system. Diversity manifested itself in several ways. (1) The Stoic scholarchs disagreed on certain doctrines even in the earliest period, sometimes on technicalities,[15] sometimes on more vital matters.[16] (2) Some significant (Platonizing) innovations were introduced in the middle period, later to be followed by the Roman Stoics.[17] (3) Individual Stoics sometimes changed their minds on certain doctrines, or at least never came to a settled opinion.[18] (4) Some doctrines within the system stood in tension, and different Stoics could gravitate in the one direction or the other.[19]

---

15. For instance, some dissented from Chrysippus's view that the "commanding-faculty" (ἡγεμόνικον) extended outward through the body from the heart, maintaining instead that the commanding faculty was located in the head. Cf. *SVF* 2:836, 879, 910–11.

16. Several Stoics came to doubt and even to reject the doctrine of cosmic conflagrations and regenerations. Diogenes of Babylon doubted it (Cicero, *Nat. d.* 2.118); Boethius of Sidon and Panaetius rejected it (Philo, *Aetern.* [15] 76–77; on Panaetius, Cicero, *Nat. d.* 2.118).

17. Christopher Gill has catalogued several areas of innovation ("The School in the Roman Imperial Period," in *Cambridge Companion to the Stoics*, 33–53, esp. 38–50). Seneca's deviations from orthodoxy in the area of psychology owe a debt to the Stoic scholarch Posidonius. J. M. Rist, "Seneca and Stoic Orthodoxy," *ANRW* 2.36:1993–2012, esp. 2011–12. For a longer discussion of innovations, see Lee, *Moral Transformation*, 271–374.

18. Seneca seemed unable to decide whether the wise man could backslide (reflecting a tension seen already in Chrysippus): for the view that the wise man could not backslide, see *Ep.* 72.6; cf. 71.34; for the view that the wise can become bad again, see *Ben.* 7.16.5–7.19.6; and for the view that he needs other wise men to help sustain him, see *Ep.* 109.10. Seneca also vacillated on the question of what happened to the individual after death: e.g., *Ep.* 24.18.

19. Although Chrysippus placed strong emphasis on the unity and harmony of things in nature (embodied in the notion of κοινωνία), this emphasis would give way in later times to the pull toward individual self-sufficiency (αὐτάρκεια).

The Diffusion and Evolution of Stoicism

Prior to the first century BCE, the philosophical schools in Athens stood apart both in their allegiances to different teachers and, quite literally, in the local spaces that they inhabited—the Stoics at the Portico; the Epicureans, the Garden; Plato's school, the Academia in the olive grove beyond the Dipylon gate; and Aristotle's school, the Lyceum.[20] For a time, they remained cloistered within their respective premises. But Rome's rout of the city in 86 BCE forced them from their enclosures and into conversation. This was the period of the philosophical diaspora. Many fled the city, scattering the seeds of their philosophies abroad, where they took root one next to another, producing hybridizations that in some ways compromised earlier forms.

Falling on fertile soil, Stoicism would shortly tower over the other philosophies through a metamorphosis resulting largely from its marriage with Roman political philosophy. A great many Roman Stoics of this period were more "advocates" than "teachers." These were those who adhered to Stoicism, and even produced Stoic literature, but did not do so from an official post in a Stoic school.[21] The marks of Stoicism are also visible in Roman poetry, both epic and satire.[22] Strong Stoic elements even appear in Jewish works composed around this time (e.g., 4 Maccabees, Testaments of the Twelve Patriarchs, Wisdom of Solomon, the works of Philo).

One could characterize the diffusion and confusion of separate philosophical traditions during this period in several ways. It was not always a case of "eclecticism." Many philosophers reflectively appropriated and merged material from other philosophies without abandoning their professed allegiances to specific philosophical schools.[23] The phenomenon known as Middle Platonism, which combined ingredients from Platonism, Stoicism, and Pythagoreanism, could be characterized in terms of this dynamic. The first identifiable representative of Middle Platonism (Antiochus of Ascalon, 130–69 BC) believed that he was reviving true Platonism, even while maintaining that Plato's philosophy was "implicit" in the works of Zeno (the Stoic) and Aristotle.[24] Also thought to represent Middle Platonism, Philo of Al-

---

20. For a topographical sketch of the locations, see Long and Sedley, *Hellenistic Philosophers*, 1:4.

21. On the sense of "teacher," see Gill, "School in the Roman Imperial Period," 33–58, esp. 36–38.

22. On Vergil and Horace, see Gill, "School in the Roman Imperial Period," esp. 56–57.

23. Troels Engberg-Pedersen, *From Stoicism to Platonism: The Development of Philosophy, 100 BCE–100 CE* (Cambridge: Cambridge University Press, 2017), 2–26, esp. 3–15.

24. Gill's word ("School in the Roman Imperial Period," 54).

exandria (ca. 20 BCE–45 CE) espoused Platonic views on protological and teleological questions (*On the Creation of the World*) but was heavily indebted to Stoicism for his ethics (esp. *That Every Good Person Is Free*). In other cases, we find Peripatetic ethics Stoicized or Stoic ethics Peripateticized.[25]

Philosophy even among those formally educated in it could take a more eclectic form. The philosophical works of Cicero reveal that not all philosophers adhered to the systematic dogmas of a particular school.[26] At the same time Cicero characterized recognized differences as being in fact no differences at all. He claimed for instance that the Stoics say the "same thing [idem]" as the Academics, although "in a different way [alio modo]," and that they differed from the Peripatetics only "in form of expression" (*verbis*), not "in substance" (*re*).[27]

Stoicism and Popular Philosophy

Cross-fertilization between schools in another form resulted in what might be called "popular philosophy,"[28] in modern parlance. Popular philosophy consisted in a loose set of ethical principles associated most recognizably

---

25. Philip Schmitz argues that Cato's Stoicism in *De Finibus* 3 reflected not orthodox Stoicism but a Stoic-Peripatetic amalgam. *"Cato Peripateticus"—stoicische und peripatetische Ethik im Dialog: Cic. fin. 3 und der Aristotelismus des ersten Jh. v. Chr* [*Xenarchos, Boethos und 'Areios Didymos'*], Untersuchungen zur antiken Literatur und Geschichte 113 (Berlin: de Gruyter, 2014).

26. Antiochus abandoned Skepticism, arguing that the Academy had lost the true doctrine of Plato, and refounded the school as the Old Academy, claiming to have restored Plato's dogmatic thinking. He was accused of being a Stoic Platonist (LS 68T). Antiochus's position is represented by Lucullus and Varro in Cicero's *Academica*.

27. On the Academics: *Tusc.* 5.11.32; 5.41.120; on the Peripatetics: *Nat. d.* 1.16.

28. Downing cites literature that equates "popular philosophy" with Cynicism or Cynic-Stoicism. F. Gerald Downing, *Cynics and Christian Origins* (Edinburgh: T&T Clark, 1992), 24. Abraham J. Malherbe makes popular philosophers, Hellenistic moralists, and the "milder" brand of Cynicism virtually synonymous. Malherbe, *Paul and the Popular Philosophers* (Minneapolis: Fortress, 1989), esp. 11–24. Kristin Divjanović uses the term *Populärphilosophie* in reference to general ancient teachings related to matters of practical relevance and widely known in the first-century Greco-Roman world. Divjanović, *Paulus als Philosoph: Das Ethos des Apostels vor dem Hintergrund antiker Populärphilosophie* (Münster: Aschendorff, 2015), 2n2. Troels Engberg-Pedersen clarifies that a phenomenon did exist that could be called "popular philosophy" and defines it as "a more or less connected set of philosophical ideas in ethics that has no distinct profile as belonging to this or that other *haeresis*, but is rather shared by all or most of them." Engberg-Pedersen, "Setting the Scene: Stoicism and Platonism in the Transitional Period in Ancient Philosophy," in *Stoicism in Early Christianity*, ed. Tuomas Rasimus, Troels Engberg-Pedersen, and Ismo Dunderberg (Grand Rapids: Baker Academic, 2010), 1–14, esp. 23.

with the Stoic and Cynic traditions but belonging to no philosophical system in particular and finding representation in a variety of public forms of discourse. The character of popular philosophy is perhaps best personified in the itinerant orator-turned-philosopher Dio Chrysostom (ca. 40/50–after 110 CE), whose teaching and lifestyle exhibited strong Cynic and Stoic affinities with an admixture of Platonism. Popular philosophy disseminated itself through many channels, public and private, and in this way reached audiences of nonprofessionals, influencing them in ways of which they were not always aware. Stoicism in particular became visible in virtually every realm of discourse by the first century CE. Ferguson's echo of Seneca summarizes the effect nicely: "everything Stoicism had to say became common property."[29]

Essentialism and Family Resemblance

Although Stoicism remained an identifiable and, in many ways, unique entity through at least the second century CE, its doctrinal amorphousness around the edges, together with the occasional divergences of opinion shown among its advocates, the evolution of some doctrines over time, and the eventual fading of Stoicism into more "popular" forms, in a way makes impossible a fully stable definition of what constituted "Stoicism" or a "Stoic."

This problem is highlighted in two recent collections of essays. In *The Routledge Handbook of the Stoic Tradition* (2016), John Sellars's introductory essay characterizes the story of the Stoa as "above all a story about a series of individual philosophers who self-identified as 'Stoics.'"[30] As Kurt Lampe puts it in his review of the book, Sellars's essay in essence considers the question whether, given Stoicism's development over time, one should define the philosophy in terms of a "core set of philosophical views," as a "set of philosophical family resemblances," or as an "arborescence that happened to be able to trace a line of succession back to Zeno's gatherings at the Painted Stoa."[31]

A second collection of essays, edited by Engberg-Pedersen (2017), has explored the development of Stoicism alongside Platonism in the period be-

---

29. Everett Ferguson, echoing Seneca: "whatever is well said by anyone belongs to me" (*Ep.* 16.7). Ferguson, *Backgrounds of Early Christianity*, 3rd ed. (Grand Rapids: Eerdmans, 2003), 368.

30. So John Sellars, introduction to *The Routledge Handbook of the Stoic Tradition*, Routledge Handbooks in Philosophy, ed. John Sellars (London: Routledge, 2016), 1–13, esp. 3.

31. Kurt Lampe, review of *The Routledge Handbook of the Stoic Tradition*, ed. John Sellars, *Bryn Mawr Classical Review*.

tween 100 BCE and 100 CE.[32] In his introduction Engberg-Pedersen calls into question the traditional category of "eclecticism" and reaffirms ancient philosophers' sense of firm, definite self-identity. On the other hand, individual essays demonstrate how Stoics engaged in "merger" and "eirenic appropriation" of alien philosophical material into the systems that they professed.

The problem of definition in the matter of ancient philosophy is one manifestation of the larger problem of "essentialism." Applied to the study of religion, essentialism consists in the belief that different religions have certain characteristics that are necessary to their identity, in other words, that they have a certain invariant "essence." In biblical studies, essentialist definitions are now widely seen as being problematic.[33] However, at a cognitive level, concept formation—whereby we separate concepts as discrete entities—is indispensable to comprehension of reality and thus also to sociological inquiry.[34]

Sociologists have proposed a plethora of ways to approach definition other than essentialism.[35] For our purposes, I adopt the notion of polythetic taxonomy as a reasonable approach to our problem in dealing with Stoicism. A polythetic approach attempts to steer between ontological deconstruction on the one hand and essentialism on the other. Whereas essentialist definitions identify certain characteristics as necessary for membership in a class, polythetic taxonomies define members in terms of clusters of overlapping characteristics that commonly occur in members of that class, without

---

32. Engberg-Pedersen, *From Stoicism to Platonism*. See also G. R. Boys-Stones, *Platonist Philosophy 80 BC to AD 250: An Introduction and Collection of Sources in Translation*, Cambridge Source Books in Post-Hellenistic Philosophy (Cambridge: Cambridge University Press, 2018).

33. A rejection of essentialism is presupposed in the treatment of "early Christianity" in James M. Robinson and Helmut Koester, *Trajectories through Early Christianity* (Philadelphia: Fortress, 1971). Against essentialist definitions of Judaism and Hellenism, see for example, J. Albert Harrill, *Paul the Apostle: His Life and Legacy in Their Roman Context* (Cambridge: Cambridge University Press, 2012), 2–3, 158; and Dale Martin, "Paul and the Judaism/Hellenism Dichotomy," in *Paul beyond the Judaism/Hellenism Divide*, ed. Troels Engberg-Pedersen (Louisville: Westminster John Knox, 2001), 29–62.

34. In any case, nominally, one cannot dispense with distinctions. For instance, almost no one has given up the terms *Judaism* and *Hellenism*. See how Daniel Boyarin struggles with this issue in "Nominalist 'Judaism' and the Late-Ancient Invention of Religion," in *Religion, Theory, Critique: Classic and Contemporary Approaches and Methodologies*, ed. Richard King (New York: Columbia University Press, 2017), 23–40.

35. John Gerring, "What Makes a Concept Good? A Criterial Framework for Understanding Concept Formation in the Social Sciences," *Polity* 31 (1999): 357–93.

making any single criterion essential. Polythetic definitions, in this regard, do not imply unique or absolute ontologies for concept entities, but they do nevertheless serve the need of taxonomic distinction.

Polythetic definitions constitute a theoretical extension of Wittgenstein's notion of "family resemblance" (*Familienähnlichkeit*).[36] As in biological relationships, resemblances fall along a spectrum of similarities and differences. By its nature, family resemblance leaves room for ambiguity since there is no stable "universal," so to speak, behind individual specimens; there are only particulars, resembling each other, but none of them identical. Approaching the concepts "Stoicism" and "Stoic" through this model, one might then define ancient Stoicism in terms of polythetic criteria that aggregate into systemic clusters of typical doctrinal characteristics, involving particularly the doctrines summarized above as teachings of Chrysippus in his systematization of Zeno. Likewise, one might define the Stoic person as one who espoused such clusters of teachings and who shared a close family resemblance with others who espoused them.

Deictic Perspective

A related issue is that of *deixis*, or subjective perspective. In sociological terms, *deictic perspective* refers to the distinction between "emic" (an insider's) and "etic" (an outsider's) perspective. In this regard, what might count as a Stoic from one person's perspective might not count as a Stoic from the perspective of another.[37] The emic-etic distinction as used in biblical studies applies typically to the distinction of perspectives between the *ancient subjects* (as they viewed themselves) and *modern observers* (as we view the ancient subjects), though in theory the distinction could also be utilized in negotiating the competing perspectives of ancient subjects.[38]

---

36. Use of polythetic definitions for taxonomy as an extension of the notion of "family resemblance" is attributed to Rodney Needham, "Polythetic Classification: Convergence and Consequences," *Man* 10 (1975): 349–69. In considering what counts as "Cynic," Downing (*Cynics and Christian Origins*, 26–56, esp. 18, 54; *Cynics, Paul, and the Pauline Churches*, 37) proposes a definition in terms of family resemblance.

37. Engberg-Pedersen (*Paul beyond the Judaism/Hellenism Divide*, 11–13) suggests that we need to interpret Paul in terms of what he is *really* doing—whether he was aware of it or not—and not in terms of what he *thought* he was doing, though Engberg-Pedersen does not explicitly use the term *etic* here.

38. A linguistic distinction coined by Kenneth L. Pike, *Language in Relation to a Unified Theory of Human Behavior*, 2nd ed. (University of Illinois, Summer Institute of Linguistics, 1954), esp. 37–72.

The Problems of Definition and Comparison

The matter of identity according to emic criteria offers an easy solution to border cases: if someone identifies as Stoic, then they were Stoic. Recent trends in how scholars talk about interaction between philosophies seems to favor this approach, for the preference for terminology like *appropriation* over *eclecticism* suggests that even in border cases the philosophy with which the proponent identified ultimately maintained the integrity of its name.[39] Yet, given both the "arborescence" of philosophical traditions in antiquity and the evolution of doctrines within each of the schools, it can be expected that philosophers did not always agree as to who counted as what, who might have been a closet member of a competing school, or who had so far compromised their allegiance to the "essential" doctrines of the founder that they became disqualified from the identity they claimed.[40] Likewise, ancient observers might have considered as "philosophers" those who did not consider themselves such at all, and vice versa.[41]

I elect here to pursue the question of identification within a robustly "historical" framework; thus, in describing identity, I will favor the self-understanding of ancient subjects, backed by the perspectives of their contemporary observers. Admittedly, this way of putting things highlights part of the problem—that of disentangling the Corinthians' self-understanding from Paul's description *of* them.[42] However, rhetoric is meant to persuade, and gross mischaracterization of one's audience is a most ineffective rhetor-

---

39. Engberg-Pedersen's choice to replace the language of "eclecticism" with that of "appropriation" allows the interpreter to preserve the integrity of each philosophy and thus to avoid expressions like *Stoic Platonism* and *Platonic Stoicism*. Engberg-Pedersen, *From Stoicism to Platonism*, 3.

40. Mauro Bonazzi considers the question of Antiochus between Stoicism and Platonism: "Antiochus' Ethics and the Subordination of Stoicism," in *The Origins of the Platonic System: Platonisms of the Early Empire and Their Philosophical Contexts*, ed. Mauro Bonazzi and Jan Opsomer, Collection d'Études classiques 23 (Leuven: Peeters, 2009), 33–54.

41. In his assessment of Cynicism and early Christians, Downing is concerned less with Christian self-identification than with the impressions of ancient observers (*Cynics and Christian Origins*, 25–30; cf. 55, 58; and again, *Cynics, Paul, and the Pauline Churches*, 8). Loveday Alexander observes that the earliest outsider's description of early Christian meetings depicts them in terms of the philosophical schools. "IPSE DIXIT: Citation of Authority in Paul and in the Jewish and Hellenistic Schools," in *Paul beyond the Judaism/Hellenism Divide*, ed. Troels Engberg-Pedersen (Louisville: Westminster John Knox, 2001), 103–27.

42. Mitchell (*Paul and the Rhetoric of Reconciliation*, 2n3) distinguishes (1) Paul's description of the situation from (2) the way the church understood their behavior and (3) the "real social conditions" in the church. Granting that this problem is unavoidable, the problem is endemic to the interpretation of any ancient source and its depictions of persons.

ical strategy.[43] It would be unfair to assume that Paul was so inept without exceptional reason to believe otherwise. In any case, I should like to argue that there was a basic match between Paul's characterization of the Corinthians, on the one hand, and the perspectives indicated in the Corinthian terminology and slogans embedded in the letter, on the other, and that this match is confirmed by the overall coherence reflected in the internal evidence of the text and the external reconstruction that I shall propose. In short, I assume that Paul's characterization of the Corinthians is rooted in their self-perceptions—or rather, that there is sufficient *family resemblance* between Paul's description of them and their self-understanding.

When it comes to nomenclature, however, I will take recourse to modern etic terminology—by proposing a new term to describe the "Stoicism" of the Corinthians.

Defining a Stoic

Despite the problems complicating the matter of definition, we can identify as a starting point a fairly simple criterion for defining philosophical identity during the Roman imperial era: in general, philosophical identity was a matter of declared allegiance. Some progressive doctrinal innovations notwithstanding,[44] according to Christopher Gill, "most philosophically committed thinkers saw themselves as having a determinate intellectual position and (unless someone was himself the founder of a new movement) an allegiance to a specific school with its own founder and conceptual framework."[45] In similar terms, Sedley has observed that, especially during the Hellenistic and Roman periods, what gave philosophical movements their cohesion and identity was "less a disinterested common quest for the truth than a virtually religious commitment to the authority of a founder figure."[46] As

---

43. For this underlying rhetorical principle, see Chaim Perelman and L. Olbrechts-Tyteca, *The New Rhetoric: A Treatise on Argumentation*, trans. J. Wilkinson and P. Weaver (Notre Dame: University of Notre Dame Press, 1969; paperback ed., 1971). Wire (*Corinthian Women Prophets*, 1–4) uses this principle as the basis for her reconstruction of the Corinthian conflict.

44. See n. 17.

45. Gill, "School in the Roman Imperial Period," 44. See also Gill's criteria for what defined Stoic teachers and nonteaching Stoics ("School in the Roman Imperial Period," 36–37).

46. David N. Sedley, "Philosophical Allegiance in the Greco-Roman World," in *Philosophia Togata*, ed. Mirian Griffin and J. Barnes (Oxford: Clarendon, 1989), 97–119, esp. 97.

Sedley has shown, the usual pattern—evident among Platonists/Academics, Peripatetics, Epicureans, and Stoics—was that followers began to venerate their founders only after their founders' deaths. In this regard, the final Stoic authority was Zeno and, to a slightly lesser degree, Chrysippus. The latter was an interpreter of the former, and an imperfect one. Chrysippus could be wrong, but not Zeno.[47]

What requires further consideration is what to call individuals who espoused Stoic doctrines but with less than "religious commitment" to the founder's whole system. As one recent collection of essays considers at length,[48] the period between 100 BCE and 100 CE saw increased interaction and exchange of ideas between Stoicism, Epicureanism, Platonism, Skepticism, and Aristotelianism. Engberg-Pedersen explains how modern perspectives on the interaction of philosophies during this period have recently changed.[49] While traditionally scholarship has described this period as one of philosophical "eclecticism," Engberg-Pedersen suggests that this term problematically connotes a loss of distinction between philosophies. Hence, scholarly discourse has begun using, in place of terms like *eclecticism*, terms like *merging, assimilation, rivaling philosophers, foreign doctrine, interaction, appropriation*—terms that connote exchange between schools without erasing lines of distinction. Innovations during this period, in other words, consisted largely in intelligent incorporation of foreign material into what individual philosophers still considered to be their originating brand of philosophy.

The Problem of Comparison

Genealogical and Illustrative Comparison

My intention to compare the σοφία of the Corinthians and Stoic philosophy may seem a bit "uncontemporary" in view of trajectories in biblical scholarship. Criticism in the last decades of the twentieth century of both "parallelomania" and that disapproved "philological" approach characteristic of

---

47. Sedley, "Philosophical Allegiance," 98–99.
48. As cited in n. 32: *From Stoicism to Platonism*.
49. Engberg-Pedersen, *From Stoicism to Platonism*, 1–26; reiterating points that he made in a 2010 article: Engberg-Pedersen, "Setting the Scene," in *Stoicism in Early Christianity*, 1–14.

the old *Religionsgeschichtliche Schule* has undoubtedly made interpreters shy of treatments that resemble such approaches. Or so the almost complete relinquishment of such approaches to 1 Corinthians would suggest.[50] Next to more recent trajectories in religious studies, the present study might also seem to run against challenges leveled against the enterprise of "comparative religions" and "genealogical" interpretations of cross-cultural comparison at large.

Since the 1980s, Jonathan Z. Smith has been a leading voice in methodological discussions about comparison in religious studies.[51] As Smith has argued, comparisons are in fact *constructions*, products of the interpreter, not *real* descriptions of similarities or differences. These constructions rely on selective and often one-sided use of the evidence and as such serve the interests of the interpreter—whether to demonstrate "identity" of the comparanda on the one hand or their individual "uniqueness" on the other. Smith has advocated for a new approach to comparison, in which the interpreter owns the fact that comparisons are constructions and the perceived similarities are not "real" while at the same time using "redescription" in the act of comparison as a tool in service of knowledge.[52] Helping to elucidate Smith's point is a distinction that has become conventional in discussions of comparison, namely, the distinction between "genealogical" and "illustrative" comparison.[53] Whereas genealogical comparison seeks to demonstrate "real" similarities resulting from a genetic relationship between comparanda, the illustrative approach is "heuristic," serving as a means through which the inquirer discovers something new about one or both comparanda through the very exercise of having juxtaposed them, while assuming nothing about their "real" relationship.

Recent methodological discussions about comparison in biblical studies, along with recent exercises in comparison, have leaned more in favor

---

50. Though there has been a resurgence in comparative studies on the NT and Greco-Roman philosophy in recent decades (see p. 16 n. 35 above).

51. Notable contributions include Jonathan Z. Smith, *Map Is Not Territory: Studies in the History of Religions* (Chicago: University of Chicago Press, 1982); Smith, *Drudgery Divine: On the Comparison of Early Christianities and the Religions of Late Antiquity* (Chicago: University of Chicago Press, 1990); and Smith, "Re: Corinthians," in *Redescribing Paul and the Corinthians*, ed. R. Cameron and M. P. Miller (Atlanta: Society of Biblical Literature, 2011), 17–34.

52. Smith, "Re: Corinthians," 27.

53. For a recent treatment of this distinction, see John S. Kloppenborg, "Disciplined Exaggeration: The Heuristics of Comparison in Biblical Studies," *NovT* 59 (2017): 390–414.

of illustrative comparison.[54] On the other hand, it should be said that the move away from genealogical approaches is partly a matter of subjective choice,[55] not a consequence of absolute invalidity in the genealogical approach. Smith's objections notwithstanding, some things in culture actually *are* genetically related—like the Stoicism of Chrysippus and of the Athenian successors who carried on his teachings. Genealogical connection can be claimed most justifiably where direct borrowing, or tradition, is involved. Genealogical descent could also be less direct. One could certainly say, from an emic standpoint, that ancient persons who claimed a particular identity (e.g., as a "Stoic") would have understood the connection between their views and those of earlier Stoics to be a "genetic" one, carried on by scholastic succession and tradition. One might even say that any person who espoused Stoic views *consciously* espoused views that descended from the Stoics "genetically."

The thesis I will be pursuing here makes a genealogical claim in a certain definite sense of the term: the Corinthians derived much of what constituted their σοφία, probably directly and probably consciously, from Stoic teaching. In this regard, it will be necessary not only to demonstrate consistency and depth of Stoic connections with the Corinthians' views but also to demonstrate the likely channels of influence.

I add that a purely "illustrative" approach would remain insufficient from the standpoint of the *historical* dimension of the Corinthian controversy. For instance, if recent scholarship is correct that the Corinthians' σοφία concerned primarily rhetorical practices vis-à-vis Paul and Apollos, or elite ideology in a general sense, or that their divided loyalties between Paul and Apollos were a result of patronage commitments, these claims affect not only the particulars of our reconstruction but also our interpretation of the text at point after point. Granting, for instance, that the conflict between oratory

---

54. A collection of essays on comparison in biblical studies can be found in John M. G. Barclay and B. G. White, *The New Testament in Comparison: Validity, Method, and Purpose in Comparing Traditions* (London: T&T Clark, 2020); see also Kloppenborg's article "Disciplined Exaggeration." For recent studies that take a heuristic approach, see Troels Engberg-Pedersen, "Stoicism in Early Christianity," in *Routledge Handbook of the Stoic Tradition*, 19–43, esp. 30, 40; and *John and Philosophy*, esp. vii, 32–34.

55. Or, in some cases, epistemological pessimism; that is, one might suggest that we cannot know for *certain* whence the Corinthians derived their wisdom (if from anywhere in particular), and hence we cannot *prove* a genealogical connection. It is this kind of uncertainty in part that has motivated a shift toward more rhetorical and textual approaches to the letter's interpretation; see p. 11 n. 24 above.

on the one hand and philosophy on the other is largely an ancient construction, by well-established sociolinguistic convention people commonly and quite consciously insisted upon a sharp distinction between the two.[56] Consequently, were we to try to "learn" something (using illustrative comparison) by juxtaposing the Corinthians' σοφία with the conventions of ancient rhetoric, the result, I believe, would be distorting from the standpoint of the historical situation and thus the meaning of the text. For if the Corinthians' wisdom *is* Stoicism, or something very like it, it is *not* rhetoric or eloquence; indeed, as we shall see, the difference between the two impacts the whole reconstruction and our interpretation of the text and its logic at many specific points. By testing the text against these respective backgrounds, one might say that we learn which background more accurately describes the historical situation and, of equal importance, that we learn whether the text means one thing or something quite different.

On the other hand, our genealogical interest is not exclusive of illustrative interest. Conzelmann's suggestion that the "position in Corinth cannot be reconstructed on the basis of the possibilities of the general history of religion" and that we gain certainty enough about the Corinthians' position from the text would seem to imply that identifying their position against any specific background adds nothing to our understanding of the text.[57] To this we would have to respond that there is a difference between saying that identifying a more specific source of influence makes no difference and simply being content to know less about it. Indeed, it may be true that one does not need to know how "Stoic" the Corinthians' σοφία was to know that they thought themselves "wise"; but this is not the same as saying that the Stoic framework that, I am arguing, grounded their thinking adds nothing to our understanding of their position or the conflict itself. I believe that my case in the coming chapters that the Corinthians' anthropology was rooted in fairly technical doctrines from Stoic physics sheds some additional light on the nature of the status distinctions and the claims that contributed to the divisions. Insofar as we learn something from our specific Stoic comparandum, our comparison will also be "heuristically" useful.

---

56. For a summary of the historical opposition between rhetoric and philosophy, see Brookins, *Corinthian Wisdom*, 17–26. The opposition continues through the Second Sophistic, as discussed in Philostratus, *Vit. soph.* §479–492.

57. See Conzelmann's full comments in *1 Corinthians*, 14–16.

Philosophical Interactivity

I referred above to various kinds of "philosophical interaction" that characterized exchange between ancient philosophical schools. Engberg-Pedersen offers terms for two different types of interaction: (1) *eirenic appropriation* (appropriation of foreign material with a conciliatory attitude toward the originating philosophy) and (2) *polemical/subordinating appropriation* (appropriation of material from a competing philosophy without full acknowledgment and with a kind of reinterpretation that serves to subvert the originating philosophy).[58]

Max Lee has built upon Engberg-Pedersen's distinction by offering a more variegated taxonomy of interaction types.[59] In *Moral Transformation in Greco-Roman Philosophy of Mind*, Lee distinguishes six types:

1. *Eclecticism.* The subject assimilates or appropriates material from another school but the rationale behind said appropriation is unclear.
2. *Refutation.* The subject cites and proceeds to disprove the source philosophy or to demonstrate that the subject's own philosophy is more correct.
3. *Competitive appropriation.* The subject takes over the meaning of the source's linguistic inventory and uses it in a "better" way.
4. *Irenic appropriation.* The author critically supplements or synchronizes the rivals' material.
5. *Concession.* The subject concedes to the rival school's teaching.
6. *Common ethical usage.* The subject appropriates language or concepts that belong to a common encyclopedia of philosophy and moral traditions.

In a more recent essay, Lee adds a seventh interaction type:[60]

7. *Doctrinal reformulation.* Adherents within a common tradition reinterpret their founder's teachings while believing that they adequately preserve the essential integrity of his original doctrines.

---

58. Engberg-Pedersen, "Setting the Scene," 10. Sterling's essay in Engberg-Pedersen, *From Stoicism to Platonism* ("The Love of Wisdom: Middle Platonism and Stoicism in the Wisdom of Solomon"), speaks of "dialectical appropriation" and "transformative appropriation" (21).

59. Lee, *Moral Transformation*, 493–516.

60. Max J. Lee, "A Taxonomy of Intertextual Interactions Practiced by NT Authors: An Introduction," in *Practicing Intertextuality*, ed. Max J. Lee and B. J. Oropeza (Eugene, OR: Cascade, 2021), 3–16, esp. 5–6.

Corinthian Wisdom as Sub(ordinated)-Stoicism

Lee's taxonomy of interaction types provides more variegated language for describing the ways in which the Corinthians appropriated contemporary philosophy and, in turn, how Paul appropriated the language of the Corinthians.

Admittedly, several obstacles stand in the way of precise classification of the Corinthians' interactions. First, we know little of the substance of their views. With very limited access to their thinking, we have little way of knowing how "eclectic" it might have been. Second, although I will argue that the σοφοί did work out their ideas at a certain level of systematicity, it is quite inconceivable that they had worked out a philosophical system on the scale of something like Chrysippus's Stoicism. Without an established "orthodoxy," the distinctions between various interaction types begin to fade. Third, it is unknown to us why the Corinthians appropriated the material that they did—that is, what their evaluation of Stoic material qua Stoic material was and what kind of polemic or irenic purposes might have driven their interactions with it.

Still, Lee's taxonomy makes possible a more nuanced assessment of the Corinthians' stance vis-à-vis Stoicism than simply a statement, in essentialist terms, that their wisdom was "Stoic" wisdom or "not-Stoic" wisdom. As I hope to show, what we do know about the Corinthians' wisdom and *habitus*—through their vocabulary and slogans, the kinds of problems addressed in 1 Corinthians, a responsible mirror-reading of Paul's response to them, and Paul's own rhetoric—evinces a certain consistency in their affinities with Stoic doctrines and discourse, a consistency that I believe is sufficient to demonstrate that the Corinthians were probably consciously, and probably directly, influenced by Stoicism. My argument in chapter 9 that their anthropology is actually informed by distinct *technical* categories native to Stoic physics suggests that their attraction to Stoicism was not merely eclectic (type 1: eclecticism), and that their views were not derived from mere commonplaces in the philosophical tradition (type 6: common ethical usage). On the other hand, if I am correct that the Corinthian σοφοί viewed Paul on analogy with the founders of the philosophical schools (chapter 10), then they did not view themselves as loyalists of Zeno—or as Stoics per se—but as members, as it were, of a new "school." This consideration of loyalty weighs against the possibility that their overall appropriation of Stoicism represents type 5 (concession to Stoicism). By the same token, their loyalty to Paul suggests that they must have regarded their theology as being grounded in the teachings of their founder. If from Paul's perspective they had gotten him wrong, we must nevertheless assume that they viewed themselves as his faithful interpreters. This is a clear case of interaction type 7 (doctrinal reformulation). Next, if the σοφοί appropriated material from Stoicism, we can eliminate the refutation interaction type (type 2). With type 3 (competitive appropriation) and type 4 (irenic appropriation) remaining, a precise description of the Corinthians' interaction with Stoicism would depend finally on greater knowledge about their critical stance toward Stoicism than we have.

Thus, my analysis in the ensuing chapters will be consistent with the view that the *habitus* of the Corinthian σοφοί was the product of a tension between interaction type 7 (doctrinal reformulation of Paul), on the one hand, and type 3/type 4 (competitive appropriation/irenic appropriation of Stoicism) on the other. In this regard, I offer as an appropriate label for the Corinthian σοφοί, *sub-Stoics*, and for their position, *sub-Stoicism*, by which I mean sub(ordinated) Stoicism.[61] On the one hand, the σοφοί appropriated the technical terminology, idioms, and often the phrasing of Stoicism; supplemented Paul's teaching with certain Stoic doctrinal points; and even relied upon a Stoic framework in how they configured some of their ideas at a more systemic level. I add the *sub-* prefix, however, to convey that for these people Stoicism was ultimately subordinate to their Christ-faith—the latter being embodied in what they believed to be the teachings of Paul.

Paul's Interactive Rhetoric

This taxonomy of philosophical interaction also supplies categories for describing the various ways in which Paul interacts with, appropriates, and subverts both Stoic and *Corinthian* language. Paul cites the Corinthians at several points in the letter (6:12, 13, 18; 8:1, 4, 8; and I argue, 2:15); he describes them in terms that appear to be based on Corinthian self-description (1:26; 3:18; 4:8, 10; 6:5); and he integrates their terminology throughout chapters 1–4 (2:6 [τέλειος; also in 13:10; 14:20], 14–15 [ψυχικός, πνευματικός]; 3:1 [νήπιος; also in 13:11; 14:20]; also σοφία, σοφός throughout). Apart from Paul's appropriation of Corinthian language, he also accommodates to their—as I argue—preferred discourse by alluding to Stoic language and ideas (2:4, 5; 3:10, 21;

---

61. This label applies to the overall characterization. It does not rule out that on specific issues or at different times they could have engaged in eclecticism (1), refutation (2), etc.

4:4, 7; 6:12, 19; 9:8–10, 18; 10:24; 11:14–15; 12:7, 12–27; 15:28, 31, 39–41, 42–49), as well as philosophical commonplaces (4:6; 6:7; 7:4, 19, 29–34; 8:6; 9:7, 24–27; 12:4–6, 12–27; 15:33), at quite a number of points. Generally these interactions reflect Paul's "competitive appropriation" of Corinthian sub-Stoicism (1:26; 2:6, 14–15; 3:18; 4:8, 10; 6:5) or Stoic concepts (2:16; 3:16, 21; 4:4, 7; 6:19; 7:37; 11:14–15; 15:28, 31), although we also frequently encounter "common ethical usage," especially in later portions of the letter (6:7; 7:4, 19, 29–34; 8:6; 9:7, 24–27; 12:4–6, 12–27; 15:33). Noted interactions that occur in 1:10–4:21 will be discussed at the appropriate points in the chapters that follow.

Stoic Sources

Some brief remarks are needed in regard to the use of Stoic sources. Ancient attestation to Stoic views includes both complete and fragmentary literary sources. Sources of the first type range from complete or mostly complete technical treatises (Cicero's philosophical dialogues, Hierocles's treatises, Plutarch's critical treatises) to nontechnical subjects on Stoic topics (Seneca's letters, Epictetus's discourses, Marcus Aurelius's meditations), doxographical "handbooks" of Stoic doctrines (Diogenes Laertius, Stobaeus), and even narrative works with didactic purposes rooted in Stoicism (Seneca's tragedies). Teachings attributed specifically to the early (Zeno, Cleanthes, Chrysippus) and middle Stoics (Posidonius, Panaetius) are almost exclusively fragmentary. Fragments survive in the works of both Stoic and non-Stoic writers.

We must bear several points in mind as we draw from these sources. First, our most complete sources are also the sources that date closest to the time of Paul and the Corinthian correspondence. These include especially, though not exclusively, the works of Cicero, Hierocles, Seneca, and Plutarch and the discourses of Epictetus and Musonius Rufus. On the other hand, due to the conservative nature of Stoicism (since a "Stoic" was one who maintained allegiance to the teachings of the school's founders), teachings that can be traced back to Zeno, Chrysippus, and the early Stoics continued to be normative and are mostly reaffirmed by the Stoics of the Roman era. Thus, I shall often cite the "Old Stoic fragments" (from *SVF* and LS) as representative of the virtually universal consensus of ancient Stoics.[62] We can also rely on

---

62. On von Arnim's collection, see n. 6 above. Long and Sedley (*Hellenistic Philosophers*) cover Stoicism in 1:158–437, with the original text in 2:163–431.

the epitomes from later antiquity (Diogenes Laertius, Stobaeus) as generally representative of Stoic consensus.

Sources from the Roman period depart from the views of the early Stoics in only a very limited range of areas. Even here, innovations basically reflect more sophisticated extensions of orthodox doctrines rather than rejection of them.[63] More to the point, these areas will not be germane to the connections that we shall draw with the Corinthian σοφία here.

Conclusion

This chapter has considered the interrelated problems of definition and comparison. First we addressed the question of how to define Stoicism and the Stoic. Despite the remarkable coherence of the Stoic system and the institutional structures that preserved its integrity over the centuries, its proponents shared some disagreement on doctrinal matters (in rare cases, on major ones); moreover, doctrine evolved as proponents interacted with the doctrines of other philosophical schools over time, and Stoic influence in realms of discourse outside the school context itself brought about more eclectic expressions of the philosophy along with a kind of weaker Stoicism that dissipated into what has sometimes been called "popular philosophy." While the flexibility of Stoicism/the Stoic makes problematic a definition of these entities in "essentialist" terms, the categories remain valid when defined in terms of polythetic criteria. For the proponent of Stoicism, these criteria include doctrinal characteristics that *typically* clustered together in some systemic fashion—especially doctrines characteristic of Chrysippus's systemization of Zeno's teaching—without making any single criterion a necessary one. Thus, various expressions of Stoicism, and various Stoics, in antiquity shared kinship rooted in family resemblances, not absolute identity.

We next considered the matter of comparison between religious and philosophical systems. Although comparisons are interpretive "constructions," claims of genealogical connection between comparanda are in certain cases legitimate, not least in cases involving philosophical succession and traditional material. If the thesis I am arguing here is correct, the σοφία of the Corinthian σοφοί was, genetically speaking, closely linked with Stoicism; yet, their σοφία was not Stoicism unalloyed. Lee's taxonomy of seven types of philosophical interaction offers us a more variegated approach for defining

---

63. See n. 17 above.

Corinthian σοφία: it is not *either* "Stoicism" *or* "not Stoicism" in essentialist terms. Rather, their σοφία can aptly be labeled *sub-Stoicism* (subordinated Stoicism), a framework that competitively (type 3) / irenically (type 4) appropriated Stoicism while also representing a doctrinal reformulation of Paul's teaching (type 7), initiated by those who considered themselves to be faithful adherents of his teaching. I draw my case for this characterization together in chapter 9. First, however, we must undertake a detailed exegesis of 1 Cor 1:17b–4:21.

PART II

Reading 1 Corinthians 1–4

3

1 CORINTHIANS 1:17B–31:
ONE λόγος AGAINST ANOTHER

The transition is almost artless. In 1 Cor 1:17b Paul slides mid-sentence from the topic of the church's divisions (1:10–17a) to the topic of σοφία (1:17b–3:23). Though the transition is distinct, the continuity of speech reveals just how closely the two topics connect. In this regard, it is a remarkable contrast how unanimous scholarship has been as to a connection between the Corinthians' divisions and their σοφία and how little they have agreed what kind of σοφία this was. In turn, it is remarkable how little interpreters have agreed about this σοφία and how consistently they have prioritized 1:17b in constructing a hypothesis about it.

In the opening words (1:17b) we encounter the first of four occurrences of the coordinated terms σοφία and λόγος (also 2:1, 4, 13), as Paul declares that he came to preach "not ἐν σοφίᾳ λόγου."[1] This expression introduces the first section (1:17b–31) of the first major unit of the letter (1:10–4:21). Following introduction of the topic in v. 17b, the section breaks down into two paragraphs, the first in 1:18–25 and the second in 1:26–31. The overarching theme is a contrast between the "wisdom of the cross/God" on the one hand, and the "wisdom of the world/humans" on the other.

The key expression in 1:17b (ἐν σοφίᾳ λόγου) is obscure, and scholars have tirelessly debated its meaning. Studies most often frame the debate around the question whether the expression refers more to the *form* of Paul's proclamation or more to the *content* of his message.[2] These options

---

[1]. Note also their coordination in 1:5; 12:8.
[2]. See summary of scholarship in Timothy A. Brookins, "Rhetoric and Philosophy

branch out into an array of hypotheses regarding what kind of wisdom this might be. Interpreters then read the remainder of the section through the respective frameworks.

Perspectives on 1:17b–31 over the last forty years have made a sharp departure from the views of earlier scholarship. Two trajectories characterize the recent period. (1) The first trajectory follows the view that σοφία refers primarily to Greco-Roman *rhetorical* culture and theorizes that the Corinthians' conflict involved criticism of Paul for lacking in "eloquence" or for lacking the high repute of the eloquent "sophists." (2) The second trajectory shifts the point of emphasis, seeing the conflict primarily as one rooted in *social stratification*. Here σοφία becomes more a general attribute of society's governing classes—the embodiment of education, or παιδεία—this being a marker of high social status for those who possessed it. In many interpretive formulations, these two trajectories intersect. In general those who follow either line of interpretation abandon explanations of σοφία that were popular through the early and mid-twentieth century, which in some form or another viewed σοφία in terms of certain religious, spiritual, or philosophical content.

The purpose of this chapter is to offer a fresh reading of 1:17b–31 by systematic movement through the text. As I hope to show, following this process exposes a number of deficiencies in newer readings, deficiencies that stem from several problems, including insufficient attention to matters of coherency in the discourse and a failure to test hypotheses against the running text.

Two Kinds of Wisdom (1:17b–25)

Form versus Content

Paul's enigmatic reference to "wisdom of word" in 1:17b (ἐν σοφίᾳ λόγου), together with the discussion of σοφία that ensues, raises a dilemma that has remained debated throughout the history of modern scholarship: Does Paul refer primarily to a σοφία of *form* or a σοφία of *content*?

Since the 1990s the former view has claimed a majority. According to the wisdom-as-form view, Paul criticizes the σοφία of Greco-Roman rhetoric and the sophistic practices of contemporary rhetorical culture.[3] Duane

---

in the First Century: Their Relation with Respect to 1 Corinthians 1–4," *Neot* 45 (2010): 233–52, esp. 233–34.

3. In addition to the literature cited below, note Edgar Krentz's comment that 1:17b

1 Corinthians 1:17b–31: One λόγος against Another

Litfin's monograph *St. Paul's Theology of Proclamation* (1994) offers an early and representative example of this view. According to Litfin, Paul rejects the use of rhetoric in preaching. Paul believed that his purpose was "to make Christ known, non-rhetorically, and the Spirit of God would take care of the rest." The problem with rhetoric, Litfin says, is that it would have "inserted a human element which would have obscured the cross's power rather than displayed it."[4] As such, Paul renounces persuasive techniques and then proceeds to offer a message presented in a distinctively unrhetorical or "plain" style, such as left persuasion to the power of God or the Spirit instead of the preacher.

Despite the sensibleness of this reading on the surface, Litfin's view that 1:17b–2:5 centers on a contrast between God and human preaching as *vehicles* of true knowledge of God faces substantial difficulties when one begins to press it. In the first place, Litfin's initial assertion that "it is tendentious to interpret οὐκ ἐν σοφίᾳ λόγου in vs. 17 primarily in terms of content" since "the context... is public speaking" is also, ironically, tendentious, for in saying this Litfin begs the very question.[5] Certainly the context is "public speaking" in the sense that Paul is "preaching" (εὐαγγελίζεσθαι) something. But one may as well say that Paul refers to wisdom as content simply because he is saying "something." Without supporting either determination through grammatical exegesis, the one argument is as vacuous as the other.[6]

It is a more telling point that the rhetorical reading of 1:17b introduces difficulties of which even the proponents of this reading seem to be aware. Indeed, a careful reading of the literature reveals a curious tendency to ob-

---

"is an explicit rejection of wisdom conveyed by rhetoric." Krentz, "Logos or Sophia: The Pauline Use of the Ancient Dispute between Rhetoric and Philosophy," in *Early Christianity and Classical Culture: Comparative Studies in Honor of Abraham J. Malherbe*, ed. John T. Fitzgerald, Thomas H. Olbricht, and L. Michael White (Leiden: Brill, 2003), 280.

4. Litfin, *St. Paul's Theology of Proclamation*, 197. Winter's view is much the same. According to Winter, Paul here refers to "the form or manner of preaching"; and Paul refused to use rhetoric in presenting the gospel so that faith would be produced not by human persuasion but by God's power (*Philo and Paul among the Sophists*, 187–88). See also Bruce W. Winter, "Rhetoric," in *The Dictionary of Paul and His Letters*, ed. F. Hawthorne and Ralph P. Martin (Downers Grove, IL: InterVarsity, 1993), 820–22, esp. 821.

5. Litfin, *St. Paul's Theology of Proclamation*, 188.

6. Stephen Pogoloff (*Logos and Sophia*, 111) takes a similar tack to Litfin. After presenting the "extensive semantic ranges" of the words σοφία and λόγος, he arrives, through several degrees of word association, at the conclusion that ἐν σοφίᾳ λόγου refers to "sophisticated speech" because this interpretation "fits the immediate context best," i.e., "since Paul is referring to his manner of speaking" (Pogoloff here begs the question).

scure difficulties that are introduced by the arguments themselves, by twists of language that are sometimes difficult to see as accidental.

We find one example in Paul Barnett's discussion of v. 17. First, Barnett states: "Wisdom from God comes *from the word of the 'cross'*, not from wisdom that arises *from eloquent speech* (1 Cor. 1:17)." Barnett's construal of ἐν σοφίᾳ λόγου as "eloquent speech" here clearly alludes to a wisdom of form. It is apparent, however, that Barnett sees the counterpart, "word of the cross," as a matter of content, for he substitutes, in place of this phrase, the expression "cross-*message.*" More notably, the careful reader will observe that in his initial words Barnett actually points us to wisdom as the *content* of speech—referring to the wisdom that either "*comes from*" or "*arises*" from God or from eloquence. In other words, wisdom *itself* is not identified with the manner of speaking but is what *comes from* the manner of speaking.[7]

Examples of such twists can be multiplied. In contrast to Litfin, Stephen Pogoloff denies that Paul's remarks have to do with a contrast between a "fancy" (rhetorical) and a "plainer" (non-rhetorical) manner of presentation.[8] On Pogoloff's reading, Paul rather presents a contrast between, on the one hand, "status-conferring" rhetoric and, on the other hand, the kind of life "marked by the worst shame and the lowest possible status."[9] One discerns a partial evenness in this antithesis—that is, an antithesis between status as reckoned by the world's standards and God's approved wisdom of lowliness. Pogoloff, however, needs σοφία to be specifically about *rhetoric*. Thus, Pogoloff works rhetoric into the antithesis by employing allusive "rhetorical" language on both sides of the equation: "What *persuades* is speech about what is ordinarily unfit for contemplation: not a life which is cultured, wise, and powerful, but one marked by the worst shame and the lowest possible status. Paul's *rhetoric* of the cross thus opposes the cultural values surrounding *eloquence.*"[10] Pogoloff's connection between status and "eloquence" or "rhetoric," as he articulates it, seems very superficial, if not misleading. In the first place, Pogoloff's reference to "*what* persuades"—this being, apparently, σοφία itself—in fact refers to a lived value system ("a life which is," etc.), not a technique. Furthermore, what could Pogoloff mean in referring to Paul's "*rhetoric* of the cross" or his "*rhetoric* of status reversal" if—according to Pogoloff—Paul is not thinking in this passage of rhetoric per se, but of "the

---

7. Barnett, *Corinthian Question*, 124 (my italics).
8. Pogoloff, *Logos and Sophia*, 121.
9. Pogoloff, *Logos and Sophia*, 119, 120.
10. Pogoloff, *Logos and Sophia*, 120 (my italics).

1 Corinthians 1:17b–31: One λόγος against Another

cultural values wedded to it"?[11] Does "rhetoric of the cross," then, not employ the term merely in the general sense of *discourse*? This realization exposes Pogoloff's use of "rhetorical" language here as a façade which obscures the fact that "status-conferring rhetoric," in his own construction, does not contrast with any alternative orientation toward rhetoric specifically or with an alternative style of speaking; rather, it contrasts with a kind of life lived ("not a life which is cultured, wise ... but one marked by the worst shame and the lowest possible status").

In another example, Dale Martin takes 1:17b as a reference to "public speech" in which is signaled that Paul "self-consciously eschewed rhetorical techniques in his presentation of his message in Corinth."[12] It is odd, then, that Martin's interpretation of 1:18–31 proceeds as if the antithesis were a different one. Martin accurately observes that this section "sets up an opposition between two realms or worlds: the realm of "this age ... and the realm ... of God,"[13] where Paul's chief point is that God in his wisdom has disrupted and reversed the status expectations assumed in secular society. While rhetorical ability was an important marker of status to be sure, one must remember that Martin takes 1:17b to mean that Paul eschewed "*rhetorical techniques.*" It must be asked then why the opposition of God's reckoning of status to the value system of the world must come with a rejection of rhetorical *techniques*? Not missing the gap, Martin pulls things together with an equivocal expression capable of evoking form but in such a way as to cloak his underlying reference to content. Martin says: "In opposition to the accomplished *rhetoric* of the educated Greek, Paul praises the '*speech* of the cross,' a term that would have struck Paul's hearers as paradoxical and perhaps ridiculous."[14] On the one hand, given Martin's assertion that Paul is "attacking rhetoric in particular" and that Paul eschews "rhetorical techniques," one cannot fault the reader for taking Martin's expression "*speech* of the cross," initially, as an attempt to evoke Paul's *form* of speech. Yet, the resulting parallel—between (1) the "persuasive techniques" that Paul eschews and (2) the "speech of the cross"—is then exposed as misleadingly superficial. As Martin has argued, the "speech of the cross" does *not* describe a method, style, or manner of preaching but a message whose *content* reverses the hierarchies constructed within the realm of the world, or what Martin calls

---

11. Pogoloff, *Logos and Sophia*, 120, 121 (my italics).
12. Martin, *Corinthian Body*, 47.
13. Martin, *Corinthian Body*, 59.
14. Martin, *Corinthian Body*, 59 (my italics).

"an alternative system."[15] In other words, Martin's interpretation straightforwardly suggests an antithesis between two *world orders* while laying a verbal veneer allusive of rhetorical techniques in its linguistic articulation.

With a different take, Joop Smit proposes that "not ἐν σοφίᾳ λόγου" refers not to "rhetoric" or "eloquence," but to "rational" or "logical wisdom."[16] From Smit's point of view the rhetorical interpretation fails both in that (1) Paul appears *not* to reject rhetoric in practice—for Paul speaks in this section "in a highly rhetorical fashion"—and (2) 1:18–31 and 2:6–16 both elaborate not a rejection of rhetoric, but a contrast between two *kinds* of wisdom. While Smit obviates the difficulties involved in the alternative view on both counts, as I will demonstrate below, this interpretation incorrectly places the emphasis on epistemology and instrumentality. Paul does not primarily set in opposition logical *methods*—logical argumentation versus the persuasion of the Spirit—but rather the respective *value* systems of God and the world.

Contrasting Accounts

The syntax of v. 17 presents, in parallel terms, the thematic contrast that Paul will begin to develop: "wisdom of word" and "the cross of Christ" (1:17). The parallel between "word" and "cross" at once prompts the reader to see "word" in relation to certain content. Immediately, v. 18 supports this inclination. Here Paul reformulates the contrast lexically through the invocation of a second kind of "word," or λόγος. That ὁ λόγος ... ὁ τοῦ σταυροῦ (v. 18) merely relabels ὁ σταυρὸς τοῦ Χριστοῦ (v. 17) is shown by the unusual attributivizing article preceding the genitive. The article is anaphoric and indicates that out of the two "words" just alluded to, "I refer to the second one, i.e., 'the one that is [ὁ] of the cross.'"[17] Thus:

1:17b–c "wisdom of word"	vs.	"word of the cross"
1:18a ["the word that is [ὁ] of wisdom"]	vs.	"the word that is [ὁ] of the cross"

---

15. Martin, *Corinthian Body*, 60.

16. Thus appearing to take the genitive in an "attributive" sense, i.e., "*logical* wisdom," on analogy with "*human* wisdom" (σοφία ἀνθρώπων) or "*divine* wisdom" (θεοῦ σοφία).

17. It hardly seems fair to assume that Paul's "formal parallelism" between *two kinds of "word"* ("wisdom of word" and "word of the cross") misrepresents his meaning, as Horsley assumes. Horsley, "Wisdom of Words and Words of Wisdom in Corinth," *CBQ* 39 (1977): 224–39. According to Horsley, although "in terms of the hermeneutics of language" there "is a formal parallelism" here, the parallelism is nonetheless not one of substance.

It is worth asking whether the indications of the syntax explain why proponents of the rhetorical thesis generally appeal to the semantics of σοφία and λόγος and their meaning in construct form to establish a reference to "rhetoric."[18] With confidence sufficient to intimidate any reader, Pogoloff asserts that *"any* urban Hellenistic reader" would have construed this language in reference to rhetoric.[19] But in fact the semantic evidence points decisively in the other direction. Usage of σοφία and its Latin equivalent *sapientia* in contemporary literary sources overwhelmingly favors specifically "philosophical" over specifically "rhetorical" denotations. This is the clear indication of every major Greek and Latin lexicon, as well as the ancient literature on which they are based. The evidence has been extensively laid out in an earlier publication and need not be repeated here.[20] This strength of evidence no doubt explains why studies resort more to multiple degrees of word association to connect rhetoric with σοφία than to more conventional semantic options.[21] Pogoloff pleads that the rhetor was also "wise," and Litfin holds that in the rhetorical tradition, "λόγος and σοφία" always went together. It is telling, however, that this supposed union of rhetoric and wisdom always breaks down again in course of Pogoloff's and Litfin's own usage: they consistently use λόγος to designate rhetoric and the coordinate term σοφία to designate philosophy.[22] This slippage is all the more deceptive

---

18. Mihaila (*Paul-Apollos Relationship*, 92) thinks on the basis of this coordination that evidence is "overwhelmingly" in favor of a rhetorical meaning for σοφία; similarly, Kwon ("Critical Review," 420) thinks that the reference to rhetoric is "clearly evident" based on this terminology.

19. Pogoloff, *Logos and Sophia*, 7.

20. Brookins, *Corinthian Wisdom*, 42–43; noting the exception of BDAG, which cites as an example the very passage under debate! We might add to Brookins's list the entry for "Σοφία, σοφός, σοφίζω" in *TDNT* 7:465ff; this article traces the concept of σοφία from the early Greek period through the philosophical schools and late antiquity, and not only does it not mention rhetoric as a standard meaning of the term, it accurately points out that from the Classical period, in the time of Plato and Aristotle, the term σοφός ceased to be a synonym for σοφιστής and these two terms became sharply distinguished (7:470); the article also points out that in the present passage Paul opposes not a particular wisdom of form but rather wisdom of content: in 1:17; 2:1, 4 (7:519).

21. For two almost humorous displays, see Litfin, *St. Paul's Theology of Proclamation*, 44–45; Pogoloff, *Logos and Sophia*, 109–13. Notably, R. Dean Anderson observes that Pogoloff "really only cites one concrete use of this word [σοφία] in a definite rhetorical context, namely, Isoc. 15.199–200." Anderson, *Ancient Rhetorical Theory and Paul*, Contributions to Biblical Exegesis and Theology 18 (Leuven: Peeters, 1999), 270.

22. This distinction is implied in Pogoloff's title, *Logos and Sophia*. The coordination of terms in this sense occurs passim in Litfin, *Paul's Theology of Proclamation*.

in Litfin's usage, for this usage belies his reading of 1 Cor 1–4: σοφία, which he consistently uses in reference to "philosophy" in his discussion of the ancient sources, cleverly becomes a reference not to philosophy but to rhetoric in his discussion of 1 Cor 1–4.

Suggestions that the conjoined terms in 1:17b refer to *both* form *and* content are not convincing on processing grounds.[23] Michael Bullmore has proposed that σοφία refers to content (philosophy), and λόγου to form (rhetoric). While there may be justification for this distinction semantically, this interpretation of the construct ἐν σοφίᾳ λόγου tightly compresses its meaning and ultimately asks too much of the construction for the processor. The result, too, is an unhelpful ambiguity: If Paul is attacking "philosophy-spoken-eloquently" (σοφία spoken with λόγος), is he attacking only this *qualified* kind of philosophy and not philosophy per se?

The least vulnerable argument that Paul refers to rhetoric in 1:18–25 is that the word λόγος has the idea of "speaking" within its range of semantic potential. Yet, as an isolated point this is a weak counter to the contextual difficulties already noted, the tortuous twists of language we have found several interpreters using to compensate for this, and more conventional usage of σοφ- language in Greco-Roman literature. As we shall see shortly, this meaning also coheres poorly with the remainder of 1:18–31.

One has still to consider the syntax of the genitive itself: ἐν σοφίᾳ λόγου. Significantly, the precise nuances of the genitive are often ignored, as if the obvious meaning of λόγος as a matter of "speech" settles that Paul refers to "rhetoric."[24] In any case, it must be said that how one decides on the genitive is not determinative for the critical point in question. Alternate construals of the syntax could be used to support opposing readings. For instance, (1) reading the genitive as attributive might yield a rendering like (a) Winter's "wisdom of rhetoric" (= "rhetorical wisdom"); but it might also support a rendering like (b) Smit's "rational/logical wisdom."[25] By the same token, (2) reading the genitive as attributed (where the head noun describes the genitive) might lead to a rendering like (a) "cleverness of speech."[26] (b) On the other hand, λόγος had

---

23. Fee, *First Epistle to the Corinthians*, 2nd ed., 66–68. Fee does not, however, explain how the language is able to accommodate a *secondary* reference to form here.

24. Litfin (*St. Paul's Theology of Proclamation*, 205) says that "the genitive λόγου specifies what aspect of σοφία Paul has in mind: it is a wisdom having to do with speech. The phrase refers essentially to the Greek eloquence."

25. Winter, "Rhetoric," 821; Smit, "What Is Apollos?"

26. Translation from Raymond B. Collins, *First Corinthians*, SP 7 (Collegeville: Liturgical, 1999), 85.

1 Corinthians 1:17b–31: One λόγος against Another

a well-established meaning of "reckoning," in the sense of one's best "account" for the total accumulation of facts. Naturally this meaning denoted in many usages something like an "explanation," a "teaching," a "statement of a theory," or a "theory" itself.[27] While some construal like "wisdom of theory [λόγου]" may be cumbersome in English, it is quite intelligible as a concept. (3) The attributed genitive as articulated in (2b) may also shade over in this case into an epexegetical genitive. In effect, the teaching/theory/account would then constitute the wisdom. One might say that this kind of λόγος indicates, generically, an ethos or philosophical outlook. On this interpretation, Paul would then be referring to two philosophies (λόγοι) or alternative wisdoms (σοφίαι). I suggest that (3) offers the best interpretation of the construction here, being, as I shall demonstrate, the most consistent with the antitheses that Paul elaborates throughout this section.

The reader receives no further clarity that λόγου alludes to *style* of "speaking" in light of the contrast itself (vv. 17–18). The counterpoint to σοφία λόγου is ὁ σταυρὸς τοῦ Χριστοῦ (v. 17), which designates not a "plain" manner of speaking, but, as becomes clear as Paul precedes, a different "account" of the world.

The Cross as Status Defying

Verse 18 confirms these insights. The attributivizing article in ὁ τοῦ σταυροῦ signifies that the introductory phrase ὁ λόγος . . . ὁ τοῦ σταυροῦ is *synonymous* with ὁ σταυρὸς τοῦ Χριστοῦ, thus restating the contrast posed in v. 17. The resulting contrast—between two kinds of "word" or two "accounts" of the world—exposes the rhetorical reading as less than natural and comparatively forced, for it produces a contrast between "eloquent speaking" and "cross speaking." On that reading, either the parallel between two kinds of speaking ("fancy" vs. "plain" speaking) is destroyed, or the word *cross* is pressed into a cipher for a style of speaking (v. 23). Does usage or context support this?

Regular usage in Paul's letters suggests that *cross* (σταυρός) serves as synecdoche for a *message*. Apart from its two occurrences in 1 Cor 1:17, 18, σταυρός occurs in Paul's undisputed letters only five times (Gal 5:11; 6:12, 14;

---

27. All of these are primary meanings listed in LSJ. Musonius Rufus, in *Diatr.* 5, uses λόγος to designate "theory" in distinction from "practice" (ἔθος). (For a translation, see Cora E. Lutz, *Musonius Rufus, the Roman Socrates*, Yale Classical Studies 10 [New Haven: Yale University Press, 1947].) Plutarch uses the term λόγος to mean "theory" while using the complementary term βίος to refer to its embodiment in "life" (*Mor.* 1033a). And see p. 200 n. 42 below.

Phil 2:8; 3:18). In all instances the cross represents the way of humiliation and shame that Jesus exhibited in his life and above all epitomized in his death. For Paul the cross also symbolized God's inversion of the world's systems of value and that God bestowed his gifts upon humanity not on the basis of worth, but *in spite of* worth. That is, in John Barclay's terms, Paul understood God's gift to humanity as being "incongruous" with human worth.[28] If the usual meaning of σταυρός holds here, then Paul speaks in 1 Cor 1:18 not about the *manner* in which his message is presented but about the message's theological *content*: to preach a message that advocates congruous gift would be to empty or destroy the cross message, with its emphasis on incongruity.

Contextually, we find that 1 Cor 1:18 grounds what immediately precedes. Paul refuses to endorse a message that runs counter to the status-inverting message of the cross, for (γάρ) it is the very status-inverting nature of the gospel that defines its "power" (δύναμις). This interpretation lends different significance to the term δύναμις than is often attributed to it. Despite the common suggestion that δύναμις reflects technical rhetorical terminology,[29] it does not here connote the "persuasive" power of the gospel as opposed to human means of persuasion, or rhetoric. The word here is metonymic and complex. Its multifacetedness is shown in vv. 23–24 by its placement in apposition not only to *Christ crucified* (Χριστὸν ἐσταυρωμένον), but also to *scandal* (σκάνδαλον), *foolishness* (μωρία), and *wisdom* (σοφία). The connotations are surely, in the broadest sense, "social," for the term alludes to the paradoxical orientation toward status that underlies the wisdom of God. In this regard, to say that the gospel is "God's *power* from the perspective of those who are being saved, i.e., for *us*" (v. 18)[30] is to say, paradoxically, that it is not "power" as normally conceived, but weakness itself—consisting in the disgraceful death of a weak Galilean peasant—through which God effected redemption. In other words, Christ demonstrated God's power not through supremacy but, ironically, through self-sacrifice, or *weakness*. God's weakness was actually strength. The gospel is God's "power" also in the sense that, through it, those who are neither distinguished nor powerful within the domain of society acquire from it wholeness and distinction of a different sort. God shows no partiality in respect to human status. In short, Paul describes his message as "foolishness" to the world not because he had preached it in words wanting

---

28. Barclay, *Paul and the Gift*, 387, etc.
29. E.g., Winter, *Philo and Paul among the Sophists*, 149–50.
30. The dative indicates perspective (the "ethical dative"), as also ἡμῖν in v. 30.

in *eloquence* ("unwise words"), but because the *message* stated the opposite of the conventional wisdom of the world.

The Shortcomings of the σοφός

Verses 19 and 20 incorporate intertexts from Isaiah that decry human "wisdom" understood in terms of its content.[31] Indeed, in v. 19 the scripture citation offers grounds (γάρ) for Paul's previous dissociation of the "word that is of the cross," on the one hand, from "foolishness," on the other. The intertext alluded to (LXX Isa 29:14–16) describes the failure of Israel's leaders in that they teach "teachings of men" (29:13)—or the "wisdom of the wise" (τὴν σοφίαν τῶν σοφῶν, 24:14)—and "set aside" God and his law (24:16). Next, Paul plays allusively in v. 20 on LXX Isa 19:11–12 and 33:18, texts that condemn the counsel of "wise" rulers. Plainly, both intertexts describe human wisdom as content.

Like Isaiah, Paul declares the "wisdom of the wise" to have been mistaken. His citation of Isa 29:14 in v. 19 echoes the wording of v. 18 but reverses the evaluation adopted by those who are "perishing": while the cross is "foolishness" to those who are perishing (τοῖς ... ἀπολλυμένοις μωρία), God will "destroy" the "wisdom" on which such thinking is based (σοφία ἀπολῶ).[32]

This line of thought explains the drift of the questions in v. 20. Paul asks "where" the σοφός, γραμματεύς, and συζητητής are. Despite scholars' bewildering lack of agreement as to the identities of these figures, it can be said with confidence that, within the intellectual domain, the term σοφός, at least, had stronger associations with the Hellenistic philosopher than anything else.[33] So sure is this identification that even Bruce Winter, although taking the "rhetorical" view of the situation, here translates the word as such ("Greek philosopher").[34] Indeed, from Socrates on σοφός became a technical

---

31. As shown by Inkelaar, *Conflict over Wisdom*, 199 (on 1:19), 195 (on 1:20).

32. Contra Smit, "What Is Apollos?" (243–44): that the two forms of ἀπόλλυμι here allude to Apollos (Ἀπολλῶς) is mere clever speculation. The verb is original to the quotation of LXX Isa 29:14; it is also used in an identical contrast outside 1 Cor (2 Cor 2:15), like its cognate ἀπώλεια in Philippians (1:28; 3:19); finally, the word is in no way unnatural here but serves the immediate argument.

33. Additionally, Markus Lautenschlager argues at length that the συζητητής is the "philosophical researcher" (philosophischen Forscher), in "Abschied vom Disputierer: Zur Bedeutung von syetetes in 1 Kor 1,20," *ZNW* 83 (1992): 276–85.

34. Winter, "Rhetoric," 821.

term for the philosopher par excellence, the so-called wise man.[35] Each of the philosophical schools worked out their own ideas of what qualities defined the wise man.[36] Yet, the σοφός paradigm had special significance for the Stoics, who laid exclusive claim to the title and whose portrait of the wise man served as the inspiration for counter portraits of this figure in the other philosophical schools.[37]

The key importance of the term σοφός in 1:20 should not be missed. Placement of the σοφός first in the list of three figures is consistent with the thematic prominence of this type across the first four chapters of the letter (the σοφ- root being passim). The σοφός is anticipated already in the preceding citation from Isa 29:14 (τῶν σοφῶν) and is the only one of the three figures to be reintroduced later. Inkelaar observes that the term σοφός "is explicitly or implicitly present in most citations" in 1 Corinthians and that the citations include four of the five occurrences of σοφός found in LXX Isaiah.[38] The term

---

35. In this case, the attempt to be gender inclusive has the adverse effect of obscuring the technical meaning of the term. Women, too, could be considered "wise" in antiquity. See H. Harich-Schwarzbauer, "Women Philosophers," in *Der neue Pauly: Enzyklopädie der Antike*, ed. H. Cancik and H. Schneider (Stuttgart: Metzler Verlag), https://referenceworks.brillonline.com/browse/der-neue-pauly; yet the term σοφός itself was gendered in the masculine because it was thought to be most properly a masculine trait. To capture the historical sense of the term, classical scholars therefore rightly persist in rendering σοφός "wise man" when it seems to carry the philosophical meaning. For one recent work that has made a case for maintaining the masculine, see Inwood and Gerson, *Stoics Reader*, ix. Runar M. Thorsteinsson also translates σοφός in this way in his recent article "Jesus Christ and the Wise Man: Paul and Seneca on Moral Sages," in Dodson and Briones, *Paul and Seneca*, 73–87.

36. Every ancient philosophy presented itself as the path to the happy life (εὐδαιμονία). Each of them also differed in their conception of how to attain it. Since one's brand of wisdom entailed a certain form of life—life *lived* in the best of all ways—the one who embodied that wisdom was truly "wise," or a "wise man" (σοφός).

37. It is widely recognized that these portraits developed as a response to the Stoic portrait of the σοφός (a kind of "competitive appropriation"); so G. B. Kerferd, "The Sage in Hellenistic Philosophical Literature," in *The Sage in Israel and Ancient Near East*, ed. John G. Gammie and Leo G. Perdue (Winona Lake: Eisenbrauns, 1990), 320–28, esp. 320–22. Long and Sedley (*Hellenistic Philosophers*, 1:138–39) observe, for instance, that parallel descriptions of the wise man suggest that the Epicurean portrait was developed as a deliberate attempt to rival the Stoic portrait (commenting on the parallel descriptions in Diogenes Laertius, *Vit. phil.* 10.117–120 [Epicureans]; apparently having in mind 7.117–124 [Stoics]); cf. Cicero, *Acad.* 2.66–67 on the Academics and Stoics.

38. Inkelaar, *Conflict over Wisdom*, 165. LXX Isa 3:3; 19:11, 12; 29:14; 3:12; four of these occur in 1 Cor 1–4 (Isa 3:3; 19:11–12; 29:14); the fifth is alluded to, i.e., Isa 31:2 (Inkelaar, *Conflict over Wisdom*, 167, 299).

σοφός occurs ten times in the first four chapters of 1 Corinthians and eleven times across the letter, more than all its other occurrences in the NT combined. It occurs as a definite substantive in 1:19, 27; 3:19, 20 ("the wise man") and as an indefinite substantive in 1:20; 6:5.[39] In at least two places Paul implies that some Corinthians think themselves σοφοί ("If anyone among you thinks he is a σοφός," 3:18; "is there not any σοφός among you . . . ?" 6:5). In view of the evidence, interpreters widely agree that some among the Corinthians applied the term σοφός to themselves and that their claim to this status was closely related to the divisions treated in chapters 1–4.[40]

We return, then, to the questions in v. 20. These three figures—the "wisest" of the world's population—cannot be found ("where?"), because the world has no "wisdom" to speak of. Verse 21 next offers grounds for Paul's underlying assertion and reveals that his emphasis in v. 20 is on "knowing" (ἔγνω) God. This emphasis suggests that the common characteristic of these figures is their ability—or inability—to arrive at knowledge of God through the investigative competencies unique to each of them: for instance, philosophical speculation (σοφός), hermeneutical insight (γραμματεύς), or dialectical acuity (συζητητής).

Paul's main emphasis in v. 20 is on the failure of the wise man, despite his clairvoyance, to have arrived at an accurate knowledge of the truth. The concluding question in v. 20 repeats the point of the prior quotation (here replacing *destroy*, ἀπολῶ, with *made foolish*, ἐμώρανεν), aiming now to force the listeners' concession: "*Did God not* [οὐχί] render foolish the wisdom of the world?" The aorist tense points to an accomplished event—the Christ event as a whole, but especially as epitomized in Christ's humility and crucifixion—as the remainder of the paragraph makes evident. It is this point—that God's wisdom is reified in the Christ event—that the wise failed to understand.

Paul's critique of worldly wisdom, however, concerns more than human epistemological limitations. Paul's language rather situates the wise persons' limitations within a more comprehensive apocalyptic framework. Their wisdom is that "of the world" (τοῦ κόσμου), or as restated, "of this age" (τοῦ αἰῶνος τούτου). It is *what* the world thinks just as much as *how* it gets there that constitutes this wisdom. We may think of this kind of complex as a *ratio*, in the sense of an "account" or "reckoning" of the world and of life. Thus Paul's critique of the σοφός and other intellectuals applies not strictly to their *methods* of knowing, but more broadly to the whole symbolic world, under-

---

39. It occurs as an attributive with ἀρχιτέκτων in 3:10.
40. See p. 21 n. 48 above.

girded by its own grammar of thought.[41] That is, the different approaches to knowing differ not just in logical processes but in the interaction of logical processes with the underlying premises that determine one's "truth," premises that interact in complex and maybe only quasi-logical configurations and that may constitute not so much reasoned truths as foundational evaluative judgments merely taken for granted. In other words, it is not simply the logical steps that determine the wise man's conclusions. On a larger scale, it is the a priori restrictions that his symbolic world sets around what kinds of conclusions can be deemed acceptable or can even be considered at all. For Paul the intellectuals' misevaluation of true wisdom as mere foolishness is a symptom of their inability to know due to their living, so to speak, "in a completely different world."

We find here that it is quite wrong to construe the wisdom of these figures (v. 20) as a matter of their ability to persuade. If Paul in some way criticizes the inadequacy of their methods, still his emphasis is not on *imparting* wisdom to *others*, but on *discovering* it for *oneself*. Confirming this reading is the causal relationship found between the two clauses in v. 21: "inasmuch as" (ἐπειδή) the world could not come to true wisdom through its various modes of inquiry (διὰ τῆς σοφίας), God "thought it good through the foolishness of the proclamation to save those who believe." The antithesis emphasizes an element of irony, even surprise. The point is that "in his wisdom" God planned the failure of human wisdom, so that wisdom might not be *found*, but rather *given*. In this respect, Paul's antithesis between the world's σοφοί and those who believe entails an antithesis between knowledge through human *discovery* and knowledge through the *revealed* paradigm of Christ. This active-passive contrast in regard to knowledge is reiterated again in 8:1 and 13:12.

It is interesting that those who affirm the "rhetorical" reading of this passage often come to our interpretation of vv. 20–21 without noticing (or noting) the discrepancy between this interpretation and their general thesis. Kuck, for instance, at the same time states that this "is a wisdom which shows itself in eloquence of speech (1:17, 20; 2:1, 4, 13)" *and* that it is a wisdom that "cannot by itself know God (1:21)."[42] Upon a moment's reflection, one notices that the two points are actually different. According to the first statement, Paul addresses eloquence and thus the inability of the orator to persuade

---

41. Echoing Berger and Luckman's term *symbolic universe*: from Peter L. Berger and Thomas Luckmann, *The Social Construction of Reality: A Treatise in the Sociology of Knowledge* (Garden City, NY: Doubleday, 1966), 114–15.

42. Kuck, *Judgment and Community Conflict*, 189.

1 Corinthians 1:17b–31: One λόγος against Another

others; according to the second, Paul addresses the inability of the inquirer to know for himself or herself. It is beside the point whether Paul could affirm both as legitimate propositions. The question is whether the same words, in the unfolding of the discourse, can be read as making both points simultaneously.

Litfin shares our reading of 1:21, though in fact it conflicts with his main thesis. Litfin reads 1:17b–2:5 as a whole as a statement about Paul's theological assumptions about preaching. Thus, for Litfin the fundamental contrast is one between the persuasion that "depended upon the speaker" and Paul's simple "placarding" of the cross, so that salvation originates solely from the agency of God.[43] This framework, however, makes Litfin's interpretation of v. 21 puzzling. Now he says: "He [God] would save, not those who everyone thought by their intellectual and verbal skills could scale the heights, but rather οἱ πιστεύοντες, that is, the ones who are able to see and humbly embrace the so-called μωρία of the placarded Christ for what is [sic] actually is, the wisdom of God."[44] Here Litfin's thesis that Paul addresses the role of the preacher in bringing about the salvation of his listeners is now inexplicably converted into a scenario involving the inability of the eloquent to bring about, it appears, their *own* salvation (God "would save, not those who everyone thought by their intellectual and verbal skills could scale the heights . . ."). This incongruity exposes precisely where Litfin's construal of this passage goes wrong. Paul's discourse has in view not the *style* used by the Corinthians' preachers or teachers, but the pretensions of the wise Corinthians as having discovered wisdom for themselves. Likewise, it concerns not human *instrumentality* in bringing about the salvation of *others* but salvation in relation to *one's own worth*. While this point becomes the unmistakable focus of vv. 26–31, as we shall now see, Paul is already developing this point in vv. 22–24.

The Wisdom of Christ Crucified

A single sentence in Greek, vv. 22–24 come as a mirror image of v. 21, now applied specifically to Paul's ministry. As the μέν-δέ construction indicates (v. 23), Paul contrasts both "Jews" and "Greeks" *together*, on the one hand (μέν), with himself and believers, on the other (δέ).[45] Paul's assertion that "Jews seek signs" undoubtedly broadens his theologically framed response beyond

---

43. Litfin, *St. Paul's Theology of Proclamation*, 191.
44. Litfin, *St. Paul's Theology of Proclamation*, 198.
45. That is, Ἰουδαίοις μὲν σκάνδαλον ἔθνεσιν δὲ μωρίαν on the one side (with δέ marking

the narrower confines of the concrete situation, where the problem more specifically is σοφία, which is said to be a "Greek pursuit."[46] Jewish earnestness for signs and Greek pursuit of wisdom, however, share something deep in common. It is true, as Lampe suggests, that for Paul the cross shattered both "Jewish" and "Greek" expectations. Paul's concern, however, is not so much the inherent insufficiency of "theo-logy" (talk about God) as it is a particular flaw that their theology entails: the cross defies human expectations about how God *should* act assuming ordinary canons of evaluation.[47]

One would need to be very committed to the thesis that "form" is "*the* crucial element in the Apostle's present argument" to hold onto the view that this is Paul's concern here.[48] Any notion that "the foolishness of the proclamation" (τῆς μωρίας τοῦ κηρύγματος) refers to the inelegance of the preacher comes into question now as Paul refers to the *content* of his proclamation—"Christ crucified" (Χριστὸν ἐσταυρωμένον). Within the developing argument, the point concerns Jews' and Greeks' inability to approve the *notion* of "Christ crucified" as "wisdom" starting from the rationalizing criteria that determine their perspectives on worth.

The common basis for Jewish and Greek rejection of Christ crucified is their common objection to the way in which Paul's message subverts ordinary human calculations of worth. Christ crucified is an "offense" (σκάνδαλον) to Jews because—as Paul indicates by the antithetical correlation between the "offense" of the cross and Christ as "power" (δύναμιν)—it characterizes the anointed one (Χριστός) entirely in terms of weakness. This weakness represents a problem undoubtedly because the messiah was expected, by many, to appear in power,[49] or if not that, certainly *not* in disgrace, meeting his end in the way he did, rejected by God himself (Gal 3:13). To the Greeks on the other hand, Christ crucified is "foolishness" (μωρία) because the message of the cross conveys God's total disregard for worth as a criterion for his

---

development or addition: "a scandal to Jews *and* foolishness to gentiles") and αὐτοῖς δὲ τοῖς κλητοῖς on the other.

46. On the assertion "Greeks seek wisdom," compare the fixed Latin expression *studia sapientiae*, "the pursuit of wisdom," as a circumlocution for philosophy (Quintilian, *Inst.* 1.pr.14; 12.2.8; Cicero, *Off.* 2.5; *Tusc.* 1.1; 4.3.5; Seneca, *Ep.* 89.4, 6; *Vit. beat.* 24.4; Tacitus, *Agr.* 4; cf. Lucretius, *De rer. nat.* 5.7–12; 1.635–644).

47. Peter Lampe, "Theological Wisdom and the 'Word about the Cross': The Rhetorical Scheme in 1 Corinthians 1–4," *Int* 44 (1990): 117–31.

48. Litfin, *St. Paul's Theology of Proclamation*, 199.

49. 1 En. 46:4–5; 4 Ezra 13:1–13; 2 Bar. 40:1–4; 70:9; 72:2; cf. 1 Macc 2:50–68; 9:21; Acts 5:33–39; 21:38; Josephus, *J.W.* 2.261–263; *Ant.* 17.269, 273–777; 20.97–98, 169–172.

benevolences or approval. Indeed, Christ lacked every marker of status as people ordinarily reckon it.

The ὅτι clause in v. 25 loosely grounds what precedes: Paul preaches Christ crucified since God's foolishness is "wiser," his strength "stronger," and so on. The statement at first appears to be an inelegant abbreviation for a comparison between the foolishness/weakness of God and "[the wisdom/strength of] humanity" (τὸ μωρὸν τοῦ θεοῦ σοφώτερον τῶν ἀνθρώπων ἐστίν). In view of Christ's description in the preceding verses, however, it seems better to see God's "foolishness" and "weakness" here not as qualities of God but as personifications of Christ himself.[50] *Christ*, whom Paul has just identified in v. 24 as God's "wisdom" and "power" (or foolishness and weakness), is wiser and stronger than humanity.

The contextual significance of v. 25 comes into clear focus in light of our interpretation of the unit as a whole. Paul presents contrary pictures of wisdom's embodiment, each centering around respective subjective orientations toward the notion of human worth. Even though it makes no sense within the rationalizing framework that the world accepts, God views the foolish and weak crucified Christ as wise and powerful. As all of this shows, the apposition of *Christ* with *power/wisdom* in v. 24 suggests that Paul wishes not to emphasize a contrast between the "simply proclaimed message" and the power/wisdom inherent in persuasive preaching,[51] but rather the paradoxical, world-shattering, commonsense-defying content of the gospel message vis-à-vis the world's common value judgments. As Paul will now develop this idea, his emphasis on Christ crucified applies to the issue of worth as a criterion for God's "calling" (vv. 26–31).

STATUS AND INCONGRUITY (1:26–31)

Although vv. 26–31 form a separate paragraph structurally, syntactically, and thematically, a continuous stream of thought connects it with what precedes. The initial γάρ in v. 26 indicates a tight connection between two premises: on the one hand, that the cross impugns the rationalizing criteria that led the world to believe that the cross is foolishness and weakness, and on the

---

50. Perhaps analogous to traditional Jewish hypostatizations of Wisdom. Wisdom: 1 En. 42:1–3; Sir. 1; 24. The Word: 1 En. 14:24; 61:7; Philo, *Spec.* 1.81. Powers (δυνάμεις): Philo, *Abr.* 119–121.

51. Litfin, *St. Paul's Theology of Proclamation*, 201.

other hand, the fact that "not many" of the Corinthians were "wise" (σοφοί), "powerful" (δυνατοί), or "well born" (εὐγενεῖς) at the time of God's "calling" (v. 26). The presence of γάρ makes it impermissible to identify a thematic shift here, as some suppose, from the unimpressiveness of Paul's gospel *presentation* (vv. 21–25) to the unimpressiveness of the Corinthians *themselves* (v. 26).[52] Rather, Paul points to the *specific case* of the Corinthians' "calling" in order to support (γάρ) the same point that he has been pressing: first, that Christ sets the standard by which we should calculate worth (vv. 21–25) and, now, that God called the Corinthians despite their lacking sufficient "credentials" (vv. 26–31). In short, Paul means "we are bound to accept the conclusion that Christ crucified establishes the criterion of evaluation, *for* [γάρ] if God followed the standards of the world, you yourselves would not even have been called."

The Wise, Powerful, and Well-Born (1:26)

Verse 26 has become a linchpin in many major studies on 1 Corinthians over the last half century. At the same time, the meaning of this verse is obscured due to several difficulties. (1) Grammatically, the clauses are verbless. (2) Syntactically, the verse could be construed as a series of either questions or statements. (3) Semantically, σοφοί, δυνατοί, and εὐγενεῖς could have either "sociological" or "religious" signification. (4) Pragmatically, Paul's tone could be either genuine or sarcastic.

Sharing a reading that goes at least as far back as Origen (*Cels.* 3.48), recent interpreters tend to repeat Theissen's view that the verse reflects a literal description of the church's socioeconomic constituency: "If Paul says that there were not many in the Corinthian congregation who were wise, powerful, and wellborn, then this much is certain: there were some."[53] Many interpreters in the past, however, have construed these attributes in a different sense. Through the second third of the twentieth century, interpreters commonly construed the three predicates in a special "spiritual" or "religious" sense, whether in specific connection with a religious tradition like

---

52. Cf. Ciampa and Rosner, *First Letter to the Corinthians*, 102.
53. Theissen, *Social Setting*, 72. Barnett (*Corinthian Question*) refers to this group as the church's "few elite members," the "haves" (92–93). Murphy-Connor (*Paul: A Critical Life*, 271) prefers this interpretation based on "common sense."

Gnosticism or Hellenistic Judaism or as understood more generally within the discourse of Greek religion or popular philosophy.[54]

In deciding the sense, Paul's addition of the qualifying phrase κατὰ σάρκα needs to be considered. Although the phrase appears in the text only after the first term (σοφοί), there are no solid grounds for denying its application to the other terms as well (δυνατοί, εὐγενεῖς). The prepositional phrase is often taken to confirm a socioeconomic interpretation. The semantic question, however, requires consideration of several intersecting issues, including (1) the syntax of κατά and the semantics of σάρξ; (2) the question whether the three predicates reflect self-ascriptions of the Corinthians; (3) the question of how, in context, the Corinthians' status as indicated relates to human "boasting" (vv. 29, 31); and (4) the question of why the Corinthians are boasting ("boasting," 1:29, 31; 3:21; 4:7; 5:6; 9:15–16; cf. 13:3; "puffed up," 4:6, 18, 19; 5:2; 8:1; cf. 13:4). We shall consider these issues amid the general discussion below.

The σοφός in Ancient Context

Many interpreters read 1 Cor 1:26–31 as a whole against the background of ancient rhetorical culture.[55] Winter sees in these verses Paul's denunciation of "sophistic boasting."[56] Finding that the adjectives referring to high status in vv. 26–28 also appear in ancient literature to describe members of the ruling class (σοφοί, δυνατοί, εὐγενεῖς, τοὺς σοφούς, τὰ ἰσχυρα), Winter concludes, "Based on the wealth of literary evidence we can conclude that 1 Corinthians 1.26 refers to the ruling class of Corinth from which orators and sophists came." While the connection between rhetorical education and high status is not to be denied, one ought not to be hasty to conclude that Paul selects his high-status terms with sophists in particular in mind. The tenuousness of the rhetorical thesis at this point is illustrated in no better way than by its proponents' mishandling of the passages used to support it. A passage from Plutarch's *How to Tell a Flatterer from a Friend* (58e) has been cited repeatedly

---

54. E.g., Pearson, *Pneumatikos-Psychikos Terminology*, 40; Horsley, "Pneumatikos vs. Psychikos," 282–83; Davis, *Wisdom and Spirit*, 75–76; and still in Finney, *Honour and Conflict*, 95–97; Demetrius K. Williams, "Paul's Anti-imperial 'Discourse of the Cross': The Cross and Power in 1 Corinthians 1–4," *Society of Biblical Literature Seminar Papers* 39 (2000): 796–823, esp. 808.

55. Beginning with Munck, "Menigheden uden Partier"; ET, "The Church without Factions: Studies in 1 Corinthians 1–4," 135–67, esp. 162n2–163n1.

56. Winter, *Philo and Paul among the Sophists*, 195.

in studies to demonstrate that the σοφός in v. 26 is the orator or rhetorically educated person.[57] The passage reads as follows:

> Again, some people will not even listen to the Stoics, when they call the wise man [τὸν σοφόν] at the same time rich [πλούσιον], handsome, well-born [εὐγενῆ], and a king [βασιλέα]; but flatterers declare of the rich man that he is at the same time an orator and a poet, and, if he will, a painter and a musician, and swift of foot and strong of body; and they allow themselves to be thrown in wrestling and outdistanced in running.

Winter includes no acknowledgment that this passage in context describes the Stoic philosopher, nor does he appear aware of the unique sense in which the Stoics understood the stated attributes. Pogoloff does acknowledge that the Stoics understood these attributes differently than their ordinary social sense; yet Pogoloff believes that "Plutarch makes clear" that people interpret the Stoic wise man's description "apart from the full system," seeing the Stoic to be "wise" only because of the external factors of wealth, high office, eloquence, honor, and power. This, however, is clearly not Plutarch's meaning.

The moral-philosophical tradition from Socrates on emphasized a distinction between different classes of goods: goods of the body (health, strength), goods of the soul (wisdom, justice, temperance), and external goods (money, friends, fame).[58] In view of these distinctions, philosophers disagreed fundamentally with ordinary society on how to define and order true "goods." Most philosophers advocated for a "transvaluation" of goods: the highest goods were not bodily or external goods, but goods of the soul. For the Stoics, goods of the soul were in fact the *only* true goods. The Stoic wise man was the man who had every good of the soul, that is, every *virtue*. Ordinary society ordered goods differently. According to the philosophers, people did so because our early socialization, under the influence especially of our parents, nurses, and tutors, taught us to value the wrong things: wealth, pleasure, civil office, popular glory—in other words, *externals*.[59] Because the philosophers' doc-

---

57. Winter (*Philo and Paul among the Sophists*, 190), in reference to members of "the ruling class"; Finney, *Honour and Conflict*, 93, seeing it as a "generic" term indicating someone "cultured" and of "high status"; Pogoloff, *Logos and Sophia*, 117. Martin (*Corinthian Body*, 51) cites Plutarch, *Mor.* 472a; 485a, d.

58. For instance, Aristotle, *Eth. nic.* 1.8.2, who also reduces the categories to two: goods of the soul and the other goods; Epictetus, *Diatr.* 3.7.2.

59. Cicero, *Tusc.* 3.1.2–3; Seneca, *Ep.* 115.11; Musonius Rufus, *Diatr.* 6.

trines were countercultural in this sense, their description of the σοφός—the one who truly possessed the highest goods—had a polemical edge. They appropriated the terminology of external goods (rich, well-born, kings) but reassigned it to the wise man in a sense that transcended ordinary semantic acceptation. The philosophers' wise man was wise, rich, well born, powerful—yes, like kings and rulers—but in a much higher sense.[60]

Plutarch's statement absolutely depends upon this distinction for its meaning. In context his succeeding statement about the kinds of things flatterers tell the rich and (further down) kings underscores that what the flatterers attribute to these men is wrong: they tell them that they are talented orators, poets, painters, and athletes when in fact they lack the requisite qualities. It is mere *flattery*. In this regard Plutarch's logic here poses a greater-to-lesser argument: ironically, people are reticent to grant to the truly wise, virtuous man (the Stoic philosopher) the *higher* qualities that he authentically possesses,[61] and yet they will fabricate admirable *external* qualities for those whose praise is deserved least (kings). Plutarch is not suggesting then that people understand the Stoic description of the wise man "apart from the full system." Rather, he is drawing from the traditional philosophical distinction of good types. Consequently, if one wanted to use this passage as an illuminating parallel to Paul's language in 1 Cor 1:26, it would not serve the rhetorical thesis; it would support the view that Paul alludes to common descriptions of the philosopher, and, more specifically, the Stoic σοφός.[62]

Plutarch's description of the Stoic σοφός is common and quite conventional. Sources ubiquitously describe the σοφός with these and similar terms. Reflecting the philosophers' countercultural evaluation of goods, the σοφός was said to possess every marker of status that was in the ordinary sense "external" but was for the σοφός a marker of status in a higher, intellectual sense. It was in this higher sense that the σοφός was "well born" (εὐγενής, *SVF* 3:594), "strong" (ἰσχυρός, *SVF* 3:567), "king" (βασιλεύς, *SVF* 3:615, 617, 619, 655), "ruler" (ἄρχων, *SVF* 3:618, 619), "rich" (πλούσιος, *SVF* 3:593, 598, 618, 655), "prudent" (φρόνιμος, *SVF* 3:655), "distinguished" (ἔνδοξος, *SVF* 3:603) and "glo-

---

60. Cicero's spokesman describes the significance of these statuses in the ordinary social sense as "a shadowy phantom glory" (*Tusc.* 3.1.3 [King, LCL]).

61. For the question whether such a man existed, see Cicero, *Acad.* 2.47.145; *Tusc.* 2.22.51; Seneca, *Ep.* 42.1; *Tranq.* 7.4–5; Epictetus, *Diatr.* 2.19.20–28; Lucian, *Herm.* 76–77; Sextus Empiricus, *Adv. prof.* 9.133–136 // LS 54D; cf. *SVF* 3:657–70.

62. Which interpreters have noted at least as far back as Grant, "Wisdom of the Corinthians," 51–55, esp. 51.

rious" (εὐκλεής), he alone being "king" (βασιλεύς) and "free" (ἐλεύθερος) (*SVF* 3:603). A Stoic allusion therefore emerges in 1 Cor 1:26, not through mere overlap of three unassociated terms, but by what is evidently a configuration of commonly associated terms. Notably, some of these terms reappear in description of the Corinthians' self-understanding later in the letter (ἰσχυρός in 1:27; βασιλεύς, πλούσιος, φρόνιμος, ἰσχυρός, ἔνδοξος, cf. 4:8–10; ἐλεύθερος, cf. 7:21).

A final comment should be added regarding the Stoics' description of the philosopher-σοφός as "rhetor" (ῥήτωρ). This is indeed a common description of the Stoic wise man,[63] but like the descriptions of the wise man as "rich," "king," and the rest, the wise man's description as "rhetor" signified not the rhetor as ordinarily conceived in society but the rhetor conceived in a higher, Stoic sense.[64] For the Stoics, eloquence was a virtue in the same sense as justice, prudence, temperance, and the rest.[65] As regarded speech, this meant no more than that words conformed with reality or, as the Stoics said, were "in conformity with Nature."[66] A connection between the Stoic σοφός and rhetoric, therefore, does not put "eloquence" back at the fore of 1 Cor 1:17b–31—neither in the sense of "fancy" rhetoric (Litfin) nor in the sense of the rhetorician's ordinarily high social status (Winter; Pogoloff).

Formal Considerations

The semantic connection that we have seen between the terminology in 1:26 and Stoic descriptions of the σοφός is, on its own, perhaps merely interesting. While not enough to establish a distinct allusion to Stoicism per se, more can be said in favor of this connection when we turn to form-critical considerations. What is found in v. 26 is not just any way of assigning attributes. Rather, Paul states his description (1) using a simple subject + predicate nominative construction and (2) using a series of predicate nominatives in a list

---

63. *SVF* 3:594, 622, 654, 655; Plutarch, *Mor.* 58e; Diogenes Laertius, *Vit. phil.* 7.122.

64. Martin (*Corinthian Body*, 51) cites evidence that the (Stoic) σοφός is the orator based on Plutarch, *Mor.* 472a; 485a, d, though he does not acknowledge the Stoic's fundamental redefinition of the role.

65. For Stoic eloquence as a virtue, see Cicero, *Or.* 3.65.

66. For a discussion of Stoic influence on grammar, see Teresa Morgan, *Literate Education in the Hellenistic and Roman Worlds* (Cambridge: Cambridge University Press, 1998), 169–74; on Stoic adaptations to rhetorical theory, see J. R. Butts, "The Progymnasmata of Theon: A New Text with Translation and Commentary" (PhD diss., Claremont Graduate School, 1986), 6–7.

(cf. 4:8–10). This way of describing the Stoic σοφός was formulaic and had wide currency in ancient literature, as several dozen passages describing the σοφός demonstrate.[67] For instance: "the *wise man* alone is *rich* and alone *good* and alone *wellborn* and alone *rhetor* [μόνον τὸν σοφὸν πλούσιον ἢ μόνον καλὸν ἢ μόνον εὐγενῆ ἢ μόνον ῥήτορα]" (*SVF* 3:594); "only the *wise man* is *free* and *ruler* [ὁ σοφὸς μόνος ἐλεύθερός τε καὶ ἄρχων]" (*SVF* 3:364); "he will most rightly be called king [rex] . . . master [*magister*] . . . rich [*dives*] . . . beautiful [*pulcher*] . . . free [*liber*]," etc. (Cicero, *Fin.* 3.75). These statements were known as the Stoic "paradoxes" (παραδόξα) because the claims that they made were "surprising." Since this syntactical structure was formulaic in the paradoxes, a rival explanation for Paul's primary allusions in 1:26 would need to offer not only alternative terminological parallels but also equally similar culturally fixed formal parallels.

Boasting

Winter's proposal that Paul responds in vv. 26–28 primarily to sophistic culture deserves further evaluation in light of Paul's prohibition of "boasting" in the verses that ensue (vv. 29–31). Paul's exhaustive reference to *"all* flesh" in his prohibition of boasting inevitably encompasses people like the sophists along with everyone else. That he primarily has a specific external group in view, however, is certainly a more strained reading of the paragraph.

(1) The paragraph is bracketed by application to the Corinthians, being framed on the one side by a denial that the Corinthians were of high status when God called them (v. 26) and on the other side by a prohibition of human boasting (v. 29) and a reminder that the Corinthians are God's in Jesus Christ (v. 30). As Paul moves from the Corinthians' qualities in v. 26 ("not wise, powerful, etc.") to his generic references to the "foolish, weak, etc." (vv. 27–28), nothing suggests a switch to a different specific group. In fact, the connectives suggest otherwise. The οὐ . . . ἀλλά construction in vv. 26–27 necessarily creates continuity of identity between the wise, powerful, and wellborn of v. 26 and the foolish, weak, and ignobly born of vv. 27–28; the sense is: "you were *not* of high status when you were called [v. 26] *but* among those of low status [vv. 27–28]." (2) If Winter's identification is correct, it would be difficult to overlook the awkwardness of Paul's logical progression. For it requires some effort to understand why Paul would begin by noting that God called the Corinthians while *they* had low status if his point is to shame the

---

67. *SVF* 3:544–656; my italics.

sophists so that *they* could not boast. (3) It would be speculation to suppose that Paul has sophistic boasting in mind and not simply the boasting of those who he tells us elsewhere are boasting. (a) Paul accuses the Corinthians of boasting repeatedly throughout the letter ("boasting," 4:7; cf. 5:6; "puffed up," 4:6, 18, 19; 5:2; see later discussion of 3:21). Moreover, (b) several pieces of evidence suggest that the predicates Paul uses to describe the Corinthians in v. 26 are actually *self*-descriptions.

In regard to (b), several points should be noted. (i) If, as interpreters assume,[68] some of the Corinthians described themselves as σοφοί, it would be natural to assume that the coordinate items—δυνατοί and εὐγενεῖς— represent self-descriptions as well. (ii) The words in v. 26 make better sense as Corinthian self-descriptions than not, for if they reflected Paul's own description (i.e., of "some but not many"), one notices that this would establish them as an exception to the theological principle being laid down, thus weakening Paul's point: he would mean that, in the case of some, God *did* choose the wise, powerful, and so forth. This reading is unlikely to be correct for at least two reasons. (α) It directly contradicts Paul's conclusion in v. 29 that *"no* flesh" can boast (μὴ καυχήσηται πᾶσα σάρξ). The absolute preclusion of boasting stands only if the called in every case constitute those who are unworthy. (β) Such an exception not only weakens the general principle, it weakens it precisely where it applies most seriously, that is, with regard to the people who *think* themselves worthy. The descriptors in v. 26 must therefore represent a *sarcastic* appropriation by Paul of the Corinthians' own claims (and boasts), intended to highlight the universal principle that God chooses irrespective of worth.

At least two further points suggest that the descriptions were the Corinthians' own. (iii) The form of Paul's remark in v. 26, where he attributes high qualities to the Corinthians using simple predication, is similar to the form of 4:8 ("Already you are satisfied, already you are rich, already are kings"), which is shown to be sarcastic by his remarks in 4:7 ("What do you have that you did not receive? etc."). (iv) The implied contrast between the Corinthians' status now as opposed to their status at the time of their calling (κλῆσις) suggests that their status has, at least from their perspective, changed. While it is not impossible that their structural social status changed in the intervening months since Paul's visit, it seems easier to believe that Paul is describing a change in their self-perceptions than some precipitous social advancement in the world.

68. See p. 21 n. 48 above.

1 Corinthians 1:17b–31: One λόγος against Another

A final determination about the meaning of v. 26 cannot be made apart from an overall reading of the situation. One cannot skip over the fact that, as the letter makes evident, many in the Corinthian community did claim for themselves an exalted spiritual or intellectual status and evaluated themselves favorably against those of allegedly lesser spiritual stature. This dynamic certainly contributed to the issues around γνῶσις and the eating of idol meat in chapters 8–10; it is central to the discussion of spiritual gifts in chapters 12–14; and as we shall later see, it is alluded to, in no uncertain terms, in 2:6–16 and 4:7–8.

Spiritual versus Social Meaning

The above considerations help us in adjudicating whether the language of v. 26 is "social-economic" or "spiritual-religious." I have argued that the latter is more likely correct. I now add further points in favor of this conclusion.

The connecting conjunction at the opening of v. 26 (γάρ) provides grounds for what Paul has said previously. Verse 26, therefore, concerns the relationship between the rationalizing *criteria* used to determine human worth on the one hand (vv. 18, 21) and the basis for human *salvation* on the other (vv. 26–31). That the status indicators in v. 26 do connect back in this fashion is confirmed by Paul's appeal to the Corinthians' "calling" as the chronological moment of evaluation. They are to consider their status *at the time of* their calling in considering the question whether status had any determining effect on God's calling or invitation to salvation. So apparent is this connection that Laurence Welborn, being intent on maintaining a socioeconomic interpretation, is left with the argument that Paul misrepresented the situation: the impetus for the divisions was social and economic inequity even if Paul has framed the problem in soteriological terms ("It is, at any rate, clear that, whatever he says, Paul *knew* better").[69]

The cumulative evidence laid out above points to the conclusion that some among the Corinthians considered themselves "wise," "powerful," and "well-born" in some way other than an *ordinary* social sense. The inclusion of κατὰ σάρκα is not a clinching argument to the contrary. The argument from κατὰ σάρκα rests upon a reduction of the domain connoted by σάρξ to *ordinary*

---

69. Welborn, "On the Discord in Corinth," 96. At best, one could argue that a socioeconomic emphasis represents one application of the broader theological principle that Paul emphasizes in chapters 1–4—that as regards "calling" to the faith, God does not regard status of *any* kind.

social qualities. Undoubtedly the phrase connotes "human standards." These standards, however, are rooted in the community's assumptions about *all* that counts as "symbolic capital,"[70] that is, about what qualities enhance the status or prestige of the subjects in the eyes of other subjects within the community. In this regard we need to distinguish between two kinds of "social" status: (1) "ordinary social status" and (2) "transcendent social status."[71] In the former sense, "social" status in the community would be measured in some ways by "ordinary" criteria, like wealth, occupation, good birth; in the latter sense, it would be measured by other factors that counted within the faith community: as later portions of the letter reveal (esp. 2:6–16; chs. 12–14), these factors included the subject's acclaimed measure of spiritual achievement.

Incongruous Election (1:27-28)

Antithesis continues as Paul carries on his response in vv. 27–28. These verses articulate the counterpoint to the point begun with οὐ πολλοί, and so on in v. 26, but with more generic application. No, God did "not" (οὐ) "call" (τὴν κλῆσιν) those of high status "but" (ἀλλά) rather "chose" (ἐξελέξατο) those of low status (τὰ μωρὰ ... τὰ ἀσθενῆ ... τὰ ἰσχυρά· καὶ τὰ ἀγενῆ ... καὶ τὰ ἐξουθενημένα ... καὶ τὰ μὴ ὄντα). We need not press the "spiritual" meaning of the terminology all the way through. The same principle that applies to spiritual status applies to every kind of status as the world measures it. God does not—indeed *did* not—choose on the basis of humanly calculated symbolic capital.

The theme of election is in no way implicated in an antithesis between the agency of God and the agency of the preacher in effecting salvation.[72] Tellingly, Winter is unable to decide whether it is status or agency that Paul has in mind, appearing to take the view that the boasters are boasting *both* in their sophistic status *and* in their ability to save through rhetoric. He states: "Paul argues that God has chosen to humble all, including the sophists, for a purpose: so that no flesh might boast before him (verse 28b). This He did by eviscerating [1] any claim to secular wisdom which could *commend* them or [2] *bring* any to the true knowledge of God."[73] It is of course conceivable that

---

70. For this expression, see Barclay, *Paul and the Gift*, 6; passim.

71. Finney (*Honour and Conflict*, 95–98) refers to "spiritual" status.

72. Winter, *Philo and Paul among the Sophists*, 188. Mihaila (*Paul-Apollos Relationship*, 19–20) says: "Their 'call' was not the result of human wisdom, power, or status, but of God's choosing and working." True as this may be theologically, the *means* by which their salvation came about is not the point of this passage (see below).

73. Winter, *Philo and Paul among the Sophists*, 194 (my brackets and italics).

Paul could affirm both points in principle. But it is not clear how to make coherent exegetical sense of the text on the premise that the same words within the given discourse structure make these two separate points at once.

That Paul's emphasis in vv. 27–28 is on God's *incongruous* call, and not on agency, is corroborated by the information structure of the clauses. In each of the five parallel occurrences of the verb *chose* (ἐξελέξατο), the direct object is placed first in its clause. This placement unmistakeably signifies that the emphasis is not on God's "choosing" (i.e., election as opposed to human initiative) but on the surprising *low status* of those whom God has elected: "*the foolish things* God chose," and not the things considered most worthy from a human perspective. Thus, Paul puts an exclamation point on the theme of the paragraph. Election to salvation is incongruous with the worth of the recipient. God, to everyone's astonishment, chose the unworthy things.

The Preclusion of Boasting (1:29–31)

Paul's meaning is now clear. "Boasting" (v. 29) is ruled out not because people are saved by means of divine election rather than eloquent preaching.[74] Rather, boasting is ruled out because of the criteria that apply, or rather do not apply, in God's act of electing. As Paul concludes in v. 29, no one can "boast" (καυχήσηται) before God since God does not elect on the basis of anyone's "worthy" qualities, but rather as a gift to the undeserving.[75] The universal applicability (πᾶσα σάρξ) of the proscription on boasting shows that the principle of incongruity is absolute: in *no* case did God call on the basis of worth. This principle is "foolish," for it flies in the face of conventional wisdom, the wisdom of the world.[76]

Again an embarrassing ambiguity results at vv. 29–31 in Litfin's construction of the situation. Here Litfin states: "God uses what the world considers unimpressive so that in the end there can be no question as to who has accomplished the result—no man can boast."[77] "God uses" seems intentionally vague. No doubt this is because Litfin's interpretation here exposes the

---

74. As Mihaila (*Paul-Apollos Relationship*, 21) believes.

75. Although Paul does not use the term *gift* (χάρις) in 1:26–31, note that he rules out "boasting" in 4:7–8 on grounds that they had "received" all that they had.

76. Funk's ("Word and Word") thesis that Paul poses an antithesis between the powerless content of the Corinthians' wisdom and the powerful Christ event misses this motif. While Paul indeed presents the Christ event ("Christ crucified") as "powerful" (1:23–24), it is specifically Christ's *way* (his "weakness")—and the message thereabout—that is powerful.

77. Litfin, *St. Paul's Theology of Proclamation*, 203.

problem that underlies his overall reading of these chapters. As noted, the οὐ ... ἀλλά construction in vv. 26–27 creates a general *continuity* of identity between the not-wise, not-powerful, and not-well-born of v. 26 and the foolish, weak, and ignobly born of vv. 27–28—the former being mere species of the genera named in the latter. Since Paul speaks in v. 26 about the Corinthians' *own* qualifications (or non-qualifications) for salvation, Paul therefore cannot mean that God uses the "not many wise" to "accomplish the result" of salvation; for this construal would result in the nonsensical notion that the low-status Corinthians (the "not many wise") effect their own salvation through the preaching that "God uses"; this is the same tension seen in Litfin's interpretation of 1:21. In sum, Litfin's construction introduces confusion between the saved Corinthians and the preacher who saves.

This kind of obscurity continues as Litfin comments on v. 29: "God has paradoxically chosen the very low-status means the world considers foolish, weak, base, despised, or 'nothing.' And the reason for this is clear: so that no mortal can claim credit for salvation." Determined to explain this verse through his model of rhetoric versus proclamation as competing "means" of salvation, Litfin again forces his reading by describing God's "means" in terms of the predicates that Paul has already applied not to those who *preach*, but to those *to whom it is preached* (the "foolish, weak, base, despised, or 'nothings'")! Should Litfin respond that v. 26 describes the low-status Corinthians, but vv. 27–28 the low-status preacher, one would have to respond that this leaves the connection in thought (οὐ ... ἀλλά) quite without meaning. Litfin's interpretation would require, in effect, the following: "Not many of you were of high status when called. Instead God used low-status preachers." The blatant incoherence of this reading results precisely from this: that Paul's point concerns not how God saves, but whom. God has elected the unworthy. For this reason, no one can boast in their election.

Regarding our larger reconstruction of the situation, it must be pointed out that Paul's discussion of "boasting" here offers no support for the view that the Corinthians were boasting in other people, for instance Paul or Apollos. The sequence of vv. 26–29 does not allow this. When we arrive at v. 29, it is evident that ὅπως must explain the purpose (or result) of God's activity across the antithesis of vv. 26, 27–28. Only with great difficulty can Paul be taken to mean that God elected low-status people so that low-status people wouldn't boast in others. With v. 26 as the antithetical counterpart to vv. 27–28, the purpose clause in v. 29 can only mean that the *Corinthians* (v. 26), like all people (vv. 27–28), have no grounds for boasting in themselves.

The same line of reasoning continues into the final verses of the chapter. Initially, the meaning of v. 30 poses difficulties on account of several grammatical uncertainties: (1) the fronting of the prepositional phrase ἐξ αὐτοῦ, (2) the discursive function of δέ, and (3) the reason for the emphatic pronoun ὑμεῖς. These issues are clarified, however, in the light of the foregoing comments. Paul has declared boasting to be unjustified for "all" (πᾶσα σάρξ) on grounds of the incongruous nature of the call. Having stated this in general terms in vv. 27–29, v. 30 now re-narrows the application to the Corinthians. Our three questions are therefore resolved as follows. (1) Ἐξ αὐτοῦ ("from him") serves to highlight that God is the gracious source of salvation against any notion that election occurs based on the worth of the individual. (2) Rather than indicating contrast, δέ develops the point ("and") from general application back again to the specific case of the Corinthians. Finally, (3) the emphatic ὑμεῖς makes the new, and more specific, subject of interest discursively prominent. To paraphrase: "Insofar as God in every case chooses irrespective of worth, *you also* are in Christ [ἐν Χριστῷ Ἰησοῦ], not based on personal worth, but due entirely to the grace of God."

The relative clause that follows (ὅς ἐγενήθη . . .) continues in this direction. In a metonymic sense, Christ "became righteousness and sanctification and redemption" (the *cause*/Christ, equated with the *effect*/righteousness and sanctification and redemption). Certainly, Paul means by this that God deserves the "credit" for salvation.[78] We should not, however, see in this an implied antithesis between the power of God and the persuasive artifices of the preacher in effecting salvation. As ἀπὸ θεοῦ shows (we received wisdom "from God"), the antithesis is between salvation "from him" (cf. ἐξ αὐτοῦ) and salvation conditioned by something in "us" (referring to hearers, not speakers!). That is, the gift of salvation is unconditioned by the prior worth of the recipients, not contingent upon it. The result (ἵνα), as Paul asserts via Jer 9:23, is that no one can boast; or rather, it is that one ought only to boast "in the Lord." As the conclusion to vv. 26–30, this plainly means: "since God always chooses irrespective of prior worth, and since salvation is from him and Christ became redemption *for* you, you cannot boast that your calling to salvation was conditioned by any qualities of your own."

Boasting and Paul's Intertexts

The reading offered above is corroborated by the intertextual allusions to LXX Jer 9:22–23 woven throughout vv. 26–31. Apart from Paul's direct citation of Jer 9:23 in v. 31,[79] we find in the background of vv. 26–28 the content of

78. Litfin, *St. Paul's Theology of Proclamation*, 204.
79. LXX Jer 9:23 reads: ἐν τούτῳ καυχάσθω ὁ καυχώμενος.

Jer 9:22: "The Lord says these things: 'Let not the wise man [ὁ σοφός] boast in his wisdom and let not the strong man [ὁ ἰσχυρός] boast in his strength and let not the rich man [ὁ πλούσιος] boast in his wealth.'" Gail O'Day has persuasively shown that this intertextual allusion to Jer 9:22–23 in vv. 26–31 preserves not only verbal, but also structural and substantive, theological parallels from the source text.[80] As she demonstrates, Jer 9:22 and 23 contain parallel language in which the author employs the same verb (*boast*), but with the *anthropocentric* pronouns in v. 22 being replaced by *theocentric* pronouns in v. 23, with a corresponding shift from *negative* to *positive* boasting. The result is an antithesis in which the negative affirmation first prohibits humans from boasting in their own wisdom, strength, and weal, and the positive affirmation then enjoins boasting in the understanding and knowledge of God (ὁ καυχώμενος συνιεῖν καὶ γινώσκειν ὅτι ἐγώ εἰμι κύριος). That Paul has Jer 9:22–23 and its content in mind is revealed conclusively in v. 31, as he quotes Jer 9:23 explicitly: "Let the one who boasts boast in this...."

This intertextual interaction provides additional substantiation for the interpretation that we have been developing: the "boasting" that Paul confronts in Corinth is neither the Corinthians' boasting in other people nor the boasting of external parties like eloquent ministers or sophists. In view of Paul's intertext in Jeremiah, it is (Corinthian) boasting in self.

Incongruity and Efficacy

While Paul's primary emphasis in vv. 26–31 is the principle of *incongruity* in divine election, this aspect of election does entail a closely related idea: that of the *efficacy* of God's initiative.[81] In this regard Paul's assertion in v. 30 that the Corinthians are "from him" (ἐξ αὐτοῦ) has not only soteriological but also anthropological implications. On the one hand, Paul's statement affirms that the calling is not conditioned by prior worth. On the other hand, the calling itself functions as a mechanism that engenders worthy qualities. The Corinthians were "not" wise, powerful, or well born prior to their calling (v. 26), but Christ has "become" for them righteousness and so on (v. 30), and as such,

---

80. Gail R. O'Day, "Jeremiah 9:22–23 and 1 Corinthians 1:26–31: A Study in Intertextuality," *JBL* 109 (1990): 259–67. As an allusion, however, this does not rule out multivalence and hence simultaneous resonances with the Stoic paradoxes.

81. Barclay (*Paul and the Gift*, 557–58) identifies "efficacy" as another "perfection" of grace in Paul's theology.

they have *become* righteous. As long as they lacked worthy qualities, they had no grounds for boasting; and since "all flesh" lacks these qualities (as no flesh can boast), all flesh possesses this same anthropological deficiency.

The efficacy of God's call illustrates what John Barclay has referred to as the "ex-centric" quality of existence in Christ: "Because this new life is sourced elsewhere, outside of human resources in the life of the risen Christ, Paul does not figure salvation as a reformation of the human person, like some newly discovered technique in self-mastery. Believers live a life derived from elsewhere, in a kind of 'ex-centric' existence (an existence whose center is outside of oneself) that draws on Jesus's life from the dead."[82] We shall return to the idea of "ex-centric" existence in chapter 9. I only note in anticipation that this idea deeply contradicts the anthropological assumptions of Stoicism, particularly with regard to human potential and the possibility of "self-sufficiency."

Conclusion

In view of this thorough exegetical treatment of 1 Cor 1:17b–31, it is difficult to resist the conclusion that the rhetorical thesis owes more of its success to the simplicity of its big idea than to close reading of the text. As such, this thesis constitutes more a *background* of the text than a background of the *text*. Advocates of the rhetorical thesis have neglected to demonstrate how their reconstructions work all the way through using detailed exegesis that addresses discursive cohesion. This situation has compelled us here to pursue perhaps an uncommonly detailed exegesis of the text. Through this I have tried to show how recent readings, upon close scrutiny, often fail to comport with the text or make coherent sense.

The conclusions we have reached through our exegesis of 1:17b–31 can now be summarized. (1) In the first subsection (1:17b–25), (a) λόγος refers to an "account," understood as something like a theory of life, a philosophical outlook, or a value system. (b) Thus Paul poses an antithesis in these verses between two value systems, which he bifurcates as two kinds of σοφία, one a wisdom of the world/humanity and the other a wisdom of the cross/God. (c) These value systems have opposing content. The wisdom of the world is defined by the pursuit of social distinction and a principle of status according to worth; the wisdom of the cross, by an ethic of humility and a principle

---

82. John M. G. Barclay, *Paul and the Power of Grace* (Grand Rapids: Eerdmans, 2020), 92.

of incongruity. (d) The principle of incongruity runs counter to humanity's most basic value judgments and can only be understood from the world's perspective as foolishness. (2) In the second subsection (1:26–31), (a) Paul narrows in on the incongruity between God's calling and the Corinthians' own status or worth. (b) The Corinthians themselves (not persuasive rhetors or orators) are boasting. (c) They boast in themselves (not in ministers or orators). And (d) they boast—as we shall explore more fully later—because they believe that their spiritual state is somehow "of themselves" (and do not boast because of their ability to persuade through rhetoric or because of their ties with certain patrons).

As to the background of this σοφία, I have begun making my case for a connection with Stoicism. Certainly, the language of σοφία has dialogistic, or layered, resonances. (1) On the level of Paul's response, σοφία refers to value systems that divide along the axis of status. This construct, however, is Paul's reframing of Corinthian σοφία. (2) In its content, the Corinthians' σοφία promotes a hierarchical model of spiritual status, adapted, I shall argue, from Stoic physics/anthropology. Some in Corinth name themselves σοφοί, understood in the mold of the Stoic philosopher. Like the Stoic wise man, they are "powerful, "well born," and "strong," elevated not by certain *ordinary* markers of status but by *transcendent* ones. Paul, however, will have none of this arrogance, for this was not the way shown by Christ—or, as we shall see, by Paul himself.

4

1 Corinthians 2:1–5:
Proclaiming Christ Crucified

If interpreters were allowed just one text in support of the rhetorical thesis, undoubtedly they would choose 1 Cor 2:1–5. Readers commonly see Paul here addressing the "form" of wisdom,[1] and they often remark that this passage represents a clear statement of Paul's "theology of preaching."[2] Recalling the language of 1:17 (σοφία λόγου), Paul brings the words λόγος and σοφία together again in 2:1 (οὐ καθ' ὑπεροχὴν λόγου ἢ σοφίας) and, possibly, 2:4 (οὐκ ἐν πειθοῖ[ς] σοφίας [λόγοις]). Interpreters again conclude that λόγος qualifies σοφία as a wisdom of "speech."[3] Many also see Paul employing a

---

1. While most interpreters see the whole of 2:1–5 as addressing the "form" of wisdom, some maintain that it does not concern form exclusively. Both Fee (*First Epistle to the Corinthians*, 2nd ed., 66–68) and Bullmore (*St. Paul's Theology of Rhetorical Style*, 220–21) see 2:1–2 in relation to content, with a switch to form in 2:3–4. A wider scan of the literature shows that the often-made claim that scholars have always understood this passage as a rejection of rhetoric apart from a parenthesis in the mid-twentieth century only partially represents the truth. With the exception of the major advocates of the rhetorical thesis at the end of the twentieth century, most exegetes have described this unit as a rejection of both Greco-Roman rhetoric *and* philosophy. E.g., J. B. Lightfoot, *Notes on the Epistles of St. Paul* (London: Macmillan, 1895), 170; Weiss, *Der erste Korintherbrief*, 23; Wilckens, "Σοφία, σοφός, σοφίζω," *TDNT* 7:522 (referencing the consensus of older scholarship); Kennedy, *Classical Rhetoric*, 131–32; Lindemann, *Der erste Korintherbrief*, 56 ("Inhalt und Form"); Bullmore, *St. Paul's Theology of Rhetorical Style*, 220–21.

2. Mihaila, *Paul-Apollos Relationship*, 1. See also Bullmore, *St. Paul's Theology of Rhetorical Style*, 4; Litfin, *St. Paul's Theology of Proclamation*, 2.

3. Krentz, "Logos or Sophia," 280; Winter on 2:4 ("Rhetoric," 821). Note, similarly, Wolff's (*Der erste Brief*, 49) translation of this phrase as "Weisheitsrhetoric."

cluster of "technical" rhetorical terminology, including ὑπεροχή (2:1), πείθω (2:4), ἀπόδειξις (2:4), δύναμις (2:4, 5), and πίστις (2:5).[4] As in 1:17b–31, interpreters feel that the passage conveys Paul's rejection of persuasive methods, so that faith (πίστις) might not be produced by "means" of human rhetorical techniques but instead by the Spirit and power of God (ἐν ἀποδείξει πνεύματος καὶ δυνάμεως . . . ἐν δυνάμει θεοῦ).[5] In short, 2:1–5 rejects the use of "persuasive rhetoric."[6]

This is an outwardly reasonable interpretation of the passage. Hence it is not surprising that interpreters since antiquity have seen some contrast being made here between human methods of persuasion and the efficacy of God's Spirit and power.[7] Nevertheless, I believe that strong reasons exist to question whether Paul's focus in this passage is on the *form* of wisdom or the techniques of *rhetoric*. Apart from the overwhelming evidence that σοφία language more conventionally denoted philosophy during this period, we shall see that the common reading of 2:1–5 relies upon a debatable under-

---

4. Cf. Davis, *Wisdom and Spirit*, 80; Hans Dieter Betz, "The Problem of Rhetoric and Theology According to the Apostle Paul," in *L'Apôtre Paul: Personalité, style et conception du ministère*, ed. A. Vanhoye, BETL 73 (Leuven: Leuven University Press, 1986), 16–48, esp. 36; Lim, "'Not in Persuasive Words of Wisdom,'" 137–49, esp. 146–47; Litfin, *St. Paul's Theology of Proclamation*, 64–65; Winter, *Philo and Paul among the Sophists*, 148–50, 159–64; Martin, *Corinthian Body*, 48.

5. Kennedy, *Classical Rhetoric*, 131–32, 151; Marshall, *Enmity in Corinth*, 389; Lampe, "Theological Wisdom,'" 117–31, esp. 127; Litfin, *St. Paul's Theology of Proclamation*, 209; Winter, *Philo and Paul among the Sophists*, 163; Mihaila, *Paul-Apollos Relationship*, 19, 53, 55, etc.; Collins, *First Corinthians*, 119–20. Bullmore (214–18) says that ἐν in v. 4 is "causal," though his gloss conveys that faith is "effected by" or "brought into being by" rhetorical ability (214). Cf. Betz, "Problem of Rhetoric," 36.

6. Winter's translation of 2:4 ("Rhetoric," 821); see n. 3 above on Wolff. Litfin says that Paul refers here to "the form of speech recommended by Greco-Roman rhetoric and practiced everywhere by the speakers of the day" (*St. Paul's Theology of Proclamation*, 205–6); "wisdom conveyed by rhetoric" (Krentz, "Logos or Sophia," 280); "the whole of classical philosophy and rhetoric" (Kennedy, *Classical Rhetoric*, 150–51); "the superiority of rhetoric" (Lim, "'Not in Persuasive Words of Wisdom,'" 147), including "the three traditional means (that is, rhetorical proofs) of persuading" (157). Cf. John R. Levison, "Did the Spirit Inspire Rhetoric?," in *Persuasive Artistry*, ed. Duane F. Watson (Sheffield: Sheffield Academic, 1991), 25–40, esp. 34–38.

7. The translation of Origen (*Princ.* 4.1.7) given in *ACC* 7:20 (= CWS 177) says: "If our Scriptures had persuaded people to believe because they had been written with rhetorical art or philosophical skill." However, the Greek text has αἱ κατημαξευμέναι τῶν ἀποδείξεων ὁδοί, "the hackneyed ways of demonstrations." John Chrysostom, *Hom. Cor.* 6.3 (*ACC* 7:20 = *NPNF*[1] 12:30) comments on this text that in human wisdom "the worse argument often overcomes the better one, because the one who argues for it has greater rhetorical skills."

standing of λόγος and other terms in this passage and leaves inadequately addressed, if at all acknowledged, some of the logical connections in the paragraph and the mechanics of several syntactical constructions. The rhetorical reading also introduces problems concerning the coherence of the passage and the consistency of Paul's claims.

A Bridge into 2:1–5

A definite transition occurs as the second chapter opens. As Paul shifts from the Corinthians and "all flesh" in 1:26–31, the crasis of καί and the explicit pronoun ἐγώ in 2:1 (κἀγώ) indicates at the same time continuity of discourse and a change of personal focus. Paul has been addressing the "saved" and the "perishing" (1:18–25), those whom God "elected" and those whom he did not (1:26–31). How one reads the shift depends largely upon how one reads the preceding sections.[8] As I have argued, the preceding sections concern God's opposition to human canons of evaluation and humanity's corresponding orientations toward status. Humanity sees "Christ crucified" as the opposite of all that counts for anything. Some among the Corinthians estimate worth according to worldly standards and view themselves—wise, powerful, and well-born as they are—as being superior to others. This, then, is the nature of the transition in 2:1: the initial καί + ἐγώ marks a transition from Paul's presentation of the wisdom of Christ crucified on the one hand to Paul and his message as being consistent with this wisdom on the other. Thus, κἀγώ means "and for *my* part."

Paul and His "Coming"

There is no reason to believe that when Paul made his first visit to Corinth around the year 50 CE, anyone there had prior knowledge of his existence. One can only imagine the interest, and perhaps suspicion, that he must have aroused in his listeners as he came propagating his shocking "good news" about a "crucified Christ." As Acts reminds us, urban dwellers were all too

---

8. If the preceding sections are read as addressing the "form" of preaching and its effect on salvation, according to Litfin, Paul's shift now focuses on himself as an illustration of "the principle that God chooses to work through unimpressive means" (*St. Paul's Theology of Proclamation*, 204).

familiar with itinerant strangers who came proclaiming "new" philosophies (17:18–21). Such itinerants often identified as "philosophers." Bruce Winter, however, has highlighted that there was also another familiar figure on the traveling circuit, namely, the itinerant "sophist."

It is against the background of sophism that Winter interprets Paul's reference to his "coming" (ἐλθών) in 1 Cor 2:1. According to Winter, 2:1–5 reflects an "anti-sophistic" stance in which Paul recalls how he had flouted the "standardised conventions" that controlled the initial arrival of a traveling sophist.[9] Drawing together data about the visits of several second-century-CE sophists to new cities, Winter argues that "upon a sophist's first 'coming' to a city," he was "expected to observe certain conventions" in order to establish his reputation as a speaker.[10] These conventions included among other things an introductory address to the city, usually delivered in a large public setting, where the sophist basically stood "trial" through his performance to determine whether the city would accept him. As Winter's repeated reference to Paul's "coming" in quotation marks conveys, Winter sees Paul's opening words in 2:1 as alluding to this "standardised" complex of events.[11] Winter believes that Paul describes his opposition to this convention also in 1 Thess 2:1, where he refers to his conduct in Thessalonica following his εἴσοδος, or "entry" ("something of a technical term for Paul").[12]

As a general idea, Winter's proposal seems sensible. Itinerant philosophers and rhetoricians were commonplace figures in the urban landscape of the Roman Empire, and Paul's career as an itinerant preacher of the gospel of Jesus Christ undoubtedly invited what would be, for him, probably unwelcome comparison with such figures.[13] Winter's more specific thesis, however, is unconvincing for several reasons. (1) Winter offers no evidence that such visits were ever referred to either as a "coming" or an "entry" in a technical sense. (2) While itinerants were naturally "coming" and "going" all the time, Winter adduces little evidence for the existence of recognizably "standardised" conventions around such arrivals. Though Winter points to

---

9. Winter, *Philo and Paul among the Sophists*, 155.
10. Winter, *Philo and Paul among the Sophists*, 147.
11. Winter, *Philo and Paul among the Sophists*, 147, 155, 161, 163.
12. Winter, *Philo and Paul among the Sophists*, 152–55. Brookins, however, argues that εἴσοδος does not refer here to Paul's "arrival" in Thessalonica but to a "visit" conceived as a whole. Timothy A. Brookins, "An Apology for Exegesis of 1 Thess 2,1–12," *Bib* 103 (2022): 89–113.
13. See Abraham J. Malherbe, "'Gentle as a Nurse': The Cynic Background to 1 Thessalonians 2," *NovT* 12 (1970): 203–17.

five examples of itinerant sophists, the pattern that he describes applies only partially or very loosely, and in two of the five cases (Polemo and Philagrus), Winter states that they "broke with convention" in certain ways; hence, they cannot be used in full support of a pattern.[14] (3) Even if Winter's examples were sufficient to establish a "standardised" pattern, he offers no evidence that these conventions were standardized, recognized, or accepted, most importantly, in Paul's own day, for the activity of all five sophists dates between roughly 100 and 180 CE.[15] Winter's comparison between Paul and others as itinerants, then, may be appropriate as to a more general phenomenon in Greco-Roman culture, but neither the cultural evidence nor the language in 1 Cor 2:1–5 justifies his specifically anti-sophistic interpretation.

Καθ' ὑπεροχὴν λόγου ἢ σοφίας AND "RHETORICAL TERMS"

Advocates of the rhetorical thesis identify further allusions to rhetoric as Paul proceeds. Beginning with καθ' ὑπεροχὴν λόγου ἢ σοφίας in v. 1, and continuing through v. 5, many technical rhetorical terms are alleged to occur.[16]

The words καθ' ὑπεροχὴν λόγου ἢ σοφίας raise several questions. Questions concern not only the connotations of ὑπεροχή, but also the meanings of λόγος and σοφία and the significance of their coordination. With noticeable circularity, Pogoloff concludes that the narrower meaning of *prolixity* is the correct meaning of ὑπεροχή, "since Paul is speaking about rhetoric."[17] Observing that the πειθ- root ("persuade") occurs just three verses later,[18] Pogoloff declares that the background is now obvious: "any reader who has been left wondering just what wisdom is at issue in the letter is now firmly guided by the implied author: the 'wisdom' or 'wise speech' is nothing other than rhetoric."[19]

The interpretive issues extending from καθ' ὑπεροχὴν λόγου ἢ σοφίας until the end of v. 1 are many and interrelated. Any attempt to explain the signif-

---

14. Winter, *Philo and Paul among the Sophists*, 146.
15. Winter, *Philo and Paul among the Sophists*, 144–47: briefly discussing Aristides, Polemo, Philagrus, Alexander of Seleucia, and Dio.
16. In addition to those cited below, note that Lim ("'Not in Persuasive Words of Wisdom,'" 147) determines that ἐν πειθοῖ[ς] σοφίας [λόγοις] in v. 4 refers to ῥητορική based on the collocation of the last three terms.
17. Pogoloff, *Logos and Sophia*, 131.
18. Several variants occur here.
19. Pogoloff, *Logos and Sophia*, 138.

icance of 2:1–5 will need to offer a solution that coherently explains all of them. I offer the following reading.

(1) The prepositional phrase οὐ καθ' ὑπεροχὴν λόγου ἢ σοφίας modifies not ἦλθον,[20] but the supplementary participle καταγγέλων. Thus, Paul states that when he came he did not *"proclaim* the mystery καθ' ὑπεροχὴν λόγου ἢ σοφίας."

(2) The meaning of ὑπεροχή cannot be decided apart from the qualifying coordinated expression λόγου ἢ σοφίας. This coordination recalls the construct expression found in 1:17, that is, σοφία λόγου. One may reasonably infer that the semantics of the terms are similar here. And so again, the terms could be construed in several different ways. The unlikelihood that (a) σοφία and λόγου refer to content and form respectively, and thus to both philosophy and rhetoric (see comments on 1:17),[21] suggests that the two terms probably do not have these respective meanings here. Moreover, a dual emphasis unnecessarily complicates Paul's point in 2:3—linked to what precedes by γάρ—on "Jesus Christ and him crucified." Most interpreters take the expression as a unified reference to *form* in some sense, whether (b) one word qualifies the other,[22] or (c) both terms refer to the same thing.[23]

The possibility that the two terms are near synonyms, in some sense, seems to me to be correct. View (b) presents the construction as a kind of "hendiadys" (two nouns used instead of a noun and an adjective or attributive genitive),[24] though it is debatable how often hendiadys actually occurs in Paul's letters. Synonymy is more prevalent, and potential examples of hendiadys could be explained as a coordination of synonyms.[25] View (c) is

---

20. According to Winter (*Philo and Paul among the Sophists*, 156), οὐ καθ' ὑπεροχὴν λόγου ἢ σοφίας modifies ἦλθον and expresses manner, thus focusing on "the stance he adopted when he arrived," that is, "not with superiority of eloquence or wisdom."

21. Taking the view that the two terms have these respective meanings are Lightfoot, *Notes on the Epistles*, 170; Pogoloff, *Logos and Sophia*, 131–32; Litfin, *St. Paul's Theology of Proclamation*, 205.

22. Collins, *First Corinthians*, 118.

23. Funk, "Word and Word," 282; Thiselton, *First Epistle to the Corinthians*, 208–9; Winter, *Philo and Paul among the Sophists*, 156n63.

24. For the definition, see Richard Upsher Smith, *A Glossary of Terms in Grammar, Rhetoric, and Prosody for Readers of Greek and Latin: A Vade Mecum* (Mundelein, IL: Bolchazy-Carducci Publishers, 2011), 99.

25. BDF §442.16 cites multiple NT examples of synonymy, but in the Pauline corpus only 2 Tim 4:1 and Titus 2:13. On the other hand, note κακίας καὶ πονηρίας . . . εἰλικρινείας καὶ ἀληθείας (1 Cor 5:8); πᾶσαν ἀρχὴν καὶ πᾶσαν ἐξουσίαν καὶ δύναμιν (1 Cor 15:24; cf. Col 1:16); ὀργὴ καὶ θυμός (Rom 2:8); μὴ κοίταις καὶ ἀσελγείαις, μὴ ἔριδι καὶ ζήλῳ (Rom 13:13); and

consistent with our interpretation of σοφία λόγου at 1:17b. Yet, a coordination of synonyms in 2:1 need not signify (i) form, rhetoric, or eloquence. Rather these will serve as (ii) rough synonyms for the *content* of Paul's preaching. Thus, as in 1:17b, both σοφία and λόγος signify a *teaching*, Paul's overall *argument* or total *explanation* for "how things are" in the world.

(3) Returning, then, to ὑπεροχή ("excellence"), this noun would appear to relate not to the quality of eloquence, but to the sophisticated or impressive quality of Paul's wisdom, or in the broadest sense, his philosophy/message. On this interpretation, Pogoloff's point that Paul's emphasis is upon status can be granted. Yet, the real antithesis, as concerns the content of Paul's teaching (or philosophy), is one of contrast between his status as a "wise" teacher (or renowned philosopher) and his contrary status as an embodiment of "Christ crucified." Put differently, the dilemma posed is whether his manner of life corresponds with the one philosophy or with the other—with a philosophy that promotes the status distinctions recognized by the world, or with one that promotes the status-denying behavior of Christ.[26]

Λόγος and σοφία in the Train of Thought

We now come to the meaning of the coordinate expression λόγου ἢ σοφίας. Though the meaning of this coordination is contested, most interpreters see at the fore a reference to the form of speech, if not to rhetoric specifically. Pogoloff's certainty is enough to shrivel the confidence of anyone who might doubt him: "any urban Hellenistic reader" would know that this is what Paul meant.[27]

Winter interprets λόγου and σοφίας consistently with his "anti-sophistic" reading of the passage. His evidence here, however, is weaker than before. As

---

several dozen examples of coordinated synonymy in the Pauline corpus cited in Timothy A. Brookins, *Ancient Rhetoric and the Style of Paul's Letters* (Eugene, OR: Cascade, 2022), 107–8.

26. This is not to say that orthodox Stoicism promoted ordinary social standards; rather, the Corinthians exploited distinctions derived from Stoic physics as grounds for self-promotion. See the conclusion to this chapter, as well as chapter 9, pp. 233–34.

27. Pogoloff, *Logos and Sophia*, 7. Litfin (*Paul's Theology*, 206) says regarding the expressions in 2:1, 4: "it is scarcely conceivable" that they "could be anything other than a reference to the rhetorical teachings of the schools and the orators"; Martin (*Corinthian Body*, 47) says on 2:1, 4: "To anyone in Greco-Roman society, the phrase [apparently both verses] would immediately recall the terminology of rhetorical training."

a parallel he cites a single reference from Dio Chrysostom (*Or.* 47). This reference, moreover, offers no support for a special coordinate meaning of λόγος and σοφία in terms of rhetoric, for the two words merely occur in the same paragraph. In context σοφία itself is coordinated with κάλλος by means of ἤ (κάλλος ἤ σοφίαν), and a disjunctive meaning is possible ("beautiful words *or* wise content"). The λόγοι mentioned further down in this paragraph are undoubtedly words of eloquence. It is not, however, the inherence of any technical connotations in λόγος that points to this meaning, but the added demonstrative pronoun, which refers back to the description of the speaker's words given previously ("*such* words," τοιούτων λόγων).

Winter's reading has allured a crowd of interpreters. Yet, not uncommonly interpreters support this reading with little more than the assertion that σοφία appears with λόγος.[28] Statements are sometimes question-begging, as to the effect that Paul must be referring to rhetoric since the terms "appear in the context of preaching."[29] Some interpreters offer support from other allegedly "technical" rhetorical terms in the passage. According to Winter, several technical terms occur in 2:1–5: πείθω (2:4), ἀπόδειξις (2:4), δύναμις (2:4, 5), πίστις (2:5). He further appeals to the "three traditional means (that is, rhetorical proofs) of persuading his [Paul's] hearers" (ἦθος, v. 3; πάθος, v. 3; ἀπόδειξις, v. 4).[30] Responding to Winter's claim that these are technical terms, R. Dean Anderson maintains that the context does not require that the terms be taken in their rhetorical sense. Winter rejoins that the terms need to be understood against the background alluded to in v. 1, where Paul alludes to the conventions of a sophist's "coming" to the city.[31] This connection I have already disputed, however. In anticipation of later discussion, I suggest based on Paul's association of πνεῦμα and δύναμις in 2:4 that his frequent references to δύναμις in 1 Cor 1–4 (1:18, 24; 2:4, 5; 4:19, 20; cf. 1:26) may actually echo not a technical "rhetorical" concept, but a technical "philosophical" one.[32] We return to this point in chapter 9.

---

28. Krentz ("Logos or Sophia," 280) says at 2:4: "the word λόγος must here mean speech; therefore I translate the phrase σοφίᾳ λόγου [in 1:17] as 'wisdom of speech,' not as 'wisdom of argument,' and the phrase ἐν πειθοῖ[ς] σοφίας [λόγοις] as 'in persuasive speeches of wisdom,' both referring to persuasive speech." See also Kwon, "Critical Review," 420.

29. Cf. Litfin, *St. Paul's Theology of Proclamation*, 189; Welborn, "Discord in Corinth," 101.

30. Winter, *Philo and Paul among the Sophists*, 157.

31. Anderson (*Ancient Rhetorical Theory*, 275–76), critiquing Winter, *Philo and Paul among the Sophists*, 1st ed., 153–55. Winter responds in his 2nd ed., 160–63.

32. Although there is nothing saliently "Stoic" in 2:1–5, the Stoics did refer to the πνεῦμα

1 Corinthians 2:1–5: Proclaiming Christ Crucified

Regarding the terms λόγος and σοφία, I submit that a different interpretation from the rhetorical one is not only possible, but that it arguably sets up the most coherent reading of 1:17–2:16. Let us consider the following points.

(1) Paul's antithesis between [A] that which is καθ' ὑπεροχὴν λόγου ἢ σοφίας and [B] τὸ μυστήριον τοῦ θεοῦ (2:1) noticeably parallels Paul's earlier antithesis between [A'] that which is ἐν σοφίᾳ λόγου (1:17) and [B'] ὁ λόγος ὁ τοῦ σταυροῦ (1:18). Observe:

	Parallel A/A'	Parallel B/B'
1:17, 18	[A] the thing ἐν σοφίᾳ λόγου	[B] ὁ λόγος ὁ τοῦ σταυροῦ
Antithesis [A] vs. [B]		
2:1	[A'] the thing καθ' ὑπεροχὴν λόγου ἢ σοφίας	[B'] τὸ μυστήριον τοῦ θεοῦ
Antithesis [A'] vs. [B']		

That [A] and [A'] in 1:17–18 and 2:1, respectively, run parallel is not a matter of dispute. It is furthermore clear that in 2:1 the "mystery of God" is the antithetical counterpart to what is said to be καθ' ὑπεροχὴν λόγου ἢ σοφίας; and this contrast is consistent with Paul's tendency toward antithetical expressions across 1:17–2:16. Together, these two observations support the impression that [B] and [B'] are roughly parallel expressions. In sum, the "word that is of the cross" (1:18), which we have seen is a matter of *content*, is in 2:1 reexpressed as "the mystery of God." The resulting parallel renders questionable the conclusion that Paul switches emphasis in this section, from content (1:17–31) now to form (2:1–5). Rather, the same antithesis recurs.

(2) That there is no shift from content to form is made further evident by the initial crasis at the transition, that is, καί + ἐγώ (2:1). This combination indicates both transition (ἐγώ) *and* continuity (καί). Specifically, Paul moves from his *general* discussion of God's wisdom as Christ crucified (1:17–31) to his own message and conduct as a *specific* embodiment of this wisdom (2:1–5).

I add several additional points. (3) "The mystery of God," to which λόγου and σοφίας are offered as a counterpoint, undoubtedly refers to content. (a) Μυστήριον refers to content in 2:7, where Paul sets in opposition "wisdom ... of this age" and "wisdom hidden in a mystery." As interpreters widely agree owing to Paul's ensuing remarks in 2:7–12, the contrast in 2:7 is be-

---

as a δύναμις, and what they called the "spiritual power" (πνευματικὴ δύναμις) constituted the active agent by which creation moved (e.g., LS 47G; Epictetus, *Diatr.* 1.1). For more discussion on δύναμις and Stoicism, see chapter 9, pp. 211–18.

tween *what* the rulers of this age know (or think that they know) and *what* Paul speaks "in a mystery." It is because they did not know this wisdom (that weakness is strength and humility is glory) that they crucified "the Lord of glory." (b) This interpretation is consistent with regular usage of μυστήριον elsewhere in Paul's letters: the mystery is the formerly concealed but now-revealed reality of God's inclusion of the unworthy among his people (Rom 16:26; Col 1:26–27; 4:3).

Christ Crucified

Paul's assertion in v. 2 that he "knew nothing but Christ crucified" could be construed in several ways. (1) Some take the assertion as a rather wooden statement about the topical scope of Paul's message: he did not preach about the resurrection or final judgment, just about the crucifixion.[33] (2) Winter suggests that Paul did not, like the sophists, take suggestions of topic from his audiences—he spoke always on the same subject.[34] (3) For those who see Paul developing an antithesis between God and eloquent preachers as opposing "means" of producing faith, Paul's preaching of "only" Christ crucified is construed to mean that he preached, as Litfin says, a "simply proclaimed" message that left the outcome to the Spirit, in other words, that he "adopted an unconventional mode of proclamation devoid of sophistication."[35]

These suggestions fail to capture Paul's meaning in the context of 1:17–2:5. As throughout chapters 1–2, the "cross" and "crucifixion" do not represent the strict and literal parameters of what Paul covered in his teaching. Rather they epitomize, through synecdoche, the *way* of Jesus as depicted in the gospel message, a way characterized by humility and self-lowering for the benefit of others—or what modern interpreters call "cruciformity." Nor is it Paul's aim to communicate *that* his "message [topic] was *fixed*."[36] Rather he indicates *what* his message *said*. Finally, it truly takes greater effort to

---

33. Both Mark D. Given and Thomas Schmeller suggest that Paul exaggerates on this point. Given, "Paul and Rhetoric: A *Sophos* in the Kingdom of God," in *Paul Unbound: Other Perspectives on the Apostle*, ed. Mark D. Given (Grand Rapids: Baker Academic, 2010; 2nd ed. 2021), 175–200, esp. 193–96; Schmeller, "Dissimulatio artis? Paulus und die antike Rhetorik," *NTS* 66 (2020): 500–520.
34. Winter, *Philo and Paul among the Sophists*, 42.
35. Litfin, *St. Paul's Theology of Proclamation*, 208; Mihaila, *Paul-Apollos Relationship*, 22.
36. Winter, *Philo and Paul among the Sophists*, 42.

1 Corinthians 2:1–5: Proclaiming Christ Crucified

construe "preached nothing but Christ crucified" as an indication of the style of preaching rather than of the content of preaching. In the first place, Ἰησοῦν Χριστὸν καὶ τοῦτον ἐσταυρωμένον, as direct object of the verb, refers grammatically to *what* Paul preached. Moreover, the substantive expression has to be understood in light of "the mystery of God" for syntactical reasons that are quite explicit. As γάρ shows at the opening of v. 2, Paul's assertion about preaching "Christ crucified" *explains* his reference to the "mystery" that he proclaims. In other words, the mysterious message now revealed *is* the message about Christ crucified.

This train of thought sheds further light on the contested expression καθ' ὑπεροχὴν λόγου ἢ σοφίας (v. 1). Paul did not speak καθ' ὑπεροχὴν λόγου ἢ σοφίας in proclaiming the mystery of God, "for" he preached only Christ crucified. If, via γάρ, "Christ crucified" *explains* Paul's "proclaiming καθ' ὑπεροχὴν λόγου ἢ σοφίας," then the content of the two clauses should exhibit some kind of referential continuity. In this regard, the words λόγου ἢ σοφίας most naturally refer to content: Paul did not preach such-and-such wisdom, *for* he preached Christ crucified, the former being contradictory to the latter. The only way to preserve an emphasis on form would be to posit an asymmetrical antithesis between speaking "eloquently" and preaching "Jesus Christ and him crucified." Of course, the unevenness of this antithesis does not make that interpretation wrong, just more awkward than the alternative.

Verse 3 strengthens our reading. While interpreters frequently observe that "weakness and fear and much trembling" reflect opposite characteristics to those expected of the public speaker,[37] the function of this description is not to contrast Paul with the orator but to compare him with Christ (and it need not be both!). Paul is an imitator of Christ, or an embodiment of Christ crucified, that is, of that very wisdom that he preaches. This emphasis is consistent with the purpose of the paragraph as a move from Paul's focus on God's wisdom generally (Christ crucified) in 1:17b–31 to himself as an example of this wisdom in 2:1–5 ("and I"), a shift of emphasis that is repeated and confirmed now by his use again of the καί + ἐγώ crasis (v. 3). The sense is that not only did he *preach* Christ crucified, *he also conducted* (κἀγώ) himself in a way consistent with this message. As is shown clearly in his concluding words to chapters 1–4 (esp. 4:16), his example as an imitator of Christ is a prominent theme in the unit.

---

37. Winter, *Philo and Paul among the Sophists*, 158; Finney, *Honour and Conflict*, 84.

The Antitheses in 2:4–5

Interpreters' perception that Paul opposes rhetoric continues at vv. 4–5. These verses are commonly read as continuing the antithesis between, on the one hand, salvation by *means* of human persuasion/rhetorical techniques and, on the other hand, salvation by *means* of God's agency/the work of the Spirit. This antithesis is thought to be confirmed in vv. 4–5 by the presence of several "rhetorical" terms, including πειθώ, ἀπόδειξις, δύναμις, and πίστις.[38] Yet, problems of coherence again confront us when we begin to scrutinize the exposition that ostensibly demonstrates this reading. While such problems are not generally blatant on the surface, they come to light when one begins to analyze the claims exegetically.

Let us take Pogoloff's reading of 2:1–5. Pogoloff's thesis stands apart from other versions of the rhetorical thesis in that he does not—he says—see Paul rejecting rhetoric per se. Thus, according to Pogoloff, Paul "is not speaking primarily of style" but of "the cultural notions of status." Thus, Paul's initial denial in v. 1 means that Paul did not "*come as a superior person in speech or (human) wisdom.*"[39] This explanation is consistent with Pogoloff's earlier remarks on 1:17 (Paul "rejects not rhetoric, but the cultural values wedded to it") and his general reading of the letter's rhetorical situation.[40] It is not, however, consistent with his subsequent commentary on 2:1–5. As Pogoloff continues, he indicates that Paul rejected not simply the *status* of the rhetor but in fact *eloquence* itself. Indeed, Pogoloff now refers to Paul's "disavowal of wise speech" in 2:1, 4, 13,[41] and he says that the truth of the gospel is demonstrated not by the preacher but by God (Paul "claims to need no eloquence"; "the 'wisdom' or 'wise speech' is nothing other than rhetoric"; "Paul contrasts ordinary human understanding through persuasion with understanding through the Spirit of God"). As Pogoloff continues, he offers in two separate places paraphrases of 2:4–5 that expose his dilemma (as it is indeed) and the unresolved tension that remains in his interpretation. I cite the two passages in full:

> Though my speech and my proclamation persuaded you so that you have πίστις, this is *not because I have used rhetorical methods to sway you to*

38. See n. 4 above.
39. Pogoloff, *Logos and Sophia*, 131; original italics.
40. Pogoloff, *Logos and Sophia*, 121.
41. Pogoloff, *Logos and Sophia*, 129.

γνῶσις based on the opinions of those who are usually honored as wise (οὐκ ἐν πειθοῖ[ς] σοφίας [λόγοις]). Rather, your faith is grounded on something far more sure than clever arguments based on opinion. Your faith is as secure as a scientific proof arising from our knowledge of the necessary truths of God's spirit and power.[42]

Though my speech and my proclamation persuaded you so that you have πίστις, *your πίστις is not a γνῶσις gained through rhetoric which swayed you on the basis of the opinions of those who are honored as possessing superior, wise eloquence* . . . (οὐκ ἐν πειθοῖ[ς] σοφίας [λόγοις]). Your faith is based on the most absolute form of proof—the sure proof of God's spirit and power.[43]

I draw attention to the italicized portions as what seem to me to be cumbersome, and somewhat convoluted, expansions specifically of the phrase οὐκ ἐν πειθοῖ[ς] σοφίας [λόγοις]. In both expansions, the prepositional phrase contains a surplus meaning. (1) On the one hand, ἐν signifies for Pogoloff a denial that the Corinthians came to faith *by* means of/because of/or sprung from rhetoric ("not because I have used rhetorical methods," "arising from our knowledge of the necessary truths," "gained through rhetoric," "based on the most absolute form of proof"). The content of Pogoloff's paraphrases so far reflects an admissible function of ἐν, and this portion of the paraphrase is unproblematic as a possible rendering of the immediate language. (2) What is added following this initial portion of the paraphrase, however, not only adds what is nowhere expressed in the language or syntax of these two verses but adds an *additional* adverbial adjunct that competes in sense with the prepositional phrase, as previously taken, in Pogoloff's attempt to explain the rise of the Corinthians' πίστις. Now it is knowledge (or faith) "*based on* the opinions of those who are usually *honored as wise*," "*on the basis* of the opinions of those who are *honored as possessing superior, wise eloquence*." If we look closely, we see that this alters the syntax and introduces a second, competing, proposition: it is now their high status that elicits faith, not their methods per se. In sum, Pogoloff conveys through his paraphrase, on the one hand, that the Corinthians' faith is a result of the speaker's rhetorical methods, but on the other hand, that it is due to the speaker's being honored as wise. Both points Pogoloff extracts from οὐκ ἐν πειθοῖ[ς] σοφίας [λόγοις] spe-

---

42. Pogoloff, *Logos and Sophia*, 138; my italics.
43. Pogoloff, *Logos and Sophia*, 140; my italics.

cifically. Hence, the problem is not whether the orator's status could theoretically serve as a kind of "proof" in argument. Rather, the problem is whether ἐν πειθοῖ[ς] σοφίας [λόγοις] can semantically mean both "by means of rhetorical techniques" and "by means of status" in a single act of expression.

A similar ambiguity surfaces when we dwell on Pogoloff's wording elsewhere. For instance: "The persuasiveness of Paul's message is not to be *attributed to the status of rhetorical skill.*"[44] What does it mean to attribute persuasion to the status of rhetorical skill? Pogoloff does not say the "status of the *rhetorician*" but the "status of rhetorical *skill.*" One may attribute persuasion to status or to skill, or to both, but it is hard to comprehend what is meant by "the status of rhetorical skill" stated in this construct formulation. The ambiguity preserved in Pogoloff's phrasing re-exposes the interpretive dilemma he is faced with and reveals that he is unable to eliminate the tension that his version of the rhetorical thesis introduces. A similar tension appears in other studies.[45]

These problems of exposition escape our notice initially because, though these verses actually involve some substantial exegetical difficulties, the relevant syntactical issues are often not addressed directly, or are even passed over entirely. Several issues need to be addressed. (1) Apart from the semantics of λόγος, σοφία, and other terms in these verses, the syntactical force of both (2) the four prepositional phrases introduced by ἐν in vv. 4–5 and (3) the genitives in v. 4 are open to question. As always, the exegetical issues are interrelated.

The Semantics of the Nouns

If the UBS[5]/NA[28] reading is correct, 1 Cor 2:4 presents us with the third instance of the coordination of λόγος and σοφία (οὐκ ἐν πειθοῖ[ς] σοφίας [λόγοις]) in the letter so far. This verse includes also the two referentially nebulous pairs ὁ λόγος μου καὶ τὸ κήρυγμά μου and πνεύματος καὶ δυνάμεως. (1) One expects the meaning of λόγος and σοφία to be similar here as in their earlier coordinations. I previously argued that in 1:17 and 2:1 these function as rough synonyms. (2) That "my word" and "my preaching" are essentially

44. Pogoloff, *Logos and Sophia*, 275 (my italics).
45. Without reconciliation, Williams ("Paul's Anti-imperial 'Discourse'") explicitly endorses Litfin's view that in 2:1–5 Paul claims that he did not use persuasive rhetoric but relied on the power of God to engender faith (808), and then immediately endorses Pogoloff's view that Paul did not reject rhetoric but rather the cultural values wedded to it (808–9).

1 Corinthians 2:1–5: Proclaiming Christ Crucified

synonymous should invite little objection. (3) Based on the precedent of the first two pairs, and the aspects of "Spirit" and "power" highlighted here, I suggest along with many interpreters that these two terms function as rough synonyms as well.[46]

The ἐν *Phrases*

Word and *preaching* need not refer to Paul's manner of speech. If v. 4 is consistent with what precedes, these terms naturally refer to the content of Paul's preaching. The ἐν phrases that follow do not provide decisive evidence against this conclusion. To be sure, instrumentality is a legitimate function of ἐν.[47] This, however, is not its only function, and the absence of any verb in the comprising clauses makes all the more uncertain a decision about its usage.

Some clarity on the ἐν phrases may be gained by turning attention to similar constructions appearing elsewhere. (1) With respect to the constructions in 2:4 (οὐκ ἐν πειθοῖ[ς] σοφίας [λόγοις] ἀλλ᾽ ἐν ἀποδείξει πνεύματος καὶ δυνάμεως), we find a closely analogous construction in 1 Cor 4:20: a simple sentence consisting of a nominative + ἐν + object, with no explicit verb (οὐ γὰρ ἐν λόγῳ ἡ βασιλεία τοῦ θεοῦ ἀλλ᾽ ἐν δυνάμει). In 4:20 the prepositional phrase is almost certainly not instrumental ("The kingdom of God is not by *means* of word but by *means* of power"), as that meaning does not work given the grounding function (γάρ) of this sentence. The phrase is more appropriately categorized as *predicative*, or more precisely, *constitutive*: "The kingdom of God is a *matter* not of word but of power." The sense is that in the kingdom

---

46. Interpreters are more inclined to see a distinction in the first pair than in the second, though most interpreters view the terms either as being coordinated in a hendiadys construction or as interchangeable. Ciampa and Rosner see *word* and *preaching* as "interchangeable" (*First Letter to the Corinthians*, 116–17); so also Garland (*1 Corinthians*, 86). Though Fee (*First Epistle to the Corinthians*, 94; 2nd ed., 99) says that the two terms "probably refer to the content and form of Paul's actual delivery (hence 'message and preaching')." Litfin says that "my word and my preaching" is a hendiadys (205n79) but then, confusingly, says that the terms indicate respectively "form and content." With regard to the second pair, Mihaila sees "Spirit and power" as a hendiadys meaning "powerful Spirit" (*Paul-Apollos Relationship*, 23n62); also Thiselton (*First Epistle to the Corinthians*, 222); Collins (*First Corinthians*, 120); Ciampa and Rosner (*First Letter to the Corinthians*, 117). Fee (*First Epistle to the Corinthians*, 95; 2nd ed., 100) says that this combination "is probably very close to a hendiadys" but understands this more or less as synonymy ("the Spirit, that is, Power"). The relationship between terms should probably be understood in the same way in each pair.

47. See citations in n. 5.

deeds have greater significance than *words* (see chapter 8). (2) A more elucidating example occurs in Eph 5:9. In this text ὁ γὰρ καρπὸς τοῦ φωτὸς ἐν πάσῃ ἀγαθωσύνῃ καὶ δικαιοσύνῃ καὶ ἀληθείᾳ does *not* mean, "the fruit of the light is *by means of* goodness, etc.," but rather, "the fruit of light *consists in* goodness, etc.," "is *characterized* by goodness, etc." (3) Romans 14:17 reflects both a similar thought and construction, though without the preposition: οὐ γὰρ ἐστιν ἡ βασιλεία τοῦ θεοῦ βρῶσις καὶ πόσις ἀλλὰ δικαιοσύνη καὶ εἰρήνη καὶ χαρὰ ἐν πνεύματι ἁγίῳ. In this example the same point-counterpoint construction occurs (οὐ-ἀλλά antithesis), again with the subject "kingdom of God," and again with no copulative; except the subject is complemented now by predicate nominatives instead of a prepositional phrase. To summarize:

1 Cor 2:4	ὁ λόγος μου καὶ τὸ κήρυγμά μου <u>οὐκ ἐν πειθοῖ[ς] σοφίας [λόγοις] ἀλλ' ἐν ἀποδείξει πνεύματος καὶ δυνάμεως</u>
1 Cor 4:20	οὐ γὰρ <u>ἐν λόγῳ</u> <u>ἡ βασιλεία τοῦ θεοῦ</u> ἀλλ' <u>ἐν δυνάμει</u>
Eph 5:9	ὁ γὰρ καρπὸς τοῦ φωτὸς <u>ἐν πάσῃ ἀγαθωσύνῃ καὶ δικαιοσύνῃ καὶ ἀληθείᾳ</u>
Rom 14:17	οὐ γάρ ἐστιν <u>ἡ βασιλεία τοῦ θεοῦ</u> <u>βρῶσις καὶ πόσις</u> ἀλλὰ <u>δικαιοσύνη καὶ εἰρήνη καὶ χαρὰ ἐν πνεύματι ἁγίῳ</u>

The overlap of features in these examples suggests that the prepositional phrase introduced by ἐν can function within an equative clause as a complement analogous to a simple predicate nominative.[48] These examples support the likelihood that the ἐν phrases do not function in 1 Cor 2:4 in an instrumental sense, but rather as predicates within simple equative clauses. In short, Paul describes what his "word and preaching" among them consisted in. His message did not "consist in persuasive words of wisdom" but "in a demonstration of the Spirit and power."[49] It remains to consider the force of the genitives in v. 4 (σοφίας, πνεύματος, δυνάμεως).

---

48. For a similar interpretation see C. F. D. Moule, *An Idiom Book of New Testament Greek* (Cambridge: Cambridge University Press, 1959), 79.

49. Ciampa and Rosner (*First Letter to the Corinthians*) say that Paul's preaching "was a demonstration" (117) and that Paul then asks, "in what, then, did *the Spirit's power* consist?" (118). The words used here for "persuasive" (πειθοῖ[ς]) and "demonstration" (ἀπόδειξις) are certainly "rhetorical" in a broad sense of the term, though they cannot be considered distinctive vocabulary of rhetoric in the technical sense of the ancient "art." Ἀπόδειξις also referred to the dialectical exercises of philosophers; see its technical usage in the context of philosophical argumentation in Cicero, *Luc.* 26; Diogenes Laertius, *Vit. phil.* 7.44, 52, 79; Sextus Empiricus, *Pyrr.* 2.135–143; Strabo, *Geogr.* 2.3.5; Lucian, *Eunuch.* 13.

The Genitives

With regard to the genitives (σοφίας, πνεύματος, δυνάμεως), interpreters have found little agreement on the syntax,[50] and indeed they are not generally even clear on how they see the genitives functioning.[51] The disarray of the manuscript tradition around ἐν πειθοῖ[ς] σοφίας [λόγοις] leaves any final decision about the syntax uncertain. The extant readings leave open a multitude of explanations. (1) If the UBS[5]/NA[28] is correct in determining λόγοις to be original, we have yet a third collocation of σοφία and λόγος (1:17; 2:1, 4). If λόγοις is indeed original, the switch to the plural against the singular in 1:17 and 2:1 (λόγου) would suggest a slight semantic shift, from the realm of teaching/system/theory/philosophy to words more generally. Σοφίας, on the other hand, might still specify the words' content. (2) The problematic alternation to the plural, though, is resolved in the reading preserved by 𝔓[46] F G, which omits λόγοις from the sentence entirely, actually leaving a more symmetrical parallel between the genitive constructions: ἐν πειθοῖ[ς] σοφίας on the one hand and ἐν ἀποδείξει πνεύματος καὶ δυνάμεως on the other. Ultimately, the syntax of σοφίας cannot be decided apart from certainty as to the original text. Still, there is sense enough in construing the *kethiv* reading as meaning that Paul's preaching did not "[*consist*] in philosophical discourse." While this gloss remains only a guess, without certainty as to the original text any translation remains a guess.[52]

Though the textual problems are less serious in the verse's final phrase,[53] the syntactical force of the genitives πνεύματος καὶ δυνάμεως remains debatable. If our reading of the paragraph is correct, we may read these as *objective*:[54] Paul's preaching consisted in a demonstrating (ἀποδείξει) of the Spirit

---

50. The genitives may be either subjective or objective. Objective: Bullmore, *St. Paul's Theology of Rhetorical Style*, 213–14; Allo, *Saint Paul: Première épître aux Corinthiens*, 2nd ed. (Paris: Gabalda, 1956), 25; according to Barrett (*Commentary on the First Epistle*, 65) they are both subjective and objective; and according to Conzelmann, the first term is qualitative, the other two possessive (*1 Corinthians*, 55).

51. So Anderson, *Ancient Rhetorical Theory and Paul*, 265–66.

52. Ambiguity remains even if the UBS[5]/NA[28] reading is correct: if λόγοις is the governing noun, σοφίας could be either attributive ("with wise words") or objective ("the speaking of wisdom"); if σοφίας governs, it could be attributed ("persuasive wisdom"), or it could express either content ("words full of wisdom") or source ("words which arise out of wisdom").

53. Though D*.2 has ἀποκαλύψει in place of ἀποδείξει.

54. This would not require that σοφίας also be objective (though it may be), for for-

and power.[55] That is, the Spirit and power are the constituent elements of Paul's proclamation or demonstration. The intertextual resonances shared with 1:17–31 should not be missed. Paul's contrast between two kinds of wisdom remains in view. In 1:23, 24, Paul has already defined God's wisdom *as* Christ crucified. In fact, Paul there puts three terms in apposition: *Christ crucified* (Χριστὸν ἐσταυρωμένον), *wisdom* (σοφίαν), and *power* (δύναμιν)! The language in 2:4 is allusive and metonymic, and exact equivalency should not be insisted upon, but the continuity of the discourse and of Paul's language in 1:17–31 and 2:1–5 lends support to the view that, in saying that his preaching consisted in a "demonstration of Spirit and power," Paul alludes to his kerygmatic *content*: as in 1:23, 24, "Christ crucified" *is* the "power" of God and *is* the "wisdom" of God. He preached this, and not some other "wisdom." Consequently, we should construe the term *power* here not as alluding to Paul's manner of speech but as alluding ironically to that weak thing—that thing which lacked all criteria by which status as status is usually determined, that thing that God ironically used to effect redemption—a man on a cross. In short, "power," or Christ crucified (equated in 1:23, 24), is the content of Paul's demonstration and proclamation.

As interpreters often note, the "Spirit" is almost synonymous with "power" (πνεύματος καὶ δυνάμεως). In turn, the Spirit is so closely associated with Christ that in speaking of the one, Paul virtually speaks of the other. One could pass over Paul's direct equation of Christ and the Spirit elsewhere ("the Lord *is* the Spirit," 2 Cor 3:17)[56] and observe that we also find a verbal parallel between Christ crucified as power in 1:24 and the "Spirit and power" now in 2:4.

In 1 Cor 2, the Spirit is also that which enables believers to accurately assess the wisdom of Christ crucified. Paul does not spell out this idea in 2:4, but it is here that he begins to make the transition to this point precisely (2:6–16): God's wisdom *appears as* wisdom only to the "spiritual" (πνευματικοί), who have "received the Spirit" (Πνεῦμα), and who think "spiritually" (πνευματικῶς).

---

mal parallelism does not always correlate with syntactical parallelism; for instance, the genitives in 2 Thess 1:11; 2:13; Gal 3:3.

55. On ἀπόδειξις and philosophical "demonstration," see n. 49.
56. Note also "the Spirit of Christ" (Rom 8:9; Phil 1:19).

Consisting ἐν Spirit and Power

In this light, v. 5 requires a different meaning than the one that many assign to it. First, the ἵνα clause no longer indicates that Paul relied on the Spirit "in order that" faith might be produced *by* God rather than *by* humans. Rather, it indicates why Paul preached the *kind* of wisdom that he did and it indicates that in which true faith is put. That is, Paul preached the wisdom of Christ crucified in order that (ἵνα) their faith might be a faith put *not in* (ἐν) human wisdom but *in* the power of God, or metonymically speaking, *in* Christ crucified, the wisdom of God and power of God (1:24).

We have already discussed the syntactical justification for taking ἐν in this way (v. 4), though the larger Greek construction in v. 5 is different. Here, the objects of the preposition ἐν (σοφίᾳ [ἀνθρώπων] . . . δυνάμει [θεοῦ]) are, as it were, objects of the verbal idea inherent in πίστις. This syntactical construction is paralleled elsewhere in Paul's letters. Πίστις + ἐν appears to have this meaning elsewhere (Gal 3:26; Eph 1:15; Col 1:4). Among the parallel texts, Col 1:4 helpfully elucidates the sense. Note how "faith . . . *in*" parallels "love . . . *toward*":

1. τὴν πίστιν ὑμῶν ἐν Χριστῷ Ἰησοῦ ("faith in . . .")
2. τὴν ἀγάπην ἣν ἔχετε εἰς πάντας τοὺς ἁγίους ("love toward . . .")

Clear examples of the "ἐν of object"—as one might call it—occur with the verb cognate elsewhere in early Christian literature: πιστεύω + ἐν, for instance, "believe in the gospel" (Mark 1:15); "believes in him" (John 3:15); "believing in him" (Ign. *Phld.* 5.2).[57] An analogous construction occurs in the combination of καυχάομαι with ἐν, which occurs, among other places (Rom 5:3; 2 Cor 5:12; 10:15; 11:12; etc.), in 1 Cor 3:21, where interpreters universally construe the syntax in the proposed sense ("*boast in* humanity," καυχάσθω ἐν ἀνθρώποις).

I mention one final point in favor of σοφία (v. 5) as content. If vv. 4–5 pose an antithesis between two different kinds of wisdom, or messages, this offers tighter coherence with the paragraph that follows, as we shall see in the next chapter.

---

57. Many examples occur with cognates followed by εἰς or ἐπί.

Paul's Use and Nonuse of Rhetoric

Having dealt with the exegetical issues, I should like to address one final point. A difficulty that has not escaped the notice of proponents of the rhetorical thesis is the contradiction between Paul's suspected rejection of rhetoric and the fact that his own letters, and indeed these very chapters, reflect considerable rhetorical skill.[58] Many interpreters offer solutions to this difficulty by appealing to the conventions of rhetoric itself: self-deprecation of one's abilities was a conventional practice of orators. Thus Paul actually consciously deployed rhetoric while ironically rejecting it.[59] The problem of Paul's (alleged) disavowal of rhetoric, however, cannot be resolved by characterizing it as a rhetorical device. It is surely not the same thing to assert modesty in one's rhetorical abilities as to say that one is rejecting the use of rhetoric. Alternatively, some interpreters see Paul rejecting only an excess or a certain flowery style of rhetoric.[60] Others see him repudiating the profession of the rhetorician without repudiating the techniques of rhetoric itself.[61] Many have been puzzled, even distressed, by the discrepancy. Mihaila sees Paul rejecting all use of rhetoric in both speaking and writing and vaporizes any apparently rhetorical features in Paul's letters by appealing to a dubious analytical distinction between rhetorical theory and the theory of letter writing.[62] Litfin, after listing several possible explanations (Paul used rhetoric unconsciously or only "descriptively"; he only used rhetorical techniques with those who were already believers; rhetorical techniques "crept unwittingly" into Paul's communication), appeals to another dubious distinction in order to preserve Paul's sincerity: persuasion, Litfin propounds, occurs in stages. Paul used rhetoric in the early, or "pre-yielding," stages of the process, but left it to the Holy Spirit to make the audience finally "yield" to the message.[63]

---

58. Lim ("'Not in Persuasive Words of Wisdom,'" 137) mentions Paul's use of rhetorical devices "especially in I and II Corinthians"; Levison ("Did the Spirit Inspire Rhetoric?," 36–37) lists examples in 1 Cor 1:17–2:10.

59. Irony: Levison, "Did the Spirit Inspire Rhetoric?," 38; self-deprecation: Martin, *Corinthian Body*, 48.

60. Lim, "'Not in Persuasive Words of Wisdom,'" 145–46, 148, 149; Bullmore, *St. Paul's Theology of Rhetorical Style*, 224.

61. Martin, *Corinthian Body*, 48.

62. Mihaila, *Paul-Apollos Relationship*, 215–17.

63. Litfin, *St. Paul's Theology of Proclamation*, 261. Joop Smit notes concerning the views of Pogoloff, Litfin, etc.: "In my view, a theological prejudice with regard to the nature of Christian preaching blinds these scholars to the highly rhetorical character of Paul's discourse"; Paul does not repudiate eloquence; rather, "the opposite is true." Smit, "Epideictic Rhetoric in Paul's First Letter to the Corinthians 1–4," *Bib* 84 (2003): 184–201.

Although these proposals offer some ingenious solutions to a perceived problem, the problem persists only when one interprets the passage as a rejection of rhetoric. In light of our arguments against this reading, I consider the problem of Paul's "inconsistency" simply as further evidence against the rhetorical reading of the passage.

Conclusion

Interpreters often point to 1 Cor 2:1–5 as the most flagrant evidence that the σοφία that Paul opposes concerns Greco-Roman rhetoric. Yet, our detailed analysis of the text and of its relationship with 1:17b–31 has given us some strong reasons to question this interpretation. Paul's elaboration in 1:17b–31 of an antithesis between two "wisdoms" or value systems, defined in terms of their respective orientations towards status, continues in 2:1–5 as Paul transitions to his own proclamation and example as consistent with God's wisdom. The "mystery of God" that he preached was the message of cruciformity, a way that he now reminds the Corinthians he himself had embodied while he was among them ("with weakness and fear and much trembling"). By preaching this message rather than its antithesis, the πίστις that the Corinthians came to accept was in consequence a πίστις "in" (ἐν) the way of the cross and humiliation, not a πίστις "in" (ἐν) the value system of the world, a system predicated upon competitive notions of worth. As Paul continues into 2:6–16, we therefore find no move from "form" (2:1–5) back again to "content."

5

1 Corinthians 2:6–16: A Spiritual σοφία

If we begin from the common reading of 2:1–5 as a statement about Paul's opposition to rhetoric, 2:6–16 becomes a problem.[1] After discussing wisdom, ostensibly as a matter of form, Paul appears to change direction again in v. 6, as σοφία becomes a matter of content.[2] Likewise, this section presents one of the most significant challenges to recent trends toward seeing the Corinthians' σοφία in connection with liberal education or secular social practices. The problem for both this line of interpretation and the rhetorical one is that not only does 2:6–16 focus on the content of σοφία, but Paul seems to be refuting a certain "spiritual" interpretation of this wisdom. Indeed, Paul here introduces as a description of the σοφοί the terms τέλειος (2:6) and πνευματικός (2:15), contrasting the latter with the term ψυχικός (2:14). A majority of interpreters conclude that these terms originate (as far as the church's conflict is concerned) with the Corinthians, that the σοφοί applied the two positive terms to themselves, and that Paul has now polemically appropriated these terms and turned them against the claimants. Until the last third of the twentieth century, interpreters commonly viewed these

---

1. Those who see 1:18–2:5 as concerning rhetoric are often surprised by the apparent "shift" to content in 2:6. As Litfin moves to 2:6–12, he seems now to see wisdom as content (*St. Paul's Theology of Proclamation*, 217); yet he sees a shift back to form in 2:13 (218). Welborn perceives in v. 6 a "massive antithesis with what precedes," only now seeing σοφία (or as he understands it, γνῶσις) as a matter of content ("On the Discord in Corinth," 104).

2. Litfin (*St. Paul's Theology of Proclamation*, 217) agrees. Welborn thinks that the word σοφία here "furnishes the slender thread of continuity" with what precedes, and that it too shifts in meaning ("On the Discord in Corinth," 104).

1 Corinthians 2:6–16: A Spiritual σοφία

terms as a key to understanding the Corinthians' σοφία, generally viewing the terms in connection with various forms of Hellenistic religiosity, from Gnosticism to the mystery religions or Hellenistic Judaism. Whether any of these connections are legitimate, one must nevertheless offer some explanation for how this section, with its appropriated terminology, fits coherently with one's overall reading and full reconstruction of the church's situation.

Tellingly, there has been a striking lack of attention to this section in most major studies of 1 Cor 1–4 over the last three decades. 1 Corinthians 2:6–16 makes up eleven of the thirty-seven verses dedicated directly to the topic of wisdom (1:17b–31; 2:1–5, 6–16; 3:18–23). And yet, when one consults the major publications that advocate for the rhetorical thesis, one finds an astonishing lack of attention to this section and its τέλειος-πνευματικός-ψυχικός terminology. In Litfin's section on 2:6–16, he relegates this topic to a footnote, saying: "In the following section we will avoid basing our conclusions on assertions about the origin of Paul's terminology." Pogoloff tries briefly to connect the terms with rhetors, though in doing so he abstracts the concepts from the plainly religious register in which the linguistic elements are here deployed.[3] In *Philo and Paul among the Sophists*, Winter touches not a single verse in 2:6–16. On the "secular-social" side, Marshall's more-than-four-hundred-page examination of "enmity" between Paul and the Corinthians explains the Corinthians' "boasting" and their predilection for ministers like Apollos on the basis of the conventions of friendship and patronage. While the monograph focuses most of its attention on 1 Corinthians, and particularly 1 Cor 4 (and 1:12), it includes only *two* references to any verse in 1 Cor 2:6–16, and both references mention only the citation formula that introduces the scripture quotation in 2:9.[4]

My suspicion is that this failure to address how the thematic emphasis of 2:6–16 dovetails with "rhetorical" or "secular" readings is due to the difficulty of integrating this section into such reconstructions. I shall pursue a complete reading through 2:6–16 here. As I hope to show, the connections between the Corinthians' σοφία and Stoicism now begin to become more prominent. In this chapter I confine attention more narrowly to the exegetical issues, touching on the Stoic background only in passing and at the most relevant points. As I shall withhold more detailed treatment of the Stoic connections until chapter 9, the reader is asked to withhold judgment

---

3. Litfin, *St. Paul's Theology of Proclamation*, 214n2; Pogoloff, *Logos and Sophia*, 140–43.
4. Marshall, *Enmity in Corinth*, 195, 203.

on the comparative aspect of our argument until we are able to address it more fully there.

The Transition into 2:6–16

If the σοφία that Paul addresses in chapter 1 pertains to rhetoric, one is compelled to explain why he transitions now to a discussion of wisdom's content. Krentz ventures a solution to the conundrum. According to Krentz, 1 Cor 1:17–2:16 parallels the debate that raged in Greco-Roman culture between rhetoric and philosophy. From the philosophers' perspective, rhetoric sought through manipulative tricks to convince listeners only of what *appeared* to be true; philosophy spoke of what *really was* true. Put differently, rhetoric was about form, philosophy was about content. Parallel to this debate, Krentz suggests, Paul condemns rhetoric as mere form in 1:17–2:5 and now advocates for content in 2:6–16,[5] thus taking the side of philosophy over rhetoric—content over form, truth over appearances.

Krentz's characterization of the ancient debate between rhetoric and philosophy is legitimate. Yet, his appeal to this dynamic here misses the nature of the transition between 2:6–16 and what precedes. Several features of the opening phrase in v. 6 (σοφίαν δὲ λαλοῦμεν ἐν τοῖς τελείοις) make evident that the transition is not a sharp one, that this is no digression, and that Paul is not moving to discuss a kind of wisdom that has not yet been introduced. (1) The placement of σοφίαν first in the paragraph lends "wisdom" prominence as the topical frame of the paragraph. In terms of discourse flow, this position is explained by the fact the subject is one that is already "cognitively available" to the participants, due of course to its prominence in the immediately preceding verses (vv. 4, 5). (2) Next, Paul's use of δέ to connect the two paragraphs indicates not strong antithesis, but only logical development, or qualification of what precedes, that is, "Now." (3) Finally, λαλοῦμεν provides a cohesive tie back to the language of "speech" that appears throughout vv. 1–5, including not only λόγος (λόγου, λόγος, [maybe λόγοις]) but also the terms καταγγέλλων and κήρυγμα.

The nature of the transition, therefore, is as follows. Paul has referred on the one hand to that σοφία that he did *not* "speak" (1:17; 2:1, 4–5); and he has referred on the other hand to a wisdom called "Christ crucified" (1:23) or "the mystery of God" (2:1). The latter he here designates again as σοφία,

---

5. Krentz, "Logos or Sophia," 280–81.

1 Corinthians 2:6–16: A Spiritual σοφία

though now uniquely qualifying it as a wisdom "spoken among the perfect."[6] σοφίαν δὲ λαλοῦμεν ἐν τοῖς τελείοις is thereby cohesively linked to the preceding paragraph, and as shown by the developmental conjunction (δέ = "now") the initial words now qualify Paul's definition of the wisdom that opposes the wisdom he has just repudiated:

vv. 1–5:   I did *not* speak human wisdom when I was among you.
v. 6:   Though, wisdom we *do* speak among the *perfect* (ἐν τοῖς τελείοις).

"Among the τέλειοι"

The older view is incorrect. Paul does not claim to have reserved a higher, esoteric wisdom for the more mature members of the community.[7] We shall take up below the question whether τέλειοι was a Corinthian self-designation. As for the occurrence of τελείοις in v. 6, Paul applies the term as a virtual synonym for *believer* (πιστός) or person "in Christ" (ἐν χριστῷ).[8]

That Paul hereby refers to the entire believing community is shown by several features. (1) The entirety of 2:6–16 is consistent with the more sweeping, cosmic framework within which Paul has framed his discussion since 1:17. The two kinds of wisdom belong respectively to God and humanity (1:25; 2:5; 3:21; cf. 3:3, 4), God and "the world" / "those of this age" (1:20, 21, 25), "those who are being saved" and "those who are being destroyed" (1:18), "those who are called" and the Jews/Greeks who reject the message of the cross (1:23–24). Paul's emphasis in 2:6 picks up thematically on the contrast introduced in 1:18–25. "The wise of this age" (1:20), even the "world" at large, were not able, at their best, to attain understanding of God's wisdom. This

---

6. Thus Inkelaar notes that the σοφία in this section is still none other than Christ crucified (*Conflict over Wisdom*, 20; citing H.-C. Kammler, *Kreuz und Weisheit: Eine exegetische Untersuchung zu 1 Kor 1,10–3,4*, WUNT 159 [Tübingen: Mohr, 2003], 245). Paul has said that he "preaches" (κηρύσσειν) Christ crucified as wisdom in 1:24.

7. That Paul refers to such wisdom is the opinion, for example, of Conzelmann (*1 Corinthians*, 60–61).

8. Paul Johannes Du Plessis, *Teleios: The Idea of Perfection in the New Testament* (Kampen: J. H. Kock, 1959), 178–85. The plural need not indicate that Paul now speaks for his coauthor, i.e., Sosthenes, 1:1; as Jerome Murphy-O'Connor believes, "Co-authorship in the Corinthian Correspondence," *RB* 100 (1993): 562–79, esp. 566–70. Nor must it indicate that he is quoting the Corinthians (Wire, *Corinthian Women Prophets*, 54).

insider-outsider contrast now continues as Paul contrasts those to whom the mystery has been revealed and those for whom it remains hidden (2:7–12). (2) Paul's focus since 1:17b has been the opposition of value systems, or how one "sees" things. One either sees through the value matrix of the world, with its notions of honor and status, or through the value matrix of Christ crucified. This contrast concerns, exhaustively, the world's way of seeing things versus believers' way of seeing things. (3) In v. 7 Paul puts eschatological glorification within cosmic context (God "predetermined it before the ages for our glory"). (4) The contrast between (a) *God's* "spirit" and (b) the *human* "spirit" in v. 11 clearly echoes the sweeping God-human contrast emphasized in 1:18–2:5. (5) In v. 12 the claim that "we did not receive the spirit of the world but the Spirit that is from God" must refer to believers universally, for at least two reasons: (a) The contrast against the spirit "of the world" evokes again the larger contrast seen in chapters 1–2 between believers and the "world" at large. (b) The idea that *all* believers have the Spirit, not just a spiritual elite, occupies a substantial portion of 1 Corinthians (12:3–14:40; cf. 3:16; 6:11, 19) and is consistently affirmed in Paul's letters (Gal 6:1; Rom 8:9; etc.).

In sum, the kind of wisdom that Paul speaks "among the perfect" is the kind that is known and discussed among "we Christ people." Paul's immediate qualification in the final words of v. 6 define his, and believers', wisdom negatively against the wisdom of the alleged "wise." He says: "but a wisdom not of this age nor of the rulers of this age." Verse 6, in short, expresses in different words the antithesis that Paul has been descanting upon all along. Implicitly, he means that *should* the σοφοί in Corinth want no part of this wisdom, they *would* not be counted among the perfect. For they *would* be aligning themselves with the "world."

To Whom It Is a "Mystery"

Paul now says more about this "wisdom among the perfect": it is a σοφίαν ἐν μυστηρίῳ ἀποκεκρυμμένην (v. 7). Initially, this expression is problematic. While most interpreters take the prepositional phrase (ἐν μυστηρίῳ) with σοφίαν, Lang has shown that ancient writers (ἐν μυστηρίῳ is restricted almost exclusively to early Christian literature) use the phrase primarily as an adverbial expression to qualify a verb of speaking.[9] In this regard, the "manner"

---

9. T. J. Lang, "We Speak in a Mystery: Neglected Greek Evidence for the Syntax and Sense of 1 Corinthians 2:7," *CBQ* 78 (2016): 68–89, esp. 69. Also holding that the phrase

of speaking indicates not necessarily "inspired" speech (or "non-rhetorical" speech), but the content formally defined *as* mystery. That is, ἐν μυστηρίῳ indicates the form in which one speaks, and μυστήριον, the *substance* of what is spoken. The sense is almost Aristotelian: its being articulated "*in* a mystery" casts wisdom *as* mystery. Thus, Lang concludes:

> The more common use of ἐν μυστηρίῳ relates the phrase not to the intention of the communicator but rather to the *nature of the thing* being communicated and the capacity of the auditor or reader to comprehend it. In other words, something is said to be spoken "in a mystery" when the matter being expressed possesses a hidden or figurative meaning that some people perceive while others do not. Thus, though all may hear it, not all can fully comprehend it.

And so, "Paul speaks about it [σοφία] 'in a mystery' because *it is* a mystery—a divine truth perceived by some but still veiled for others."[10] As Paul therefore states in 2:7, wisdom comes in the form of "a mystery" in the sense that wisdom *as such* was once hidden from human understanding until it was revealed to some people *as* wisdom.[11]

The relative pronoun that follows (ἥν) grammatically agrees with σοφίαν; yet the relative clause itself indicates that the pronoun refers not to the qualified phrase "wisdom that was hidden," but simply to "wisdom." It is the "wisdom" itself that is "for our glory." At this point, wisdom as Christ crucified converges with wisdom as God's plan of salvation: God's wisdom consists in the kind of counterintuitive—or mysterious—rationality embodied in the cross.

By describing the "rulers" as being "of this age" (v. 8), Paul puts them on the earlier end of the two ages, as those to whom this wisdom has remained hidden (recalling the "wise" etc. "of this age" in 1:20). Again the framing of chapters 1–4 is important. Paul has consistently drawn a contrast between God's wisdom and that of humans (1:25; 2:5; 3:21; cf. 3:3, 4). This scheme undoubtedly lends favor to the view that the rulers of this age are not exactly "demonic" or "spiritual" powers, but the human authorities (or more gener-

---

is adverbial is Bo Frid, "The Enigmatic ΑΛΛΑ in 1 Corinthians 2:9," *NTS* 31 (1985): 603–11, esp. 605.

10. Lang, "We Speak in a Mystery," 89 (my italics).

11. Or simply until God revealed it, as elsewhere in Paul's letters (Rom 16:26; Col 1:26–27; 2:2 [the mystery as "Christ"!]; 4:3) and other Second Temple texts (Dan 2:18–19, 27–28; 1QpHab VII, 4–6 [plural רז]; 2 Bar 81:4).

ally, the human regime) that were responsible for Jesus's death.¹² Paul's invocation of the rulers need not indicate that the Corinthian "wise" belonged to the ruling class; and it is indeed quite a stretch to identify the "rulers" here with rhetoricians.¹³ The rulers rather are paradigmatic of people "of this world," whom Paul selects for mention because he refers to Jesus's historical crucifixion. If, to their shame, they crucified, ironically, the "Lord of *glory*," this can only mean that those responsible for his crucifixion, like humanity in general, failed to comprehend the "wisdom of the cross." This descriptive appellation ("Lord of *glory*") echoes Paul's affirmation in v. 7 that God had planned to reveal this wisdom "for *our* glory." Believers receive "glory" through the crucified man of "glory." In this way the ironic subversion of the stigma attached to the cross undermines the honorific criteria that the σοφοί in Corinth endorse. It is not those who are honored in the estimation of humans who receive glory (especially eschatologically), but the crucified one, and together with him, the lowly.

The logical connection that Paul draws between vv. 8 and 9 is hardly "enigmatic."¹⁴ In v. 9, ἀλλά introduces a contrast with the preceding words, "if they had known." Consequently, the composite citation that follows (LXX Isa 64:4; 65:16e + free adaptations) responds to the contingency of their *having* known by means of the solemn assertion that they did *not*, and could not, have known; that is, "they did not *know*, *but rather* [ἀλλά], 'eye has *not* seen and ear has *not* heard.'"¹⁵ In this regard, a contrast emerges in v. 10 between those whose eyes remain blind, on the one hand, and emphatically "*us*" (ἡμῖν), on the other, that is, those to whom God has revealed his wisdom.¹⁶

---

12. Despite the prevalence of the *non*human-entities view in ancient interpretation, and despite some modern advocacy for it, the *human*-entities view is on firmer ground exegetically; note Gene Miller, "Archontōn Tou Aiōnos Toutou: A New Look at 1 Corinthians 2:6–8," *JBL* 91 (1972): 522–28; Williams, "Paul's Anti-imperial 'Discourse.'" Against Robert Ewusie Moses, there is no "dramatic turn" here from humans to "superterrestrial" beings (90). Moses, *Practices of Power: Revisiting the Principalities and Powers in the Pauline Letters* (Minneapolis: Fortress, 2014), 84–94. Despite Paul's (continued) use of apocalyptic language, he maintains his antithesis between God and "human" (v. 11), God's wisdom and "human wisdom" (v. 13), and the opposing epistemic outlooks of believers and nonbelievers (vv. 14–16).

13. Pogoloff (*Logos and Sophia*, 142) says: "Nor is it difficult to understand the connection of rulers to rhetoric." That may be true culturally speaking, but there is nothing to make one believe that is relevant here.

14. Frid, "Enigmatic ΑΛΛΑ."

15. It is here that the emphasis lies, not on the final portion, "for those who love him."

16. De Witt sees Paul using the quotation to undermine the Epicurean criterion of

To Whom It Was "Revealed"

In vv. 10–12 Paul continues to elaborate upon the difference between these two kinds of people, now focusing on those to whom God has "revealed" his wisdom. A person knows the things of God through the "Spirit," which "searches out all things"; and since "we" (believers) have received God's Spirit and not the "S/spirit of the world," "we" (believers) know God.

The existence of partial parallels to this language in a variety of philosophical or religious systems of antiquity (as also in Judaism) is not to be denied.[17] It is worth noting, however, that several features of these verses closely echo the ideas of one philosophical system in particular that flourished in the Corinthians' day and environment, namely, Stoicism.

Especially apparent are parallels with Stoic physics.[18] Contrary to Paul's Jewish monotheism, Stoicism was fundamentally pantheistic. God existed as part of the material universe and "extended through" it in the form of an "airy power" (πνευματικὴ δύναμις) called "breath," or πνεῦμα.[19] As this divine power was in a sense a part of the material world, the Stoics could refer to God himself as "the world" (κόσμος).[20] At the same time, Stoic physics was in a sense pan-*en*-theistic. While God *was* the world, he also penetrated and *inhabited* the world, as its "soul" (ψυχή).[21] Conceived in terms of its intelligent quality, this divine pervading power was known as "mind" (νοῦς).[22] Hence, because God, or Spirit, was rational (λόγικος), intelligent (νοερός), wise (σοφός), and perfect (τέλειος), so was the world that God inhabited.[23]

---

truth, the senses (*St. Paul and Epicurus*, 110–11), and as setting up a new criterion, the Spirit. However, the Stoics too viewed the senses as the criterion of truth.

17. R. Reitzenstein thinks that Paul's words derive from the Hellenistic mystery religions. Reitzenstein, *Die Hellenistischen Mysterienreligionen: Ihre Grundgedanken und Wirkungen* (Berlin: Teubner, 1927), 340.

18. See LS §47A–T.

19. LS §45H; 46A; 47C, L, O; 48C; LS §47G.

20. LS §44F; 54B.

21. "God is the world-soul [ὁ θεὸς ἡ τοῦ κόσμου ψυχή]" (*SVF* 1:532; cf. LS §46E). The world "is endowed with soul [ἔμψυχον], as is clear from our several souls [τῆς ἡμετέρας ψυχῆς] being each a fragment of it" (Diogenes Laertius, *Vit. phil.* 143 [Hicks, LCL]). The "soul extends through the whole world [τὴν ψυχὴν δι' ὅλου τοῦ κόσμου διήκειν]" (*SVF* 1:495); etc. On the theory of "mixture," or inter-envelopment, of God and matter, see LS §48.

22. LS §46B.

23. God as λογικός (LS §54A), νοερός (LS §54A; 46A), τέλειος (LS §54A); the world as λογικός (LS §54F), νοερός (LS §54F), perfect (LS §54H), sapiens (LS §54H); see also

And since God inhabited the whole world, God also inhabited humanity, who in turn shared in his divine rationality, or "reason" (λόγος).[24]

One might contend that nothing Paul says here need be seen against any background other than the Jewish Scriptures. Yet, several peculiar aspects of these verses offer compelling reasons to believe that Stoic resonances are intended. (1) While v. 10 contains a clear echo of Prov 20:27, Paul makes two significant adaptations to this text: (a) he changes the subject of the verb ἐρευνᾷ ("searches out") from φῶς κυρίου ("the light of the Lord") to πνεῦμα (Spirit); and (b) he adds πάντα ("all things") as the direct object. Now the *Spirit* searches out "*all things*." Paul must have some motivation for these changes, and the rationale for both could lie in the resonances of this language with the Stoic physics just sketched: the divine "Spirit" "extends through" "all things."

(2) If present, the Stoic allusions will have been polemically motivated, for Paul's subsequent comments are unmistakably subversive. The Stoic would agree, as Paul indicates in v. 12, that this inhabiting power endows people with the faculty of understanding ("no one knows the things of God except the Spirit of God"). Paul's denial that "we received the Spirit [πνεῦμα] of the world [τοῦ κόσμου]," however, runs directly counter to the Stoic doctrine that people (or the Corinthians) have within them the kind of πνεῦμα that inhabits *all things*. In this regard, we should be careful to reflect upon the curious significance of the linguistic asymmetry created in v. 12, as Paul departs from a genitive construction to an attributive one:

they ("we") did not receive:	τὸ πνεῦμα	τοῦ κόσμου
they received:	τὸ πνεῦμα	τὸ ἐκ τοῦ θεοῦ

The one Spirit inhabits the world. The other comes "from" (ἐκ) God. The ensuing purpose clause (ἵνα) confirms that the article + preposition construction specifies the indwelling Spirit as a *special endowment* conferred upon believers, not a connatural presence immanent in all people and things: "in order that we might know the things *given* to us by God."[25] In sum, Paul emphasizes that the Spirit is a special "gift" (not natural) and its endowment

---

SVF 2:633–45. For the reasoning connecting God and the world with respect to these attributes, see LS §54H = Cicero, *Nat. d.* 2.37–39.

24. Seneca, *Ep.* 41.1; 66.12; Epictetus, *Diatr.* 1.14.11–14; 2.8.9–17.

25. While Stoics sometimes describe the inherent divine portion as something "given" (Seneca, *Ep.* 31.9; 49.12; 124.7), the language of "giving" is in a sense catachrestic: just as the world *is* God, so the divine portion of the human being *is* the human being, the essential

1 Corinthians 2:6–16: A Spiritual σοφία

an "eschatological event" (not original).²⁶ Believers do not have the Spirit of the world (Stoic pantheism) but the Spirit that comes from God (a spiritual endowment received by believers).

(3) Verse 16 offers further evidence that the echoes are intentional. The first part of the verse consists in an unintroduced, reworked citation of LXX Isa 40:13. Departing from the Hebrew reading רוח ("spirit"), the LXX substitutes νοῦς:²⁷ "who has known the *mind* of the Lord?" Paul's divergence from the Hebrew version—which contains the "spirit" terminology—is not noteworthy on its own; yet, he has spoken throughout this section not of the divine "mind" (νοῦς), but of the divine "Spirit" (πνεῦμα), and we must suppose that he now departs to the alternative term with deliberation.²⁸ A reasonable motivation would be that νοῦς introduces an echo of the Stoic "intelligence." This echo would suggest that Paul's language works on two levels. Just as the Stoics described a πνεῦμα that "extended through all things" (διῆκον πάντα), this same πνεῦμα, when conceived in terms of the quality of "intelligence," was called νοῦς. In the same respect, νοῦς was *God* conceived in terms of intelligence;²⁹ and it was this pervading νοῦς that gave humanity the faculty of reason. As we shall see, Paul however will conclude in summary that "we have" not the νοῦς of the *world*, but rather the "νοῦς of *Christ*" (νοῦν Χριστοῦ).

"Taught Words" of Wisdom

At 2:13 we encounter our next configuration of σοφία and λόγος,³⁰ as Paul says, οὐκ ἐν διδακτοῖς ἀνθρωπίνης σοφίας λόγοις. Again the expression comes in the form of a denial (οὐκ), now corrected in the counterpoint ἀλλ' ἐν διδακτοῖς πνεύματος. On both sides of the antithesis, the syntax of the genitives is difficult to explain with precision, though both genitives function loosely to indicate the source of what is "taught"—that is, whether it is "from human wis-

---

part of the person that has always existed in them (at least in seed form) from conception (Seneca, *Ep.* 124.10).

26. Pearson, *Pneumatikos-Psychikos Terminology*, 40.

27. While Paul usually cites from the LXX tradition, his citations sometimes seem to interact with a Hebrew Vorlage (e.g., Rom 9:17; 10:15; 1 Cor 3:19; 14:21; 15:54, 55).

28. Inkelaar, *Conflict over Wisdom*, 238, 267–68.

29. LS §46B; 470.

30. Ἐν σοφίᾳ λόγου, 1:17; λόγου ἢ σοφίας, 2:1; though λόγοις may not be original in ἐν πειθοῖ[ς] σοφίας [λόγοις].

dom" or "from the Spirit." Several considerations indicate that the contrast, again, is not one between uninspired rhetoric and inspired preaching.[31]

(1) The plurals in vv. 10–12, as demonstrated above, clearly refer to believers generally, and the discourse is not marked for an abrupt change in v. 13. Therefore, it is not specifically ministers, but *believers* who "speak, etc." in this way; it is not, therefore, legitimate to view Paul here as defending specifically *his* nonuse of rhetoric.

(2) The rhetorical reading would require yet another shift of emphasis, from content (2:6–12) back to form (2:13), within a section (2:6–16) that, by common agreement, lays thematic emphasis on content.[32]

(3) The view that the ἐν phrases indicate the *manner* in which the subject speaks misses Paul's point of emphasis. Litfin is nearly correct when he says that "the λόγοι represent the *external form*, even in a sense the '*container of the content*'" of what the Spirit teaches. Nevertheless, Litfin's assertion that Paul's comment concerns "where one may learn the most appropriate *form*, from man or from God" reflects a vain attempt to counter the more obvious implication of his "container" interpretation.[33] The "form" represents not the style of delivery but the content subjectively defined in terms of its formal appearance, in the same way that one might speak of a "package" when referring to the content that it contains. Thus, by saying that he speaks "*in* the taught things of the Spirit," Paul indicates the form in which the content, that is, the teachings of the Spirit, is outwardly constituted.

(4) Confirming this interpretation are the cohesive ties by which v. 13 links back with the initial words of vv. 6 and 7. (a) The adverbial καί in v. 13, "which things *also* we speak" (ἃ καί λαλοῦμεν) joins the act of "speaking" (λαλοῦμεν) here with the act of speaking either as first expressed in v. 6 (λαλοῦμεν) or, more directly, in v. 7 (λαλοῦμεν), where Paul asserts that we speak "in a mystery" (ἐν μυστηρίῳ). (b) Further strengthening the tie between vv. 7 and 13 is the parallel form of the prepositional phrases in the respective verses (ἐν μυστηρίῳ and ἐν διδακτοῖς πνεύματος), a parallel that may suggest similar syntactical functions: just as Paul presented "wisdom *in mystery form*," so now he presents his message "*in* the taught (words) of the Spirit."

---

31. E.g., Davis, *Wisdom and Spirit*, 112.

32. Litfin (*St. Paul's Theology of Proclamation*, 217–18) sees vv. 6–12 as addressing content, but then he says that in 2:13 "we pick up again the continuing thread of Paul's argument. It is the same argument about the form of his preaching he has been hammering from the outset" (218).

33. Litfin, *St. Paul's Theology of Proclamation*, 219 (my italics).

1 Corinthians 2:6–16: A Spiritual σοφία

The terms in which Paul describes the one kind of wisdom—wisdom that is "taught" (διδακτός) and "human" (ἀνθρωπίνη)—are vague and have a wide range of potential significations. While the art of rhetoric was, indeed, "taught" by humans,[34] so was every kind of science or philosophy. In line with our reading of chapters 1–2 so far, it may be offered that this language alludes recognizably to philosophical traditions as *passed on*, or "taught," in schools of philosophy.[35] Several special points of contact are salient. (1) As Abraham Malherbe has shown, compounds of διδακτός were common in philosophical discourse.[36] Cynic philosophers described themselves as αὐτοδίδακτοι ("self-taught"), claiming that their wisdom derived from practice rather than from study. And Epicureans claimed to be "untaught" (ἀδίδακτος), their knowledge being innate rather than imparted. (2) On the other hand, most philosophers (Epicureans included) claimed allegiance to the teachings of school founders, whose doctrines (διδασκαλία) were passed down, or taught, through successors (διάδοχοι) to succeeding generations of students.[37] A student's identification with a particular philosophy was, in this regard, a matter of "allegiance" to the received teachings (as will be discussed at length in chapter 10). (3) Apart from the importance of "doctrine" in the philosophical schools, it was a matter of debate "whether virtue could be taught" (διδακτός). This is a question that Plutarch treats in a brief though apparently fragmentary treatise by that very title (*Mor.* 439a–440c).

Many philosophers would have objected to a characterization of philosophy—to use Paul's term—as "human" (ἀνθρωπίνη). Philosophers in the tradition of Plato described wisdom as something "divine" (θεῖος) (Philo, *Det.* 1.117; *Her.* 1.129; *Fug.* 1.195; *Post. Cain.* 1.138; *Gig.* 1.147), and they sometimes even disparaged its counterfeit as mere "*human* wisdom" (ἀνθρωπίνη σοφία) (Plato, *Apol.* 23a.8–9). For the Stoics, the very definition of wisdom was "knowledge of things *divine* and human" (θείων τε καὶ ἀνθρωπίνων ἐπιστήμη).[38] Indeed, one could not dissociate divine and human things given the Stoics'

---

34. Martin, *Corinthian Body*, 48; cf. Pogoloff (*Logos and Sophia*, 142): "taught in human schools."

35. The handing down of tradition as practiced in the rabbinic schools could also qualify as an example.

36. Abraham J. Malherbe, *The Letters to the Thessalonians: A New Translation with Introduction and Commentary* (New Haven: Yale University Press, 2004), 244.

37. Sedley, "Philosophical Allegiance," 97 and throughout.

38. *SVF* 2:35–36; cf. Cicero, *Off.* 1.153; a definition also shared by Philo, *Congr.* 1.79; 4 Macc 1:16.

pan(en)theistic assumptions. Yet, "human" is *Paul's* assessment of things; and very possibly it is a slight. At the primary level of discourse, the term functions to characterize the Corinthians' wisdom and the behavior resulting from it as "fleshly" in the most negative sense (cf. 3:1, 3). This is because the Corinthians' σοφία, as "human" wisdom, entails a value system that is antithetical to that of the cross.

The Speaking of "Spiritual Things"

The final portion of 2:13 (πνευματικοῖς πνευματικὰ συγκρίνοντες) introduces several grammatical difficulties, which combine to open up a multitude of interpretations.[39] It seems best, in view of (1) the proximity of πνευματικοῖς to the masculine plural λόγοις and (2) the common function of συν- + dative as indicating sharing ("with") to understand the phrase to mean "combining spiritual things with spiritual words." In sense, this amounts to "using spiritual words when discussing spiritual matters." This is spiritual content delivered as "spiritual" discourse. It is "language" that only Spirit people understand.

Humanity and the Spirit act in v. 13 as opposing "sources" of wisdom. There is either wisdom taught by humans or wisdom taught by the Spirit. Paul's stress here leans in the direction of the wisdom now "possessed." In this regard Paul emphasizes not the *inception* of wisdom as received through the Spirit (the beginning of wisdom), but rather the *epistemic outlook* adopted by those who possess the Spirit (qualitative wisdom). The implication of this conclusion for the rhetorical reading is clear: this section does not have at its center the competing agencies of "human rhetoric" and "divine inspiration" as opposing *means* of salvation. Rather it concerns two resulting *perspectives*. If one does not have the Spirit, one cannot comprehend God's wisdom, for God's wisdom contradicts not just the values of secular society but the rationalizing criteria that underlie them and compel people to view God's wisdom as foolishness. "Spiritual things" (πνευματικὰ) only make rational sense through the cipher of the "language" of that rational universe (God's universe of thought).

---

39. (1) πνευματικοῖς could be either masculine or neuter. (2) If masculine, it could refer either (a) attributively to words (λόγοις) or (b) substantively to people (ἀνθρώποις). (3) Συγκρίνοντες could mean "interpreting/explaining," "comparing," or "bringing together."

1 Corinthians 2:6–16: A Spiritual σοφία

DISTINCTIONS OF STATUS

The final verses of chapter 2 elaborate the thesis that Paul has pursued throughout 2:6–13.[40] He now illustrates the divergent epistemic outlooks of those who possess God's Spirit and those who do not through application of the Spirit principle to two types of persons, namely, the ψυχικός person and the πνευματικός person. Verses 14, 15 offer parallel descriptions of these figures:

ψυχικὸς δὲ ἄνθρωπος οὐ δέχεται τὰ τοῦ πνεύματος τοῦ θεοῦ μωρία γὰρ αὐτῷ ἐστιν, καὶ οὐ δύναται γνῶναι, ὅτι πνευματικῶς ἀνακρίνεται (v. 14)

ὁ δὲ πνευματικὸς ἀνακρίνει [τὰ] πάντα, αὐτὸς δὲ ὑπ' οὐδενὸς ἀνακρίνεται. (v. 15)

These verses present several difficulties. First, it must be decided whether the key terms originated with Paul or, as most scholars believe, with the Corinthians.[41] Second, it must be decided whether all or any portion of these verses cite, as some believe,[42] a "Corinthian slogan." Finally, it must be decided what Paul, or the Corinthians, or each of them, meant by the pertinent terms ψυχικός and πνευματικός and the contrast that they convey.

Ψυχικός and πνευματικός as Corinthian Terms

There is solid justification for the view that—whether ψυχικός-πνευματικός, as a pair, was historically *original* to the Corinthians—it has at least come to Paul through them. (1) The terms are not characteristically Pauline. Ψυχικός

---

40. Here, δέ = "now" in a transitional sense, though the continuity with what precedes has led many translations and commentators to omit the conjunction.

41. See p. 22 n. 52 above. Additionally, Martin (*Corinthian Body*, 63n68) has a note on πνευματικός-ψυχικός in which he expresses reserved agreement that this terminology belongs to the Corinthians. One wonders whether his reservations, like those of others (below), are due to the difficulty of making sense of these self-designations in light of the thesis that σοφία refers to rhetoric.

42. Among those who view 2:15 as a Corinthian slogan are Thiselton, *First Epistle to the Corinthians*, 271–72; Horsley, *1 Corinthians*, 61; Talbert, *Reading Corinthians*, 18; Wire, *Corinthian Women Prophets*, 21–22; and 2:15 is listed as a text that some take to be a quotation in Roger L. Omanson, "Acknowledging Paul's Quotations," *BT* 43 (1992): 201–13, esp. 212–13. This verse is not addressed in the recent reassessment of slogans in Watson and Culy, *Quoting Corinthians*.

occurs nowhere else in the Pauline corpus (only Jas 3:15; Jude 19 in the NT). Πνευματικός occurs only once (Gal 6:1). (2) The contrast itself—between two levels of spiritual status among *believers*—finds no place in Paul's theology. (3) Looking elsewhere in 1 Corinthians, we find conclusive evidence that some of the Corinthians did consider themselves πνευματικοί.[43] (a) In 14:37 Paul says this obliquely ("if anyone thinks he is a πνευματικός"). (b) In 14:12, Paul notes that the Corinthians are "zealous for spiritual things" (ζηλωταί ἐστε πνευμάτων) (14:12). (c) Paul's response to the Corinthians across chapters 12–14 contains clear indications that some considered themselves more "spiritual" than others. Paul discusses "spiritual gifts" (or is it "spiritual people"?; πνευματικῶν, 12:1);[44] he condemns individualist (12:12–26; 14:6–25) and competitive (14:4, 26–33) practices around the deployment of the gifts; he challenges the assumption that the gift of tongues is superior to the other gifts (14:1–5); and he opposes the apparent view that some believers have spiritual gifts while others do not (12:4–11).

Other Corinthian Contrasts

Apart from ψυχικός and πνευματικός (2:14, 15), Paul employs in 2:16–3:3 several other terms that describe the (im)maturity level of believers. Positive terms include τέλειος (2:6) and πνευματικός (2:15); negative terms include ψυχικός (2:14), σάρκινος (3:1), and νήπιος (3:1).

These terms fall into pairs and together constitute a set of contrasts. In 3:1 Paul puts πνευματικός in direct contrast with σάρκινος and νήπιος. The first term distributes with the other two to express basically synonymous dualities.[45] Paul articulates these in the form of an οὐκ . . . ἀλλά construction, with the two negative terms σαρκίνοις and νηπίοις standing in equal apposition, in contrast with the term πνευματικοῖς.[46]

---

43. Only Baird ("One against the Other,'" 127), it seems, has doubts regarding a connection between the πνευματικοί in 2:6–16 and the discussion of spiritual gifts in chs. 12–14. His refusal to connect them surely stems from the fact that he divides up the letter into discrete and disconnected problems in reaction to studies that have tried to trace a more overarching thread (like over-realized eschatology).

44. In the introductory formula, περὶ δὲ τῶν πνευματικῶν, the substantive could be either masculine or neuter.

45. Against Davis's view (*Wisdom and Spirit*, 124) that they were working with a three-stage schema.

46. σάρκινος (v. 1) and σάρκικος (v. 3) are probably synonymous here, as suggested by ἔτι in v. 3 ("as to σαρκίνοις . . . for you are *still* [ἔτι] σαρκικοί." Mikeal C. Parsons has shown that Paul and the NT writers use these terms more or less indiscriminately (although F

Paul does not oppose τέλειος (2:6) to the other terms directly. However, his description in 2:6 of the τέλειοι as those who comprehend God's wisdom undoubtedly establishes this term as a synonym for πνευματικός.[47] Moreover, placement of the term in direct antithesis to νήπιος twice later in the letter firmly establishes νήπιος-τέλειος as a coordinate pair (13:10–11; 14:20).[48] This same pairing occurs elsewhere in ancient literature, as shown below.

When one reads 2:14–15 against the primary theme of 1:17b–2:16, it becomes evident that the self-professed πνευματικοί/τέλειοι who believe themselves spiritually superior are one and the same as the σοφοί. Verses 2:6–16 continue to elaborate the theme of *two wisdoms*, and a similar bifurcation of perspectives appears. Paul had said in 1:17b–31 that God has abolished the wisdom of the "wise" (σοφοί) and per the foolishness of the cross elected the "foolish things" (μωρά = foolish people). In different terms, it is now the πνευματικοί who understand God's wisdom, and the ψυχικοί who do not. We have, in sum, at least four antitheses either articulated or implied:

	Lower Status	**Higher Status**
2:6	-	ἐν τοῖς τελείοις
2:14–15	ψυχικός ... ἄνθρωπος	ὁ <u>δὲ</u> πνευματικός
3:1	<u>ἀλλ'</u> ὡς σαρκίνοις, ὡς νηπίοις	<u>οὐκ</u> ... ὡς πνευματικοῖς
3:3	<u>ἀλλ'</u> ὡς σαρκίνοις, ὡς νηπίοις	<u>οὐκ</u> ... ὡς πνευματικοῖς
13:10–11	ὅτε ἤμην νήπιος ... νήπιος, ... νήπιος, ... νήπιος	ὅταν <u>δὲ</u> ἔλθῃ τὸ τέλειον ὅτε γέγονα ἀνήρ
14:20	τῇ κακίᾳ νηπιάζετε	ταῖς <u>δὲ</u> φρεσὶν τέλειοι γίνεσθε

The Language of Moral Status

The pull of scholarship over the last several decades has made interpreters reticent to connect this moral language with any religious or philosophical system in particular. Yet, the language of the "spiritual" and its opposite surely have some kind of "religious" meaning. For exponents of the rhetorical thesis, this language presents an obstacle that the interpreter must make some effort to surmount. The πνευματικός-ψυχικός distinction, if the *Corinthians* endorsed

---

and G do not). Parsons, "Sarkinos, Sarkikos in Codices F and G: A Text-Critical Note," *NTS* 34 (1988): 151–55.

47. A point noted as early as Weiss, *Der erste Korintherbrief*, 74; see also Funk, "Word and Word," 298.

48. For example, Horsley, "Pneumatikos vs. Psychikos," 282.

it, has no perceptible relevance to a rhetorical reconstruction of the circumstances. The spiritual emphasis of 2:6–16 presents a similar set of problems for explanations that have sought not simply to supplement, but rather to supplant older "theological" explanations by contending that the Corinthians' problems were, "*rather*, sociological." Indeed, it is surely forced to take τέλειος here as a reference to the "'perfect' citizen" in a political sense, just as it would be to take πνευματικός as a reference to the "'spiritual' citizen" in the same sense.[49] Hence, in deciding the background of the relevant language, it seems that the choice is not between a rhetorical/political interpretation and a spiritual/religious one, but between competing spiritual/religious options.

I delay until chapter 9 a fuller demonstration of uniquely "Stoic" connections. However, several observations about the Corinthians' language should be noted for purposes of exegesis. As discussed, allusions to Stoic physics are already salient in the context of 2:10–13 (the "spirit of the world" as a pervading and intelligence-giving power; "taught" wisdom; distinction between "Spirit *of*" and "Spirit that is *from*"; adaptations to Prov 20:27 that introduce the terms πνεῦμα and πάντα; the substitution of νοῦς for רוח in the citation of Isa 40:13). I now add that the Corinthian pairs with which we are dealing find parallels in Stoic ethics. We shall treat the τέλειος-νήπιος and πνευματικός-ψυχικός pairs more fully in chapter 9. Here I only note that the τέλειος-νήπιος pair is endemic to discussions of moral development in the Greek philosophical tradition, and in Stoic discourse in particular. As Horsley has noted, Philo of Alexandria applies this distinction in several passages,[50] sometimes identifying milk as the nourishment for the νήπιος and solid food as the nourishment for the τέλειος.[51] Though a Hellenistic Jew, Philo himself is cited on this point in von Arnim's collection of old Stoic fragments (*SVF*) as being a witness to the views of the Stoics, for his scheme is derived from them.[52] The evidence of Philo finds parallel in several other Stoic witnesses, who repeatedly affirm the ideas that children (νήπιοι) are figurative for the morally immature,[53] milk is nourishment for the unadvanced, solid food is nourishment for the mature,[54] and the σοφός is τέλειος.[55] As we shall later see, this twofold ethical distinction is inseparable from the doctrines of Stoic physics.

---

49. Welborn, "On the Discord in Corinth," 105.
50. *Sob.* 9–10; *Agr.* 9; *Migr.* 1.29, 33.
51. Philo, *Migr.* 29; *Somn.* 2.10; *Agr.* 9; *Quod omnis* 1.160.
52. The Stoic system of moral development is mapped out in detail in Lee, *Moral Transformation*, 228–45.
53. *SVF* 3:519 (= Philo, *Leg. all.* 1.93–94); *SVF* 3:512 (Philo, *Leg. all.* 3.210); *SVF* 3:754.
54. Epictetus, *Diatr.* 2.16.39; cf. 3.24.9.
55. Another one of the Stoic "paradoxes": the wise man is τέλειος (*SVF* 3:548; cf. 1:566),

1 Corinthians 2:15 as a Corinthian Slogan

Interpreters do not always include 1 Cor 2:15 among the so-called Corinthian slogans.[56] However, as good a case can be made for this verse as any other. Interpreters widely agree that both πνευματικός and, in 2:14, ψυχικός are Corinthian terms.[57] That ἀνακρίνειν is also a Corinthian term is suggested by its pattern of usage across the NT. Apart from its six occurrences in Luke-Acts (Luke 23:14; Acts 4:9; 12:19; 17:11; 24:8; 28:18), this term appears nowhere else in the NT, including the Pauline corpus, with the exception of its *ten* occurrences in 1 Corinthians (2:14, 15 [x2]; 4:3 [x2], 4; 9:3; 10:25, 27; 14:24).[58] Finally, the point that the spiritual man "evaluates" (ἀνακρίνειν) all things asserts the *opposite* of Paul's own policy. For as he says in 4:3, "I do not even evaluate [ἀνακρίνω] myself."

What has, surprisingly, remained hitherto unnoticed is that 2:15 has a more exact extrabiblical parallel than any other putatively Corinthian slogan. It comes from a Stoic author: Paul's contemporary Seneca. The two texts read as follows:

Seneca, *Ep.* 71.20 "[Such is virtue], which passes judgment on everything, but nothing passes judgment on virtue."
Haec [virtus] de omnibus rebus iudicat, de hac [virtute] nulla [iudicat].

1 Cor 2:15 "The spiritual man passes judgment on all things, but he himself is judged by nothing/no one."
ὁ δὲ πνευματικὸς ἀνακρίνει [τὰ] πάντα, αὐτὸς δὲ ὑπ' οὐδενὸς ἀνακρίνεται.

Any prejudice against "parallels" of this kind should be allayed when one notices the comprehensiveness of the similarities; for the similarities comprise the exact form and the same conceptual and verbal content. Formally, (1) both lines are structured as antitheses (labeled below as Point [*P*] and Counterpoint [*C*]). (2) In both texts the Point and Counterpoint exhibit mu-

---

possessing "perfected virtues" (τέλειοι ἀρεταί) (*SVF* 3:522 = Philo, *Cain* 43; *SVF* 3:609 = Philo, *Cain* 111), having "perfect wisdom" (*perfecta sapientia*) (Cicero, *Tusc.* 2.51). Cf. discussion of 1:26 above.

56. Widely regarded as Corinthian slogans are 6:12, 13; 8:1, 4; often 6:18; 8:8; cf. 15:12. 1 Cor 2:15 is sometimes included. See p. 22 nn. 50 and 52 above.

57. See pp. 21–22 n. 49 above.

58. Davis (*Wisdom and Spirit*, 127) and Fee (*First Epistle to the Corinthians*, 117; 2nd ed., 125) view this as a Corinthian term.

tual structural parallelism, with each of the elements of the Point being paralleled by a corresponding element in the Counterpoint (*P1/C1*, *P2/C2*, etc.). (3) Both texts include three components on each side of the antithesis (with ellipsis of the verb in Seneca's Counterpoint). (4) Four of the six elements in each of the two texts are identical Latin-Greek verbal equivalents (*P2*, *P3*, *C2*, *C3*), while the elements in the fifth and sixth portions (*P1*, *C1*) parallel each other conceptually, as I shall demonstrate.

P1	*P2*	*P3*	*C1*	*C2*	*C3*
ὁ πνευματικὸς	ἀνακρίνει	[τὰ] πάντα	αὐτὸς	ἀνακρίνεται	ὑπ' οὐδενὸς
Haec [virtus]	iudicat	de omnibus rebus	de hac [virtus]	[iudicat]	nulla

P1, C1

Despite the lexical variance in *P1* (ὁ πνευματικός = *virtus*) and *C1* (αὐτός = *virtus*), when we examine the meaning behind the lines themselves, we find that the parallel items in *P1* and *C1* remain conceptually equivalent. This point requires demonstration.

The line from Seneca occurs in the context of a larger discussion about "virtue" (*virtus*), in which Seneca characterizes virtue as a "rule" or "standard" (*regula*). This description reflects the Stoics' understanding of virtue as "non-scalar."[59] Just as the quality of straightness cannot be intensified or reduced (what is straight cannot become straighter), so it is with virtue. Dispositions of mind are either virtuous (in the shape of virtue) or not.[60] There is no sliding "scale." Accordingly, a person either has all the virtues ("virtues perfected") or one has none of them.[61] The one who possesses virtue perfected, that is, the wise man (*sapiens*), is the embodiment of virtue and so represents in himself the natural "standard" and becomes the absolute measure against which everything and everyone else is judged.

In this light, we find that the striking correspondence between 1 Cor 2:15 and Seneca, *Ep.* 71.20 extends not only to their formal and linguistic features but also to their functionally one-to-one conceptual content. The two subjects ὁ πνευματικός and *haec* [*virtus*] are the only terms in the two texts

---

59. Lee, *Moral Transformation*, 337–38.
60. Virtue is defined as a "disposition of the soul" (*SVF* 3:197–213).
61. *SVF* 3:295–304.

that do not constitute exact Greek-Latin equivalents, and yet we find that these components directly correspond when understood against the Stoic framework just described. Here is how. Stoic virtue is a disposition of the soul, and the wise man the one whose soul has this disposition. Since virtue is "the soul in a certain condition," and the soul is a living thing, virtue also is a living thing.[62] In this sense, the soul of the wise man *in the shape of virtue* and virtue *itself* are identical. Both the wise man and virtue, therefore, "pass judgment on all things" because both conform with nature and thus constitute the universal "rule," against which all else must be judged. The correspondence of the (Corinthian) "spiritual man" with (Stoic) "virtue," therefore, is much closer than it might at first appear. The πνευματικός/σοφός figure in Corinth embodies the natural "standard" (2:15) in the same way that Stoic virtue/the σοφός does. As I shall argue in chapter 9, this structural analogy with Stoicism also links into a larger configuration of systemically related Stoic ideas that the Corinthian σοφοί appear to have shared with the Stoics.

P², C²

The semantic equivalency between ἀνακρίνει ("examine," "evaluate") in 1 Cor 2:15 and *iudicare* in Seneca's text is corroborated by use of the Latin term to render ἀνακρίνειν in the Vulgate, both in this verse and elsewhere.[63] Thus, the "spiritual man" passes judgment on, or "evaluates," all things, just as "virtue" does. This is not mere "judgment," but *perfect* judgment.[64] Virtue evaluates all things, and because it is the "rule," it offers always a perfect evaluation.

P³, C³

The verbal complements match in *P3*: "evaluates *all things*" ([τὰ] πάντα), and "passes judgment *concerning all things*" (de omnibus rebus). The components in *C3* match as well, but with Paul's text substituting the passive "by *no one/nothing*" (ὑπ' οὐδενός) for Seneca's active "*nothing* passes judgment" (*nulla* [*res*]). The gender of Paul's οὐδενός is ambiguous. Despite the common rendering of the word as masculine ("no one," "anyone"), it may be better taken as a neuter for two reasons: (1) the corresponding neuter [τὰ] πάντα in the first half of 2:15 (if the article is original) naturally suggests a matching

---

62. Seneca, *Ep.* 113.2. See also *SVF* 3:305–7.
63. Including 1 Cor 2:15 (×2); 4:3 (×2); 4:4; though for some reason *examinare* in 2:14.
64. This signification holds here not by fixed semantics but by the identity of the agent.

neuter in the second half ("all things," "nothing"), and (2) Seneca's line refers to impersonal "things" in both halves of the antithesis (*omnibus rebus* and *nulla* [*res*]).

Summary

The Corinthian assertions embedded in 1 Cor 2:14–15 epitomize the mindset that we have seen represents the Corinthians' σοφία, a wisdom that Paul has branded the "wisdom of the world." For the Corinthians, the σοφός/τέλειος/πνευματικός person is a person of higher spiritual rank, who stands above the νήπιος/ψυχικός. The πνευματικός is the measure of all things; the ψυχικός the one measured by him.[65] This kind of personal comparison, Paul suggests, embodies the spirit of the world's mindset about worth and status and defies the wisdom of the cross—or what Paul will now call "the mind of Christ."

The Mind(set) of Christ

We now consider the relationship between 2:15, as a Corinthian slogan, and the two clauses paratactically adjoined to it in 2:16. (1) Through γάρ, Paul specifies that v. 16 grounds the general thesis argued throughout vv. 6–15—specifically that comprehension of God's wisdom *as* wisdom requires the subject to experience an epistemological transformation. The specific grounds that he offers consist in an unintroduced, reworked citation of LXX Isa 40:13, in which he substitutes the Greek term νοῦς ("who has known the *mind* of the Lord?") in place of the Hebrew רוח ("spirit"). (2) Following the

---

65. Despite the strong arguments of Laura B. Dingeldein, in v. 14 ψυχικός is probably not to be inferred as the subject of ἀνακρίνεται. Dingeldein, "'Ὅτι πνευματκῶς ἀνακρίνεται': Examining Translations of 1 Corinthians 2:14," *NovT* 55 (2013): 31–44. While Dingeldein is correct that elsewhere Paul consistently uses ὅτι, after γινώσκειν, to introduce a content clause, this point misses the fact that γινώσκειν already has a complement here, which is simply not repeated ("all things" = "it" [collectively] as "foolishness" = "these things"), as usual when the complement is readily understood from what precedes (Rom 7:11; 1 Cor 2:8; 2:10; 3:13; 4:7; 6:5; 7:3; etc.). Dingeldein reasonably assumes based on the common placement of the verb that πνευματικῶς ἀνακρίνεται here parallels αὐτὸς δὲ ὑπ' οὐδενὸς ἀνακρίνεται in v. 15, making the subject in both cases personal—i.e., ψυχικός in the one instance and πνευματικός in the other. Yet, this construal misses the difference between the content of vv. 14 and 15, for the contrast in v. 15 between "evaluating" and "being evaluated" is not at hand in v. 14. Moreover, the referent of οὐδενός is probably not masculine, but neuter (see above).

citation Paul summarily adds a *correction* via δέ and the explicit pronoun ἡμεῖς, saying, "*but we* have the mind of Christ."[66]

The sequence of thought (γάρ ... δέ) in v. 16 is difficult to account for when one pauses to consider it.[67] The problem initially is that "who has known the mind of the Lord" in v. 16a (introduced by γάρ) seems to respond *negatively* to—rather than as *grounds* for—the preceding claim that the "spiritual man evaluates all things," that is, perfectly *understands* them. If, moreover, the quotation in v. 16a ("*no one* has known the mind of the Lord") indeed constitutes Paul's response to the slogan in v. 15, why does he then *counter his counter* in v. 16b with the assertion that, in fact, "we [*do*] *have*" the mind of Christ?

The solution to these difficulties lies not only in identifying the slogan in v. 15 but also in correctly correlating the elements of Paul's response with the slogan's respective parts. If *both* of the claims made in vv. 14a, 15 reflect (originally) Corinthian slogans, the two parts of v. 16 fall into place as a two-part response—v. 16a responding to v. 14a and v. 16b responding to v. 15:

	Corinthian Slogan	**Paul's Response**
2:14a, 16a	"The unspiritual man is not able to receive the things of the Spirit of God" (2:14a)	"*for* [γάρ] 'who has known the mind of the Lord?'" (2:16a)
2:15, 16b	"The spiritual man evaluates all things" (2:15)	"*but* [δέ] *we* [in contrast with your "spiritual man"] have the mind *of Christ*" (2:16b)

The first point in favor of this structure is that it offers a coherent solution for a logical sequence that is otherwise difficult to explain. Second, this solution offers an exact parallel to Paul's handling of another, widely accepted Corinthian slogan, that in 6:13. While the boundaries of this slogan are difficult to delineate, Jay Smith has expertly demonstrated that the slogan comprises both 6:13a ("Food is meant for the stomach and the stomach for food") and b ("God will destroy both one and the other") and that the two portions of the slogan pair with corresponding Pauline responses in 13c (answering 13a) and 14 (answering 13b):

---

66. If this is another Corinthian slogan (Wire, *Corinthian Women Prophets*, 21–22), Paul has again appropriated and applied it to "we Christ people."

67. Note a general neglect of the conjunctions in the commentaries.

	Corinthian Slogan	**Paul's Response**
6:13a, c	"Food is meant for the stomach and the stomach for food" (6:13a)	"The body is meant not for fornication but for the Lord and the Lord for the body" (6:13c)
6:13b, 14	"God will destroy both one and the other" (6:13b)	"And God raised the Lord and will also raise us by his power" (6:14)

Consistent with the antithesis that Paul has been developing since chapter 1, it appears then that in 2:16b Paul counters the Corinthians' πνευματικός-ψυχικός distinction/slogan by appealing again to the example of Christ, though now replacing the expression "Christ crucified" (1:23; 2:2) with "mind of Christ," or νοῦν Χριστοῦ. Vis-à-vis the Corinthian *habitus*, νοῦς seems to be an intentional echo of Stoicism, for reasons already noted. There is, however, a noticeable layering of meaning at this point. Paul himself intends the term primarily in the sense of a "mindset." While the term νοῦς does not appear in Phil 2:5–10, this passage makes the same point as the one made both here and throughout 1 Cor 1:17b–2:16. Christ's followers are to imitate Christ's "thinking" (τοῦτο φρονεῖτε, Phil 2:5), and not just his patterns of thought in a cognitive sense but the *habitus* that directs his life and orientation toward others, his taking the form of a servant (Phil 2:7) and his humbling himself and becoming obedient to the point of death (2:8). In view of Paul's opposition between Corinthian wisdom and his theology of the cross, this bifurcation between the Stoic and the cruciform meaning involves a damning irony. The "wise Corinthians" who boast that they have reached a *comparatively* higher level of intellectual (νοῦς) or spiritual (πνεῦμα) insight, by virtue of their comparative or competitive outlook, actually exhibit qualities *opposite* those who truly possess the νοῦς of Christ, or the wisdom of God.

Paul's "Competitive Appropriation" of the Corinthian Framework

The interpretation just offered poses a challenge to the older view that Paul speaks in 2:6–16 of an "esoteric" wisdom that he withheld from the immature and revealed only to the advanced. Initially, it was not Paul but the Corinthians who drew distinctions in maturity.[68] Within Paul's apocalyptic framework as seen consistently throughout 1:17b–2:16, the only real distinction is be-

---

68. Talbert, *Reading Corinthians*, 17–18.

tween "those who are perishing" and "those who are being saved" (1:18).[69] Yet, Paul now expediently appropriates the Corinthians' distinction and reverses the applications of the respective terms (thus, "competitive appropriation") with ironic effect.[70] Indeed, Paul says, it is true that only those who have the Spirit can comprehend the things of the Spirit. Since, however, the self-proclaimed πνευματικοί prove themselves to be σοφοί not in God's sense but in the world's sense, ironically it is they who are truly ψυχικοί. Moreover, *if* they do not understand God's wisdom, Paul insinuates, it *would* follow they do not have the Spirit. In this regard, Paul's indirect, negative characterization of the Corinthians that comes in 3:1–3 is not tantamount to outright denial that they are Christ people. Only, as he regrets, he is still not able to speak to them "*as* [ὡς] to πνευματικοῖς." At worst, their status is in jeopardy. If they are Christ people, they are not acting the part, to their peril (cf. 3:15).

THE THEMATIC FOCUS OF 2:6–3:4

Before concluding, I should like briefly to examine the remarks of one representative of the rhetorical thesis who attempts to relate 2:6–16 to the church's controversy. According to Corin Mihaila, the "central theme" of 2:6–3:4 is that of competing agencies in effecting salvation, that is, the agency of preachers versus the agency of God.[71] In this regard Mihaila thinks that Paul's purpose here is "to warn the Corinthians that, by their assessment of preachers according to the worldly canons of wisdom, they place themselves in a dangerous spiritual condition."[72] The difficulty with this interpretation, as we have seen, is that "perfect" and "spiritual" are attributes that the Corinthians assign to *themselves*,[73] not to their "preachers." This point reproduces an obscurity that we have found repeatedly in iterations of the rhetorical thesis, an obscurity that is difficult to unravel and therefore generally remains hidden. If the Corinthians consider *themselves* wise, spiritual, and perfect, how then

---

69. Du Plessis (*Teleios*, 178–85) rightly insists that for Paul the contrast is an intra-extra one, as in 1:17–31, and that τέλειος is just another word for πιστοί or people ἐν χριστῷ. Du Plessis, however, does not acknowledge that Paul derived the term from the Corinthians before redefining it.

70. Lee, *Moral Transformation*, 498–503.

71. Mihaila, *Paul-Apollos Relationship*, 26.

72. Mihaila, *Paul-Apollos Relationship*, 31.

73. Actually Mihaila (*Paul-Apollos Relationship*, 30–31) agrees on this point, though he does not recognize the resulting discrepancy.

does the "central theme" of 2:6–16 become the wisdom (or eloquence) of the *preachers*? There are no grounds exegetically for distinguishing human actors here—as if Paul is talking now about "wise preachers," now about "spiritual/unspiritual" listeners. This, however, is what Mihaila's reading seems to require. Rather, the one who has the Spirit is also the one who has God's wisdom (vv. 10, 12); and as we have seen, the first-person plural in 2:6–16 concerns "we believers" against "those who are perishing." We do not have distinct groups of actors.

It is hard to resist the conclusion that, for interpreters who take such a line, their preconstruction of the Corinthian conflict has here taken priority over the source that bears witness to it. Paul does not rebuke the Corinthians because they consider him or Apollos or some preacher to be wise, but because they consider themselves to be such.

Conclusion

As Paul moves from 1:17b–2:5 into 2:6–3:4, the transition is neither abrupt nor sharp. Paul continues to elaborate upon the antithesis between God's wisdom and the wisdom of the world, understood as two different *mindsets* about worth and status. Like the world, the σοφοί in Corinth ascribe honor based on stratifying criteria of worth and thereby divide the community into tiers. The main difference is an addition of new terms. We find that the Corinthians—or some of them—describe themselves not only as σοφοί but also as τέλειοι and πνευματικοί and disparage others in the community as νήπιοι and ψυχικοί. It is the σοφοί who introduced these distinctions. While Paul appropriates their language, he does so "competitively." Offering a redefinition of wisdom, contrary to that of the world, Paul redraws the lines of identity. Those who consider themselves "spiritual" (πνευματικοί), by this very fact, prove themselves to be "unspiritual" (ψυχικοί), for their comparative personal outlook defies the way of Christ. In this regard, Paul recasts the wisdom of "Christ crucified" here as "the mind of Christ," a mindset characterized not by reach for status but by self-lowering in the interest of others.

These two mindsets are, literally, "worlds" apart. This is the framework within which Paul's reference to the "taught words of human wisdom/the Spirit" finds its meaning. To outsiders, God's wisdom remains incomprehensible when judged by ordinary canons of status and can only appear as "mystery." Thus, Paul's emphasis on the Spirit in regard to God's wisdom is not essentially about agency, or the *inception* of salvation. Rather, it is about the indwelling Spirit as the faculty through which one "goes on seeing" God's wisdom as wisdom *qualitatively*.

Finally, we saw in the course of Paul's response substantial interplay with the language and ideas of Stoicism, particularly from Stoic physics. As I have tried to confine attention in this chapter to exegetical concerns, a final evaluation of the plausibility of the proposed background must await more complete demonstration in chapter 9. As we shall find, the Stoic allusions, together with the Corinthian vocabulary incorporated into 2:6–16, offer key evidence of the wise Corinthians' anthropological assumptions and thus provide us with some of our most direct evidence of the Corinthians' *habitus* and self-understanding.

6

1 Corinthians 3:1–4:5: The Apostles and the σοφία of God

With a brief transition in 3:1–3, the discourse moves into a new section that integrates the two facets of the controversy that interpreters must endeavor to relate: σοφία and partisanship (3:4–4:5). Holding this section together is discussion on either end of the relationship between Paul and Apollos. Enclosed are several subsections in which personal referents are not always patently identified. In summary, the constituent subsections cover the following:

3:1–4	Paul blames (explicitly) the Corinthians who claim allegiance either to himself or Apollos.
3:5–10b	Paul describes (explicitly) his and Apollos's activities of tending and building as ministers.
3:10c–17	*Paul discusses the person (τις) who lays a different foundation, builds upon it, or destroys the temple of the church.*
3:18–23	*Paul warns the person (σοφός) who espouses the wisdom of the world.*
4:1–5	Paul discusses (explicitly) his and Apollos's roles as assistants and stewards of God.

Because of the indefinite nature of the personal references in 3:10c–17 and 18–23, the identity of Paul's target(s) of criticism in these subsections is debatable. Even Paul's open discussion of Apollos in 3:5–10b and 4:1–5 could be explained in terms of a range of motives and varying levels of transparency. Consequently, several readings of this unit are possible. Across the history

1 Corinthians 3:1–4:5: The Apostles and the σοφία of God

of scholarship interpreters have sometimes offered completely opposite pictures of Apollos's role in the divisions. While more recent reconstructions tend to envisage a two-party rivalry between partisans of Paul and partisans of Apollos,[1] in the past some interpreters have even viewed the Apollos party as Paul's biggest ally.[2]

Especially prevalent since the 1970s, the Paul-vs-Apollos reading has had three primary variants, all of which build around our (meager) biographical information about Apollos supplied from Acts.[3] (1) Through the 1970s and '80s several interpreters highlighted Apollos's roots in Alexandria (Acts 18:24) and hypothesized that Apollos had been the conduit of Hellenistic Jewish wisdom in the tradition of Philo of Alexandria. (2) A slightly more recent theory capitalizes on the remaining biographical data offered in Acts, specifically, the description of Apollos as ἀνὴρ λόγιος and δυνατὸς ὢν ἐν ταῖς γραφαῖς (Acts 18:24). Taking λόγιος to mean "eloquent," interpreters in this line envisage a conflict between the partisans of Paul and the partisans of Apollos over the two men's respective rhetorical abilities. (3) On a third reading (sometimes combined with the second reading), some more affluent members of the church had offered a monetary gift to both Paul and Apollos. Apollos accepted, Paul refused, and the Corinthians became offended at his rejection of their patronage. Overall, while proponents of a Paul-versus-Apollos view disagree as to whether Apollos contributed to the divisions wittingly or unwittingly,[4] they almost invariably view the Apollos party as Paul's primary opposition.

The interpretive difficulties involved in this section, and in relating it to the data in Acts, leave us with an array of explanations for how the Paul-Apollos discussion functions within 1 Cor 3:4–4:5. I distinguish the following readings:

---

1. Note an important article representing the shift: Sellin, "Das 'Geheimnis' der Weisheit."

2. Paul-with-Apollos vs. Cephas-with-Christ: Schmidt, *Bibliothek für Kritik und Exegese*, 263–64; and Baur, "Die Christusparti"; and still in Goulder, "Σοφία in 1 Corinthians"—Paul-with-Apollos against Cephas: Gerd Lüdemann, *Paulus der Heidenapostle, II: Antipaulinismus im frühen Christentum* (Göttingen: Vandenhoeck & Ruprecht, 1983), 118–21—mainly Paul against a Christ party: Lütgert, *Freiheitspredigt und Schwarmgeister*; Wilckens, *Weisheit und Torheit*; Schmithals, *Die Gnosis in Korinth*.

3. For the literature, see p. 10 n. 22 above.

4. Mihaila (*Paul-Apollos Relationship*, 183–90) overviews the history of scholarship under the headings "Paul and Apollos Are Rivals," "Apollos' Unintentional Role in the Dissensions," "Apollos' Neutral Role in the Dissensions."

1. Paul views Apollos as the very source of the Corinthians' σοφία and blames him for the factions, for laying a different "foundation" than the one he had laid, and for destroying the "temple" of the church. Thus, this section is apologetic and represents a fairly straightforward attempt on Paul's part to subordinate Apollos to himself.
2. Paul views Apollos as a minor threat and suspects that he may be responsible for dividing the church and damaging it in some way. Though in 3:5–10b Paul appears to speak of Apollos positively on the surface, in fact these verses reflect a subversive attempt to return Apollos to a subordinate role.
3. Paul speaks only positively of Apollos and their partnership. He sees Apollos neither as the source of the Corinthians' σοφία nor as culpable in the formation of the factions, despite the allegiance to Apollos declared by some in the church. Any condemnation of Apollos, if present, applies only at the level of Paul's generically applicable point about destructive wisdom as perpetuated by any person. The main targets of criticism are either completely indefinite or a different group. (a) In the first instance, Paul applies his criticism not specifically to ministers but to anyone who damages the church with the "wisdom" that they purvey. (b) Alternatively, the warnings in 3:10c–21a are semantically indefinite though situationally applicable especially to certain members of the Corinthian church. Paul speaks only positively of Apollos in 3:5–10b and discusses their relationship so as to present their amity as a paradigm for the Corinthians to imitate.

As I hope to show, the third option in the (b) variant offers the most likely interpretation of the situation. Both internally and within the context of 1 Cor 1–4, this reading makes the most sense and is less dependent upon presumed innuendos or the intrusion of preconceived suspicions about Apollos influenced largely by Acts. Paul lays no blame on Apollos and his censures are directed primarily at the Corinthian σοφοί and those who may be tempted by their brand of wisdom.

3:1–10B

The Transition from 1:17–2:16

Κἀγώ again introduces the transition (cf. 2:1). Here the καί + ἐγώ combination implies that the perspective voiced throughout 2:6–16 did not just represent

Paul's perspective. It represented the perspective of Christ people, that is, of people who have the Spirit (2:12) and who thereby appreciate God's wisdom. Only now does Paul re-narrow the application to his own teaching specifically (cf. 2:1). Thus, κἀγώ = "And for *my* part."

Looking back on his visit, Paul recalls how he "was not able" to speak to the church "*as* [ὡς] to πνευματικοῖς," but spoke to them "*as* [ὡς] to σαρκίνοις, *as* [ὡς] to νηπίοις" (3:1). With this remark Paul does not concede to the view that there are two stages of Christian maturity.[5] His characterization, rather, competitively appropriates the stance of the *wise* and applies it ironically back to his initial teaching: yes, perhaps his message *was* too "elementary" (tongue in cheek). Meanwhile, distinguishing between milk and solid food as graded forms of nourishment, Paul places himself in the role of the philosophical teacher, who, as they say, adapts his instruction to suit the respective levels of his students—milk for some and solid food for others.[6]

First Corinthians 3:1–3 provides a natural bridge from the discussion of wisdom back to the theme of intra-community strife (ἔριδες), mentioned first in 1:11. The intervening verses from 1:17b to 2:16 can hardly be considered an interruption.[7] A clear logical sequence is evident: having said that the wisdom of the world is opposite the wisdom of God (1:17–2:5) and that the wisdom of God is understood only among the "spiritual" (2:6–16), Paul now indicates (3:3) that he cannot address the Corinthians *as* spiritual people for the reason that there is "rivalry" (ζῆλος) and "strife" (ἔρις) among them (3:4). With the reintroduction of strife, Paul cites again two of the four Corinthian "slogans" encountered in 1:12—"I am of Paul" and "I am of Apollos" (3:4). Noticeably, Paul ties together the topics of σοφία and factionalism directly via the common term *human*: just as their *wisdom* is "human" (1:25; 2:5, 13), so also is their *partisan attitude* ("do you not walk in accord with humanity?").

Rivalry and Strife Again

Winter here seeks to explain the connection between σοφία and rivalry in the letter's background. Extending his thesis about the background of 1:17b–2:16,

---

5. As James M. M. Francis correctly notes, νήπιος here is wholly negative, not a status defined by partial progress: "'As Babes in Christ': Some Proposals regarding 1 Corinthians 3:1–3," *JSNT* 7 (1980): 41–60.

6. Seneca, esp. *Ep.* 33.7; 94.50. Cf. Abraham J. Malherbe, *Paul and the Thessalonians: The Philosophic Tradition of Pastoral Care* (Philadelphia: Fortress, 1987), 45–46, 81–88.

7. As taken by Branick, "Source and Redaction Analysis."

Winter locates the language of 3:3 against the backdrop of the sophistic tradition. According to Winter, the terms *student* (μαθητής) and *emulator* (or *follower*, ζηλωτής) occur abundantly in Greek sources beginning "in the first century A.D. with the rise of the Second Sophistic." Crucially, Winter does not say how many of these occurrences "in the first century" actually refer to students/followers *of sophists*.[8] It hardly bears mentioning that the student of a philosopher would also be called a μαθητής, generic as this designation was.[9] Ζηλωτής is a more exceptional term. Paul refers to the Corinthians' partisanship here with one of the term's cognates, that is, ζῆλος. Significantly, Winter adduces only one text that uses the term ζηλωτής in reference to the student of a sophist.[10] He cites Dio Chrysostom (*Or.* 55.1–5) as another example (in reference, as he says, to the "sophists"), though in fact this passage clearly concerns the identity of Socrates as a philosopher, as he is called here explicitly (φιλόσοφος in 55.6) and as is indicated by the analogy to philosophical succession in the context, where several philosophers are named explicitly (and note τῶν σοφῶν of philosophers in 55.1!). Otherwise, Winter is able to locate three examples that attest to conflict between sophists or their students,[11] although the terms ζῆλος and ἔρις do not occur.[12]

By contrast, a preliminary search reveals that ζηλωτής was a remarkably common designation for students of the philosophers. Diogenes Laertius speaks of ζηλωταί of Stilpo (*Vit. phil.* 2.113), Lacydes (*Vit. phil.* 4.59), Parmenides (*Vit. phil.* 8.55), Pyrrho (*Vit. phil.* 9.64), and the Pythagoreans (*Vit. phil.* 9.38). Epictetus encouraged his students to become ζηλωταί of Socrates (*Diatr.* 3.7.34) and in one place defines a philosopher as a "ζηλωτής of the truth" (*Diatr.* 3.24.40). Josephus recalls how he submitted himself to the way of life of each of the three major Jewish "philosophical sects" (*J.W.* 2.119; *Ant.* 18.11) and notes that he became a ζηλωτής of his Essene teacher, whom

---

8. Winter, *After Paul Left Corinth*, 32.
9. E.g., Diogenes Laertius, *Vit. phil.* 10.2, 22; referring to a student of Epicurus.
10. Dio Chrysostom, *Or.* 8.9. See Winter, *After Paul Left Corinth*, 32–40; Winter, *Philo and Paul among the Sophists*, 125–27, 172–78.
11. Students fighting with one another (Dio, *Or.* 8.9); a rivalry between a sophist in Ephesus and a sophist in Smyrna (Philostratus, *Vit. soph.* 490–491); a verbal attack on a sophist by students of another sophist (Philostratus, *Vit. soph.* 208).
12. Winter, *After Paul Left Corinth*, 36–38. Winter appeals here (p. 38) in general terms to a chapter in Bowersock that treats "professional quarrels," though offering examples only from Philostratus in the second century, when the Second Sophistic was well underway. See also Winter, *Philo and Paul among the Sophists*, 125, 133, 136–37. Winter's examples from Philo (*Philo and Paul among the Sophists*, 90) actually concern "striving" in opposing arguments about philosophical doctrines, where "sophist" seems to be a pejorative term for petty intellectuals, rather than orators per se.

he describes as a philosopher (*Vit.* 1.10–12).¹³ The term ζηλωτής could also be used in reference to a philosophical "rival" (Lucian, *Peregr.* 15). Relatedly, we find instances where "strife" (ἔρις) arises over philosophy (Lucian, *Symp.* 1)—this being the coordinate term used in 3:3.

Apart from the terminology, and of equal note, Luke Timothy Johnson has investigated the "conventional rhetoric of slander" in the Hellenistic world and catalogs several dozen examples from Dio Chrysostom, Epictetus, Aelius Aristides, Lucian, Plutarch, and Philostratus that describe "rivalry" between rhetoricians and philosophers and between members of opposing philosophical schools; but he includes no examples of rivalry between *sophists*.¹⁴ While Winter has pointed to at least three examples of sophist-vs.-sophist rivalry (noted above), the content of Johnson's catalog no doubt reflects the more prevalent tendencies of the polemical climate, the tumultousness of which is attributable largely to the nature of philosophical schools as sectarian and philosophical identity as being inherently a matter of personal allegiance (thus the prevalence of ζηλωτής). We shall discuss the dynamics of philosophical allegiance further in chapter 10.

Paul's double reference in vv. 3, 4 to the "human" behavior of the Corinthians undoubtedly characterizes them as acting, per Winter's suggestion, in a "secular" way.¹⁵ This characterization, however, almost surely includes a disparagement of their self-assessment at an *anthropological* level. Specifically, it attacks their elevated estimation of themselves as "wise," "perfect," and "spiritual" in a kind of intellectual, religious, and, obviously, spiritual sense (1:17–2:16). That Paul indeed implies more here than merely an acceptance of ordinary cultural practices is suggested by the more conspicuous wording of v. 4: it is not now "are you not *acting* like ἄνθρωποί?" Rather, it is "*are you* not ἄνθρωποί?"¹⁶

Paul and Apollos as Coworkers

While thematically continuous with what precedes, 3:5–10b constitutes a new subsection, in which Paul discusses his and Apollos's roles as ministers

---

13. Other references to ζηλωταί of philosophers include Lucian, *Herm.* 14.7; *Dem.* 48.6.

14. Luke Timothy Johnson, "The New Testament's Anti-Jewish Slander and the Conventions of Ancient Polemic," *JBL* 108 (1989): 419–41, esp. 430–34.

15. Winter, *After Paul Left Corinth*, 40. The expression κατὰ ἄνθρωπον περιπατεῖτε occurs only here in Paul's letters; the wording evokes the contrast of chapters 1–2 between "God" and "humanity."

16. The expression is odd enough to have given rise to the variant reading καὶ κατὰ ἄνθρωπον περιπατεῖτε.

to the Corinthian community. Paul's intentions here are widely debated. If an Apollos party—and thus indirectly Apollos himself—constitutes the chief opposition to Paul, then this section could be read as an apology calculated to put Apollos in his place and to restore Paul to his rightful place of higher authority.[17]

At the opening of 3:5, two rhetorical questions imply Corinthian misapprehension of the persons of Paul and Apollos ("What *then* [οὖν] are we, i.e., if we are not what you had thought?"). Two features in context reveal that Paul's concern is not how the Corinthians have assessed his or Apollos's *abilities*, but how they understand their *roles*. (1) Paul asks "what" (τί) they are; and (2) he answers in substantive terms (they are διάκονοι, "servants").

The shape of this answer calls into question at the outset any suspicion that Paul's primary intention is to set himself *above* Apollos. Paul's answer defines their roles in terms of which he will depict himself and Apollos throughout vv. 6–10: he will speak of the two of them as coworkers, just as he describes them now as "servants."[18] This characterization at the same time does nothing to support the view that Paul—this "servant"—intends to bolster his apostolic *authority* against the threat of his counterpart.

The remainder of the paragraph lays out a series of weak antitheses, which consistently separate not Paul and Apollos, but (a) Paul-with-Apollos on the one hand and (b) God on the other. The initial individuation of Paul and Apollos in v. 5d, as καί shows, highlights not their differences ("*but* each . . .") but the fact that God has given an assignment to both in common ("servants . . . *and* [καί] to each"). Next, vv. 6, 7 share an almost identical structure. While Paul "plants" and Apollos "waters," these descriptions juxtapose each other asyndetically and stand together against a counterpoint (δέ) that emphasizes *God's* role as distinct from the role that they themselves have in common: God "causes the growth."

	Point	Counterpoint
v. 6	ἐγὼ ἐφύτευσα, Ἀπολλῶς ἐπότισεν	ἀλλὰ ὁ θεὸς ηὔξανεν
v. 7	οὔτε ὁ φυτεύων ἐστίν τι οὔτε ὁ ποτίζων	ἀλλ' ὁ αὐξάνων θεός

Paul's thematic focus in v. 7 on "the one who causes the growth" is reinforced by the over-specifying addition θεός, which is unnecessary for clarity

---

17. Smit, "What Is Apollos?"
18. Benjamin Fiore thinks that Apollos's "subordination to Paul is clearly stressed" in the laborer's analogy. Fiore, "'Covert Allusion' in 1 Cor 1–4," *CBQ* 47 (1985): 100.

1 Corinthians 3:1–4:5: The Apostles and the σοφία of God

and is delayed, against the pattern of v. 6, until the end of the clause, thus making the constituent "God" more emphatic in the contrast.

Verse 8 again coordinates "the one planting and the one watering" but, different from v. 5d (καί), now adds a qualification (δέ) that serves to distinguish the two men: "each [ἕκαστος] will receive his own reward according to his work." That the word *reward* (μισθός) alludes to Apollos's practice of taking pay for his ministry is wholly speculative.[19] Nor need one presume that Apollos will receive (or is in danger of receiving) a lesser reward. Rather, the sentence in v. 8 is, both in thought and in structure, like Paul's statements in 12:12, 20 about unity and diversity in the body: "the body is one and has many members, *but* [δέ] all the members of the body ... are one body" (v. 12), and "there are many members *but* [δέ] one body" (v. 20). In the same way, Paul and Apollos are one, but (δέ) they play complementary roles. Moreover, Paul's greater emphasis in 3:8 cannot be one of distinction, for γάρ prohibits this in v. 9. Γάρ here grounds Paul's comment about his and Apollos's work and their respective rewards with the assertion that Paul and Apollos are God's "*coworkers*" (συνεργοί) ("*for* we are coworkers"). It is they as coworkers (no distinction here) who have cultivated the "field," who have built the "edifice," that is, the Corinthian church.

Likewise, the view that the purpose of this section is "to determine the correct order between [Paul and Apollos] on the basis of the status each of them is credited with" seems doubtful in light of Paul's initial handling of the divisions in 1:13–17.[20] An intent to assert a proper *ranking* here would be, at the very least, inconsistent with the approach taken in 1:13–17, where Paul's first and only counter was to target those who claimed allegiance to *him*.

In this light, we may conclude that 3:5–9 emphasizes two complementary points. (1) Paul and Apollos work together as *one* (ἕν), and (2) the relative value (τι) of Paul or Apollos—either of them—is slight, for it is God who brings about the effect. This meaning is transparent from the sentence structure and sequence of thought, and one must presume some profound subtlety of meaning to construe Paul's intentions otherwise.[21] Yet, such subtlety is the opposite of what one expects from Paul in such circumstances. Paul was hardly shy of confrontation (Gal 1:6–7), and he was not unwilling to issue harsh indictments against individuals when he found them blame-

---

19. A view taken by Chow (*Patronage and Power*, 107–10).

20. Smit, "Epideictic Rhetoric," 194.

21. Bitner (*Paul's Political Strategy*, 202) sees 3:5–4:5 as a response to criticisms of Paul; Paul is concerned here with "proper evaluation of his authoritative ministry" (245).

worthy (e.g., the adulterous man in 5:1–11). In the present situation he cannot have believed that the most effective way to remove the threat of Apollos and restore the allegiance of an opposing Apollos party was to hide subtle criticism beneath none too subtle praise.

Rather, vv. 5–10b make more sense if Paul's intentions are not so much apologetic as hortatory. Margaret Mitchell's argument that 1 Corinthians is a "deliberative" letter designed to advocate concord as a solution to factionalism has been widely accepted as more or less correct.[22] Mitchell shows extensively that a key convention in deliberative argumentation was appeal to "examples" (*exempla*, παραδείγματα) for imitation,[23] a feature that we encounter frequently in 1 Corinthians. Appeals to Paul's positive example are found in 4:16–17; 7:7, 8; 8:13; 9:1–27; 10:33–11:1; 13:11; and 14:18–19; appeal to the example of Timothy, in 4:17. Twice Paul directly asks his audience to imitate him (1 Cor 4:16–17; 11:1). He also appeals to external examples that model desired behavior (9:7; 10:1–13; 13:4–7). If therefore Paul's chief rhetorical purpose in 1 Corinthians is to reestablish concord in the church, 3:5–10b offers another obvious *exemplum* in service of this purpose: having appealed to the church to be "of the same mind" (1:10; cf. "one body," 12:12–26), he now offers the example of himself and Apollos, who "are one" (3:8).

3:10c–17

The Shift to an Indefinite Referent

An abrupt change between vv. 9b and c from an agricultural metaphor ("God's field") to a building metaphor ("God's edifice") provides a new thematic point of departure, from which Paul begins to develop a more extended building analogy. Stoic resonances return as Paul describes himself using the typical description of the philosopher as "wise architect" (σοφὸς ἀρχιτέκτων)—so called because the philosopher laid down the "standard" by which to measure good and bad.[24] While vv. 10a, b seem merely to reiterate the point of vv. 6–9 in the form of the new metaphor ("I laid the foundation,

---

22. Mitchell, *Paul and the Rhetoric of Reconciliation*. I have encountered serious criticism only in R. Dean Anderson, *Ancient Rhetorical Theory and Paul*, 254–65.

23. Mitchell, *Paul and the Rhetoric of Reconciliation*, 39–60.

24. Aristotle gives this as the reason for the title (*Eth. nic.* 1152b; cf. *Pol.* 1260a: "rational principle is master-craftsman," ὁ δέ λόγος ἀρχιτέκτων). Seneca states without elaboration that "the wise man is an architect [ille prudens atque artifex]" (*Ep.* 31.5). The correlation

but another one builds"), it is not just the metaphor that changes. Now the name of Apollos disappears and Paul speaks indefinitely of "each person" (ἕκαστος, vv. 10, 13), "no one" (οὐδείς, v. 11), or "anyone" (τις, vv. 12, 14, 15, 17).

While it might seem plausible on the face of it that the indefinite references point to Apollos,[25] the switch away from his name is surely significant.[26] The change can hardly be explained as a "covert allusion" to Apollos,[27] for Paul has already discussed him openly, and in positive terms. Ker's suggestion that τις cannot refer to the Corinthians since "the Corinthians can hardly be both the building and the builders" misses even more so the fact Apollos cannot be both "Paul's coworker," responsible for producing "God's building" (v. 9), and someone who is laying a "different foundation" and "destroying" God's temple (vv. 11, 17).[28] The most convincing solution to the dilemma is that the indefinite references refer specifically to the σοφοί group.[29] Paul and Apollos are God's coworkers; the Corinthian church is the edifice that Paul and Apollos have built; the σοφοί now build on that foundation, and their work is not "up to code." God's coworkers have departed the city, and a new wisdom threatens to destroy these ministers' building, or as Paul will shortly call it, God's "temple" (3:17).

To see Apollos as the referent one must look past not only the positive portrait Paul paints of the former's role in producing (both watering and building) the Corinthian church but also the fact that Paul has just, for a second time, censured for factional behavior the Corinthians themselves (1:12; 3:3–5). This factionalism is self-evidently rooted in a wisdom (read: "other foundation") that the *Corinthians* have espoused. Evoking this wisdom indirectly, Paul's reference here to the foundation "which is Jesus Christ" (3:11) surely alludes to the wisdom of God that is earlier called "Christ crucified" (1:23; 2:2). In sum, if the Corinthians are *known* to have espoused this human wisdom, and Paul has *openly* censured them for "dividing Christ" (1:13), it seems unwarranted to prefer the hypothesis that "someone" refers instead

---

between God and reason means that the wise man is "architect" in the same way that God is; cf. Philo, *Opif.* 1.24; *Mut.* 1.30.

25. So Wire, *Corinthian Women Prophets*, 42.
26. A point noted long ago by Weiss, *Der erste Korintherbrief*, 88, 104.
27. As Smit ("Epideictic Rhetoric," 198–99) takes it.
28. Ker, "Paul and Apollos," 89.
29. So also Munck, *Paul and the Salvation*, 67–68. Inkelaar (*Conflict over Wisdom*, 292; cf. 304) says these are "appointed or self-appointed leaders in Corinth"; Bitner (*Paul's Political Strategy*, 266–70) thinks that "anyone" may refer to one specific person—likely a partisan of Apollos, possibly Crispus specifically.

to the one whom Paul has just described as his coworker who with him built the "edifice" of the church.

It is not only the change from *Apollos* to *someone* that indicates a change in reference, but also the sequence of the historical narrative that Paul retraces. The Corinthians "believed" through Paul and Apollos, and Apollos "watered," just as Paul "planted" and "laid" the foundation (vv. 5–6). Paul expresses all of this using the aorist tense. But with the change to "someone" in v. 12, Paul now expresses the subject's activity in the *present*: "another person *builds* upon it [ἐποικοδομεῖ]." Consistent with this, Paul indicates in v. 18 that this someone is still "among" them—and a person whom Paul identifies as a σοφός.

Verses 13–17, then, describe the threat of judgment that hangs over those Corinthians whose incompetent (as it were) architectural design after the pattern of human wisdom jeopardizes the stability of the structure first laid on the firm foundation of Jesus Christ by Paul *and* Apollos. As to the finished construction, "fire" will test its quality (v. 15). As Paul works out the metaphor, it proves to be consistent with his earlier remarks about the spiritual status of the Corinthians. He could not speak to them "*as*" (ὡς) to "spiritual people" (3:1), although perchance they still remain Christ people. Now, as fire tests their work,[30] even if it consumes the building they have constructed and they lose their reward,[31] still they will be "saved" (σωθήσεται).

The Church as Temple

Verse 16 contains the first of ten occurrences in 1 Corinthians of the expression "do you not know [οὐκ οἴδατε ὅτι]." This formula occurs outside of 1 Corinthians only once in Paul's letters (Rom 6:16). In view of the Corinthians' pretensions of "wisdom" and, later, "knowledge" (8:1), this expression is evidently sarcastic and devised specifically for this audience. Interestingly, this formula introduces a comment that is found nowhere else in the NT but that, like Paul's comments in 2:10–12, intriguingly parallels ideas from Stoic physics.

Paul says: "You are a temple of God and the S/spirit of God dwells in you." Despite faint echoes here of Ezek 37:26, and a partial parallel with "house"

---

30. For fire as a means of testing quality, see Zech 13:9; 1 Pet 1:7; Wis 3:6; T. Ab. 12:14; Herm. Vis. 24.4.

31. The parallel apodoses point to a complementary parallel as regards *rewards*: "If the work of anyone ... he will *receive a reward*.... If the work of anyone ... it [that reward] will be lost."

1 Corinthians 3:1–4:5: The Apostles and the σοφία of God

language occurring in the DSS,[32] Paul's language brings together three elements that are not found together in these or any other Jewish text: (1) God's presence among his people (2) as if in a house/temple, where (3) God's presence takes the form of the Spirit. Paul's remark, moreover, departs from the language of the Jewish texts precisely where it overlaps with Stoicism. As noted in chapter 5, for the Stoics not only nature but also each human being is a household or temple *filled with a "holy spirit"* (*sacer spiritus*). As Seneca said: "God is near you, he is with you, he is within you."[33] Since Stoicism was in this respect pan(en)theistic, each and every person had divinity within as a *property* of their very humanity.[34] In this connection, Paul's sarcasm in v. 16 establishes a double entendre in which he affirms the indwelling presence of the S/spirit in believers by alluding *subversively* to the Stoic doctrine of the universal Spirit. For Paul, it is neither the cosmos nor the individual but, as the plural references show, the believing *community* that constitutes God's temple: "*You all are* [ἐστε] a temple of God," and God's Spirit "dwells in *you all* [ἐν ὑμῖν]."

A clear picture has now emerged from this portion of Paul's argument. The Corinthian σοφοί build on the foundation laid by Paul and Apollos with a different σοφία, and in so doing *they*, and not Paul's coworker Apollos, destroy God's temple/community.

3:18–23

Linking 3:10c–17 and 3:18–23

In what some see as a sudden switch, Paul is back to the topic of wisdom in 3:18–23. The apparent parenthesis in 3:1–17 between the "wisdom" sections of 1:18–2:16 and 3:18–23 has remained a general source of perplexity, and no consensus has been reached as to the relationship between these sections. Kuck suggested that the impasse is due to an inordinate focus on "the question of the background of the Corinthian theology in the history of religions, a question

---

32. The community as a "house" of God's dwelling: 1QS VIII, 5; XI, 7–8; 1QH XIV, 15; XVI, 6; cf. 1QS XI, 8.

33. Seneca, *Ep.* 41.1. See also citations on the πνεῦμα in nature discussed in chapter 5.

34. Marcus Aurelius frequently refers to the divine "genius" (*Med.* 3.12; 8.45), the divine "genius within" (δαίμων ἔνδον) (*Med.* 2.13; 2.17; 3.16; 5.10), or the "God within you" (ὁ ἐν σοὶ θεός) (*Med.* 3.5). Seneca says that the human is a "part of God," and we are his "members" (*Ep.* 92.30). Cf. Epictetus, *Diatr.* 1.14.6–17; 2.8.9–29.

that has found chapters 1–2 much more fertile ground than chapters 3–4."[35] For Kuck, "the rhetorical structure of 1:10–4:21 clearly shows that Paul's main concern is the factional strife and that the discussion of the false valuation of wisdom is complementary."[36] Branick sees so sharp a division between these sections that he determines 1:18–3:23 to be a pre-Pauline homily into which Paul has inserted 3:1–17 (and 2:1–5) and reapplied it to the Corinthian church.

The transition into 3:18–23, however, is only difficult when we insist upon reading 3:10d–17 in reference to Apollos or Cephas or "party leaders." At the widest level of application, Paul's censure in 3:10d–17 would of course apply to division universally, and thus to any in the church or any aspiring leader. Yet, the chief targets are those who consider themselves to be "wise." This is why the references in vv. 11–17 to "someone" are substituted, in v. 18, with σοφός. Reinforcing the connection between the two terms is the parallel wording in vv. 17, 18, "if *anyone* . . ." (v. 17), and now, "if anyone [τις] thinks he is a *wise man* [σοφός]" (v. 18).

It remains clear here that the σοφός cannot be Apollos. In 3:18 we find the first of three occurrences in the letter of the formula "if anyone [τις] thinks that he. . . ." In all cases it is evident that Paul attributes to the subject some quality that the Corinthians have claimed for themselves: "If anyone thinks he *knows* [ἐγνωκέναι] something" (8:2), and "If anyone thinks he is *spiritual* [πνευματικός]" (14:37).[37] In 6:5 Paul's leading (οὐκ) rhetorical question—"Is there not a *wise man* [σοφός] among you . . . ?"—provides firm evidence of this self-attribution among the Corinthians. In 3:18 Paul affords us with added certainty that he does not indicate Apollos: he refers to the "wise man *among you*" (ἐν ὑμῖν). Apollos is no longer among them (16:12).

Read within the train of thought, 3:18–23 must be seen as specifying the *cause* of the community's destruction (v. 16) and the grounds on which the perpetrator(s) of vv. 11–17 will be judged. It is the σοφός who will be judged because his wisdom destroys the church. Ironically, this makes him a "fool." In this way wisdom is not just responsible for the church's divisions indirectly, that is, because the Corinthians see a Paul or an Apollos as wise; rather, the church deteriorates from within because of their own professed wisdom, which consists in an ideology of competition and distinctions of status, through which a separation emerges between the wise and their alleged spiritual inferiors.

---

35. Kuck, *Judgment and Community Conflict*, 153.
36. Kuck, *Judgment and Community Conflict*, 154.
37. "We know that we all have knowledge [γνῶσιν]" in 8:1 is almost universally taken as a Corinthian slogan. See the tabulation of commentators' views in Brookins, *Corinthian Wisdom*, 92. On *spiritual*, see the discussion in chapters 5 and 9 in the present volume.

1 Corinthians 3:1–4:5: The Apostles and the σοφία of God

Paul reiterates again the invertedness of God's definition of wisdom. The world's status-oriented wisdom is foolishness to God. This is because, as Paul has repeatedly said, God's wisdom is defined by status denial, as embodied by Christ crucified.

Allusive Adaptation of Wisdom Language

Just where Paul reprises the language of σοφία, we find again that he adapts the theme specifically for this church and its situation.

(1) Verse 18 exudes echoes of the Greco-Roman philosophical tradition. (a) Paul not only reintroduces the figure of the "wise man" (σοφός), but with the expression "wise man *in this age*" (ἐν τῷ αἰῶνι τούτῳ), (b) he quite possibly alludes to the Stoic idea that the wise man was historically rare. Seneca remarked that a wise man comes onto the scene very rarely and "after great spaces of ages [magnisque aetatium intervallis unum]" (*Const.* 7.1), or perhaps, like the phoenix, only once every five hundred years (*Ep.* 42.1). Thus, Paul wryly suggests, to be "a wise man in this age" would be an exceptional achievement indeed. (c) As v. 18 concludes, Paul speaks in the persona of Socrates, who had memorably said that the beginning of wisdom was the realization of one's own ignorance (Plato, *Rep.* 354c; *Charm.* 175a–b; *Lys.* 222d–e; *Prot.* 361a–b; Epictetus, *Ench.* 46.2). Speaking as Socrates, Paul advises that one "must become a fool in order to become wise."

(2) The scripture citations in vv. 19, 20 provide further evidence that σοφός was a definite Corinthian self-ascription. In v. 19 Paul cites LXX Job 5:13 but makes what appears to be an original adaptation by adding the article τούς. Thus, Paul refers not to "wise people" but "*the* wise." If this is indeed a Pauline adaptation, Christopher Stanley proposes, Paul may have introduced it to link σοφός here with its articular usage both in 1:27 and in the next verse, 3:20.[38] At 3:20 the evidence is again suggestive. The citation is from LXX Ps 93:11, though as Stanley argues, Paul again introduces an original adaptation. Now Paul substitutes in place of the generic τῶν ἀνθρώπων words that are reflected in no extant tradition of the source text: τῶν σοφῶν.[39] In this way the citations in vv. 19 and 20 both introduce original adaptations that create articular references to "the wise man," functioning as a definite substantive.[40]

---

38. Christopher D. Stanley, *Paul and the Language of Scripture: Citation Technique in the Pauline Epistles and Contemporary Literature* (Cambridge: Cambridge University Press, 1992), 192.

39. Stanley, *Paul and the Language of Scripture*, 194–95; Stanley calls this a Pauline adaptation "beyond reasonable doubt."

40. See also 1:19.

If the thesis we have been pursuing is correct, this adaptation offers further confirmation that some of the Corinthians did not just consider themselves "wise" in a generic sense but that they conceived of themselves on analogy with the concept of "the wise man" in the technical philosophical sense.

Boasting in Self

Paul has worked his way to a conclusion, and it is a major one: ὥστε μηδεὶς καυχάσθω ἐν ἀνθρώποις (3:21). This conclusion manifestly follows from the preceding "wisdom" sections. Interpreters, however, universally see in Paul's conclusion a link between the Corinthians' infatuation with wisdom and their "boasting in *apostles*."[41] For proponents of the rhetorical thesis, this boasting relates to the apostles' respective rhetorical abilities or sophistic status.

It would be foolish to quickly dismiss a consensus. What is difficult to understand on this interpretation, however, is the relationship between (a) the Corinthians' *self*-understanding as wise people and (b) their boasting in *apostles*; difficult also is the linking of these ideas with the inferential conjunction ὥστε. It is not sufficient to advocate, merely as a hypothesis, that the Corinthians viewed their own status as being enhanced by their connection with renowned leaders. One must be able to support this connection of ideas exegetically.

There arises at this point another instance where the reconstruction appears to have overwritten the text. Margaret Mitchell poses in summary terms that Paul here *combines* boasting in leaders and boasting in gifts.[42] While this combination undoubtedly overcomes the dilemma, Mitchell's suggestion cannot be sustained exegetically. Certainly, it is possible that Paul means, "do not boast in *your leaders/apostles*, for *they* belong to you [all things are yours] rather than you to them [I am of Paul, etc.]." Were we to assume, however, that "all things" refers, more broadly, or perhaps also, to spiritual gifts, this would actually create a different connection of ideas. Paul links μηδεὶς καυχάσθω ἐν ἀνθρώποις with what follows by means of γάρ. As such, "let not anyone boast in humans" is *explained* by "all things are yours." This connection of propositions forces a decision between the more restrictive (humans/apostles) and the more expansive construal of "all things" (humans/apostles *and* spiritual gifts): if "all things are yours" grounds

---

41. Pogoloff, *Logos and Sophia*, 213; note also Litfin, *St. Paul's Theology of Proclamation*, 226; Winter, *Philo and Paul among the Sophists*, 195.

42. Mitchell, *Paul and the Rhetoric of Reconciliation*, 94.

1 Corinthians 3:1–4:5: The Apostles and the σοφία of God

the prohibition not to boast *and* includes spiritual gifts, then why does the prohibition mention only boasting in "human leaders" (ἐν ἀνθρώποις); and if Paul specifically prohibits boasting in "human leaders," how does his prohibition of boasting remain *grounded* (γάρ) by an assertion that "all spiritual gifts" are yours? In other words, the one meaning and the other seem to be exclusive of each other, for the alternatives alter the referentiality of terms and therefore the sense of the propositions and their logical connection. While Mitchell's suggestion, then, offers a nice summation of a particular reading of the unit's general themes, the discourse itself cannot bear the load of this double meaning.

I suggest that v. 21 fits most coherently with what preceeds if Paul refers not to the Corinthians' boasting in *others*, but to their boasting in *self*. This reading finds support in both the features of the context and in the intertexts with which Paul here interacts.

(1) Paul's assertion in 3:21, "let not humanity boast in humans," clearly echoes 1:31, "let the one who boasts, boast in the Lord." This correspondence in turn draws an *inclusio* around 1:31–3:21. One way of reading this interplay is to see 1:31 as a command to boast exclusively in the *Lord* and 3:21 as a command not to boast in *human leaders*. Were it not for the deeply entrenched popularity of this reading, however, it would be difficult to come to this reading given the flow of 1:17–3:20. In the first place, the putative leaders are, according to this theory, Paul, Apollos, and Cephas, as mentioned in 3:22. That Paul would use the word *human* now in reference to the apostles—who according to Paul do *not* preach "human" wisdom—after his lengthy discussion framed precisely around the antithesis between Christ's wisdom and "human" wisdom seems doubtful. Likewise, if we restrict the contrast to one between God and human *leaders*, this would be to depart from the sweeping apocalyptic contrast that these chapters have consistently drawn: between God and humans at large. In short, the common interpretation introduces a departure and local anomaly in Paul's use of a term (ἄνθρωπος) that has figured in a central and fairly specialized way in these chapters.

Among English translations, the better reading may actually be reflected in the KJV: "let no man glory in men." By rendering μηδείς as "man," one may suspect that the translators intend to establish μηδείς as in some way co-referential with, or hyponymic of, ἀνθρώποις. Whether this is in fact the translators' intention, this interpretation of the text seems to be quite correct. That is, the subject ("no one") is now included as a member of the class "men" (or "humans"). The resulting sense is that Paul conceptualizes the boasting subject/person *qualitatively* as a representative of the genus "humanity." Thus the prohibition addresses not human boasting in *others*, but human boasting in self *as* human, that is, in *one's own* nature, strength, abilities, or qualifications.

(2) Not only is this reading consistent with chapters 1–2 as a rebuke of self-proclaimed "wise" and "spiritual" church members. It is easy to overlook just how clearly this interpretation is indicated by the pre-text alluded to in 1:31, namely, Jer 9:23. As was discussed in chapter 3, Jer 9:23 draws a contrast between boasting *as* a human, in one's own wisdom, strength, and weal, on the one hand, and boasting in the knowledge of God, on the other. The boaster in Jeremiah is not boasting in *other* human beings. The boaster is boasting in himself or herself *as* human.[43]

(3) The linking of v. 21a with vv. 21b–23 via γάρ further confirms our reading. The latter portion, as a unit, furnishes the syntactical grounds for the prohibition on boasting: no one can boast, as a human, *for* (γάρ) while they "have all things" (πάντα ὑμῶν ἐστιν), God "has" them (ὑμεῖς δὲ Χριστοῦ, Χριστὸς δὲ θεοῦ). In short, "all things are yours, to be sure, . . . *but* [δέ] you are *Christ's* and Christ is *God's*." In this respect 3:21–23 quite fully parallels 1:29–31. In both texts Paul prohibits boasting, while also stating similar grounds for this prohibition: all things come ultimately from God (ἐξ αὐτοῦ . . . ὑμεῖς ἐστε ἐν Χριστῷ Ἰησοῦ, ὃς ἐγενήθη σοφία ἡμῖν ἀπὸ θεοῦ, 1:30).[44]

"All Things Are Yours"

Interpreters since Lightfoot and Weiss have noted that πάντα ὑμῶν ἐστιν (v. 21b) echoes a Stoic claim about the wise man: πάντα σοφῶν ἐστιν.[45] The Stoic assertion represents a particular iteration of a widely used philosophical commonplace. From as far back as Pythagoras, philosophers had said that "friends hold all things in common." Some philosophers joined this maxim with the premises "the wise man is a friend of God" and "God owns all things" to get to the conclusion "all things belong to the wise man."[46]

---

43. This humanity-vs-God emphasis is not unique to Jer 9:23 but is a prevalent theme throughout the Jewish scriptures: LXX Pss 8:4; 144:3; Eccl 6:10; Ps Sol 2:28–32; 2 Macc 5:21; 9:8, 12; cf. LXX Ps 82:6–7; Sir 18:1–10; Acts 12:21–23 // Josephus, *Ant.* 9.346–50.

44. Finney (*Honour and Conflict*, 104) views 3:21–23 in terms of reward and honor: all things are "gifts of God, not attained through merit, and therefore not to be used as public claims to honour."

45. Lightfoot, *Notes on the Epistles*, 195; Weiss, *Der erste Korintherbrief*, 89–91. See also Kuck, *Judgment and Community Conflict*, 190.

46. That friends hold all things in common: Plato, *Phaedr.* 279c; Diogenes Laertius, *Vit.*

1 Corinthians 3:1–4:5: The Apostles and the σοφία of God

Despite the wide currency of such premises among philosophers, a comparison with the discourse of Stoicism merits special attention:[47]

1 Cor 3:21	πάντα ὑμῶν [σοφῶν] ἐστιν
	"all things belong to you"
SVF 3:590	πάντα σοφῶν ἐστιν
	"all things belong to wise men"

Remembering that the Corinthians claimed to be σοφοί, the parallel in 1 Cor 3:21 is shown to be exact: σοφοί + the copulative verb εἶναι (or Latin *esse*) + a Greek genitive of possession.[48] Ordinarily there would be nothing striking in a verbal parallel of just three words. The present instance, however, acquires added significance when one recognizes that the expression is not just a one-off verbal configuration but formulaic in the Stoic's description of the wise man.[49]

For the Stoics in particular, the claim that "all things belong to the wise man" was a claim, astonishingly, of his "perfection." The wise man lived in perfect conformity with the dictates of divine reason within, and so he had not one but all of the virtues.[50] A consequence of this reality was that the wise man "owned" the world—but in quite a special sense. In the first place, he alone could truly "own" anything since he alone knows "how to use" things, that is, how to use them as nature dictates. Second, since God is a friend (φίλος) of the wise man, and friends hold all things in common (κοινά), what belongs to God belongs also to the wise man.[51] Therefore, just as God is perfect, so also is the wise man.

In alluding to the Stoic claim, Paul employs the same kind of competitive appropriation of language that appeared throughout chapters 1–2, where he appropriated the Corinthian terms *wise*, *perfect*, and *spiritual*. As Lightfoot cleverly put it, "Instead of assigning all virtues to the wise, it is just to the

---

phil. 10.11 (of Pythagoras and Epicurus). We find the whole series in Diogenes Laertius, *Vit. phil.* 6.37, 72 (of Diogenes the Cynic); Crates, *Epistle 26*, 10–11; *Epistle 27*, 15–17; Diogenes, *Epistle 10*, 5–6; Philo, *Mos.* 1.156.

47. The parallels noted from the Cynic epistles (see the previous note) concern more specifically nature's provision for the necessities of survival.

48. For the equivalent Latin expression, see Cicero, *Acad.* 2.136: *omnia sapientis esse*.

49. E.g., Seneca, *Ben.* 7.2.5; 7.3.2–3; *SVF* 3:590, 597, 599; etc.

50. See *SVF* 3:295–304, 557–66.

51. On "having all things" because of correct use, see *SVF* 3:591; on friendship see *SVF* 3:351, 631. The idea is also captured by the Cynic saying in Diogenes Laertius, *Vit. phil.* 6.37.

wise that St Paul denies them."[52] That is, the self-proclaimed wise man is in fact here a "fool" (vv. 18–20) and so has not *all* virtues, but *none* of them. It is rather the one who embraces God's foolishness (God's wisdom) who "has all things."

It can hardly be accidental that in the next verse Paul joins this Stoic slogan with the language of the party slogans of 1:12 and 3:4: "All things are yours, *whether Paul or Apollos or Cephas.*" The statement in 3:22 mirrors the possessive genitive construction of 1:12 and 3:4, but noticeably, it reverses the order of the relationship: the Corinthians do not now belong to the ministers (1:12), but the ministers to the Corinthians (3:22). As such, the ministers are among the things that the Corinthians have at hand in Christ. Here a deeper function of the Paul-Apollos discourse comes into focus. Paul and Apollos do not just function as a paradigm of concord that the factious Corinthians ought to imitate. Paul's portrait of himself and Apollos as ministers to the church presents them as counter examples to the honor-seeking Corinthians and situates Paul—together with Apollos and Cephas—within a wholly different kind of hierarchy than the one that the Corinthians have constructed.

In 2:6–16 we saw that the σοφοί promoted a hierarchy that included two levels of believer. First Corinthians 1:17b–3:23, and 3:21–23 specifically, now offer evidence that their hierarchical schema may also have involved a reduction in the distance between themselves and God. Stoic physics may prove illuminating on this point. The Stoics classified things in nature in the following order: gods, humans, irrational creatures, plants. Gods and humans were rational, the other two entities irrational (Seneca, *Ep.* 113.17; 124.14; *Ben.* 2.29.3). While the Stoics regarded humanity as "second" to God from one point of view,[53] from another point of view humanity was equal, if not *superior* to God.[54] In the gods, reason is perfect by nature; humans must perfect reason in themselves, and this they can do. Understood within this framework, Paul's insistence in 1:17–3:23 on an *antithesis* between God and humanity would suggest that, from Paul's point of view, the wise Corinthians have transgressed in their estimation of human potential, putting themselves too close to the level of God.

Paul replaces this distorted hierarchy by reaffirming a God-vs-all-humanity antithesis. In what structurally mirrors the kind of natural hier-

---

52. Lightfoot, *Notes on the Epistles*, 195.
53. Humans are in a sense "second" to the gods: Seneca, *Ben.* 2.29.3; 7.2.2; *Ep.* 76.9; 92.7; 120.14.
54. Seneca, *Ep.* 53.11; 73.13; 92.28; 124.14; Cicero, *Nat. d.* 2.36, 153.

1 Corinthians 3:1–4:5: The Apostles and the σοφία of God

archy of Stoicism, Paul establishes a different hierarchy, one that reorders things according to the gospel: God, Christ, the church, apostles. (1) By setting God at the top, Paul establishes God unequivocally as preeminent, above humanity and those who pretend to be wise, spiritual, and perfect. (2) At the same time, Paul reaffirms the counterintuitive, inverted ordering that characterizes the wisdom of God: it is the *lowly* whom God honors—like God's ministers who preach and embody Christ crucified (2:1–5). This is paradoxically spoken. The apostles *are* not less than others in the church, but *make themselves* less for the sake of the church, after the way of Christ.

Following the names *Paul, Apollos*, and *Cephas*, Paul adds *the world, life, death, things present*, and *things to come*. Fee remarks that one is "not quite prepared for the sudden expansion of the list" and poses that the factions around the three named figures "of course is the point of everything."[55] On the contrary, the list becomes comprehensible when one recognizes that 1:17b–3:23 focuses not directly on the factions, but on their cause: the Corinthians' σοφία and self-boasting due to spiritual status ("humans" in 3:21 referring qualitatively to what they themselves are). The expanded list summarizes what "all things" includes. (1) While inclusion of the "world" (κόσμος) at first seems puzzling, the reference is comprehensible as a double reference that amalgamates (a) the Stoic notion that the wise man "has all things" and (b) the traditional Jewish conception of the descendants of Abraham as "heirs of the world" (Rom 4:13; cf. 8:32).[56] The two pairs that conclude the list, (2) "life and death" and (3) "things present and things to come," represent in a sense "the whole of existence" in Christ, but articulated it seems to accord with a more balanced *eschatological* framework. The effect is to put a check on the Corinthians' conceited conception of their redemptive state. If they now have "life" in Christ, life must be complemented by "death." This is death not just in the literal sense that one day their corruptible existence will come to an end, but even more so, in the sense that they must "live," that is, "die" (Rom 6:2–11; Gal 2:19–20), according to the wisdom of the cross and Christ crucified. As regards the *now-then* pair, although they are already "being saved" (τοῖς σῳζομένοις, 1:18), still the culmination of salvation lies in the future.[57] All of this is theirs. But it is not of themselves. For they are God's.

---

55. Fee, *First Epistle to the Corinthians*, 154; 2nd ed., 166.
56. The idea that God created the world for Israel is widely attested in Second Temple literature, e.g., Sir 44:21; 4 Ezra 6:55–59; 7:10–11; 1 En. 5:7; 2 Bar. 14:13; Jub. 22:14; T. Mos. 1:12; Sib. or. 3:767–769.
57. We will encounter the same emphasis in 4:8.

4:1–5

The puzzle of the background continues. First Corinthians 4:1–5 permits two very different readings. (1) Assuming a rivalry between Paul and Apollos, a majority of interpreters read these verses as if the Corinthians have "evaluated" Paul and Apollos (many would add, according to the criterion of eloquence) and Paul here expresses indifference to their judgment, confident that the only judgment that matters is that which comes from God.[58] On this interpretation, the paragraph serves as an "apology" in which Paul defends his value as a minister or defends his apostolic authority.[59] While this reading may appear "plain" from one point of view, in fact this reading commends itself only when one brings prior assumptions to the text. That the Corinthians have (a) *already* "evaluated" Paul and (b) *compared* him with Apollos, with the result that (c) he has *lost* prestige or authority in the eyes of an influential faction within the church, owes a great deal to speculation. (2) A different reading is not only possible but in my view offers a more coherent reading of the paragraph in 4:1–5.

Counterexamples to Personal Comparison

Several features of 1 Cor 1–3 present obstacles to the apologetic reading of 4:1–5. First, if Paul's intention is to defend himself against an Apollos faction (1:12) and thereby to restore his place of preeminence as the church's founder and proper authority, this approach would not be consistent with the approach he took when first mentioning the factions in 1:10–17. There he did nothing to consolidate support but rather did the opposite: he condemned his own supporters (1:13–16). Second, it seems questionable that if Paul is dealing with a loss of authority by dint of some negative evaluation, he can have believed that he was in a position to ask his judges to imitate him (as he will do explicitly in 4:16 and 11:1).[60] Third, Paul makes no reference here to any special (apostolic) privilege but assigns the same role, and titles, to Apollos as he assigns to himself: both (ἡμᾶς) are "servants of Christ and stewards of the mysteries of God" (ὑπηρέτας

---

58. E.g., Kuck, *Judgment and Community Conflict*, 200; Barnett, *Corinthian Question*, 71–75.
59. According to Dahl, "the entire section [chs. 1–4] contains an apology for Paul" and his apostolic authority. Dahl, "Paul and the Church at Corinth according to 1 Corinthians 1:10–4:21," in *Studies in Paul: Theology for the Early Christian Mission*, 40–61 (Minneapolis: Augsburg, 1977), 55. In a final footnote, Dahl says that this is evident especially in 4:2–5 and 18–21 (61n50). Marshall (*Enmity in Corinth*, 217) also reads 4:1–5 in this way, citing Dahl.
60. A point raised by Mitchell, *Paul and the Rhetoric of Reconciliation*, 55n156.

1 Corinthians 3:1–4:5: The Apostles and the σοφία of God

Χριστοῦ καὶ οἰκονόμους μυστηρίων θεοῦ, 4:1). As in 2:2, 7, the construct expression "mysteries of God" refers to the gospel message about Christ crucified. This was not only the message revealed to Paul but also the message that, he says, "*we* [apparently believers] speak among the perfect" (2:6). Fourth, Paul's description of himself and Apollos as "ministers" and "stewards" continues to underscore their *servile* roles, similar to διάκονοι in 3:5.

The servile connotations of Paul's self-description are confirmed by two additional points. (a) 4:1–5 is continuous with what immediately precedes and carries further several of the main themes of 2:6–3:23. At 4:1 the introductory οὕτως refers the listener back to Paul's description of himself and Apollos in v. 22 (we "are yours"); thus, οὕτως indicates "things being as they are [i.e., inasmuch as *we are yours*], let a person consider us to be ministers."[61] (b) That both ὑπηρέτης and οἰκονόμος here indicate some level of servility is generally agreed upon,[62] although the social connotations of the terms have been debated. Οἰκονόμος in particular had a wide range of meanings, which commentaries reference indiscriminately but which have more recently been distinguished and clarified by John Goodrich.[63] As Goodrich convincingly shows, Paul does not here describe himself as a *municipal* οἰκονόμος, that is, a financial city magistrate with usually high socioeconomic status. Rather, he describes himself in terms of the *domestic* οἰκονόμος, that is, a servile household figure, being normally a freedman or slave.

If Paul has any subtextual apologetic intentions here, these do not harmonize well with the rhetorical function of this section within the unfolding argument. As Mitchell observes, 4:1–5 is consistent with the "deliberative" purpose of the letter and constitutes "another instance of Paul's use of himself as an example of proper behavior."[64] Specifically, Paul does not "evaluate" (ἀνακρίνειν) other people. He deals in 4:1–5 with a comparison, then,

---

61. Οὕτως is not correlative with ὡς (4:1), as Fee thinks (*First Epistle*, 1st ed., 158). The thematic continuity suggests a syntactical connection, not asyndeton and a fresh start with a new topic. Sharing our view is Conzelmann, *1 Corinthians*, 82. The fronting of ἡμᾶς does not introduce "Paul and Apollos" as a new topic, but rather reestablishes them as the thematic point of departure, in continuity with what precedes.

62. John Byron, "Slave of Christ or Willing Servant? Paul's Self-Description in 1 Corinthians 4:1–2 and 9:16–18," *Neot* 37 (2003): 179–98; and Dale B. Martin, *Slavery as Salvation: The Metaphor of Slavery in Pauline Christianity* (New Haven: Yale University Press, 1990), 15, 34, 85; agree that this language describes lower-status individuals but disagree as to the intended social significance of it here.

63. John Goodrich, *Paul as an Administrator of God in 1 Corinthians*, SNTSMS 152 (Cambridge: Cambridge University Press, 2012), 27–102.

64. Mitchell, *Paul and the Rhetoric of Reconciliation*, 55.

not between himself and Apollos, but between the example of himself and Apollos, on the one hand, and the practices of the *Corinthians*, on the other. This kind of comparison, Mitchell reminds us, "*depends* upon Paul's assumed stature as an illustrious person worthy of comparison and emulation (along with all the apostles)."[65] In other words, Paul's whole argument depends upon the Corinthians' generally high estimation of him, alternative factions notwithstanding (1:12).

As ὧδε λοιπόν shows, 4:2 takes Paul's preceding claim about his and Apollos's common role as a point of departure for what now comes.[66] This formula introduces what appears to be a conventional maxim: as regards stewards, it is required that such a person be found "faithful" (ὧδε λοιπὸν ζητεῖται ἐν τοῖς οἰκονόμοις ἵνα πιστός τις εὑρεθῇ).[67] One could suppose that this maxim implies that the criteria that determine the steward's worth exclude the requirement that he be "wise" (cf. σοφός in 1:19, 20, 25, 26; 3:18, 19, 20; σοφία in 1:17, 19, 20, 21, 22, 24; 2:1; etc.). But the underlying point is broader.[68] Paul's fronting of the predicate nominative (πιστός) shows that he places particular emphasis on the quality of "faithfulness" in the absolute, the effect being to stress simply *fulfilling one's duty*, as opposed to doing it *so as to distinguish* oneself against others. This interpretation results in a close parallel with 2:14–16, but with antithetical application: there the "spiritual" Corinthians (πνευματικοί) are found "evaluating" (ἀνακρίνειν) others and vaunting themselves as superior. Here Paul and Apollos neither evaluate others nor compare themselves with others.

Tracing the Train of Thought

Paul formulates v. 3 in parallel terms to v. 2, thereby moving from the general axiom of v. 2 to the specific case of himself.[69] His own situation places him

---

65. Mitchell, *Paul and the Rhetoric of Reconciliation*, 220n181.
66. Here, ὧδε λοιπὸν = "in this regard, furthermore"; BDF §451.6; Conzelmann, *1 Corinthians*, 82n2; Fee, *First Epistle to the Corinthians*, 1st ed., 160; Garland, *First Corinthians*, 126.
67. The passive *it is sought* with a prepositional phrase indicating the person from whom certain responsibilities are sought ("from *x*," "from *y*") is formulaic in Latin; e.g., Quintilian, *Inst.* 2.5.1; Seneca, *Ot.* 3.5; Tacitus, *Dial. or.* 20.5; Seneca Maior, *Controv.* 2.3.7. Also suggesting a maxim is Paul's application of the principle to an indefinite "someone" (τις) rather than to himself.
68. Indeed, the question is not likely to have occurred to someone whether "wisdom" (in either a rhetorical or a philosophical sense) was an important characteristic of the "steward."
69. Note the parallel structure:

1 Corinthians 3:1–4:5: The Apostles and the σοφία of God

outside the scope of the maxim's application. Generally speaking (v. 2), it is sought that stewards be found faithful by human masters. In Paul's own case, he is not concerned with the prospect of any "human" evaluation (v. 3b). In v. 4c, *God's* evaluation (ὁ δὲ ἀνακρίνων με κύριός ἐστιν) is introduced as a conceptual complement to *human* evaluation (ὑφ' ὑμῶν ἀνακριθῶ ἢ ὑπὸ ἀνθρωπίνης ἡμέρας). Thus, Paul is concerned not to establish whether wisdom is a necessary qualification for the steward but to establish who is in position to evaluate whether the steward has been "faithful" (πιστός).

The remainder of the paragraph can be readily understood as a development of this point. Verse 3c ("I do not even evaluate myself") introduces a transition from Paul's implicit condemnation of interpersonal comparison through "evaluation" (vv. 2–3b) to the question of prerogative in evaluation (vv. 4–5). It is in v. 4a that Paul reveals the grounds for his refusal to self-evaluate: οὐδὲν γὰρ ἐμαυτῷ σύνοιδα. A crucial point is missed if we fail to account for the contribution of γάρ.[70] Since Paul has said that he does *not* evaluate himself (v. 3c), he cannot mean in v. 4a—where γάρ offers grounds for what precedes—that he is not aware of having done anything wrong, for that would necessarily imply that he has evaluated himself. Similarly, if we take v. 4a to imply that Paul recognizes *limitations* in his self-awareness, we must still take his statement to be establishing a tentative verdict of innocence that could only be the result of self-evaluation. I suggest a new interpretation of v. 4a.

Paul and Self-Evaluation

In v. 4a Paul states: οὐδὲν γὰρ ἐμαυτῷ σύνοιδα. Interpreters commonly render this as "I am not aware of anything *against myself/me*." Interpreters supply the final words ("against myself") either on the basis of the dative pronoun (ἐμαυτῷ) or on the basis of perceived sense. (1) Garland explicitly labels ἐμαυτῷ a "dative of disadvantage" ("against myself").[71] (2) Others understand the negative idea as being required by sense. Frederich Grosheide

| ὧδε λοιπὸν ζητεῖται <u>ἐν τοῖς οἰκονόμοις</u> | ἵνα πιστός τις <u>εὑρεθῇ</u> |
| ἐμοὶ δὲ εἰς ἐλάχιστόν ἐστιν | ἵνα ὑφ' ὑμῶν <u>ἀνακριθῶ</u> |

70. Fee, having decided that Paul is addressing charges that he had hidden motives, is now troubled by γάρ and unjustifiably concludes that γάρ must here be equivalent to δέ (*First Epistle to the Corinthians*, 176n482). According to Fee, Paul has renounced self-evaluation of his stewardship (v. 3c) and now effectively adds, "I do not intend to suggest that I really do have hidden agendas that have yet to be revealed" (176).

71. Garland, *1 Corinthians*, 128.

suggests that while Paul's words literally mean "I am not conscious of anything *with regard to myself,*" innocence is implied according to the rule *in dubiis pro reo* ("in doubtful cases, in favor of the defendant").[72] Robertson and Plummer take the verb + pronoun combination as an expression simply of *self-awareness*, so that the pronoun does not, itself, convey a negative idea; yet, they continue: "as conscience can condemn more surely than it can acquit, the word [σύνοιδα], when used absolutely, has more frequently a bad sense, and hence comes to mean to 'be conscious of guilt.'"[73] Still differently, Bullinger sees a negative idea as being latent within an ellipsis, and suggests that we should supply "unfaithful" (ἄπιστον) as an echo of "faithful" (πιστός) in v. 2.[74] Other commentators offer no elaboration on the syntax, although it would appear from the usual translation that they understand the expression to convey a similar negative meaning.[75]

I suggest that the negative interpretation is incorrect. In both Classical and Koine Greek, ἐμαυτῷ σύνοιδα means simply "I am self-aware," and no negative idea is either inherent in the dative pronoun or necessarily implied by the construction. The dative reflexive pronoun occurs normatively after σύνοιδα as a supplement to the prepositional prefix (συν-) to express *self-awareness*; thus, ἐμαυτῷ σύνοιδα = "I am aware."[76] The equivalent Latin expression *conscius sum* also takes a dative reflexive pronoun as a complement (i.e., *mihi conscius sum* = "I am aware"). I note the following variations of these constructions.

(1) *Σύνοιδα + dative reflexive + agreeing dative participle*. We find in Plato ἐμαυτῷ γὰρ ξυνῄδη οὐδὲν ἐπισταμένῳ, "For I was aware that I knew nothing" (Plato, *Apol.* 22d.1). Note that the added οὐδέν is not the direct object of σύνοιδα (i.e., "aware of *nothing*"), but the object of the dative participle ἐπισταμένῳ. The dative pronoun ἐμαυτῷ supplements the main verb (ξυνῄδη) and does not carry negative meaning. The speaker refers only to ignorance itself. In this construction, the participle may even indicate awareness of

---

72. Frederick Grosheide, *Commentary on the First Epistle to the Corinthians* (Grand Rapids: Eerdmans, 1953), 100–101.

73. Robertson and Plummer, *First Epistle of St. Paul to the Corinthians*, 76.

74. E. W. Bullinger, *Figures of Speech Used in the Bible* (London: Eyre & Spottiswoode, 1898; repr. Grand Rapids: Baker, 1968), 79.

75. For the translations, see the ASV, ESV, KJV, NKJV, RSV, NRSV, NAB, NASB, NIV; representative of commentators are Collins, *First Corinthians*, 173; and Friedrich Lang, *Die Briefe an die Korinther* (Göttingen: Vandenhoeck & Ruprecht, 1994), who has "keiner Schuld" (59).

76. H. W. Smyth, *Greek Grammar* (Cambridge, MA: Harvard University Press, 1920), §2108.

something positive, as in συνίσασι . . . ἐμοὶ δὲ ἀληθεύοντι, "they were aware that I was telling the truth" (Plato, *Apol.* 34b).

(2) *Σύνοιδα + dative reflexive + nominative supplementary participle.* LXX Job 27:6 is often cited as a parallel to 1 Cor 4:4. However, the construction in Job does not parallel our syntax exactly: οὐ γὰρ σύνοιδα ἐμαυτῷ ἄτοπα πράξας, "For I am not aware of having done anything out of line." As usual, ἐμαυτῷ conveys not disadvantage, but self-awareness, serving to supplement σύνοιδα. It is rather the direct object of πράξας (i.e., ἄτοπα) that indicates wrongdoing. A similar example occurs in Plato (*Apol.* 21b.4): ἐγὼ γὰρ δὴ οὔτε μέγα οὔτε σμικρὸν ξύνοιδα ἐμαυτῷ σοφὸς ὤν, "I am aware that I am wise neither very much nor even a little." Adjoined to the participle are a predicate nominative (σοφός) and two adverbial adjuncts (μέγα, σμικρόν); it is the latter additions that negatively qualify the content of the speaker's self-knowledge, not the dative pronoun or the σύνοιδα + dative reflexive construction itself.

(3) *Σύνοιδα + dative reflexive + accusative direct object.* Note the following examples from Plato: συνειδὼς ἐμαυτῷ ἀμαθίαν, "I am aware of my ignorance" (*Phaedr.* 235c.7); and μηδὲν ἑαυτῷ ἄδικον ξυνειδότι, "the man who is aware as to himself of no wrongdoing" (Plato, *Rep.* 331a.2). The second example offers a closer parallel to 1 Cor 4:4, though importantly, the notion of wrongdoing is again expressed by an explicit complement (ἄδικον) and is not inherent in the dative pronoun or implied by the verb + pronoun construction. The same construction occurs in Stobaeus with similar wording: τὸ μὴ συνειδέναι γὰρ αὐτοῦ τῷ βίῳ ἀδίκημα μηδέν (*Flor.* 3.24.7; the negative term being ἀδίκημα; here with the dative τῷ βίῳ in place of a dative pronoun). Euripides (*Orest.* 396; also cited in Plutarch, *Mor.* 476e) likewise indicates the negative content of the subject's knowledge with an explicit term (δείν', "terrible things").

(4) *Sum conscius + dative reflexive + genitive.* Similar to the Greek construction, the dative reflexive pronoun in this Latin construction complements the term *conscious (conscius)*. That of which a person is "conscious" may be added in the genitive case, as "*in huius rei conscius mihi sum,*" "I am aware of this thing/task" (Seneca, *Ep.* 71.36); or "*animi, imbecillitatis sibi conscii,*" "a spirit conscious of its own weakness" (Seneca, *Ira* 1.20.3). This self-awareness could, but need not, concern a negative object.

(5) *Conscius + dative reflexive + accusative direct object.* There is one Latin text I am aware of that at first seems to parallel the syntax of 1 Cor 4:4 exactly (Horace, *Ep.* 1.1.61). The line consists of two parallel expressions:

nil conscire sibi,	*nulla pallescere culpa*
to be aware of no (fault),	to turn pale from no fault

The implied meaning in the first half of the line appears undeniably to be "to be aware of no (fault)," and the syntax exhibits an exact Latin equivalent of the Greek text in 1 Cor 4:4a. The notion of "fault," however, appears again neither to be inherent in the dative pronoun nor implied by the construction per se; rather, it is an inference that depends upon the explicit material supplied in the synonymously parallel unit that follows. That is, the single occurrence of *nulla... culpa* ("no fault") in the second part of the line applies distributively to both *nil conscire sibi* and *pallescere*.

In sum, the dative reflexive pronoun (ἐμαυτῷ) when conjoined with σύνοιδα does not carry the force of disadvantage (and likewise for the equivalent Latin constructions), nor does the verb + pronoun construction itself imply awareness of fault or guilty conscience. The construction expresses only self-awareness. Where any notion of wrongdoing is present, some additional word usually expresses this (e.g., LXX Job 27:6; Plato, *Rep.* 331a.2), or clear parallelism signals its ellipsis (Horace, *Ep.* 1.1.61). Hence, we do not have sufficient grounds for preferring the negative meaning based on the construction. If we have correctly traced Paul's train of thought, moreover, the negative reading is not required by the context either.

The thought is naturally understood when heard in the more continuous unfolding of vv. 3c and 4a in the arrangement of the source language. The cohesive structure of the Greek reveals a certain parallelism, and within the parallelism an ellipsis in the thought:[77]

| v. 3c | οὐδὲ | ἐμαυτὸν | ἀνακρίνω |
| v. 4a | οὐδὲν γὰρ | ἐμαυτῷ σύνοιδα | [--] |

Allowing ourselves to be carried along by the parallelism, we then get the following:

| v. 3c | Nor | myself | do I evaluate |
| v. 4 | for nothing | am I aware of | [to evaluate] |

The structural parallelism invites us to supply in v. 4a a new form of ἀνακρίνειν in the ellipsis. In English, the emphasis might be placed on the word *to* ("... nothing am I aware of [*to* evaluate]"). If this correctly captures Paul's emphasis, then Paul refers to self-awareness *absolutely*. His meaning

---

77. Ellipsis of verbs in parallel expressions is very common in Paul's letters. For a host of examples see Brookins, *Ancient Rhetoric*, 32–34.

is: "I am not qualified to evaluate myself; for *I do not know myself in this way.*" Only God does. Admittedly, no modern English version appears to reflect this interpretation. The KJV at first seems to support it ("I know nothing *by myself*"), though this translation could be an archaism for "*against* myself."[78]

In order to further validate our reading, we shall need to explain what Paul might mean in denying self-awareness. As I will now show, Paul's language creates an allusion that is fitted specifically to the proclivities of his audience: he alludes to the Stoic practice of self-evaluation.[79]

Stoic Self-Evaluation

As early as Plato, philosophers began to interpret the well-known Pythian dictum "know thyself" (γνῶθι σαυτόν) as a philosophical precept about the necessity of self-knowledge for moral progress.[80] Self-knowledge was thought to establish the basis for moral improvement in all the philosophical schools, thus the maxim "The knowledge of sin is the beginning of salvation" ("Initium est salutis notitia peccati").[81] The Stoics of the Roman era are credited with an important development in the philosophers' concern with self-knowledge. Their special contribution was the development of self-evaluation as a habitual "spiritual exercise."[82]

Paul's contemporary Seneca offers the earliest surviving extended discussion of this practice.[83] We find the idea later in the works of Epictetus and

---

78. As both Lightfoot (*Notes on the Epistles*, 198) and Robertson and Plummer (*First Epistle of St. Paul to the Corinthians*, 77) think.

79. As far as I have found, only Hays makes this connection. Assuming that the Corinthians were likely "entranced by Stoic 'wisdom,'" Hays suggests that the Corinthians may have engaged in "the sort of self-examination that Seneca recommends." However, Hays does not elaborate or share our interpretation of the syntax. Richard B. Hays, *1 Corinthians* (Louisville: John Knox, 1997), 66.

80. On moral progress through self-knowledge among the Platonists, see Lee, *Moral Transformation*, 156–58. Plato cites the Pythian oracle in several places (*Phaedr.* 229e; *Charm.* 164d–165b; *Prot.* 343b; *Phileb.* 48c; *Leg.* 11.923a; *Alc. I* 129a).

81. Seneca quotes Epicurus as holding this view: Seneca, *Ep.* 28.9.

82. Lee (*Moral Transformation*, 356) explains that this is a traditional translation of the phrase ἀσκήσεις τῆς ψυχῆς. Lee summarizes exercises common among the Neostoics on pp. 360–62.

83. For a discussion of Seneca's practice of self-scrutiny, see Catherine Edwards, "Self-Scrutiny and Self-Transformation in Seneca's Letters," in *Seneca*, ed. J. G. Fitch, Oxford Readings in Classical Studies (Oxford: Oxford University Press, 2008), 84–101.

Marcus Aurelius.[84] According to Seneca, most people remain ignorant of their sins because they fail to reflect upon them—or else, we refuse to admit them because we think that no one else sees them. Seneca recommends as a first step to improvement that we select imaginary witnesses, who might witness not only our actions (*Ep.* 32.1) but even our thoughts (*Ep.* 11.9; 25.4–7; 83.2). He suggests, however, that we ought also to play the role of judge for ourselves. One should be one's own witness and "judge" (*Ep.* 43.5; *Ira* 2.28.1) and every night examine oneself (*Ep.* 83.2; *Ira* 3.36.1–4), "hunting up charges" ("inquire in te"), playing the part "first of accuser, then of judge, last of intercessor" (*Ep.* 28.10). Seneca describes this exercise at some length in *Ira* 3.36.1–4:[85]

> This [the mind (*animus*)] should be summoned to give an account of itself every day [*ad rationem reddendam vocandus est*].... "What bad habit have you cured to-day? What fault have you resisted? In what respect are you better?" ... how delightful the sleep that follows this self-examination [*recognitionem*]—how tranquil it is, how deep and untroubled, when the soul has either praised or admonished itself, and when this secret examiner and critic of self [*speculator sui censorque secretus*] has given report of its own character. I avail myself of this privilege, and every day I plead my cause before the bar of self [*apud me causam dico*]. When the light has been removed from sight, and my wife, long aware of my habit, has become silent, I scan the whole of my day and retrace all my deeds and words. I conceal nothing from myself, I omit nothing. For why should I shrink from any of my mistakes, when I may commune thus with myself? (*Ira* 3.36.1–3 [Basore, LCL])

For Seneca and the Stoics, examiners identify through this exercise where they have failed and where they have made progress. From this knowledge

---

84. Lee, *Moral Transformation*, 362, citing in n. 102 Marcus Aurelius, *Med.* 4.24; 5.11; 8.2, 36; 10.13; 11.2; and John Sellars, *The Art of Living: The Stoics on the Nature and Function of Philosophy*, Ashgate New Critical Thinking in Philosophy (Aldershot: Ashgate, 2003), 147–49, 163–66; Gretchen Reydams-Schils, *The Roman Stoics: Self-Responsibility, and Affection* (Chicago: University of Chicago Press, 2005), 10–11. Lee states that Marcus Aurelius "has devoted his entire *Meditations* to the premise of self-examination and evaluation, where in the process of self-dialogue with oneself he writes out his train of thought as part of the spiritual exercise." Lee also cites in n. 102 Epictetus, *Diatr.* 4.12.15–21; *Ench.* 1.5; 48.2–3. On the idea "get it from yourself," see Epictetus, *Diatr.* 1.9.31–32; 1.29.4; 4.1.51. On the idea that nothing is shut off from the sight of God, see Epictetus, *Diatr.* 1.14.13–14; 1.30.1–2; 2.14.11.

85. See also Seneca, *Ira* 2.28.1–8; *Tranq.* 6.1–2; *Ben.* 6.38.5; *Ep.* 16.2; 68.6–7.

1 Corinthians 3:1–4:5: The Apostles and the σοφία of God

they then made gradual moral improvements (*Ep.* 5.1; 16.2), with a final end of moral perfection (*Ep.* 35.2), a state of "consistency with oneself" (*Ep.* 35.4), at which point one became a σοφός, or "wise person" (*Ep.* 85.5; 109.1). Only at this point could one turn to evaluate *others*, namely, when they had progressed beyond them (*Ira* 2.28.6–8; *Ep.* 27.1; 68.8; 118.2–3).

To be sure, God played a key role in this process. As Seneca said, one must always remember that God sees whatever secrets we keep hidden, even from ourselves: "Nothing is shut off from the sight of God" (*Ep.* 83.1; cf. 41.2). This point, however, must be set within the context of the larger Stoic system. What is implicit in Seneca's discussion of self-evaluation is that, since the faculty of divine reason inhabits humans by nature (as "mind," *animus*), humans are capable of examining themselves with the same objective and comprehensive insight as God.[86] The notion that "God sees all" therefore has equivocal meaning. On the one hand, it means that nothing escapes God's knowledge, even what we refuse to admit; on the other hand, it means that through thorough and penetrating self-evaluation, we too can identify every sin.

Paul's rejection of self-evaluation as a basis for interpersonal *comparison* in 4:1–5 is not a matter of generic Christian parenesis. Tying in with the theme of 2:6–16, this discussion of evaluation in 4:1–5 appears to address concretely a practice carried on in this particular church. The theme of 2:6–16 is succinctly captured in the maxim of 2:15: "The spiritual person evaluates all things [or everyone] but he himself is evaluated by no one" (ὁ δὲ πνευματικὸς ἀνακρίνει [τὰ] πάντα, αὐτὸς δὲ ὑπ' οὐδενὸς ἀνακρίνεται). As discussed in chapter 5, this is the perspective of the Corinthian πνευματικοί,[87] who also consider themselves to be σοφοί (3:18; 6:5; see also 1:19, 20, 25, 26; etc.). These distinguished themselves as πνευματικοί from others as ψυχικοί, their spiritual inferiors. The separation of believers by the σοφοί into "classes" began from this very thing: the practice of evaluation—evaluation of self and others—followed by comparison.

This practice explains the context behind Paul's critique of self-evaluation in 4:4–5. Paul does not "evaluate" (4:3, 4) either himself or other people, as the Corinthian πνευματικοί do (2:15). They should, rather, follow his example,

---

86. The connection of these ideas is the main subject of *Epistle* 41. Seneca here connects God's witness of our actions (*Ep.* 41.2) and the divine soul as a property of the human per se (41.4–9). Note also that we have reason by nature, in Seneca, *Ep.* 73.16; that reason makes us divine/is a portion of the divine, in Seneca, *Ep.* 31.11; 66.12; 92.27–31; 120.14; that the wise man has a God's-eye perspective, in Seneca, *Ep.* 53.11.

87. See chapter 5, pp. 121–24.

and Apollos's. He does not evaluate himself (v. 3c) because he lacks the requisite self-awareness (v. 4a); he is not like the Stoic wise man, who by virtue of innate divine reason and his God's-eye perspective can accurately "evaluate all things." This, then, is what Paul means by τούτῳ, "not by means of *this* am I justified [οὐκ ἐν τούτῳ δεδικαίωμαι]": that is, he will not achieve justification at the bar of judgment through having practiced penetrating self-introspection and making gradual moral improvements. For he does not have the kind of faculties requisite for this kind of evaluation. And so he leaves evaluation to God (vv. 4c), whose attention nothing escapes (v. 5).[88]

Summary of 4:1–5

I have offered a different reading of 4:1–5 than the common one. Verse 1 reiterates the *common* character of Paul and Apollos as servants of God (3:5) and ministers to the Corinthians (3:22). In v. 2 Paul critiques the practice of "evaluating" others by establishing a single criterion of worth as viewed in the eyes of God: it is sufficient to be a "faithful" steward of the master, without having to stand out in comparison. Finally, in vv. 3–5 Paul offers a decisive critique of "evaluation" by declaring impossible the kind of *self*-evaluation requisite for establishing a benchmark for comparison. In the final words of the paragraph (v. 5), Paul's reference to "praise from God" implies not his vindication against opponents, but the point that final judgment of the *Corinthians'* worth—high as they may have estimated themselves—will be God's to determine.

CONCLUSION

It has been the contention of this chapter that 1 Cor 3:1–4:5 speaks more about the Corinthians' evaluation of self and personal comparison with others than about their evaluation of and comparison between Paul and Apollos or any other apostle. In this respect, the purpose of Paul's extended narrative about himself and Apollos is to offer the two as a positive exemplum that sets them against the negative example of the Corinthians. Paul and Apollos work

---

88. There is apparently no specific allusion to the scriptures here. Inkelaar (*Conflict over Wisdom*, 280) notes a connection between our text and βουλή, σκότος, and the stem κρυπτ- in LXX Isa 29:15 but determines that we have here only a common scriptural "topos," not an allusion.

1 Corinthians 3:1–4:5: The Apostles and the σοφία of God

together in harmony (3:5–10b); they are but ministers of God on behalf of the church (3:5, 22; 4:1); together they have constructed the edifice of a church (3:6–10b). They are content to fulfill their charges as ministers without assessing their own worth in comparison with others (4:2–5). In short, Paul and Apollos prove by their character to be devotees, as it were, of the wisdom of God. Opposite them are those among the Corinthians who, in accordance with their own wisdom, evaluate and compare, fancying themselves better than others. Paul refers to such persons indefinitely in 3:10c–17 as "someone" or "each person" before reverting back in 3:18 to the label used in 1:17b–31, namely, the "wise man" (σοφός). Such persons undermine the work of Paul and Apollos, destroying the edifice/temple that God's coworkers have built. While claiming to be wise, they expose themselves as fools, for just as the wisdom of comparison elevates some above others, so it also divides.

This section contains what may seem to be a surprising abundance of allusions to Stoicism and the ancient philosophical tradition. I have sought to highlight where the *configurations* of ideas and *formal* correspondence involved in the proposed parallels resonate palpably with Stoic discourse. Notable examples include the commonplace usage of the milk/solid-food distinction among the Stoic moralists (3:1–2); the notion of God's dwelling in a human temple in the form of the Spirit (3:16); various remarks about the σοφός in 3:18–23, where Paul also adds the σοφός into two OT citations (3:19, 20); and a polemical response to the Stoic practice of moral improvement and vindication through self-evaluation (4:2–5).

7

1 Corinthians 4:6–13:
The Apostles and the Corinthian σοφοί

In the foregoing chapters, I have argued that reconstructions of the Corinthians' conflict that assume a Paul-Apollos rivalry—whether over respective rhetorical abilities, financial practices, or leadership potential—begin to encounter problems when one presses the arguments at an exegetical level. The same kinds of issues continue in 4:6–13.

Over the last several decades, two main lines of interpretation on 4:6–13 have prevailed. (1) Those who see the Corinthians' wisdom against the backdrop of Greco-Roman rhetoric or sophistry take Paul to mean that the Corinthians should not boast in Apollos for his eloquence. (2) Others locate the preference for Apollos in other factors, in particular his/Paul's conformity or nonconformity with social conventions around friendship and patronage.

We shall interact with these viewpoints as we discuss the text. As I shall argue, neither line of interpretation stands up to exegetical scrutiny. While 4:6–13 does not mention "wisdom" explicitly, it does reprise the main themes of 1:17–2:16 and 3:18–23—chiefly boasting (4:6–8, 10) and the antithesis between the Corinthians' regard for status and the apostles' example of lowliness, which embodies the wisdom of God (4:8–13). Moreover, even though Paul's main points surely have "social" import, his criticism of the Corinthians addresses more properly their status in respect to intellectual or spiritual qualities than ordinary markers of status. Finally, I shall argue that Paul does not here address Corinthian boasting in himself or Apollos—"one against the other"—but the Corinthians' boasting in their own qualities over against others.

1 Corinthians 4:6–13: The Apostles and the Corinthian σοφοί

THE FUNCTION OF THE PAUL-APOLLOS DISCUSSION

A "redundant" vocative in v. 6 (ἀδελφοί) marks a transition and calls the Corinthians to full attention at a critical juncture in the argument. That much is clear. Every other portion of v. 6 is subject to serious debate.

Μετασχημάτισα

Verse 6 opens as follows: Ταῦτα δέ, ἀδελφοί, μετεσχημάτισα εἰς ἐμαυτὸν καὶ Ἀπολλῶν δι' ὑμᾶς. In a very true sense this statement is the "key" to understanding Paul's intentions in 3:5–4:5, for he offers this sentence as his clarification. The interpreter, however, is at once frustrated by the apparent semantic obscurity of the verb, μετεσχημάτισα. The meaning of μετασχηματίζειν is widely debated. Summaries of the possibilities are difficult to reconcile,[1] though this seems to owe partly to incongruities between interpreters' translational glosses and their explanations for the meaning of the whole clause, including the referent of ταῦτα and the sense of the preposition εἰς. All seem to agree that the verb's root supplies us with the fundamental meaning of "change [μετά] the form [σχημ-]" of something. Further clarity, however, is needed on several issues: (1) what it is that is "changing," (2) whether the verb is a technical term for the rhetorical device of "covert allusion," (3) what the referent of the verb's object (ταῦτα) is, and (4) what the function of the preposition εἰς is. As these issues interrelate, we shall discuss them together.

Ταῦτα clearly refers to what precedes. Yet, the pronoun's precise referent remains uncertain. Recognition that "these things" apply *to Paul and Apollos* (εἰς ἐμαυτὸν καὶ Ἀπολλῶν) only gets one so far, for although Paul discusses himself and Apollos explicitly in 3:4–9 and 4:1–5, I have argued that Apollos is not in fact in view in 3:10–17. Moreover, one still has to decide whether the church's conflict is a matter really of a two-party rivalry rather than four, and a rivalry specifically between Paul and Apollos. Hooker concludes from the fact that the pronoun is neuter that the "change" cannot be between people—that is, from the Corinthians (X) to Paul and Apollos (Y).[2] Based on the verb's σχημ- root, Hooker considers the possibility that the "change" refers to

---

1. Thiselton, *First Epistle to the Corinthians*, 348–50; Mihaila, *Paul-Apollos Relationship*, 202–12; BDAG, s.v. "μετασχηματίζειν"; Bitner, *Paul's Political Strategy*, 294.

2. Morna D. Hooker, "'Beyond the Things Which Are Written': An Examination of I Cor. IV. 6," *NTS* 10 (1963): 127–32.

a change of *shape*, as in *figures* of speech (the Latin *figura* means "shape"). In this regard, Hooker argues that what "changes" are the figures of speech in chapter 3, as Paul moves from one to another: "the figures of gardeners, builders and stewards." Hooker concludes: "The meaning seems to be: 'I have applied these figures of speech to myself and Apollos.'"[3]

David Hall, however, has pointed out that μετασχηματίζειν "normally" meant "'to change the σχῆμα (form or appearance) of' something into something else" and that when εἰς follows, the preposition "introduces the end product of the transformation."[4] If Hall's generalization holds, then the problem with Hooker's view is twofold. First, although she argues that the verb refers to a "change of figures" based on the σχημ- root, as she herself notes, "the verb is not used in this sense elsewhere."[5] Second, her rendering of the clause differently construes the contribution of εἰς. In her rendering it does not indicate the *end product of* the transformation, but the people *to whom* the transformation of the product applies.

Hall suggests that the normal meaning of the construction applies. Paul refers to "a transformation in his [Paul's] argument from statements about something or someone else into statements about himself and Apollos."[6] While Hall's rendering ("statements *about*") seems to imply that the verb in fact means "apply to" (in common with Hooker), this gloss merely reflects a translation adjustment to account for the neuter form of ταῦτα. That is, in Hall's view it is the *statements* (ταῦτα) that apply to Paul and Apollos. Thus, "changed these things to myself and Apollos" does not mean "only the *names* are changed" (which, Hooker rightly notes, cannot be the meaning). Lest we retreat to Hooker's anomalous rendering of the verb and anomalous understanding of εἰς, we must conclude that the pronoun indicates, in certain loose terms, the subject matter that precedes *together with* the people to whom it applies. In short, 4:6a is an abbreviated way of saying: "I have changed this

3. Hooker, "'Beyond the Things Which Are Written,'" 131.

4. David R. Hall, "A Disguise for the Wise: Μετασχηματισμός in 1 Corinthians 4.6," *NTS* 40 (1994): 143–49, esp. 143, 144. Compare the Greek text here (ταῦτα . . . μετεσχημάτισα εἰς ἐμαυτὸν καὶ Ἀπολλῶν) with the following examples: "change the appearance of [acc. noun] into (εἰς) [acc. noun]," and the Latin, "change [acc. noun] into (*in*) [acc. noun]" (e.g., "change these circumstances into opposite things [*sortem in contraria mutet*]," Ovid, *Met.* 3.329; "Acis . . . having been changed into a river" [*Acis . . . in amnem versus*], 13.896–897; "bodies changed into shapes that are not to be believed [*in non credendos corpora versa modos*]," Ovid, *Trist.* 2.63–64).

5. Hooker, "'Beyond the Things Which Are Written,'" 131. Making the same criticism is Anderson, *Ancient Rhetorical Theory and Paul*, 248–50.

6. Hall, "Disguise for the Wise," 144.

discussion about you into a discussion, *mutatis mutandis omnibus* [with all the things needing to be exchanged having been exchanged], about myself and Apollos."

This clarity on the construction does not yet resolve the question of the pronoun's bounds of reference (ταῦτα). On this point we must consider not only what precedes,[7] but also how the preceding material connects with what follows, part by part. Here is the syntactical sequence:

v. 6a <u>That which</u> (ταῦτα) applied to Paul and Apollos in the preceding discussion, <u>this</u> Paul discussed . . .
v. 6b "in order that" (ἵνα) the Corinthians might learn:
v. 6c τὸ Μὴ ὑπὲρ ἃ γέγραπται,
v. 6d "in order that" (ἵνα) they should not be "puffed up" (φυσιοῦσθε).

Despite the many difficulties involved in v. 6, these difficulties are elucidated greatly by v. 7 and what follows. The first item of significance is the linking of vv. 6 and 7 by means of γάρ. Paul grounds his prohibition of boasting in v. 6, via γάρ, in the specific assertion that the Corinthians have received from God everything that they have (v. 7). From this connection we find that Paul's purpose (ἵνα) in "changing these things into myself and Apollos," evidently, has been to teach them not to boast in *themselves*. As Paul proceeds in vv. 8–10, he criticizes the Corinthians' high estimation of themselves as "rich," "kings," "prudent," and so on, in comparison with the apostles, who are "fools," "weak," "undistinguished," and so on. All of this recalls the discussion of human versus divine wisdom that extends from 1:17 to 3:4, where Paul descants upon God's inversion of human criteria of worth, reverses determinations about who is spiritual/unspiritual or mature/immature, and explicitly prohibits anyone and everyone from boasting. With these themes still echoing in the background, Paul's announcement in 4:6 that he uses himself and Apollos as an example *in order to* (ἵνα) teach against boasting and the worldly pursuit of status shows that the referent of ταῦτα cannot be limited only to the "figures of speech" in 3:5–4:5.[8] Rather, ταῦτα refers loosely to the whole discussion in 1:17–4:5.

---

7. The aorist tense of μετεσχημάτισα indicates that ταῦτα is anaphoric.
8. Contra Ker, "Paul and Apollos," 92; E. Coye Still III, "Divisions over Leaders and Food Offered to Idols: The Parallel Thematic Structures of 1 Corinthians 4:6–21 and 8:1–11:1," *TynBul* 55 (2004): 17–41, esp. 20; and Hooker, "'Beyond the Things Which Are Written,'" 131.

The Saying "Not Beyond the Things That Are Written"

The purpose of the Paul-Apollos discussion, as indicated in v. 6b, is so that the Corinthians "might learn in us [μάθητε ἐν ἡμῖν]."[9] This assertion conveys rather transparently that Paul offers himself and Apollos as an example. But an example of what? The object of μάθητε specifies the content of the lesson in the obscure expression τὸ Μὴ ὑπὲρ ἃ γέγραπται. The history of the interpretation of this expression is rich with disagreement and speculation.[10] Apart from the few who see the phrase as a textual gloss, most interpreters agree that its form lends it the character of a maxim. The neuter article (τό) often signals an ensuing quotation,[11] and the succinct and elliptical form of the expression renders its meaning too open-ended apart from some prior familiarity with the idea. We find no exact parallels with our maxim in ancient evidence. Yet, its meaning is elucidated by two items in the immediate context. (1) The content of what is "written" corresponds with the example of Paul and Apollos as already discussed. (2) The purpose or result of the audience's learning it is "so that" (ἵνα) the Corinthians might no longer be "puffed up" (μὴ ... φυσιοῦσθε). In light of 1:17–4:5, both points suggest that the content pertains primarily to a requirement of humility.

The critical point is the question of *what* is "written." The verb form γέγραπται (perfect middle/passive indicative) is of course Paul's most common introductory formula for a citation of scripture.[12] The significance of this point, however, is put into question by the fact that no citation is forthcoming. What kind of "written" texts, then, might Paul be alluding to? Proposals

---

9. Hooker's view that μετεσχημάτισα indicates a change in figures of speech seems a bit off point in light of ἐν ἡμῖν. Hooker's "I changed the figures of speech to myself and Apollos so that you might learn *in us*" would seem to indicate that it was *changing* the figures of speech that allowed them to learn. But that is not exactly the point. The point is that they learned *by the example* of Paul-Apollos, not by the changing of the rhetorical forms in which Paul presents it.

10. See the history of interpretation in James C. Hanges, "1 Corinthians 4:6 and the Possibility of Written Bylaws in the Corinthian Church," *JBL* 117 (1998): 275–98, esp. 275–80 (supplemented with a fresh proposal of his own); see also a history of interpretation in Ronald L. Tyler, "The History of the Interpretation of τὸ μὴ ὑπὲρ ἃ γέγραπται in 1 Corinthians 4:6," *RQ* 43 (2001): 243–52; and a proposal of his own in Ronald L. Tyler, "First Corinthians 4:6 and Hellenistic Pedagogy," *CBQ* 60 (1998): 97–103. For a more recent proposal, see Bitner, *Paul's Political Strategy*, 294–99.

11. Examples include Rom 13:9; Gal 5:14; among other texts cited in Tyler, "First Corinthians 4:6," esp. 98n6.

12. Rom 12:19; 14:11; 1 Cor 1:19; 3:10; Gal 3:10; 4:22, 27; and some two dozen other examples.

1 Corinthians 4:6–13: The Apostles and the Corinthian σοφοί

include (1) "the rules" in a proverbial sense, (2) a community charter, (3) the rules of a teacher's commissioning, and (4) the stipulations of civic law.[13] The last three options can be summarized as descriptions of a "written" text that is basically legal or contractual in nature. Proponents of these options have marshaled some intriguing examples that offer conceptual parallels to our text, though none of the examples approximates our text formally.[14]

In addition to formal considerations, a critical factor in evaluating these options is that of contextual "register." Paul's appeal to a maxim about the binding stipulations of law or about contractual obligations is most apropos if the larger context—or contextual register—of the discourse is basically *political* in resonance.[15] As many have noted, however, Paul's language in 1:10–4:21 resonates extensively with the register of *education*. Language and images from the domain of education occur throughout chapters 1–4 (e.g., 3:1–4; 4:14–15, 16, 17, 21).[16] Interpreters have commonly understood 4:6c along the same lines. Perhaps the most frequent suggestion has been that "not beyond what is written" alludes to elementary school instruction, where teachers wrote the letters of the alphabet as "models" (παραδείγματα) for students to trace.[17]

I find the connections with education throughout chapters 1–4 persuasive, though I would like to offer a different take on the saying in 4:6. I propose that the saying refers, not to the tracing of letters, but to the *teachings* passed down by the teachers of "schools," and particularly of *philosophical* schools. In this respect the saying correlates closely with the kind of perceptions that lie behind the Corinthians' cries of allegiance (e.g., those who say, "I am of Paul," 1:12). We shall later consider how the concept of philosophical "allegiance" relates to these slogans. Here, I offer a few points in favor of this background as an explanation for 4:6c.

(1) The verb introducing the slogan in 4:6c, "that you might *learn* [μάθητε]," naturally evokes a school setting. (2) The appeal to example (*exemplum*, παραδείγματα) "in us" (ἐν ἡμῖν) was commonplace in philosophical instruction.[18] (3) Other considerations point to philosophy more narrowly.

---

13. Tyler, "History of the Interpretation," 247–48.
14. See esp. Welborn, *Politics and Rhetoric*, 56–75; Hanges, "1 Corinthians 4:6," 284; most recently, Bitner, *Paul's Political Strategy*, 294–99.
15. See for example Bitner, *Paul's Political Strategy*, 42.
16. For a recent monograph, see White, *Teacher of the Nations*.
17. E.g., Benjamin Fiore, *The Function of Personal Example in the Socratic and Pastoral Epistles*, AnBib 105 (Rome: Biblical Institute Press, 1986), 165–66.
18. E.g., Seneca, *Ep.* 6.5; 25.5–6; 52.7–8; 104.20–33; Plutarch, *Mor.* 119d.

Philosophical schools were traditionally sectarian. To be an aspiring Stoic, Epicurean, Platonist, or what have you was to commit to the teachings of the school's founder, which were safeguarded generation after generation through a succession of scholarchs.[19] While we have no evidence that Μὴ ὑπὲρ ἃ γέγραπται was a common slogan in any of the schools (as we have no parallel for this slogan anywhere), the slogan encapsulates the spirit of the schools' culture of allegiance to the doctrines of their teachers (as we shall discuss in chapter 10).[20] (4) Both the nature of instruction in Paul's communities and Paul's emphasis on prior instruction correspond most closely with the parenetic practices of the philosophical schools.[21] The philosophical schools were deeply interested in shaping behavior and inculcating new habits holistically, through repeated instruction and persistent accountability.[22] Students needed to be constantly pointed back to the standard in order to complete deconstruction of their pre-conversion worldview and to reinforce the process of resocialization into a new *habitus*.

In view of these considerations, I suggest that the injunction in 4:6c not to go "beyond what is written" works as a maxim about the binding importance of the teachings handed down to students by teachers in the philosophical schools. Yet, both Paul's remarks in 4:1–5 and his introductory remark in 6b impose an important caveat: the Corinthians should not adopt an attitude of exclusive allegiance to a single teacher (minister) as if in a philosophical *sect*, for this divides the community. Rather, they should adhere to the example of Paul and Apollos, as *co*workers, who do not view themselves as rivals, as the Corinthians do each other.

The Subject and Object of "Boasting"

After much disagreement over vv. 6a–c, interpreters come back in v. 6d to what appears to be a consensus. According to the *communis opinio*, v. 6d con-

---

19. See Sedley, "Philosophical Allegiance," 97–119.
20. On the culture of philosophical allegiance, see chapter 11.
21. Malherbe, "Exhortation in First Thessalonians," 169–70; Malherbe, *Paul and the Thessalonians*, 61–94; Abraham J. Malherbe, "Hellenistic Moralists and the New Testament," *ANRW* 26.1:267–333. For a new look at the "protreptic" genre of philosophical literature, see Daniel Markovich, *Promoting a New Kind of Education: Greek and Roman Philosophical Protreptic*, International Studies in the History of Rhetoric 16 (Leiden: Brill, 2021).
22. See Malherbe, *Paul and the Thessalonians*. This is not to deny that there was some interest in the associations on "rules" or "ethics" (*IG* 2.1368, 1369; *SIG* 985), but the evidence is too slight to argue that ethics was a major concern, much less in comparison with the philosophical schools.

veys that individuals in the Corinthian church are "puffed up" (φυσιοῦσθε), each (εἷς) on behalf of one minister (Paul/Apollos) against the other (Apollos/Paul).[23]

One would be justified in hesitating toward any suggestion that such a rare consensus is wrong. One must, however, always be open to the possibility that it is. Exegetically, I believe a different interpretation is not only defensible, but that it is more likely in the context of the unfolding argument. Specifically, I contend that Paul refers here not to Paul/Apollos on the one hand (τοῦ ἑνός) and Apollos/Paul on the other (τοῦ ἑτέρου). Rather, in keeping with earlier discussion, Paul refers to Corinthian *self*-boasting (1:29–31; see also discussion of 3:21) and mutual comparison *between members of the church* (1:18–31; 2:6–16). In other words, the "one" (εἷς) person boasts on behalf of *oneself* (τοῦ ἑνός) against *the other* (τοῦ ἑτέρου).

While I am aware of no one who has made a sustained argument for this interpretation, William Baird appears to share this reading,[24] and it has been mentioned as a grammatical possibility by both Fee and Marshall, though Fee ultimately rejects it. Fee provides an exact parallel in favor of the consensus in Matt 6:24 (also noting Luke 17:34; 18:10; though these are not identical to our construction). No verbal parallel, however, is decisive, since the question is not one of grammatical possibility (more than one interpretation is grammatically possible) but also of sense in context.[25] Oddly, Marshall seems to interpret the text in both ways simultaneously, offering that a reference to boasting "against *each other*" is "also possible." That Marshall indeed wishes to preserve both interpretations is made clear further into his discussion, where he summarizes Paul's meaning as "against an apostle *or each other* (4:6)."[26] A similar kind of ambiguity is sometimes evident in commentaries.[27]

Let it be noted: the issue is not whether it is phenomenologically possible for Corinthians to boast in both the apostles and themselves, but whether this combination of facts can be squeezed from the language of "puffed up,

---

23. Pogoloff, *Logos and Sophia*, 222; Clarke, *Secular and Christian Leadership*, 111; Still, "Divisions over Leaders," 20; Finney, *Honour and Conflict*, 87; Martin, *Corinthian Body*, 65; Ker, "Paul and Apollos," 91; and others cited below.

24. Baird ("'One against the Other'") thinks that the "search for opponents in 1 Corinthians may be misguided." He suggests that it is not a case of Paul against Corinthians but "Corinthians 'one against the other' (4:6)" (116).

25. Fee, *First Epistle to the Corinthians*, 2nd ed., 185.

26. Marshall, *Enmity in Corinth*, 204 (my italics).

27. For example, Thiselton summarizes v. 6d as addressing both "taking sides" and "self-affirmation" (*First Epistle to the Corinthians*, 355).

one on behalf of the one against the other," and what follows. As we shall discuss, how one interprets the duty of the preposition ὑπέρ is of vital importance. Despite lacking strong support in the history of interpretation, a different interpretation than the usual one makes, I believe, more sense both in light of the language of v. 6d and a careful exegesis of vv. 6–9. I offer the following arguments.

The Language of 4:6d

(1) The common reading of v. 6d views ὑπὲρ τοῦ ἑνός ... κατὰ τοῦ ἑτέρου as referencing Paul/Apollos on the one hand (τοῦ ἑνός) and Apollos/Paul (τοῦ ἑτέρου) on the other. This interpretation of the pronouns, while sensible, is not self-evidently correct.

(a) Τοῦ ἑνός ("the one") is reasonably taken as a reference to the same person as the one designated by the subject, εἷς ("one"). That they represent the same entity is suggested by at least two considerations. (i) The designation employs in both instances the same "pronoun" (εἷς), followed by a different one only where the referent clearly changes (τοῦ ἑτέρου). (ii) The article τοῦ, repeated with both ἑνός and ἑτέρου, need not point back anaphorically to the two individuals just mentioned (Paul, Apollos). The first article just as easily indicates a reference back to the co-referent of εἷς ("one on behalf of *the* one" just mentioned, i.e., "of *oneself*"), with the second article functioning as a "generic" article indicating "the *other*" as a class.

(b) Paul speaks of "the other" as a generic entity in at least two other passages in the undisputed letters, and in both instances the term explicitly complements "oneself" in an antithetical construction: "let no one seek the interest of *oneself* [τὸ ἑαυτοῦ] but the interest of *the other* [τὸ τοῦ ἑτέρου]" (1 Cor. 10:24); and "with each person looking not to the interests of *oneself* [τὰ ἑαυτῶν] but to the interests of *the others* [τὰ ἑτέρων]" (Phil. 2:4). The same self-other dynamic is implied in other passages: "[love] does not seek the things of itself [τὰ ἑαυτῆς]" (1 Cor 13:5; cf. 14:1; Rom 15:1–2). The substitution of ἑνός for the reflexive ἑαυτοῦ in 1 Cor 4:6 would be due to Paul's emphasis on Corinthian individualism.

(c) The contrast between enlarging (inflating) oneself and enlarging (building up) the community is a prominent theme across the letter. Paul discusses this theme at length in chapters 12–14 (e.g., "the one who speaks in a tongue builds up *oneself*, but the one who prophesies builds up *the church*," 14:4).

1 Corinthians 4:6–13: The Apostles and the Corinthian σοφοί

(d) Elsewhere Paul accuses the Corinthians of boasting in themselves. This is clearest in 1:29–31 and 8:1, though as argued previously, this is likely Paul's meaning in several other passages as well, including 3:21 (note also 13:4).

In sum, Paul does not say here that "the one" (Corinthian) boasts on behalf of "the one" (i.e., Paul/Apollos) against "the other" (i.e., Apollos/Paul), but that "the one" (Corinthian) boasts on behalf of "the one" (that same one) against "the other" (Corinthian).

Corinthian #1	Corinthian #2
εἷς	τοῦ ἑτέρου
τοῦ ἑνὸς	

(2) A further point in favor of this interpretation concerns the function of ὑπέρ. The common interpretation understands Paul to mean that the Corinthians boast in one apostle or another *and*—indirectly from their connection with their respective apostle—also in themselves. One must ask, then, what ὑπέρ is doing that would make this double meaning possible.

The usual interpretation, it seems, involves equivocation between two incompatible syntactical options. In this light, it is unsurprising that commentators do not address the function of ὑπέρ specifically. Or rather, one suspects that they do not address ὑπέρ specifically because their interpretation of its function is equivocal. Indeed, when one considers the matter, it seems that one is asking for the preposition to do two things at once: (i) to indicate that the Corinthians boast "in" ("on behalf of") the apostles and (ii) to indicate that the Corinthians boast in themselves "due to" ("on behalf of") the apostles. If, however, *on behalf of* means that the Corinthians boast "in" the apostles, then the phrase cannot simultaneously be taken to mean that they boast "in" themselves, for, whereas the first meaning makes the apostles the *object* of boasting, the second makes the apostles the *source or cause* of (self-)boasting. Conceptually, syntactically, and contextually speaking, these two functions of this single preposition are mutually exclusive. Moreover, the second syntactical interpretation ("due to," "from our relationship with") is not an admissible function of ὑπέρ. The lexicon BDAG correctly categorizes ὑπέρ in this verse under the sense "to be for someone," where all examples cited indicate the subject's support of or favorable disposition toward someone, as "for their [the object's] benefit."[28] In short, "puffed up, one on behalf of the one against

---

28. BDAG, s.v. "ὑπέρ."

the other" cannot mean both "puffed up *on behalf of/in* Paul/Apollos" (advantage) and "puffed up in oneself *due to* Paul/Apollos" (cause).

1 Cor 4:6d and Exegesis of 4:6–7

The usual view encounters additional problems when we examine its implications in context. In the next verse (v. 7), Paul asks three rhetorical questions that address the Corinthians' boasting. The singular form of address (σε) emphasizes difference and individual distinction. The first question calls their self-evaluation into question on grounds that only God (τίς) is in position to judge between the comparative merits of the one and the other (διακρίνει), while the second and third questions emphasize that everything the Corinthians have to their credit has been received, as gift (ἔλαβες), from God.

The interpreter is obligated to offer an exegetically grounded explanation for what would be an abrupt shift between vv. 6 and 7 if v. 6d refers to boasting in *ministers* on the one hand and v. 7 to the Corinthians' estimation of *self* on the other. Such an explanation must account for the fact that, being linked to what precedes by γάρ, v. 7 provides the *grounds* for the assertion in v. 6d about boasting ὑπέρ and κατά. Paul's implied reminders in v. 7 that the Corinthians' qualities are gifts from God quite naturally ground a prohibition of Corinthian self-boasting as stated in v. 6d. But these reminders are—if not impossible—much more difficult to understand as grounds for Corinthian boasting in *others*. Fee freely paraphrases v. 7a: "Who in the world do you think you are, anyway? What kind of self-delusion is it that allows you to put yourself in a position to judge another person's servant?"[29] Apart from its very free rendering of the text, this paraphrase complicates the train of thought given the two immediately succeeding questions about what the Corinthians have "received" from God. The assiduous reader will notice that Fee, apparently, locates a critical shift from boasting in Paul/Apollos to boasting in self between v. 7a and vv. 7b–c: that is, v. 7a asks why the Corinthians feel privileged to boast in Paul/Apollos, while 7b and c ask why the Corinthians feel they can boast in themselves. As such, a first instance of δέ introduces what seems to be an abrupt shift between 7a and b, and then a second δέ links two closely related questions in 7b and c. Our interpretation of 6d offered above presents a smoother train of thought as one moves through the three questions in v. 7. Specifically, v. 7 grounds v. 6d (γάρ) using a series of questions that highlight (1) God's prerogative in distinguishing

---

29. Fee, *First Epistle to the Corinthians*, 2nd ed., 186.

1 Corinthians 4:6–13: The Apostles and the Corinthian σοφοί

the comparative merits of "the one" and "the other" and (2) God's role in engendering the qualities on the basis of which he distinguishes between them. In short, the chain of clauses from v. 6d through v. 7a, b, and c is most comprehensible when read as a continuous thread that concerns Corinthian boasting in self over others:

> Do not be puffed up, *the one* on behalf of *oneself* against the
> other (6d)
> *For* [γάρ]
> God is the judge of who among you is better than another
> (7a)[30]
> *and* [δέ] everything you have you have received from him
> (7b)
> *and* [δέ] if you received these things you have no grounds
> for boasting (7c)

The logic follows a natural circle from the initial injunction against self-boasting, to Paul's grounds for this injunction, to the conclusion that they indeed *have* no grounds for such boasting: in short, they boast in themselves (6d), but since they have no grounds for this, they ought not boast (7a–c).

Winter seems to treat γάρ as if it were not there, simply juxtaposing the respective statements in v. 6d and 7 with "and" (= γάρ?). He states: "These questions [in v. 7] vigorously rebuke the Corinthians for comparing Paul and Apollos [apparently v. 6d], *and* for boasting as if gifts originated from themselves [apparently v. 7]."[31] This comment fails on two exegetical points already discussed: first, it fails to explain why vv. 6 and 7 are linked by γάρ; second, it fails to explain how the same set of three questions can function as a rebuke for boasting both in the apostles and in the Corinthians at the same time.

We reencounter in this last point a problem that was encountered earlier in interpretations of 3:21–23. Interpreters often *assert* that Paul is condemning "both" Corinthian boasting in their leaders "and" Corinthian boasting in self but do not demonstrate how the words can be made to mean both things exegetically. Given the thematic parallels between 3:21–23 and 4:6–7, it is un-

---

30. τίς here is God, who is also the ultimate agent in 7b, c. For this rendering of διακρίνω, see BDAG, s.v. "διακρίνω."

31. Winter, *Philo and Paul among the Sophists*, 198 (my italics).

surprising that Marshall replicates exactly the same error here.[32] According to Marshall, it is "possible" that v. 6d refers to the Corinthians themselves ("the one ... the other"), but it is "better" to view it as a reference to boasting in Paul and Apollos. As this comment shows, Marshall correctly recognizes that we are faced with mutually exclusive options ("better") as to the boasting in v. 6d. Yet, because v. 7 so clearly refers to distinctions that the Corinthians have made among themselves (where γάρ grounds what precedes!), Marshall unavoidably finds himself redescribing v. 6 itself as a reference to the Corinthians' attitude for or against "an apostle *or each other*"; and then he goes on consistently to explain vv. 6–7 as addressing the Corinthians' "*self*-knowledge"![33]

In the abstract, the idea that the Corinthians could boast both in themselves and their leaders is not an impossible combination of facts. The problem, again, is that one cannot make the text mean both things exegetically.

"Theological" versus "Sociological" Explanations

Many interpreters venture explanations as to the alleged connection between boasting in self and boasting in the apostles. Like others, Coye Still argues that the Corinthians exalted themselves on the basis of their connections with the leaders in whom they boasted.[34] Marshall and Litfin argue the reverse: that the Corinthians boasted in leaders based on their high conceptions of themselves.[35] A typical problem with such proposals is that the explanation is a "historical," but not an "exegetical," one. I mean this distinction in a special sense. I do not mean that an exegetical approach excludes history. I mean that the historical approach comes functionally to exclude exegesis. In this regard, the interpreter paints a background of these chapters, or of a section within, in terms of some general state of affairs (usually with copious discussion of the social world of first-century Corinth) but then does not demonstrate the mechanics of their reading in context. They offer a *background* of the text rather than a background of the *text*.

Close consideration of the context in 4:6–7 raises further problems for the line of interpretation that I am opposing. Many interpreters explain the Co-

---

32. Marshall, *Enmity in Corinth*, 204.
33. Marshall, *Enmity in Corinth*, citations on p. 204 (my italics); see longer discussion on pp. 203–5.
34. Still, "Divisions over Leaders," 21.
35. Marshall, *Enmity in Corinth*, 204; Litfin, *St. Paul's Theology of Proclamation*, 233.

1 Corinthians 4:6–13: The Apostles and the Corinthian σοφοί

rinthians' alleged boasting in leaders as being grounded in certain "external" markers of status perceived in their leaders: eloquence, education, wealth. This line of interpretation has two common variants.[36] (1) One sees the Apollos party "judging" Paul for his comparably inferior rhetorical skills. (2) According to another, some well-to-do Corinthians had offered both Paul and Apollos financial gifts. Paul rejected the offer, preferring to support himself through manual labor. The Corinthians took umbrage at his rejection of their "friendship" (understood in terms of patronage) and at his preference for the "mean" life of a laborer as opposed to the respectable life of a client.

Both lines of interpretation neglect to address that the *grounding* questions in v. 7 (γάρ!) are *soteriologically and anthropologically* oriented. That Paul's reference to the gifts "received" from God refers not to externals or social qualities but to soteriological or spiritual realities is settled conclusively by the fact that Paul refers not simply to qualities that people *think* they have (like high social status), but to the fact that *God has given* them these qualities (they have "received" them). The point of v. 7, moreover, reiterates what Paul had said in 3:21–23, specifically, that "all things are yours" in Christ and in God (see chapter 6).

The soteriological nature of the assertions in 4:7 further increases the difficulty that interpreters find in explaining the connection between v. 6d and v. 7. For the transition is now made more problematic as Paul is perceived as moving from (1) the high social status of the apostles based on *"externals"* like wealth and eloquence (v. 6d) to (2) Corinthian boasting in the ostensibly *spiritual* qualities that (Paul suggests) they have "received" as gifts from God (v. 7). Against this line of thought, there must be some continuity of qualities since the Corinthians' having "received" these qualities is supposed to explain (γάρ) the prohibition against boasting.

Having considered the relevant exegetical issues, let us return to Paul's initial statement in v. 6a: "I have changed these things to myself and Apollos." As I have read vv. 6–8, this statement means that Paul had discussed his and Apollos's roles not because the Corinthians were boasting in their leaders, but because the Corinthians were boasting in and comparing themselves and required an example of godly humility and interpersonal concord against which to correct their behavior. Paul had "changed the terms" of the discussion so as to rebuke the Corinthians, not by direct censure, but indirectly, through his example.[37]

---

36. See p. 10 n. 22 above.
37. As early as John Chrysostom, interpreters have construed Paul's statement as im-

Corinthian Self-Sufficiency

In 4:8–10, Paul continues his attack on the Corinthians' boastful pretensions. With unmistakable sarcasm, he exclaims in 4:8: "Already you are satisfied! Already you are rich! Apart from us you have become kings!" One need not strain to see the parallel between this language and a common saying about the Stoic wise man: "Only the wise man is rich, only the wise man is king."[38] This echo of Stoicism is salient and widely recognized.[39] The Stoic connection, moreover, is not merely incidental to the language of 4:8 but also underlies Paul's characterization of the Corinthians throughout 4:6–10. His point, specifically, is that the σοφοί in Corinth, as wise men, boast in their *self-sufficiency*.

For the Stoics, "self-sufficiency" (αὐτάρκεια) was not a matter of bodily wholeness or financial independence. It was a transvalued kind of self-sufficiency. The σοφός was "self-sufficient" (αὐτάρκης) because he possessed in himself all the moral resources and intellectual qualities necessary for contentedness and happiness.[40] The Stoic ideal of self-sufficiency began from their physics (φυσικὸς λόγος), or theory of nature (φύσις). By nature humanity had within all that was necessary for the good life. This convic-

---

plying that, in course of his earlier discussion, he had used "covert allusion." According to Chrysostom, Paul had discussed himself and the other apostles only so as to conceal the actual dividers of the church, thus making his criticism feel less severe (*Hom. Cor. 3* 4). Now in 4:6, Paul "removes the mask, and shows the persons concealed by the appellation of Paul and Apollos," that is, the divisive Corinthians (*Hom. Cor. 12* 1). Fiore ("'Covert Allusion'") argues that μετασχηματίζειν itself was a technical rhetorical term for covert allusion in which one spoke in some sense indirectly, usually to soften criticism, though Fiore also notes that Paul's explicit exposure of the "covert" allusion here spoils the function of the device.

38. For example, Cicero, *Fin.* 3.75; *SVF* 3:655; see also *SVF* 3:615, 617, 618, 619, etc.

39. Among older scholarship, see Lightfoot, *Notes on the Epistles*, 200; Weiss, *Der erste Korintherbrief*, 89–91, 157–59; Grant, "Wisdom of the Corinthians," 52. See also Paige, "Stoicism, *Eleutheria*, and Community," 184; Kuck, *Judgment and Community Conflict*, 217; Hays, "Conversion of the Imagination," 408–9. Parallels can also be found in Philo (e.g., *Migr.* 197), though it was from Stoicism that Hellenistic Judaism borrowed its description of the wise man. Note also Grant's observation ("Wisdom of the Corinthians," 54) that some Hellenistic Jews described the Essenes on analogy with the Stoic wise man. Downing (*Cynics, Paul, and the Pauline Churches*, 101) thinks that Paul's description of the Corinthians reflects "Cynic rather than Stoic usage" and that Paul has in view Cynic antinomianism, or the view that as "kings" they were "free" from convention. On this claim, see chapter 9 below.

40. *SVF* 3:272, 276.

1 Corinthians 4:6–13: The Apostles and the Corinthian σοφοί

tion gave rise to the commonplace precept that one "should not seek from another what one could get from oneself."[41] Indeed, one should not even ask God. As Seneca challenges us, "What need is there of vows? Make yourself happy through your own efforts [*fac ipse felicem*]."[42] For the Stoic this self-sufficiency was possible because one had God already available within, as a *part* of oneself—in the inborn faculty of divine reason.[43] In this respect the moral resources needed for the happy life were not "exogenously" effected—or supplied from without—they were a faculty intrinsic to human nature. The faculty of divine reason was the peculiar quality of the human being, a faculty that no other creature had but God. As such, living according to reason—or nature—was the highest and distinct end, or τέλος, of human existence.

The discourses of Epictetus play on these ideas extensively, often in ways that overlap conspicuously with the language of 1 Cor 4:7. Several passages are worth transcribing in full:

> He [God] says, "If you wish any good thing, get it from yourself [παρὰ σεαυτοῦ]." You say, "No, but from someone else." Do not do so, but get it [λάβε] from yourself. (*Diatr.* 1.29.4 [Oldfather, LCL])

> For, in fact, it is foolish and superfluous to try to obtain from another that which one can get [ἔχει] from oneself [ἐξ αὑτοῦ]. Since, therefore, I am able to get greatness of soul and nobility of character from myself, am I to get a farm, and money, or some office, from you? Far from it! I will not be so unaware of what I myself possess [τῶν ἐμῶν κτημάτων]. (Epictetus, *Diatr.* 1.9.31–32 [Oldfather, LCL])

> Seek and you will find. For you have from nature [ἔχεις . . . παρὰ τῆς φύσεως] resources to find the truth. (Epictetus, *Diatr.* 4.1.51)

> This is the position and character of a layman: He never looks for either help or harm from himself, but only from externals. This is the position

---

41. Cf. *Ep.* 41.1–2; 80.4–5; 92.2; 98.1; also Epictetus, *Diatr.* 1.9.31–32; 1.29.4; 4.1.51; 4.9.17; *Ench.* 48; Marcus Aurelius, *Med.* 7.59.
42. Seneca, *Ep.* 31.5 (Gummere, LCL).
43. Seneca, *Ep.* 41.1–2. While Seneca could say "no one can be good without the help of God," his point is that God, indeed, is a part of us.

and character of the philosopher: He looks for all his help or harm from himself [ἐξ ἑαυτοῦ]. (*Ench.* 48 [Oldfather, LCL])

For the Stoics the implications of these doctrines were far-reaching. Since humans possessed the faculty of reason *qua* a human quality, and since reason was a distinctive quality of human creatures, and since living according to reason was the highest end of human existence, humans who lived according to reason had every right to boast in their own achievement. Seneca spells out this logic fully in *Epistle* 41. At 41.6, he begins to describe a human soul (*animus*) as that which is "resplendent with no external good, but only with its own [*bono suo*]." He then asks: "For what is more foolish than to praise in a man the qualities which come from without [*ad alium transferri*]?" Indeed, "No man ought to glory except in that which is his own [*suo*]." Seneca applies the same point, *mutatis mutandis*, to other living things. We ought to praise each thing for accomplishing that for which it is intended by its nature. We do not praise a lion for wearing decorations or a horse for its bit. So in the case of humans, we should praise only "that which is his own [*ipsius*]." Externals can be snatched away—a retinue of handsome slaves, a beautiful house, a farm as large as one's income. One should praise, then, the quality in a person that is "the peculiar property of the person," namely, "soul, and reason brought to perfection in the soul."

I propose that this framework provides a tightly integrated explanation for the connection between the Corinthians' σοφία, their attitude of self-sufficiency, and their self-boasting. We shall now discuss this further.

"Received" It from Another

Paul's characterization of the Corinthians in 4:7 resonates well with this picture and includes some conspicuous terminological overlap with the passages from Epictetus just cited. Yet, Paul himself *rejects* the Corinthians' kind of self-sufficiency. He refers to what the Corinthians "have" (ἔχεις) but challenges the assumption that it is "from themselves," reminding them that they have rather "received" it from God. The word *received* (ἔλαβες) probably reflects the language of benefaction (with God as benefactor), though the conceptual complex here suggests a possible play on the dynamics of "having" and "receiving" as paralleled in one of the passages cited from Epictetus. In *Diatr.* 1.29.4, Epictetus commits for rhetorical effect a kind of semantic catachresis in his use of the verb λάβε: the "receiver" also becomes his own "giver." As he says, if you want something, "receive [λάβε] it from yourself"

1 Corinthians 4:6–13: The Apostles and the Corinthian σοφοί

(*Diatr.* 1.29.4). This play on the idea of "receiving" underscores the way in which the Stoic idea of self-sufficiency flouts the common conception of "receiving" as ordinarily involving the help of someone external. The rhetorical effect of Epictetus's malapropism is to underscore more emphatically the "paradoxical" (or "astonishing") truth of the Stoic doctrine of self-sufficiency. In this light, Paul's own opposition between gifts that the Corinthians "have of themselves" and gifts as "received" from God appears to undercut this bold and extraordinary Stoic point using precisely the kind of terminology that we find in Epictetus.

Corinthian Qualities

Verse 8 expands directly upon v. 7 and describes, as it were, the content of the Corinthians' boasts: "Already you are satisfied! Already you are rich! Without us you have become kings!" The tone is sarcastic, for Paul adds that they have reached this state "without us"; and the ensuing "wish" ("would that you did reign as kings!") reveals that his assertions are, in some sense, contrary to fact. If the description is his own, doubtless it captures the Corinthians' view of themselves, or there would be nothing to gain by it.

As a direct and censorious description of the Corinthians, this verse has been thought to reveal much about the nature of the Corinthians' claims and the dynamics of the church's conflict. Until the final decades of the twentieth century, most interpreters saw behind their claims religious influences from Gnosticism, Hellenistic Judaism, popular religiosity, or something akin to these. Since then there has emerged a dominant new trend toward viewing Paul's description against the backdrop of secular social practices.[44] Marshall, for instance, argues in his lengthy monograph that Paul had rejected an offer of patronage (see above) and that it is this issue that Paul addresses in 4:6–13. Paul depicts the Corinthians as "hybrists" who were "puffed up" in their high status. In 4:8–10 he caricatures them with such terms as *rich*, *kings*, *prudent*, and so on.[45] Finding these same terms used in sources in a sociological sense, Marshall concludes that the contrast between the Corinthians and apostles in 4:10 "is primarily a social one and the terms belong to the rhetoric of status."[46]

---

44. In addition to our discussion of Marshall below, see Clarke and Pogoloff (both cited in Hiigel, *Leadership in 1 Corinthians*, 78–79).
45. Marshall, *Enmity in Corinth*, 194–218.
46. Marshall, *Enmity in Corinth*, 210.

It would be wrong not to credit Marshall for his extensive (for lack of a stronger term) research into the social conventions of Paul's environment, which takes up in excess of one hundred pages of his substantial tome. Were the reader not prohibited by the book's length, however, it would be apparent how inadequate Marshall's actual treatment of 1 Cor 4 is. The way he situates his thesis within the history of scholarship is stated, from the preface, in equivocal terms and somewhat inconsistently with how he approaches his argument. Specifically, Marshall's preface presents his explanation of the conflict as a *complement* to earlier theses and announces that "to do full justice to the matter [the Corinthian conflict], the religious and philosophical dimensions would need to be investigated as well." What is easy to miss if one is eager to accept his novel suggestions is that Marshall's interpretation does *not* then serve to complement other explanations but, if correct, effectively supplants them. Moreover, he advocates for his reading without examining its *comparative* merits. The only thesis to which he explicitly offers his reading as a better alternative is the old gnostic thesis,[47] which interpreters widely acknowledge has been defeated. Given both Marshall's intent to complement theological readings and his refusal to deal with them, it is then a giant and highly unjustified leap to his conclusion that "the conflicts in Corinth are primarily social *rather than* theological or religious in character."[48]

These deficiencies are evident in Marshall's treatment of 4:8 specifically. As Hiigel notes, Marshall at no point deals with earlier interpretations of the verse.[49] Moreover, his interpretation excludes rather than complements earlier interpretations. If in 4:8 *rich* and *kings* indicate that these people were wealthy and held power in the civic sphere, and if this status relates to their observance of cultural conventions that themselves stimulated the conflict, then Marshall has ruled out a "spiritual" interpretation of this verse, not supplemented it.

That Paul's description of the Corinthians in fact does not refer to social status in the ordinary sense is shown by several points.[50] (1) Marshall's examples in which "kings" are criticized for their presumption of absolute

---

47. Marshall, *Enmity in Corinth*, ix, xiii.
48. Marshall, *Enmity in Corinth*, xiii (my italics).
49. Hiigel, *Leadership in 1 Corinthians*, 77–79.
50. Several others agree. Horsley ("Pneumatikos vs. Psychikos," 282) takes these in reference to "exalted [religious] status"; Hyldahl ("Paul and Hellenistic Judaism," 210) refers to the spiritually "rich." Murphy-O'Connor (*Paul*, 283) says that it is "debatable" whether 4:8 refers to social status and that this depends on whether the "spirit-people" were drawn "predominantly from the wealthier."

1 Corinthians 4:6–13: The Apostles and the Corinthian σοφοί

freedom apply to *actual* kings and tyrants.[51] Since the Corinthians were not kings or rulers in any equivalent sense, we must suppose from the beginning that Paul's remarks involve some level of departure from the *literal* "social" meaning of the terms. (2) Paul's description of the Corinthians in v. 8 is an elaboration of the rhetorical questions asked in v. 7. As we have already seen, the implication in v. 7 that *"God* gave you what you have" indicates that the gifts in view are nothing but the gifts received in respect to salvation. (3) Interpreters since Lightfoot and Weiss over a century ago have noted that the vocabulary of v. 8 most audibly echoes the Stoic and Cynic description of the wise man.[52]

Ironically, 1 Cor 4:8 is an example where "parallelomania" looks less applicable to "history-of-religions" interpretations than to "social" ones. For instance, Dale Martin acknowledges that the Stoic sayings about their "wise man" in fact offer the most salient parallels to 4:8; yet he adds that "the same terms function more broadly in the terminology of patron-client structures of the Empire" and that "patrons were sometimes called *rex* ('king')."[53] Martin includes no citations, and while one could no doubt turn up examples, the individual terms are not significant on their own, for the contextual applications of the word *king* in the cultural encyclopedia would certainly be too numerous to count.[54] Similarly, Winter's observation that sophists belonged to the same class as the "wealthy" and "rulers" (he does not say "kings") is correct but hardly a strong connection.[55] The main criticism to emphasize is that arguments grounded in the observation that *"x* word could be used" can hardly be granted the same significance as arguments based on overlap at the level of some kind of standard usage, overlapping configuration of terms, formal-syntactical similarities, and surely most importantly, the stream of thought in context.

We have already examined the Stoic formula "only the wise man is $x \ldots y$" (chapter 3). As shown, this standard formula assigns attributes to "the wise man," usually in a list, and in the syntactical form of simple predication. So conventional were these statements that the Stoics had a name for them—

---

51. Marshall, *Enmity in Corinth*, 189, 209.
52. See n. 39 above.
53. Martin, *Corinthian Body*, 66.
54. Similarly, Miller's observation ("Not with Eloquent Wisdom," 344n89) that we find the political *ekklēsia* being called "king" in first-century discussions of democracy may be an interesting sociolinguistic point, but we are concerned with the most probable meaning in context, not with every possible meaning.
55. Winter, *Philo and Paul among the Sophists*, 198–99.

the "paradoxes" (παράδοξοι)—so called because the claims they conveyed were "astonishing." One may take for granted that some of the Corinthians considered themselves σοφοί. I have noted that the series of predicates encountered in 1:26 (σοφός, δυνατός, εὐγενής) all occur as typical attributes of the Stoic wise man in the paradoxes. Here again Paul returns to his Stoical description. His description of the Corinthians in 4:8 uses simple predication and multiple predicates (now using predicative verbs). The precise description of the Corinthians found here, moreover, is typical in descriptions of the Stoic wise man:[56]

> Some think that the Stoics are jesting when they hear that in their sect the *wise man* [σοφόν] is termed . . . *a rich man and a king* [καὶ πλούσιον καὶ βασιλέα]. (*SVF* 3:655)

> More rightly will *the wise man* [*sapiens*] be called *king* [*rex*] . . . more rightly will he be called *rich* [*dives*]. (Cicero, *Fin.* 3.75)

> *Wealth* [πλοῦτος] . . . *kingship* [βασιλείαν] . . . *good birth* [εὐγένεια] . . . *freedom* [ἐλευθερία] belong only to *the wise man* [σοφός]. (*SVF* 3:619)

Inadvertently, Winter actually confirms that the paradoxes supply the most salient cultural resonances with 1 Cor 4:8. Although he relates Paul's language to the sophists, the passage that he adduces, from Plutarch, in fact describes none other than the Stoic wise man. We have already examined his misuse of this passage in chapter 3.[57]

The allusions to Stoicism in Paul's language continue in the final portion of v. 8: "without us you reign . . . would that you did reign, so that we might reign together with you." The Stoics held that friendship was best among those equal in virtue, and that among true friends there existed fellowship and a sharing of all possessions (κοινωνία).[58] They extended the principle of κοινωνία among friends to include the relationship between the σοφός and God. The wise man and God also were "friends," so that the wise man ruled together with God.[59] Philo articulates the philosophers' point clearly and

---

56. Among countless other examples, see for the wise man as "king" (βασιλεύς) also *SVF* 3:615, 617; Philo, *Somn.* 2.244; and as "rich" (πλούσιος), *SVF* 3:593, 598, 603, 618.

57. Winter, *Philo and Paul among the Sophists*, 190; citing Plutarch, *How to Tell a Flatterer from a Friend* (58e). See discussion in chapter 3 of Pogoloff's misuse of this passage (*Logos and Sophia*, 117).

58. Seneca, *Ben.* 7.12.2; cf. *Mos.* 1.158; Diogenes Laertius, *Vit. phil.* 7.124.

59. See discussion of "all things" and Stoic self-sufficiency in chapter 6.

concisely: "He alone [the wise man] is king, having received from the All-ruling the power of rule, without rival, over all things."[60]

Paul's description of the Corinthians in v. 8 therefore depicts them again as affecting a high estimation of their humanity, professed without due credit to the originating (incongruous grace) and enabling work of God (efficacious grace). That is to say, their self-assessment reflects again the notion of the σοφός, or of themselves, as αὐτάρκης, or self-sufficient.

I must add a final word regarding the relevance of this passage to the older thesis that the Corinthians' problem was one of "(over)realized eschatology."[61] According to this view, Paul's description of the Corinthians as having "already" (ἤδη) become rich/kings indicates that they had transferred eschatological realities into the present, seeing all that would happen as having already happened, including the arrival of the fullness of the Spirit (chs. 12–14), even final glorification and, in some form, the resurrection itself (15:12). Against this view, the philosophical underpinnings of the Corinthians' views, rooted as they are in an optimistic humanism, suggest that from Paul's perspective the Corinthians had in some sense *no*,[62] or at least too *little*, eschatology. Within this framework, the temporal adverb ἤδη (4:8) serves not as a reflection of the Corinthians' theology but as a Pauline insertion added to *reframe* their thinking in eschatological terms. Set in the context of 1:18–3:23, Paul's eschatological reservation in 4:8 asks the Corinthians to make space for the *cross*, a synecdochic symbol of the ethos that believers ought to embody during the present era. The implications are largely anthropological. The wise Corinthians' self-conception transgresses *human* limits, puffs them up, and bursts the model of cruciformity. They view themselves, like the wise man, as having everything and needing nothing. They, like the philosopher, did not have their sights set on a higher future state.

Two Kinds of Wisdom

This reading of Paul's invective is confirmed as he shifts in the second half of v. 8 from the Corinthians to himself and the apostles ("us"). Though the Corinthians may "reign as kings," they do so "without us [apostles]" and Paul

---

60. *SVF* 3:603 = Philo, *Sobr.* 57. See also *SVF* 3:359.
61. For a fuller treatment of this view, see Thiselton, "Realized Eschatology at Corinth."
62. Darrell J. Doughty, "Presence and Future of Salvation in Corinth," *ZNW* 66 (1975): 61–90; Kuck, *Judgement and Community Conflict*, 16–25, 216–19; Hays, "Conversion of the Imagination"; Chester, *Conversion at Corinth*, 218.

can only "wish" that he and the apostles "reigned together with" them. In v. 9 Paul contrasts his (feigned) wish with the actual state of affairs: he does not, like the Stoic wise man, share now in God's rule. Far from that, God has displayed him and the apostles as "people condemned to death" in a "spectacle" witnessed by heaven ("angels") and earth ("the world").[63] This image sets off a description of the apostles in vv. 9–13 as despised in the eyes of the world and as plagued by constant hardship: they hunger and thirst, are poorly clothed, are virtually homeless, are abused, and grind out a living by the toil of their hands.

These verses offer no support for the view that the Corinthians directed their boasting toward Paul or Apollos. These verses suggest only that the Corinthians thought well of themselves. In v. 10 Paul contrasts the apostles and the Corinthians in a set of three antitheses. The apostles are "foolish" (μωροί), "weak" (ἀσθενεῖς), and "dishonored" (ἄτιμοι); the Corinthians are "prudent" (φρόνιμοι), "strong" (ἰσχυροί), and "distinguished" (ἔνδοξοι).

It is not immediately clear whether these terms apply in the ordinary "sociological" sense. The fact that Paul goes on to describe his socioeconomic condition in vv. 11–13 offers partial support to this reading. Hock proposes that Paul's self-description relates specifically to his vocation as a manual laborer and that it was this vocation that caused some of the Corinthians to turn against him. In this regard Hock sees Paul's reference to "working with the hands" against the backdrop of debates among philosophers about how to support themselves. While most philosophers earned a living by charging fees, taking up residence in the households of the well-to-do, or even by begging, Paul chose the least common path, that of self-support through manual labor.[64] Similar to Marshall, Hock thus imagines that other itinerant preachers had agreed to take pay from members of the church and that Paul had refused the offer, which the Corinthians then took as a rejection of their patronage and friendship.[65]

Hock's reading is another example of how a hypothesized social background can become so inflated as to overshadow the text. Paul's reference to "laboring" is listed in a polysyndetically arranged series of items that describe his abject condition ("hungry, thirsty, etc."). Paul does not subsume

---

63. Such spectacles are described for example in Seneca, *Ep.* 7.2–5; Dio Chrysostom, *Or.* 31.121; Suetonius, *Claud.* 34.1–2.

64. E.g., Musonius Rufus, *Diatr.* 11.

65. Hock, *Social Context*, 52–65; cf. Still, "Divisions over Leaders," 22–26.

1 Corinthians 4:6–13: The Apostles and the Corinthian σοφοί

hungering and thirsting and being abused (and the earlier items in the list) beneath his occupation as a manual laborer (the last item in the list). Rather the former conditions derive, equally in the list with his occupation, from his vocation as an apostle of cruciformity. It is hard, moreover, to see how Paul's decision to work could be responsible for a conflict between him and the church given the context of vv. 6–13. What does Paul's work have to do with the Corinthians' boasting in things they have received from God (v. 7) or in their thinking that (closely related to v. 7) they are "rich" and "kings" (v. 8)? And why, if the issue is Paul's difference of financial policy from other ministers, does he elaborate instead upon the difference between himself and the Corinthians while describing the apostles as being just like him ("we apostles")? Above all, how does his policy about work integrate with the matter of "wisdom," around which most of the first four chapters focus?

The likelier reading is that in vv. 9–13 Paul addresses, more generally, opposing orientations toward "status," as weighed by all kinds of qualities, both *social and spiritual*. Yet, in contrast to Paul's description of himself, we have solid justification for taking the Corinthian attributes in v. 10 in a spiritual sense.[66] Paul's differentiation of prepositions in his qualification of the first antithesis—"foolish διὰ Christ" (apostles) and "prudent ἐν Christ" (Corinthians)—should not be overlooked. The terms on the apostles' side are easily understood in the sociological sense, given the qualification: the apostles are foolish, weak, and dishonored *because of* their imitation of Christ. The Corinthians, however, are said to be prudent, strong, and distinguished *in* (ἐν) Christ. That is, they are such *by virtue of their spiritual condition*. Naturally, these characteristics contributed to the Corinthians' "social" status in a sense. Indeed, the σοφοί do enjoy an increase in social status in a certain domain of existence. Yet, it is a status that accrues to them within the "social" domain of the church and on the basis of their spiritual qualities that they possess, as Paul says, "ἐν Christ" (cf. 2:15).[67] This is "transcendent social status." In sum, Paul describes his own status against criteria of "ordinary social status" (as attributed within the domain of the world) while describing the Corinthians' "social" status in reference to certain transcendent criteria (as attributed

---

66. Horsley ("Pneumatikos vs. Psychikos," 282) takes these in reference to "exalted [religious] status."

67. Thus Wire (*Corinthian Women Prophets*, 62–68) is correct that those who lacked ordinary status indicators within the domain of society acquired a new status in Christ, placing them on "a new *cursus honorum* within the community" (65). This is not a status tied to their roles in an institutional sense, as if Paul had said not ἐν Χριστῷ, but ἐν ἐκκλησίᾳ.

largely within the fellowship of believers). The encompassing point remains the same: the Corinthian emphasis on eminence and distinction reflects the wisdom of the world and the lowliness of the apostles reflects the wisdom of the cross.

It is not a random coincidence that Paul's self-characterization here resembles the *peristasis*, or "hardship," catalogs that were typical in descriptions of the philosopher or wise man.[68] Similar to 4:9–13, these catalogs present the hardships of the wise man as being ordained by God and visible on the cosmic stage.[69] They depict the wise man's perseverance (ὑπομονή) through hardships as evidence of his virtue, as he learned to properly distinguish things "indifferent" (externals) from things "good and bad" (virtue and vice). Different from the wise man, however, Paul endures not because externals are a matter of indifference, but because in hardship he becomes an imitator of Christ. In this, Paul describes the "wisdom of the cross" as articulated in 1:18–31 yet again, in the embodied form of his and the other apostles' lowly way of life.

Paul's description of the Corinthians in v. 10, too, is consistent with the Stoic description of the wise man. As in v. 8, Paul here parodies the Corinthians' pretensions of wise-man status (or else repeats their claims) by characterizing them with the language, and in the form, of the Stoic paradoxes. Note again the language of the paradoxes and the coordination of attributes in simple predication, including terminology already encountered in 1:26 and 4:8:

> Some think that the Stoics are jesting when they hear that in their sect the wise man [σοφόν] is termed *prudent* [φρόνιμον] . . . a rich man and a king [καὶ πλούσιον καὶ βασιλέα]. (*SVF* 3:655)

> And that the wise man . . . is great and full and exalted and *strong* [ἰσχυρόν]. (*SVF* 1:216 // 3.567).

---

68. See for example Epictetus, *Diatr.* 3.22.45–49; Dio Chrysostom, *Or.* 8.16; Seneca, *Const.* 2.3; 15.1; 19.3. For a discussion of this theme, see John T. Fitzgerald, *Cracks in an Earthen Vessel: An Examination of the Catalogues of Hardships in the Corinthian Correspondence*, SBLDS 99 (Atlanta: Scholars, 1988).

69. For a connection between the Stoic metaphor of the "contest" and the contestant's struggle as taking place on the world "stage," see Courtney J. P. Friesen, "Paulus Tragicus: Staging Apostolic Adversity in First Corinthians," *JBL* 134 (2015): 813–32, esp. 823–27.

> He alone is well-born [εὐγενής] ... is not just rich [πλούσιος] but all-rich [πάμπλουτος] ... being a man not just *distinguished* [ἔνδοξος] but glorious [εὐκλεής]. ... He alone is king [βασιλεύς]. ... He alone is free [ἐλεύθερος]. (*SVF* 3:603 // Philo, *Sobr.* 56–57)

Culturally, such claims about the wise man overturn conventional sociopolitical definitions of terms and redefine them in an inward sense.[70] For the Corinthians, like the Stoics, the terms offer not just a "social" description; rather, they apply in a transvalued sense.

Conclusion

This chapter has offered a reading of 1 Cor 4:6–13 that differs substantially from dominant readings of late. I have tried to offer a reading that is consistent with the text's finer details, including the critically significant conjunctions that determine its logic (so often γάρ!). Paul announces in 4:6 that he had discussed himself and Apollos (3:5–4:5) in order to provide the Corinthians with an example—an example of believers who taught and lived the wisdom of God and who worked together in harmony. The axiom "not beyond what is written" (4:6c) then cast Paul in the role of a philosophical teacher, whose teachings remain binding and should be preserved and imitated by his students—a further warning to those who might be "laying a different foundation" (3:11) with a contrary wisdom.

At vv. 6d–7, I offered the bold proposal that these verses address not Corinthian boasting in apostles, but Corinthian boasting in self over against others in the church. As little support as this reading has garnered among interpreters, it is grammatically sensible (εἷς = τοῦ ἑνός), and it more adequately accounts for the function of ὑπέρ in v. 6d, provides the needed transition into vv. 7–8, and preserves overall greater coherence in the passage.

As Paul continues, his comments in vv. 8, 10 function as a condemnation of Corinthian boasting, which they ground in their αὐτάρκεια ("self-sufficiency"). They exaggerate their spiritual qualities, and in this regard, they fail to acknowledge that their gifts are received from God (v. 7). This state of affairs is consistent with the picture of the controversy that I have been developing. A contingent within the church viewed themselves on analogy

---

70. See for such redefinition *SVF* 1:216 // 3:567.

with the Stoic "wise man," believing that they had reached a higher state than others in the church. Like the wise man, they were "rich," "kings," "prudent," "strong," and "distinguished" (vv. 8, 10). Only, in variation from the Stoic view, they believed that they had reached this state "ἐν Christ."

Finally, vv. 9–13 elaborate the same antithesis that appeared from 1:18 to 3:23, namely, that involving a contrast between the status-driven wisdom of the world and the cruciform wisdom of Christ. In this light, the antithesis between "us apostles" and the Corinthian σοφοί need not be seen primarily as a "defense" against criticisms of Paul from the Corinthians or as an indication that Paul had lost prestige in the church while others gained it. Rather, the antithesis displays Paul and the apostles as a cruciform *example*, against which the Corinthians' σοφία is exposed as being rooted not in the wisdom of the cross, but in that of the world.

8

1 Corinthians 4:14–21:
Paul as Founder and Teacher

Asyndeton and a change of subject in 4:14 signal a new paragraph, and it is the last of the unit (1:17b–4:21). As in 4:6, Paul points back to "these things" (ταῦτα) and explains his purpose in discussing them (ἐντρέπων and νουθετῶν), thus marking the paragraph as a conclusion to the foregoing. In the flow of the argument, ταῦτα will be recognized unambiguously as a reference to what immediately precedes.[1] Paul's rebuke against the Corinthians' boasting in vv. 6–8, as well as his sarcastic characterization of them and his sharp contrast between them and himself in vv. 9–13, no doubt dealt a blow to their self-esteem, and he must now reassure them that his criticisms had constructive purpose.

Interpreters' reconstructions of the occasion have played a formative role in shaping interpretations of this particular passage. Interpreters commonly affirm several points that, while plausible as hypothetical realities, rely less on the obvious meaning of the text than on a series of assumptions: that Paul is here defending himself or his apostolic authority, that he is still contending to win back partisans who have gone over to Apollos, that these have gone over to Apollos because of Paul's inferior rhetorical abilities, that they are "puffed up" in Apollos, that they are offended at the likelihood that Paul will not return or else boast *because* he will not return. As I demonstrate below, reconstructions sometimes assert the "facts" but do not clearly articulate

---

1. Verses 6–13, however, continue the general theme of chapters 1–4: the Corinthians, with their pursuit of honor and status, embody the wisdom of the world; Paul (and the apostles), the wisdom of God/Christ crucified.

how they integrate. I shall offer a different reading here. In this reading the domain of "education" provides the controlling matrix within which Paul's language works. The scholastic resonances in this section, I contend, offer us additional clues about the Corinthians' conception of the parties and of Paul himself.

Paul as an Example

The shift in 4:14 from the first-person plural amid discussion of "us apostles" (v. 9) now to the first-person singular (γράφω, "I write") is critically related to Paul's point: Paul and only Paul can claim the Corinthians as his "children" (τέκνα μου) (v. 14). While the Corinthians may have "myriad pedagogues" in Christ, still they have "not many fathers" (v. 15). The first expression is hyperbolic. The second is litotic, for it is explained (γάρ) in terms of the singular ἐγώ ἐγέννησα ("for *I* begot you"). The reason for the singular is open to various explanations.

The terms *pedagogue* (παιδαγωγός) and *father* (πατήρ) both require elucidation. The "pedagogue" (παιδαγωγός) was a familiar figure in the world of education. The sources offer varied and in some ways conflicting explanations of his role.[2] The pedagogue typically belonged to the slave class, though some were freedmen, and some took pride in their position as one of relative prestige (for members of their class). To the extent that pedagogues played a role in curricular instruction, this was limited to the elementary level. Their broader responsibility was to serve as children's guardians, conducting them safely to and from school, holding them accountable for staying on task, and facilitating their progress in their studies.

Paul's use of the "pedagogue" metaphor is mildly pejorative. These connotations come not so much from the general reference as from the contrast that Paul draws between the Corinthian pedagogues and himself, and by his pointing to his *singular* role as father. This distinction, driven to an extreme by hyperbole ("ten thousand" pedagogues), serves rhetorically to amplify the uniqueness and greater relative importance of his role.

But why his emphasis on singularity? The pedagogues here must be members of the Corinthian church. They can hardly be itinerant minis-

---

2. For a longer treatment of the pedagogue role, see Norman Young, "Paidagogos: The Social Setting of a Pauline Metaphor," *NovT* 29 (1987): 150–76; and for a brief, recent discussion, see White, *Teacher of the Nations*, 84n416.

ters like Apollos or Cephas. (1) In the first place, the contrast pedagogues versus father is entirely unlike the pairing of Paul and Apollos in 3:5–9. As noted, Paul and Apollos there played complementary roles. Paul never set the two in opposition, but together, on one side of a contrast, with God on the other (3:6–7). Where Paul described himself and Apollos in titular terms, he assigned them not different titles but the same: both were διάκονοι (3:5), ὑπηρέται, and οἰκονόμοι (4:1). (2) Next, one must consider the inappropriateness of the tally—"ten thousand" pedagogues—if the reference is to only *two* other party leaders—Apollos and Cephas—much less to Apollos alone. While clearly hyperbolic, Paul's reference makes more sense the greater the multitude he has in view.[3] (3) Finally, it is by all means clear, and most immediately from vv. 6–13, that Paul believes that some of the Corinthians advocated a wisdom other than the one he taught them. By contrast, Paul has at no point attributed any sort of wisdom to Apollos. The more judicious approach is surely to construe Paul's meaning in terms of what he has said, over and above suspected innuendos. On all grounds, it makes the most sense to view the pedagogues, like the kind of person discussed in 3:10–18, as being identifiable with the Corinthian σοφοί who build unsoundly upon the work of the apostles and thereby "destroy" God's temple, the church.

The connotations behind the term *father* (πατήρ) require examination as well. The term is at once seized upon by those whose reconstructions envisage a Paul who has lost his grip on the community he founded.[4] Some see in the term strong authoritarian connotations, with Paul exploiting the advantages of the patriarchal culture in order to reassert his authority.[5] Patriarchal dominance, however, is not always a primary resonance, nor is this connection sensitive to the context. We are, first of all, surely helped in identifying the register by the fact that Paul describes his children as "beloved" (ἀγαπητά). Williams accepts that Paul plays on the political connotations of the term, and specifically the kind of hierarchical-patriarchal arrangements legitimated by Roman imperial ideology; yet, he observes based on

---

3. Johannes Munck presents these as members of the Corinthian church in "Church without Factions," excerpted in Adams and Horrell, *Christianity at Corinth*, 68; so also Paul Holloway, "Religious 'Slogans' in 1 Corinthians: Wit, Wisdom, and the Quest for Status in a Roman Colony," *JTS* 72 (2021): 125–54, esp. 126.

4. According to Dahl ("Church at Corinth," 55), Paul's appeal to his paternal role is a claim to his authority, which he needs to reestablish before addressing the problems that occupy chapters 5–16.

5. Elizabeth Anne Castelli, *Imitating Paul: A Discourse of Power* (Louisville: Westminster John Knox Press, 1991), 99–111.

"Paul's preceding arguments on servanthood (4:1–5) and the catalogue of suffering (4:9–13)" that Paul "appears to aim at a redefinition of the father image," appealing not to power and authority but to his cruciform example.[6] In other words, Paul actually *rejects* the status hierarchies of the "world" that he himself echoes, in advocacy of a wisdom of the cross.

Williams's attentiveness to Paul's status-inverting message puts us on the right track. Still, the sociolinguistic register seems to be other than political. The term *father* also had resonances in the discourse of ancient education, both Jewish and Greco-Roman. Devin White has shown that the duties of parents as educators are a prevalent theme in Second Temple Jewish literature and that the duties of the father especially are emphasized.[7] In Greco-Roman education, parents were not only involved in choosing the "teachers" who reared their children in their earliest years (nurses, pedagogues), but actually instructed their children in basic literacy. Plutarch offers a lengthy description of the ideal father-educator in his biography of Cato the Elder.[8] So important was the role of parent as teacher that Quintilian could say, when students later graduated to study rhetoric with hired teachers, that teachers were to play the role of "parent" for their students and that students were to regard their teachers as "parents."[9]

White observes that the likelihood of an allusion to Paul's paternal role as educator increases in light of the multiple pedagogical allusions present in the context of vv. 14–21. In addition to the explicit reference to "pedagogues" and Paul's, countering, self-characterization as a parent-teacher (v. 15), White identifies several other connections with primary- and secondary-level education: "imitation" of teachers (v. 16), "teaching" in all the churches (v. 17), "remembering" what was taught (v. 17), and the "rod" of discipline (v. 21).

White's comparanda from the matrix of early education seem generally appropriate. On the other hand, Abraham Malherbe has demonstrated extensively that Paul's practices of pastoral care often resemble the practices of the schools in the tradition of the *philosophers*.[10] (1) Malherbe observes that it was conventional for philosophers to exhort their listeners in the manner

---

6. Williams, "Paul's Anti-imperial 'Discourse,'" 821–22.

7. White, *Teacher of the Nations*, 87; citing Sir 2:1; 3:1, 17; 6:23; etc.; 1 En. 81; Josephus, *Vit.* 7–9; Jub. 47:9; Philo, *Spec.* 2.228; and others.

8. Plutarch, *Cat. Maj.* 20.1–4.

9. Quintilian, *Inst.* 2.2.5; 2.9.1; cited in White, *Teacher of the Nations*, 89.

10. Malherbe, "'Gentle as a Nurse'"; "Exhortation in First Thessalonians," *NovT* 25 (1983): 238–56; *Paul and the Thessalonians*.

of fathers and to think of their listeners as their children.[11] The kinship metaphor "was thought particularly apt because of the favorable disposition of fathers to their children."[12]

The paternal metaphor is not the only allusion to the philosophical moral tradition evident here. Several other features in vv. 14–21 reflect the conventions of the "parenetic" style of moral instruction, as Malherbe further discusses.[13]

(2) Rhetorically, vv. 14–21 serve one of the fundamental purposes of parenesis, namely, that of admonishment. The language of admonishment in fact occurs in the opening verse: "in order to admonish you" (νουθετῶ[ν]).

(3) Despite wide cultural currency of the rhetoric of "imitation,"[14] Paul's direct exhortation in v. 16, "become imitators of me," evokes most clearly the mimetic tradition rooted in moral philosophy. Philosophy in the Hellenistic and Roman periods was "theoretical" only insofar as theory articulated the dogmatic basis for practice,[15] and it was often said that the best way to absorb the doctrines (*doctrinae*) of philosophy was by following examples (*exempla*) that best embodied them.[16] It was recommended that students imitate their teachers.[17] For philosophers in both the Stoic and Platonic traditions, imitation proceeded in a series in which the principal model was Nature, God, or the gods, a model imitated by the wise, who in turn became a model for others.[18] We find an analogous series in 1 Cor 11:1, where Paul says, "become imitators of me, just as I also am of Christ."

(4) Paul's sending of Timothy so that the Corinthians might, as he says, "*remember* my ways in Christ Jesus" (v. 17) reflects a conventional strategy

---

11. Malherbe, *Paul and the Popular Philosophers*, 54; citing primary and secondary literature in n. 54.

12. Malherbe, *Paul and the Thessalonians*, 150.

13. Malherbe, "Exhortation in First Thessalonians," 169–70; Malherbe, *Paul and the Thessalonians*, 61–94; Malherbe, "Hellenistic Moralists."

14. James R. Harrison, *Paul and the Ancient Celebrity Circuit: The Cross and Moral Transformation* (Louisville: Mohr Siebeck, 2019), 217–55.

15. See for example the following remark from Cicero: "if it be true that all the doctrines of philosophy have a practical bearing [referuntur ad vitam], I may claim that in my public and private conduct alike I have practiced [praestitisse] the precepts taught by reason and by theory [ratio et doctrina]" (*Nat. d.* 1.7 [LCL, Rackham]). See also *Tusc.* 2.4.11–13; Musonius Rufus, *Diatr.* 4.

16. Seneca, *Ep.* 6.5; 52.8; 104.20–33.

17. Philo, *Mos.* 1.158–159; Seneca, *Ep.* 6.5–6; 84.8.

18. Seneca, *Ep.* 66.39; 95.50; *Clem.* 1.7.1; Epictetus, *Diatr.* 3.3.34; Plutarch, *Mor.* 780e–781a; Galen, *Aff. pecc. dig.* 10.41.5–11.

in the parenesis of the philosophical schools. "Reminders" were important for a similar reason as *exempla*. Philosophy was a way of life, and to pursue it one had, as Seneca said, to "devote yourself wholly" to it.[19] One could not pursue it with only casual commitment because the values it advocated differed fundamentally from the ones into which popular culture socializes us from birth. For the Stoic the pursuit of philosophy meant a singular focus on virtue, the one and only "good," and a renunciation of all those "external" things ordinarily called good (health, offspring, wealth, success) as being now a matter of "indifference." This transition requires a radical reorientation of values, away from those socialized into us by our earliest teachers (our nurses, pedagogues, even parents), reinforced through public opinion and habit, legitimated through society's various institutions (schools, the state, cults), and modeled for us by the crowd (virtually everybody) that surrounds us.[20] The philosophers saw that resocialization of values could be achieved only by immersion in one's new doctrines, inculcated by constant repetition and nourished by persistent practice.[21] In this regard it was often said that the precepts of philosophy bear repeating, for they "refresh the memory,"[22] and they help recondition the mind and reprogram habits.[23] Thus teachers constantly "reminded" their students about what they already "know" and applied positive reinforcement for appropriate behavior.[24] Paul's "reminder" about his own "ways in Christ Jesus" here serves a parallel function in that, like the philosophers, he is dealing with students who have converted to a new value system, different from the system that they, evidently, still struggled to move beyond. They still live according to the values of the crowd (the "world") and have not been sufficiently indoctrinated into the habitus of God's wisdom, embodied in the way of Christ. Paul's call to imitation is an appeal to his own cruciform example.[25]

In short, the images employed in vv. 14–16 cluster as a consistent set of cultural significations that fit within the domain of ancient education and moral

---

19. Seneca, *Ep.* 53.8. See also Cicero, *Tusc.* 5.2.5.
20. The philosophers often blamed vice on bad socialization: the influence of the crowd (Seneca, *Ep.* 94.55; 123.6–9; Musonius Rufus, *Diatr.* 6) or how we were taught by our parents (Seneca, *Ep.* 115.11); Cicero lists nurses, parents, masters, the poets, and public opinion (*Tusc.* 3.1.2–3).
21. Epictetus, *Diatr.* 2.9.12–14.
22. Seneca, *Ep.* 94.21; cf. 30.7, 15.
23. Seneca, *Ep.* 94.48.
24. Note Seneca, *Ep.* 25.4: "as indeed you are doing"; see also 30.7, 15; 94.21.
25. So also Hiigel, *Leadership in 1 Corinthians*, 118.

1 Corinthians 4:14–21: Paul as Founder and Teacher

formation. Paul disparages *Corinthian* teachers as mere "pedagogues" and characterizes himself, by contrast, as the "father" who not only established the community but who also, in the manner of the philosophical teacher, took chief responsibility for their spiritual and moral development.

Puffed Up in Themselves

Though he calls the Corinthians to imitate him, Paul is not able to be with them at present. His mention of a visit from Timothy gives him occasion to address his own travel plans (v. 18). Here he says: "As if I were not coming to you some of you are puffed up" (ὡς μὴ ἐρχομένου δέ μου πρὸς ὑμᾶς ἐφυσιώθησάν τινες).

Dahl assigns this verse critical significance in his reconstruction of the conflict, proposing that "the quarrels and the slogans at Corinth were related to the assumption that the apostle would not return."[26] Connecting 4:18 back with the first mention of the parties in 1:12, Dahl proposes that the slogans in 1:12 are declarations of "independence *from* Paul" and that their independence is expressed in 4:18 in terms of their being "puffed up."[27]

How interpreters connect the facts of these verses with an overall picture of the conflict is not always clear. It is unclear, for instance, how Marshall integrates, on the one hand, his theory that the Corinthians were offended at Paul's rejection of their offer of friendship (patronage) and, on the other hand, the cause of the Corinthians' arrogance as mentioned in 4:18–19. Marshall infers from 4:18 that the Corinthians had criticized Paul for his absence, and from 4:18–19 that they are puffed up "against him," but from 4:19 that they are puffed up on account of "an over-confidence in eloquence." Marshall concludes, based on all the facts, that their chief objection was his "refusal of financial assistance (9:1–23)."[28] Perhaps Marshall's many claims could be assembled into an ingeniously integrated situation, should one carefully consider. His inferences, however, are impossible to reconcile exegetically. For one, his interpretation assigns to "puffed up" in 4:18 two meanings at once: the Corinthians are puffed up *against* Paul, and they are also puffed up because of an overconfidence in their *own* eloquence (we witnessed the

---

26. Dahl, "Paul and the Church at Corinth," 46.
27. Dahl, "Paul and the Church at Corinth," 49 (my italics).
28. Paul's absence (Marshall, *Enmity in Corinth*, 217); puffed up against him (204); overconfidence in eloquence (346); his refusal of financial assistance (217).

same overexploitation of language in Marshall's interpretation of 4:6). Furthermore, Marshall leaves unanswered how their arrogance relates to Paul's absence: does Marshall imply, or not, that the Corinthians are puffed up against Paul on the basis of their "criticism" that he would not return?

It is difficult also to tie Litfin's reading of the situation together. According to Litfin, "in 4:18 Paul relates their [the Corinthians'] inflated self-image to his own absence; it was when Paul did not come to them that 'some' were puffed up." Then Litfin says, "in 4:19 their being puffed up is associated with their speech, or perhaps better, their [the Corinthians'] eloquence." Finally, Litfin states that the Corinthians criticized Paul for his rhetorical deficiencies after the eloquent Apollos came to town.[29] This list of assertions leaves Litfin's explanation for how Paul's absence inflated the Corinthians' self-image, for me, somewhat scattered. It also leaves unclear whether Litfin sees the Corinthians puffed up *both* over their own eloquence *and* on behalf of Apollos against Paul, with regard to *their* eloquence. While both could be true from the standpoint of conceivable scenarios, as we explore below, this construal overloads ἐφυσιώθησαν and the immediate assertions with signification.

Similarly, Winter poses that the Corinthians whom Paul has in mind are those who supported Apollos as the superior "sophist" and that v. 18 implies their "obvious relief" that "Paul's promised return had not eventuated."[30] Winter further remarks that they had become puffed up "in the face of" Paul's failure to return."[31] According to Winter, the relationship between the two events (Paul's failure to return and the Corinthians' being puffed up) was a causal one.[32] Yet, it remains unclear how to put all of this together. What does it mean for the Corinthians to be puffed up "in the face of" Paul's failure to return? That is, in whom or in what are they puffed up? How does Paul's failure to return precipitate this attitude? And if they boast now "because" Paul will not return, does this boasting refer *at the same time* to boasting in Apollos's eloquence?

Fee detects a parallel here with 4:6 and thus interprets 4:18 to mean that some of the Corinthians are puffed up "for Paul over against Apollos." Like Winter, Fee sees the Corinthians questioning Paul's eloquence,[33] though Fee notes that they also question his authority and theology. At the same time,

---

29. Litfin, *St. Paul's Theology of Proclamation*, 170.
30. Winter, *Philo and Paul among the Sophists*, 177; see also 200, 203.
31. Winter, *Philo and Paul among the Sophists*, 142, 200.
32. Winter, *Philo and Paul among the Sophists*, 203 ("because Paul was unable to return").
33. Fee, *First Epistle to the Corinthians*, 191; 2nd ed., 207.

Fee says that "the precise nuance of the qualifying clause 'as if I were not coming to you,' lacks certainty." He is inclined to the view that this implies that the Corinthians, believing Paul would not return, were offended.[34] With that, however, the clarity of Fee's explanation begins to falter. If ἐφυσιώθησαν means that the Corinthians are offended ("puffed up") because they believed Paul would not *return*, how does ἐφυσιώθησαν *also* mean that they are proud ("puffed up") on behalf of *the eloquent Apollos*? These amount to two different propositions and yet emerge from just one predicate. The truth that comes to light is that Fee exploits his "lack of certainty" about the qualifying words "as if I were not coming to you" as an opportunity to maintain both meanings, rather than deciding between them.

Two main issues emerge from this survey, issues that are not always addressed or answered in a clear and coherent way. (1) Are the Corinthians "puffed up" about themselves or about someone else? Relatedly, whose eloquence is meant? (2) What is the causal relationship between Paul's "not coming" and the Corinthians' alleged attitude about him or Apollos? As shown, some interpreters answer the first question as a both-and by a combination of assertions that are often left logically unexplained. While such bidirectional boasting is not a phenomenological impossibility, it will not do as an explanation for the occurrence of ἐφυσιώθησαν in *this* verse, for the term is set within a context and a sentence.

The critical exegetical point is that since the Corinthians' puffed-up state is conceptually and syntactically *qualified* by a genitive absolute—"as if I were not going to come to you"—the interpreter must provide an explanation for the relationship between these logically related propositions. Of the readings surveyed above, only Dahl offers an explicit explanation: the Corinthians are puffed up in belief that ("as if," ὡς) Paul will not return; *for* with his failure to return, they *have now completed their independence* from him.[35]

Having reviewed the issues, I would like to propose a different interpretation as being more satisfactory. (1) As wise and spiritual people, the Corinthians have boasted in their own qualifications. That the Corinthians boast in their spiritual qualifications has been evident throughout chapters 1–4: they consider themselves "wise," "powerful," and "well-born" in an inward sense, and Paul prohibits their boasting in this (1:26–31); they consider themselves

---

34. Fee, *First Epistle to the Corinthians*, 190; 2nd ed., 207.

35. Note BDAG, s.v. ὡς, meaning 3b: "w. focus on a conclusion existing only in someone's imagination or based solely on someone's assertion." Fee (*First Epistle to the Corinthians*, 190; 2nd ed., 207) says that the "precise nuance" of the phrase "lacks certainty."

"perfect" and "spiritual"; as "rich," "kings" (4:8), "prudent," "strong," and "distinguished" (4:10); they "boast" as if what they have (from God) they did not receive (4:7–8). I have argued both from these texts and through exacting exegesis that it is a boasting in self that Paul refers to also in 3:21 and 4:6. The weight of evidence for self-boasting leaves us good reason to consider it as a probable scenario here. If this interpretation is correct, the "some" (τίνες) who are boasting (4:18) would again be the "wise." (2) As for Paul's "coming," he refers to this not because the Corinthians have criticized him for his failure to return, or for his being comparatively ineloquent, or because the Corinthians are relieved at his absence (which are actually three different points!), but because the flagrance of their arrogance suggested to him that they were heedless that they would ever be held accountable. This interpretation explains why he does not, in fact, say, "as if I will not *return*" (as interpreters often say), but rather, "as if I will not *come* [ἐρχομένου]." The arrogant Corinthians rest in a state of blithe self-satisfaction and no authority is present to call them out. It is *"as if"* (ὡς) they had not considered the prospect and consequences of a visit. But (δέ) Paul indeed *will* come, and they *will* be held accountable (v. 19).

Intriguingly, this interpretation suggests an analogy with Jesus's teaching about "preparedness." The thought is similar to the sayings and parables of Matt 24:42–51 // Luke 12:41–48, where Jesus advises faithfulness in doing as the master has instructed, since the servant does not know when the master is "coming" (ἔρχεται).[36] Even if Paul's remarks are redolent of the Jesus material only accidentally, this connection proves to be heuristically helpful. Paul's threat is directed not—like most of 1 Corinthians—to the church as a whole. It is directed at "some" (τινες). There is no good reason to identify this group with any other than those who boast as σοφοί. Paul's threat, then, depicts the σοφοί as *teachers* who, similar to the slave set over the master's household, have not safeguarded his teachings/done as he instructed in his absence. These teachers have departed from his message, building, as it were, "on another foundation" (3:11). Paul asks: Have they not considered what will happen when the master returns?

Word versus Power

Paul's train of thought following v. 18 helpfully confirms this reading. Indeed, vv. 19–21 reflect an interest not in proving the Corinthians' assumptions

---

36. The verb in Matt 24:42, 43, 44, 46; Luke 12:43, 45.

about his unwillingness to "return" wrong but in the *accountability* that a visit might bring. In vv. 19 and 20, two terms found repeatedly in the first two chapters of the letter resurface. Paul declares that, when he comes, he will discover "not the λόγον of those who are puffed up, but their δύναμιν," and observes that "the kingdom of God is not ἐν λόγῳ but ἐν δύναμιν."[37] Paul continues to play with the meaning of these terms. Many interpreters construe λόγος again as meaning "eloquence."[38] On this interpretation, Paul warns that what matters is not their "eloquence" (λόγος) but the "power" (δύναμις) associated with the kingdom of God (4:20). The interpreter's construal of the sense, however, needs (1) to make clear both *whose* eloquence is meant (if Paul indeed refers to eloquence) and *whose* power is meant and (2) to provide an adequate explanation for the balance of the stated antithesis. Litfin's reading exposes a coherency problem that is inherent in many versions of the rhetorical thesis. According to Litfin, λόγος now refers to the eloquence not of Paul and proclaimers of the gospel, but of the *Corinthians*. At the same time, Litfin appears to understand the "power of God" still in reference to God's agency in conversion.[39] In this way, we not only lose Litfin's overarching contrast between (a) the agency of the *preacher*/the role of rhetoric in *preaching* on the one hand, and (b) the agency of *God* in engendering salvation on the other. We are also left with an oddly asymmetrical contrast between the Corinthians' personal aspirations to eloquence (rather than the preachers' eloquence) and God's power to save. This result replicates the same problem encountered in Litfin's interpretation of 1:26-29. Litfin here has become a victim of a tension introduced by his own reconstruction. It is clear that Paul refers now to the *Corinthians'* λόγος, and yet the conflict, Litfin tells us, is to be about the comparative quality of the λόγος of *Paul and Apollos*. Perhaps the Corinthians focused both on their own eloquence and on Apollos's, but the interpreter would need to make clear which is Paul's concern at each specific point in the text.

Winter rightly interprets λόγος and δύναμις as reflecting the commonplace duality of "word" versus "deed." There is no reason, however, to take the words as "rhetorical terms."[40] Winter relates the pairing to accusations made against sophists, to the effect that they were eloquent (λόγος) but not

---

37. Λόγος in 1:17, 18; 2:1, 4 (×2), 13; δύναμις in 1:18, 24; 2:4, 5.
38. Litfin (*St. Paul's Theology of Proclamation*, 235) says that this "surely must be translated here 'eloquence.'" Winter proposes that both λόγος and δύναμις are "rhetorical" terms. Note also Fee, *First Epistle to the Corinthians*, 191; 2nd ed., 208.
39. Litfin, *St. Paul's Theology of Proclamation*, 235.
40. Winter, *Philo and Paul among the Sophists*, 200-201.

virtuous (δύναμις). Yet, it was the *philosophers* who typically made this accusation. Moreover, this pairing figured in a central way in the moral discourse of the philosophers, as they emphasized that philosophy was fundamentally a practical discipline, not just a theoretical one.[41] They emphasized repeatedly that the doctrines of philosophy should be lived, a point that they often expressed as a call to "conformity of words and deeds." Sources employ a variety of roughly equivalent terms for this pairing:[42]

Word	Deed
λόγος	ἔθος
λόγος	ἔργον
λόγος	πρᾶξις
λεγών	πράττων
θεωρία	πρᾶξις
dicta	*facta*
legere	*facere*

It became conventional to brand those who did not live by their doctrines as philosopher-counterfeits, that is, "those who are called philosophers [τῶν καλουμένων φιλοσόφων]" (Dio, *Or.* 13.11), or not "true" (ἀληθῶς) but "spurious" (πεπλασμένως) philosophers (Plato, *Rep.* 485d), or "philosophers in name only [οὐκ ὀνόματι μόνον ἀλλ' ἀληθῶς φιλοσόφοις]" (Musonius Rufus, *Diatr.* 17.14–16). Within this framework, Paul's contrast between "word" and "power" would not, then, be a "parting shot at rhetoric,"[43] but at *would-be philosophers*. It was they above anyone whose deeds ought to conform with their words.

In v. 20 Paul relates the commonplace precept about conformity of words and deeds with the "kingdom of God": "the kingdom of God is not in *word* but in *power*." The wording is vague,[44] and the terms rich with resonances. Verse 19 shows that the present application is to the *Corinthians'* "power," or rather, to a lack thereof. The terms βασιλεία and δύναμις seem to play on multiple meanings. (1) With *kingdom* Paul may echo, secondarily, the

---

41. See p. 59 n. 27 above.

42. Dio Chrysostom, *Or.* 18.17; Musonius Rufus, *Diatr.* 5 (λόγος vs. πρᾶξις); Seneca, *Ep.* 20.2 (*legere* vs. *facere*); 34.4 (*dicta* vs. *facta*); all the others in Musonius Rufus, *Diatr.* 1; 5; 6; 8.

43. Martin, *Corinthian Body*, 48.

44. The prepositional phrases (with ἐν) function as simple predicates and are thus *descriptive*. See chapter 4, pp. 97–98 and n. 47.

1 Corinthians 4:14–21: Paul as Founder and Teacher

pretensions of the Corinthians as "kings" (4:8), after the pattern of the Stoic wise man (see chapter 7). (2) While *power* here refers primarily to "deeds" or *praxis*, secondarily it evokes "Christ" *as* God's "power," as referenced earlier (1:24). Since the wisdom-of-God *habitus* is embodied in "Christ crucified" (1:24; 2:2), and since Paul has presented himself as an embodiment of this wisdom (2:4; 4:9–13), and since Paul has now called the Corinthians to "imitate" him (4:16–17), indeed the word *power* here must refer both to the *works* characteristic of God's wisdom and the specific paradigm that embodies it: that of Christ crucified.

Two Philosophical Approaches

Paul concludes with an offer of alternatives: "What do you want? Should I come to you with a rod or in love of spirit and of meekness?" Paul has no intention of literally thrashing the Corinthians with a rod (ῥάβδος). Yet, both the cultural associations of the ῥάβδος intended here and the *pragmatic* force of the question could be debated. It is indeed commonly believed that the "rod" (ῥάβδος) here is a symbol of Paul's authority, which the Corinthians have challenged to their imminent peril.[45] For several reasons, however, this seems unlikely to capture Paul's meaning.

(1) As we have found repeatedly, Paul's overwhelming concern in chapters 1–4 is the behavior of the Corinthians, not clearly their criticism of Paul (although some undoubtedly had their criticisms). This concern is now reaffirmed in the context of 4:14–21, as Paul presents his "ways in Christ Jesus" as an example. His intentions are parenetic. (2) It is very difficult to accept the conclusion that Paul means to assert his authority by forcible means (even if figuratively) after his self-descriptions as "minister" (3:5), "assistant," and "steward" (4:1) and after four chapters depicting "power" as "Christ crucified" and Paul himself as "weak" in imitation of Christ. (3) Paul does not declaratively threaten the Corinthians here but poses a disjunctive rhetorical question. In this respect, the expected answer obviously is that they would prefer Paul to come "in love and a spirit of gentleness." Thus, the pragmatic purpose of the question is to provoke *reflection* on the better alternative, which they will surely take to be the latter. In a way the question evokes the very dilemma that is at the center of Paul's discussion of wisdom: given the

---

45. Dahl, "Paul and the Church at Corinth," 46. Cf. Still, "Divisions over Leaders," 27–28.

choice between power and a spirit of gentleness, would they not now agree that "weakness" is better than "power"?

(4) Paul's question is naturally understood in association with the cultural domain of education. (a) Several studies have argued that the semantic context that explains the "rod" is that of Hellenistic education and the practice of corporal punishment.[46] Interpreters have proposed a variety of contexts besides (the rod carried by Roman imperial authorities, the rod of discipline in the OT/LXX, paternal discipline). Out of these options, the domain of education makes better sense in the immediate context of 4:14–21. As noted, White has shown that Paul makes several other allusions to ancient education here: the pedagogue, parent-teachers (v. 15), "imitation" of teachers (v. 16), "teaching" in all the churches (v. 17), "remembering" what was taught (v. 17).

(b) I should like to suggest an alternative, yet related, framework to (a). Specifically, Paul alludes to the commonplace contrast between two kinds of philosophical teacher and their divergent approaches to instruction. Malherbe popularized this contrast in relation to the Cynic tradition, proposing that there were "two types of Cynicism: an austere, rigorous one, and a milder, so-called hedonistic strain."[47] According to Malherbe, one finds the epitome of this contrast in Lucian's depictions of the two Cynics Peregrinus (the austere type) and Demonax (the milder type).[48] From the perspective of the harsh Cynic, human beings were deeply depraved and so bereft of reason and self-control that their condition could only be cured by extreme abuse. The harsh Cynic thus took upon himself the responsibility of curing this disease through "bold" reprimand (παρρησία).[49] The milder Cynic was less pessimistic about humanity and therefore less extreme in his reforming efforts. The mild Cynic recognized that ailments were often best treated with gentleness, as with the touch of a nurse.[50] The latter approach could aptly be described as "parenetic."

Recent evaluation of Malherbe's proposal has challenged his taxonomy on grounds that the distinction between Cynics was not one between two types of *Cynicism* but rather of two types of *personality* found among Cyn-

---

46. White, *Teacher of the Nations*, 96–99; Dutch, *Educated Elite*, 263–68.

47. Malherbe, *Paul and the Popular Philosophers*, 14.

48. Also representing rigoristic Cynicism are the Cynic letters attributed to Crates, Diogenes, Heraclitus, and Hippocrates; and representing gentler Cynicism, the Cynic letters attributed to Socrates. So, Malherbe, *Paul and the Popular Philosophers*, 17, 20.

49. Ps.-Diogenes, *Epistle 28; 29*.

50. Malherbe, "'Gentle as a Nurse,'" 210–14.

1 Corinthians 4:14–21: Paul as Founder and Teacher

icism's representatives.[51] The contrast of dispositions remains nonetheless. Cynics like Diogenes and Demetrius were known for their austerity; those like Crates, Demonax, and Dio, for their gentleness.[52]

The two alternatives that Paul offers in 4:21 map onto this contrast well. It is not immediately clear what Paul means by coming ἐν ῥάβδῳ, owing to the wide range of possible meanings for ῥάβδος.[53] It is a further point in favor of the background I am proposing, however, that ῥάβδος is evocative of one of the Cynic's most defining qualities: his carrying of a "staff." Defining who counted as a "Cynic" has proven to be notoriously difficult;[54] yet, in antiquity the Cynic's manner of dress was so recognizable as a defining characteristic that, regardless of his creed or behavior, a man might be considered a "Cynic" if only he wore a beard and a rough cloak and carried the light accoutrements of only a wallet and a staff.[55] It is said that the founder of Cynicism, Antisthenes,[56] established the cloak, wallet, and staff as the Cynic's standard equipment (Diogenes Laertius, *Vit. phil.* 6.13). Sources commonly mention the staff, although there is no standard term for this accessory. It is variably called a βακτηρία (Diogenes Laertius, *Vit. phil.* 6.21, 32; Diogenes, *Epistle 30*, 30; Theon, *Prog.* 99 [Spengel]; Lucian, *Symp.* 16; 19), βάκτρον (Diogenes Laertius, *Vit. phil.* 6.13; Lucian, *Peregr.* 24), σκῆπτρον (Diogenes, *Epistle 7*, 20), ξύλον (Lucian, *Peregr.* 15; Lucian, *Phil.* 7; cf. Diogenes Laertius, *Vit. phil.* 6.21; Lucian, *Pisc.* 24), or ῥόπαλον (Lucian, *Peregr.* 36). Notably, it is also called a ῥάβδος (Diogenes Laertius, *Vit. phil.* 6.102; Diogenes, *Epistle 7*, 3; cf. Diogenes Laertius, *Vit. phil.* 6.4; Matt 10:10 // Mark 6:8 // Luke 9:3). In the Gospels Jesus refers to the ῥάβδος when sending out his disciples to the villages (Matt 10:10 // Luke 9:3; cf. Mark 6:8), instructing them not to carry a "wallet" or a "staff" (ῥάβδος). These instructions are widely regarded as having the preemptive purpose of precluding confusion between the disciples and the Cynics. By foregoing the staff, they would not be earmarked by the Cynic's defining equipment.[57]

---

51. Marie-Odile Goulet-Caze, *Cynicism and Christianity in Antiquity* (Grand Rapids: Eerdmans, 2019), 59–71.

52. Goulet-Caze, *Cynicism and Christianity*, 59–71.

53. White, *Teacher of the Nations*, 96–99; Dutch, *Educated Elite*, 263–68.

54. See discussions in Malherbe, *Paul and the Popular Philosophers*, 11–16; Downing, *Cynics and Christian Origins*, 26–56; Goulet-Caze, *Cynicism and Christianity*, 53–107.

55. Diogenes, *Epistle 30*, 25–34; Diogenes, *Epistle 7*, 17–21; cf. Epictetus, *Diatr.* 3.1.24; Lucian, *Dem.* 13.

56. Diogenes Laertius (*Vit. phil.* 6.2, 13) describes him as the founder, but some regard his student Diogenes as the true founder. See debate about the founder in Goulet-Caze, *Cynicism and Christianity*, 6–9.

57. Though in Mark 6:8 Jesus advises that they should take a staff.

That the Cynics used their staff as a weapon against their students and listeners is amply attested.[58] Diogenes Laertius relates two stories describing how Antisthenes had used a "rod" against his listeners; in one instance the term used is ῥάβδος. When asked why he had only a few students, Antisthenes replied, "Because I use a silver rod [ῥάβδος] to drive them away" (*Vit. phil.* 6.4), though this does not seem to be the characteristic "staff." Strangely, it was under such circumstances that Diogenes became Antisthenes's pupil. On this occasion Antisthenes extended his staff to strike him, and Diogenes only "offered his head with the words, 'Strike, for you will find no wood [ξύλον] hard enough to keep me away from you'" (*Vit. phil.* 6.21 [Hicks, LCL]). Theon relates a chreia in which Diogenes, witnessing a boy eating fancy food, beat the child's pedagogue with his staff (βακτηρία), thinking of course that the child's behavior was due to poor training.[59] In the same spirit, Lucian refers to the Cynic's staff as a "Herculean club" ('Ηράκλειον ῥόπαλον), in this way not only alluding to the Cynics' idealization of their traditional hero (Hercules carried a club), but also characterizing the Cynic's staff in terms of what seems to have been one of its common functions—cudgeling one's listeners. Indeed, it is facetiously said in the *Cynic Epistles* that that is in fact what the Cynic's staff was for.[60]

Complementing Paul's image of himself as an austere Cynic brandishing his staff is a portrait of a gentler Paul. Like the Cynic of milder disposition, Paul would wish to come in "love" (ἀγάπη) and a spirit of "gentleness" (πραΰτητος). Using the adjectival form of πραΰτητος, Lucian describes the philosophy of Demonax—the epitome of the gentle Cynic—as "kind" (πρᾶος), "gentle" (ἥμερος), and "cheerful" (*Dem.* 10). In another work from Lucian (*Pisc.* 24), Diogenes the Cynic describes philosophy as "kindly and gentle [ἥμερος καὶ πρᾶός]" (though Diogenes himself can hardly be described as such).

If this distinction in philosophical approach resonates in the background here, the final verses of 1 Cor 1–4 do not seek to reestablish Paul's apostolic authority. Rather, Paul draws upon the distinction between contrasting philosopher types as a final, illustrative example of the difference between, one might say, *two types of wisdom*. The one approach relies on dominance and power, the other on gentleness and love. Paul asks which is better, but the answer is already obvious. As he has been saying all along, it is the latter.

---

58. In addition to the examples below, see Lucian, *Symp.* 16; 19; Diogenes Laertius, *Vit. phil.* 6.32.

59. Theon, *Prog.* (Spengel, 98–99).

60. Diogenes, *Epistle 30*, 4.

CONCLUSION

First Corinthians 4:14–21 brings the first major unit of the letter to a close. This paragraph reprises many of the themes encountered in the preceding sections: Paul as founder of the community (3:6–10; 4:15); the presence of other, aspiring teachers in the community (3:12–18; 4:15); Paul as an example (2:1–5; 4:1–13, 16–17); Corinthian pride (1:26–31; 4:6–10, 18–19); weakness and power (1:22–28; 2:4–5; 4:18–21). In its own allusive way, this section also furnishes some of the most helpful linguistic context for elucidating the Corinthians' conception of the parties and the roles of their respective leaders. The imagery, tropes, and commonplaces of this section are consistent with the reconstruction of the situation that we have been developing and will develop more fully in part 3: Paul's partisans viewed him as a kind of schoolteacher, as of a philosophical "school," and they themselves as his students. Paul playfully embraces this role. He is, as it were, his students' "father." In that role he "admonishes" them and carries on the necessary work of parenesis. They are to remind themselves constantly of his teachings and example, to imitate him and others who imitate him in turn. Yet, they are puffed up in themselves, heedless that he could appear when they do not expect it and find them unfaithful to his teachings. No, they would not want him to arrive brandishing his Cynic's staff. He reasserts the essential point one more time: they ought to choose weakness (gentleness) over power (the rod).

9

The Sub-Stoic Wisdom of the Corinthians

I have argued that a prominent group among the Corinthians viewed themselves in the mold of the Stoic σοφός, or "wise man." The σοφός was the living embodiment of the Stoic system, the person who lived in perfect conformity with nature. In this state the σοφός remained supremely happy (*SVF* 3:582–88); never erred in judgment (*SVF* 3:548–56); "did all things well" (*SVF* 3:557–66); "has all things" (*SVF* 3:590, 597, 599; etc.), including all the best intellectual qualities (he was rich, king, free, powerful, and more; *SVF* 3:589–603). In a word, he was "perfect" (τέλειος; *SVF* 3:548, 522, 609; Cicero, *Tusc.* 2.51). As we have seen, descriptions of the Stoic σοφός came to be articulated in concise formulas known as the Stoic "paradoxes" (παράδοξα), so called because they made "surprising" claims: "*only the wise man* is rich, *only the wise man* is king, etc." (e.g., *SVF* 3:364, 594; Cicero, *Fin.* 3.75). The wise man's description as such depended upon a *transvaluation* of ordinary social values. The σοφός was not rich or king in the ordinary social sense, but in an inward or intellectual sense.

Some of the Corinthians defined themselves according to this model. They considered themselves σοφοί, "wise men," in the technical, substantive, philosophical sense of the term (esp. 1 Cor 1:19, 20; 3:19, 20; 6:5).[1] They assigned to themselves the qualities assigned to the wise man in the paradoxes. Paul describes them using not just the terminology but also the formulas of the paradoxes: wise man + stative predicate + predicate complement ("were wise, powerful, well born," 1:26; "you are rich, kings," 4:8; "you are prudent,

---

1. See esp. chapters 3 (on 1:20) and 6 (on 3:19, 20).

strong, honored," 4:10; "all things are yours," 3:21). The Corinthian σοφοί also consider themselves to be, like the wise man, τέλειοι and contrasted themselves with those whom they considered νήπιοι (2:6; 3:1).

Admittedly an overlap of language, however striking, is not sufficient to prove that the Corinthians were influenced by Stoicism at a deep doctrinal level. Our preceding chapters have restricted attention primarily to a running exegesis of 1 Cor 1:17b–4:21 and have refrained from demonstrating the necessary doctrinal connections with Stoicism at a deeper level. In order to demonstrate distinct Stoic influence, we shall now need to demonstrate that the Corinthians' self-understanding was consistent with Stoic distinctives at some level of substance, technicality, and interrelation of parts. In this chapter I argue that it was. Specifically, the views of the σοφοί were rooted in a distinctly Stoic anthropology, at a point of intersection between Stoic physics and Stoic ethics. In this regard we shall examine (1) the connection between Stoic "tonic" physics and the two pairs of contrasting terms that the Corinthians used to describe themselves and their believing counterparts (τέλειος-νήπιος and πνευματικός-ψυχικός), (2) the Stoic theme of "self-sufficiency," and (3) the Stoic classification of valuables into things good, bad, and indifferent.

Corinthian Wisdom

Contrasting Pairs and Stoic Anthropology

The Corinthian σοφοί employed at least two pairs of terms to describe themselves and their believing counterparts: τέλειος-νήπιος and πνευματικός-ψυχικός. While interpreters widely agree that the Corinthians employed these pairs to distinguish levels of spiritual status within the believing community, the question of the *cultural* source of this language has remained debated. The history of modern scholarship is rich with speculation. We can now dismiss the thesis that the language derived from Gnosticism of the sort that Schmithals and others imagined since no solid evidence exists for this kind of pre-Christian Gnosticism.[2] Nor does this language closely approximate the language of the mystery religions.[3] As we shall review below, the possibility

---

2. Against Wilckens, *Weisheit und Torheit*, 52–60. For the evidence against Gnosticism, see Edwin M. Yamauchi, *Pre-Christian Gnosticism* (Grand Rapids: Eerdmans, 1973).

3. Pearson (*Pneumatikos-Psychikos Terminology*, 28) argues that this is not the language of the mystery religions.

that the language derives from the discourse of Hellenistic Judaism remains plausible in many respects.[4] Yet, most interpreters are now content with the view that the language represents the religious and philosophical "spirit of late antiquity" more broadly.[5]

It must not be quickly concluded that a lack of absolute uniqueness implies a lack of specific background. For one must not confuse a plurality of "semiotic *potential*" with the "significant *situational* value" of language in context. Nor need we assume from the outset that partial novelty of usage implies a lack of specific influences.[6] As I shall demonstrate, the τέλειος-νήπιος pairing not only occurs within Stoicism but as a pairing best fits the conceptual framework of Stoic ethics. Moreover, this terminology and pairing, when understood in relation to other doctrinal points, is sufficiently specific to this philosophical context to justify the view that it is specifically "Stoic" and not merely a commonplace of the moral milieu.

Whether cultural antecedents exist for the second pair of terms (πνευματικός-ψυχικός) has remained a matter of more serious debate. Extant sources offer no instances where πνευματικός and ψυχικός occur either in juxtaposition or in direct contrast prior to the Corinthian correspondence. A strong case can be made, however, that this pair constitutes but a very minor modification of an already-existing distinction made within Stoic physics.

Τέλειος versus νήπιος

The terms τέλειος and νήπιος were well-established correlates in the discourse of the Greek philosophical tradition. Horsley notes that Philo of Alexandria, a Hellenistic-Jewish philosopher, borrows this pairing in several passages in his corpus,[7] sometimes identifying "milk" as nourishment for the νήπιος and "solid food" as nourishment for the τέλειος.[8] Elsewhere, Philo appropriates this language as part of a threefold moral distinction: (1) the τέλειος person, formed after the divine image and not in need of instruction; (2) the μέσος

---

4. Horsley, "Pneumatikos vs Psychikos"; Davis, *Wisdom and Spirit*, 113–31; Pearson, *Pneumatikos-Psychikos Terminology*, 7–30. See further discussion below.

5. Pearson, *Pneumatikos-Psychikos Terminology*, 83. Cf. Martin, *Corinthian Body*, 72–73; Betz, "Problem of Rhetoric and Theology," 26; Conzelmann, *1 Corinthians*, 15–16; Barclay, "Thessalonica and Corinth," 49–74, esp. 65n29.

6. Barclay cautions that we must not underestimate what was "different and new" in Corinth ("Thessalonica and Corinth," 65n29).

7. Philo, *Sobr.* 9–10; *Agr.* 9; *Migr.* 1.29, 33.

8. Philo, *Migr.* 29; *Somn.* 2.10; *Agr.* 9; *Quod omnis* 1.160.

or νήπιος person, who is neither bad nor good but requires exhortation and teaching in order to do good and refrain from evil; and (3) the φαῦλος person, who requires instruction in the form of both prohibition and injunction.[9] Following this system of classification, several interpreters see the Corinthians also as distinguishing between three types of people.[10]

Von Arnim's collection of Old Stoic Fragments (*SVF*), however, cites Philo on this point as a witness to the views of the Stoics, for Philo's basic scheme is derived from them.[11] Like Philo, Stoic sources reflect a tension between a twofold and threefold classification of moral development. Yet, official Stoic doctrine specified that a person fit *technically* into either of only two categories: that of the wise person (σοφός) or that of the foolish person (the inferior, φαῦλος; the imprudent, ἄφρων; or the insane, μαίνεσθαι).[12] For the Stoics there was no middle state. One's moral disposition either "agreed with nature" or it did not.[13] And so one was either wise or one was not, and one was perfect or one was not, just as a line is either crooked or straight and there is no state between,[14] and just as the man submerged in water is either drowning or is not, no matter how near he is to the surface.[15] Virtue is not a matter of degree. The straight stick cannot be made any straighter.[16]

---

9. *Leg. all.* 1.93–94; a three-fold distinction also in *Prob.* 1.160 (the enslaved, the immature, the prudent); *Agr.* 1.157–162 (beginnings, progress, and perfect), 165 (the beginner, the progressing, the perfect); *Somn.* 2.234–236 (the foolish, the progressing, the perfect); *Leg. all.* 3.159 (man of pleasure, the progressing, the perfect).

10. Davis (*Wisdom and Spirit*, 124–25) adopts a three-fold distinction: πνευματικός is the mature believer, νήπιος is the immature believer, and ψυχικός is the nonbeliever. Pearson (*Pneumatikos-Psychikos Terminology*, 29, 39) distinguishes three kinds of people: the τέλειος, the νήπιος, the φαῦλος ("Hellenistic-Jewish Wisdom Speculation," 53–55). Hyldahl ("Paul and Hellenistic Judaism") distinguishes three kinds: pneumatic, psychic, and sarcic (214), the pneumatic also being perfect. Inkelaar identifies three groups: pneumatikoi, psychikoi, sarkikoi (*Conflict over Wisdom*, 173).

11. The *SVF* cites Philo's use of this language in *SVF* 3:519 (= Philo, *Leg. all.* 1.93–94); *SVF* 3:512 (Philo, *Leg. all.* 3.210); *SVF* 3:754. Epictetus (*Diatr.* 2.16.39; cf. 3.24.9) asserts that milk is for the unadvanced and solid food for the mature. It is another one of the Stoic "paradoxes" that only the wise man is τέλειος (*SVF* 3:548; cf. 1:566), having the "perfect virtues" (τέλειοι ἀρεταί) (*SVF* 3:522 = Philo, *Cain* 43; *SVF* 3:609 = Philo, *Cain* 111), having "perfect wisdom" (*perfecta sapientia*) (Cicero, *Tusc.* 2.51). Cf. discussion of 1:26 above. The Stoic system of moral development is mapped out in detail in Lee, *Moral Transformation*, 228–45.

12. *SVF* 3:657–84.

13. LS §63.

14. Diogenes Laertius, *Vit. phil.* 7.127; Cicero, *Fin.* 3.10.34.

15. *SVF* 3:539; Cicero, *Fin.* 3.48.

16. Diogenes Laertius, *Vit. phil.* 7.125–126; cf. Cicero, *Fin.* 3.34.

For the Stoics these distinctions in *ethical* class were rooted in their theory of *physics*. The soul was material, being nothing but the divine "Breath" (Πνεῦμα), itself a corporeal entity.[17] In a veritably material sense, then, wisdom was "the soul in a certain shape,"[18] a shape that was either "in conformity with nature" or not in conformity with it.[19] The Neostoics made room for the possibility of progress between these extremes; yet, even these later Stoics maintained that everything short of wisdom was technically not wisdom at all, just as the man who finds himself submerged in water drowns no matter how near he is to the surface.[20] In that respect the φαῦλος ("inferior man") and the νήπιος ("immature man") fell on the *same* side of the divide, short of the threshold for σοφός status. There remained only *two* types of person.

First Corinthians offers strong evidence that the Corinthians were working within a similar, two-class, framework. Some considered themselves to be σοφοί, and as σοφοί, also τέλειοι, while considering the others in the church to be νήπιοι. While the former may have acknowledged that the latter had made "progress" (perhaps beyond the unbelieving), nonetheless the latter lacked the requisite understanding to be considered "perfect." This was no "middle state." We shall soon see what this meant for these Christ followers in Corinth.

Ψυχικός versus πνευματικός

Unlike the νήπιος-τέλειος pair, ψυχικός and πνευματικός occur nowhere as a *pair* in ancient sources prior to or contemporary with Paul. Several studies through the 1970s made promising arguments in favor of a Hellenistic Jewish background. Pearson proposed that the Corinthians derived the ψυχικός-πνευματικός distinction from traditional exegesis of LXX Gen 2:7. According to Pearson, the distinction parallels one found in Philo between the lower (ψυχή) and the higher soul (νοῦς), one the "mortal soul" shared by Adam and all living creatures, the other the "immortal spirit" breathed into man and capable of contemplating God.[21] Horsley built upon Pearson's thesis, agreeing that the Corinthian view reflected a development of the tradition behind LXX Gen 2:7 and acknowledging that we find the terminology of both the *soul* (ψύχη) and the *spirit* (πνεῦμα) in Philo. Yet, Horsley observed that

17. As "breath," or πνεῦμα (LS, §53); as corporeal (LS, §45C–D).
18. LS §29; 33P; Diogenes Laertius, *Vit. phil.* 7.89 (calling this shape an "arrangement," διάθεσις).
19. LS §63.
20. *SVF* 3:539; Cicero, *Fin.* 3.48.
21. Pearson, *Pneumatikos-Psychikos Terminology*, 18–20.

while Philo makes a distinction between the "soul" (ψυχή) and the "*mind*" (νοῦς), neither Philo nor any extant Greek source employs precisely our contrast between "soul" and "*spirit*" (πνεῦμα) or the adjectives ψυχικός and πνευματικός. Broadening the scope of comparison, Horsley pointed out that the ψυχικός-πνευματικός distinction conceptually parallels two pairs of terms found elsewhere in 1 Corinthians (2:6; 3:3; 13:11; 14:20; 15:47–49): immature-mature man (νήπιος-τέλειος) and earthly-heavenly man (χοϊκός-ἐπουράνιος). According to Horsley, the first pair shares the same "conceptual apparatus" as the other two, and all three pairs distinguish "two different levels of religious-ethical ability and achievement."[22] From these correlations, Horsley drew the conclusion that the ψυχικός-πνευματικός distinction indicates a contrast not between lower soul (ψυχή) and higher soul (the νοῦς breathed into humanity by the "spirit"), but between "mortal *body*" and "immortal *soul*."[23]

The proposals of both Pearson and Horsley are intriguing. They offer, via Philo and Hellenistic Jewish exegesis, thematic parallels that incorporate the semantic roots ψυχ- ("soul") and πνευμ- ("spirit"). Horsley's criticism of Pearson, however, is damaging. Moreover, neither proposal successfully locates parallels that include the exact terms or the direct terminological distinction that we seek. I would like to propose that a closer parallel exists in Stoicism.[24] Specifically, the ψυχικός-πνευματικός pair is rooted in the "tonic" theory that underlies basic Stoic physics.

According to the Stoics, the "spiritual power" (πνευματικὴ δύναμις) that extended through the universe penetrated nature's substances at four levels of "tension" (τόνος). The tension of each object accounted for its peculiarly qualified properties and its available faculties.[25] The first three kinds of substances were irrational. The πνεῦμα penetrated (1) logs, stones, and objects moved from the outside at the level of "cohesion" (ἕξις, ἑκτικόν); it penetrated (2) plants at the level of "physique" (φύσις, φυσικόν), giving them the capacity of growth; and it penetrated (3) irrational animals at the level of "soul" (ψυχή, ψυχικόν), giving them the faculties of both movement and sense perception. Finally, there were (4) "rational" substances (λογικά, νοητικά), things through which the πνεῦμα passed as "reason" (λόγος); this last category included God and humanity alone.[26]

22. Horsley, "Pneumatikos vs Psychikos," 278.
23. Horsley, "Pneumatikos vs Psychikos," 273.
24. A thesis briefly considered in Brookins, *Corinthian Wisdom*, 169–71.
25. LS §47M–R; 53A–P.
26. See especially LS §47N, P, Q; 53A; *SVF* 1:158; 2:459, 460. Philo (LS §47P) lists the first three types of tenor, followed by two terms that seem to be synonyms for the fourth type,

My proposal is that the Corinthian σοφοί developed a distinction between the ψυχικός and the πνευματικός on analogy with the third (ψυχικόν) and fourth (λογικόν) kinds of tension identified in Stoic physics. Ψυχικός served for the Stoics as the standard technical term for natural bodies at the *third* level of "tension," bodies considered to be *animal but irrational*. The *fourth* kind of tension, which the Stoics described as λογικός or διανοητικὴ δύναμις, referred to bodies endowed with *rational faculties*. For us the problem remains that, while the Stoic and Corinthian pairs share the first term exactly (ψυχικός), they do not share the second (λογικός/πνευματικός). I hope to demonstrate, however, that the adjectival form πνευματικός ("spiritual"), while not appearing in Stoic sources as a technical term for the fourth type of "tension," functioned for the Corinthian σοφοί analogously to the Stoics' description of the fourth tension type, the λογικόν ("rational").

It is critical to note that the Stoic ψυχικός-λογικός (third-fourth) distinction was not a matter of antithesis, but of *variable degrees* tension. For the Stoics, πνεῦμα was the "intelligent" (νοερόν), or "reasonable" (λογικόν), designing power that pervaded the entire universe (LS §47; 48; 54A). This pneumatic material, conceived in terms of its intelligent quality, was considered to be λόγος. As the πνεῦμα pervaded the whole κόσμος, so did the λόγος. The λόγος "extended through all of nature [rationem quondam per omnem naturam rerum pertinentem]" (*SVF* 1:161); it "ran through all matter [διὰ ταύτης δὲ διαθεῖν τὸν τοῦ παντὸς λόγον]" (*SVF* 1.87), was "the active agent in matter [τὸ δὲ ποιοῦν τὸν ἐν αὐτῇ λόγον]" (*SVF* 1:85); it "extended through the whole of what is [τὸν δι' ὅλης τῆς οὐσίας διήκοντα λόγον]" (Marcus Aurelius, *Med.* 5.32). Thus, the Stoic view was not that reason (λόγος) per se inhabited only humanity, but that, while filling *all things*, it filled only humanity at a level of *tension* (τόνος) sufficient to constitute the *faculty* of reason.[27] Among things in the universe filled with λόγος, in other words, some acquired from this source lower faculties (e.g., ψυχικόν), others higher (λογικόν).

The Corinthian ψυχικός-πνευματικός distinction borrows from Stoic tonic theory the doctrine of pneumatic tensions together with the idea of correlating facultative distinctions. Inspiring this distinction, in the first place, was the shared premise of an immanent πνεῦμα. As in Stoicism, the Corinthian

---

the "rational" (λογική, διανοητική δύναμις). Long and Sedley (*Hellenistic Philosophers*, 2:285) call the fourth and fifth terms "Philonian amplifications of the Stoic triad," the terms λόγος and διάνοια being used "indifferentially to refer to the faculty of reason." Cf. Hierocles // Stobaeus, *Anth.* 4.67.22. See νοῦς for the rational kind also in *SVF* 1.158.

27. *SVF* 2:879; Seneca, *Ep.* 41.8–9; 76.9–10; 92.27–28.

distinction between ψυχικός and πνευματικός was not one of sharp dualism, but of degree. Just as Stoic λόγος resided in all things but was constituted as the *faculty* (δύναμις) of reason only in gods and humanity, so πνεῦμα resided in all believers but manifested as pneumatic *power* (δύναμις) only in some special few. These qualified as πνευματικοί by virtue of the greater "strength" (τόνος) of their union with πνεῦμα. They considered others in the church to be ψυχικοί, that is, as constituted by a lower level of pneumatic strength. The πνευματικοί were "perfect" (τέλειος) in wisdom, the ψυχικοί were "immature" (νήπιος).

	Level 3 Tension	Level 4 Tension
Stoic Pneumatic Tension	ψυχικός	λογικός
Corinthian Pneumatic Tension	ψυχικός	πνευματικός

In sum, the Corinthian distinction maps—partly verbally and entirely functionally—onto the Stoic tonic distinction between "irrational animal" and "rational animal"—ψυχικός correlating with ψυχικός and λογικός with πνευματικός. The Corinthian substitution of the "spiritual" (πνευματικός) for the "rational" (λογικός) represents their chief modification of the Stoic theory. As we shall see, this difference is not merely a semantic one. At the same time, the substituted concept appears to perform an analogous function within the larger framework, working within a similar set of systemically related doctrinal points.

I should now like to demonstrate that even the term πνευματικός may not reflect merely an overlapping emphasis on πνεῦμα. It may reflect a new appropriation of a term not without antecedent connection to the Stoics.

Πνευματικός and the Pneumatist Medical School

We find a terminological connection in accounts that describe the Stoic-influenced medical sect known as the Pneumatists, or Πνευματικοί.[28] The connection between the Stoics and the Pneumatists is consistent in the ancient sources, though a recent study on the Pneumatists by Coughlin and Lewis allows for more nuanced assessment.[29] Ancient sources connect

---

28. While Martin (*Corinthian Body*) does not explore this connection, it could further support his thesis that Paul is responding in 1 Corinthians to a higher-status group, educated in philosophy and having a view of the body common in medical theory.

29. Brookins, *Corinthian Wisdom*, 169–71. A new study in Sean Coughlin and Orley

the Pneumatist school with Athenaeus of Attaleia (in Pamphylia), naming him as the school's founder, as pupil of the Stoic philosopher Posidonius and as having the Stoic Chrysippus as his "grandfather" and describing his medical theories as being based on Stoic doctrines.[30] While the activity of Athenaeus would date to the mid-first century BCE if he was indeed a pupil of Posidonius (135–51 BCE), his description as pupil of Posidonius could imply no more than his debt to Posidonius's teachings. Coughlin and Lewis date the Pneumatist school "roughly between the first and second centuries CE" and caution that, while sources designate the Pneumatists with such labels as Πνευματικοί, ἡ πνευματικὴ αἵρεσις, οἱ ἀπ' X, and οἱ περὶ X, the school may have consisted only of a "loose-knit group" with a basically common medical theory.[31]

The Pneumatists' doctrines survive only in fragments, many of them found in the works of Galen (b. 129 CE), who was himself said to have been a partisan of Athenaeus's views. What can be gleaned from the fragments is that the Pneumatists viewed the πνεῦμα as a kind of "fifth element" which permeated the universe, holding all things together and supplying the power of movement. While medical theorists commonly theorized πνεῦμα as a kind of "breath" that flowed through vessels, hollow channels, and pores that ran throughout the body, the πνεῦμα of the Pneumatists was akin not to the conventional kind of πνεῦμα but rather to the Stoic "compositional" πνεῦμα. As such, πνεῦμα did not consist of air ("breath") flowing through channels but not itself a part of the body; rather it was a power (δύναμις) that permeated the body as a "connate" (σύμφυτον) or "vital" (ζωτικόν) force holding its parts together.[32]

The summary of the sources offered by Coughlin and Lewis demonstrates strong connections between the Pneumatists and the Stoics. (1) The sources explicitly reflect a consensus that Pneumatist theory was borrowed directly from the Stoics. (2) The sources connect Pneumatist theory specifically

---

Lewis, "What Was Pneumatist about the Pneumatist School?," in *The Concept of Pneuma After Aristotle*, ed. Sean Coughlin, David Leith, and Orley Lewis (Berlin: Freie Universität Berlin, 2020), 203–36. Note the older studies of F. Kudlien, "Poseidonios und die Ärzteschule der Pneumatiker," *Hermes* 90 (1962): 419–29; and F. Kudlien, "Pneumatische Ärtzte," in *Real-Encyclopädie der classischen Altertumswissenschaft, Supplement 11*, ed. A. F. von Pauly and G. Wissowa (Stuttgart: Metzler, 1968), 1097–1108.

30. Galen, *Caus. cont.* 1.1–2.4; *Dig. puls.* 3.641–642.

31. Coughlin and Lewis, "What Was Pneumatist about the Pneumatist School?," 204, 208.

32. Coughlin and Lewis, "What Was Pneumatist about the Pneumatist School?," 212–16.

The Sub-Stoic Wisdom of the Corinthians

with the notion of the πνεῦμα as a fifth element and "connate" force. (3) The sources elaborate this theory using technical Stoic terminology: "permeating through everything" (διῆκον δι' αὐτῶν), "holding things together" (συνέχεσθαι), "cohesive cause" (συνεκτικὸν αἴτιον). (4) They indicate that the Pneumatists connected all of these concepts in the same way as the Stoics and adapted the concepts to their medical theory.[33] In the end, Coughlin and Lewis register some hesitation: "While our sources almost universally assert that the Pneumatists take Stoic physics as a starting point in physiology, it remains unclear to what extent the Pneumatists portrayed or even considered themselves to be following Stoic physics."[34] That is to say, we cannot know for certain whether the Pneumatists thought of themselves as Stoics, only that the sources consistently depict them as such.

It is needlessly speculative to suppose that the Corinthian σοφοί were members of the Pneumatist medical school or that they derived their views from the Pneumatists directly. In any case, some creative combination of elements would be necessary in order to bridge the gap to the Corinthians' conception of the πνευματικός, not least as it applied within the framework of their new Christ-faith. For (1) the sources do not reveal whether the Pneumatists, like the Stoics, described the πνεῦμα as "intelligent" (νοερόν). (2) The Pneumatists (Πνευματικοί) were so called not because they considered *themselves* to be uniquely "spiritual" but because they viewed human physiology from within the framework of the Stoic doctrine of the πνεῦμα. (3) The Stoics themselves did not use the adjectival form πνευματικός *technically* in reference to the highest, rational level of tension (the λογικόν kind of tension), though they did refer to the πνευματική "power" (δύναμις) that penetrated all things and supplied their respective faculties.

The Pneumatist material, however, may prove relevant on at least three counts. (1) The activity of the Pneumatist school was roughly contemporary with the activity of Paul's missions (mid-first century CE) and operated within close geographical proximity to Corinth (Pamphylia and elsewhere). (2) It provides a link between Stoic tonic theory and the term πνευματικός. (3) It reflects a parallel instance of the *personal* use of πνευματικός.[35]

---

33. Coughlin and Lewis, "What Was Pneumatist about the Pneumatist School?," 228–29.

34. Coughlin and Lewis, "What Was Pneumatist about the Pneumatist School?," 229.

35. Athenaeus in Pamphylia, with other representatives of the school, including Claudius Agathinus of Sparta, Herodotus, Magnus, and Archigenes of Apamea.

1 Corinthians 2:15 as a Stoic-Corinthian Slogan

A further point of connection between the term πνευματικός and Stoicism comes in 1 Cor 2:15: "The spiritual man [ὁ πνευματικός] evaluates all things, but he himself is evaluated by no one/nothing." Many studies cite this verse as a "Corinthian slogan."[36] Even among those who do not identify a full slogan, many see Paul incorporating Corinthian language. Most agree that both πνευματικός and (in the previous verse) ψυχικός are Corinthian terms,[37] and some identify ἀνακρίνειν as a Corinthian term, based largely on its pattern of usage across the NT.[38]

In chapter 5, I made the case that 2:15 in fact does cite a Corinthian slogan. I also noted there the striking parallel between this slogan and a line from one of Seneca's letters, which context helpfully clarifies amid larger discussion of the pertinent doctrine:

Seneca, *Ep.* 71.20   "[Such is virtue], which passes judgment on everything, but nothing passes judgment on virtue."
Haec [virtus] de omnibus rebus iudicat, de hac [virtute] nulla [iudicat].

1 Cor 2:15   "The spiritual man passes judgment on all things, but he himself is judged by nothing/no one."
ὁ δὲ πνευματικὸς ἀνακρίνει [τὰ] πάντα, αὐτὸς δὲ ὑπ' οὐδενὸς ἀνακρίνεται.

As demonstrated, the two lines are both formulated as point-counterpoint antitheses and include the same conceptual constituents on either side while using almost entirely equivalent terms. Consequently, the general meaning of the assertions is the same: *X or Y* embodies the "standard" against which all else is judged. The nature of the respective standard differs in name, but as we saw previously, the pertinent terms stand for equivalent concepts. For the Stoics, "virtue" (*virtus*) was a "rule" that admits of no degree. The rule is always perfectly straight and so serves as an absolute standard for judging what is or is not virtuous. As the embodiment of virtue, the wise man also embodies the standard. In place of "virtue"/the wise man, the Corinthians

---

36. See p. 22 n. 52 above.
37. See pp. 21–22 n. 49 above.
38. See chapter 5, p. 121. Davis (*Wisdom and Spirit*, 127) and Fee (*First Epistle to the Corinthians*, 117; 2nd ed., 125) view this as a Corinthian term.

substituted "spiritual man" (πνευματικός)/wise man. Thus, whereas the Stoic wise man embodied *virtue*, the Corinthian wise man embodied the *spiritual*. Through the indwelling Spirit the Corinthian σοφοί possessed a higher knowledge, even "perfected" knowledge, making their perspective normative and qualifying them, like Stoic virtue and the wise man who embodied it, to measure everything else. Those who did not, or could not, see things from this higher perspective were lower down on the scale of rational—or rather, *spiritual*—tension. These people were ψυχικοί.

Summary of the ψυχικός-πνευματικός Distinction

In my view, this Stoic background offers a more compelling explanation for the Corinthian ψυχικός-πνευματικός distinction than the alternatives. (1) Despite the strength of the parallels Horsley adduces from Philo, given the choice between a Hellenistic-Jewish and a Stoic background, there is nothing more inconvenient for Horsley's thesis than the fact that Paul explicitly states that "*Greeks* seek *wisdom*," while "*Jews* search for *signs*" (1:22). Hence, a non-Jewish background should be preferred as a starting hypothesis. (2) The ψυχικός-πνευματικός distinction as the Corinthians used it maps conceptually onto the distinction made in Stoic tonic theory between "irrational animal" and "rational animal." (3) The specific technical term ψυχικός is used to describe the former type of tension in both the Stoic and the Corinthian material. (4) While the Stoics did not use the term πνευματικός technically to describe the highest level of tension, they did describe the pervading rational "power" (δύναμις) that determined tension as πνευματική ("spiritual").[39] (5) The Pneumatists provide an instance in which the adjective πνευματικοί applied substantively to persons, and to persons whose views on the πνεῦμα were indebted to Stoic physics. Likely, the Corinthians either coined the term πνευματικός as a natural extension of Stoic tonic theory, parallel with the Pneumatists, or the currency of a kind of Pneumatist medical theory around the Aegean environment disseminated the basic doctrines of the school or this Stoic-associated term more widely. (6) The ψυχικός-πνευματικός distinction runs parallel to the Corinthians' νήπιος-τέλειος distinction, which we have seen was indeed a technical distinction made within Stoicism. (7) Prominent resonances with Stoic physics (competitively appropriated in Paul's discourse) are already prominent in the context of 2:10–13, as demonstrated in chapter 5: the "spirit of the world" as a pervading and

39. LS §47G.

intelligence-giving power, "taught" wisdom, distinction between "Spirit *of*" and "Spirit that is *from*" the world, adaptations to Prov 20:27 that introduce the terms πνεῦμα and πάντα, the substitution of νοῦς for רוח in the citation of Isa 40:13. (8) Finally, the exact parallel between 1 Cor 2:15 and Seneca's line in *Ep.* 71.20, where the Corinthians substitute only ὁ πνευματικός for *virtus*, supports the view that πνευματικός in the Corinthian framework paralleled λογικός in Stoic tonic theory: the Corinthian spiritual man, like the Stoic wise man, was constituted by the highest-tension πνεῦμα and in that state became the standard by which all else is evaluated.

Conclusion on Contrasting Pairs and Stoic Anthropology

I have argued that the two pairs of terms that the Corinthian σοφοί used to distinguish themselves from their lower-level counterparts distinguish two "orders" in respect to spiritual stature. This distinction of orders does not imply a Platonic-type *dualism* such as Horsley found in the works of Philo. Rather, these orders stem from Stoic physics, with its conception of *graded* orders within creation, where the respective faculties available to each order depend upon variant degrees of Pneumatic "tension" (τόνος). The Corinthian distinctions, in other words, are not *Pla*tonic, but "tonic." The σοφοί find themselves constituted at the highest level of pneumatic tension, making them "perfect" in a way similar to the Stoic wise man, except qualifying them as fully πνευματικοί ("spiritual") rather than as fully virtuous.

Yet, we must return to an important point: the adjective πνευματικός was not exactly a standard term for describing pneumatic tension in Stoicism. While I have shown that the term is cognate with language native to Stoic physics (πνεῦμα, δύναμις πνευματική), this aberration is noteworthy and reveals one of the key reasons why the Corinthian viewpoint cannot be reduced to unalloyed "Stoicism": whereas the Stoic σοφός was, above all, "rational," the Corinthian σοφός was "spiritual." We now explore the fuller significance of this modification.

Stoic Anthropology and Self-Sufficiency

The picture of the Corinthians that emerged in our exegesis of 1 Cor 1:17b–4:21 suggests that the parallels between the views of the Corinthian σοφοί and the doctrines of Stoicism run even deeper than the aspects of Stoic physics just sketched. One might say that there is a further "systemic" quality to the parallels. This quality falls at the intersection of Stoic physics and Stoic ethics.

Ancients credited the Stoics for devising what became the traditional threefold division of philosophy's departments: logic, physics, and ethics.[40] At the same time, the Stoics regarded these divisions as inseparable. The parts of philosophy were like the parts of a body, whose individual members could not subsist as such independently of the whole (Seneca, *Ep.* 33.5; 89.1–2).[41] Because each part had to be referred to the whole for its meaning and existence, the parts of Stoic philosophy were only "Stoic" to the extent that they related to the whole Stoic system. In this respect, "physics" and "ethics" were inseparable, as ultimately all the parts were.

It follows that the Stoic anthropological framework considered in its "physical" aspects (physics) fully *entailed* certain "ethical" principles (ethics). Specifically, the pantheistic rationalism of Stoic anthropology entailed an anthropology of ethical "self-sufficiency," or αὐτάρκεια. By definition, αὐτάρκεια was "a condition which is satisfied with what is necessary, and by itself furnishes what contributes to the blessed life" (*SVF* 3:272 [p. 67, line 3], 276 [p. 68, line 5]). This definition had unique meaning within philosophical, and especially Stoic, doctrine. For the philosophers, αὐτάρκεια was a divine attribute.[42] God—or if one prefers, Nature—lacks and needs nothing.[43] Nature is self-sufficient (αὐτάρκης) because it is a complete system, containing everything necessary to nourish itself and being capable of recycling its parts in perpetuity (Marcus Aurelius, *Med.* 8.50). In this state of self-sufficiency, the world (a living thing) is happy. Nature (or the World or God) in turn offers a model of self-sufficiency that is imitated by the "wise man." Having God as a part of himself, the wise man possesses reason, and through reason virtue, the only thing necessary for happiness (Seneca, *Ep.* 85.1), all externals being indifferent. And so the wise man is self-sufficient (Seneca, *Ep.* 9.3). And since reason is a *proper* quality of the human *qua* human, right use of reason earns the wise man a right to "boast," for he has used well what is properly his own (Seneca, *Ep.* 41.6).

---

40. Diogenes Laertius, *Vit. phil.* 7.39–40; *SVF* 2:35–40. Some attributed the arrangement to Plato (Apuleius, *Dogm. Plat.* 1.3; Aristocles in Eusebius, *Praep. ev.* 9.3.6; Diogenes Laertius, *Vit. phil.* 3.56; Hippolytus, *Refutatio* 1.18.2; Augustine, *Civ.* 8.4), though others suggest that Plato did not invent the divisions but only discussed their substance (Cicero, *Acad.* 1.19; but Sextus Empiricus, *Adv. math.* 7.16).

41. For other analogies see Diogenes Laertius, *Vit. phil.* 7.40.

42. David N. Sedley discusses this claim as one shared by Empedocles, Plato, and the Stoics. Sedley, "Self-Sufficiency as a Divine Attribute in Greek Philosophy," in *Ecology and Theology in the Ancient World: Cross-Disciplinary Perspectives*, ed. A. Hunt and H. Marlow (London: Bloomsbury, 2019), 41–47.

43. For *Nature* (φύσις) as another word for God (θεός), see Seneca, *Nat. qu.* 45.1–2.

This framework is consistent with the picture of the Corinthian σοφοί that emerged in our treatment of 1 Cor 1:17b–4:21. We found the clearest evidence of αὐτάρκεια in 4:7–8 (note also 1:26–31).[44] As discussed, Paul's rhetorical questions there confront directly both Corinthian self-sufficiency ("what do you have that you did not receive?") and their boasting on this basis ("if you did receive it, why do you boast as if you did not receive it?") in language that both parallels and strikingly clashes with the claims of self-sufficiency that we found articulated in several passages from Epictetus (whatever you need, "*receive* it from yourself").[45] One might reasonably infer that the Corinthian presumption of inherent human potential explains in part why Paul so persistently uses, in a *polemical* way, the word *human* as a characterization of the Corinthians' σοφία (1:25; 2:5, 13; 3:3, 4). The Corinthian σοφοί ground their ethic of self-sufficiency in an *anthropology* that understands the qualities that they allege not as extrinsically given, but as intrinsically abiding.

In short, the Corinthians' σοφία owes a debt to Stoicism that involves a complex of ideas located at the *intersection* of Stoic physics and ethics. They possess connate πνεῦμα at the highest level of tension and in that state are wise, perfect, and spiritual. These are qualities of "their own." And naturally, every creature has a right to boast in what is its own.

The Spiritual, the Unspiritual, and Indifference

Striking as these Stoic parallels are, one would not wish to overlook what was "different and new" in Corinth.[46] Something indeed was different. For the Stoics, the σοφός was perfect *in virtue*. The σοφός accurately assessed through reason what was in every situation good, bad, or indifferent. Yet, anyone who has read 1 Corinthians is only too familiar with its portrait of the Corinthian church as—at least by Pauline standards—shockingly immoral and ill-behaved.

One must be careful not to assume at the outset that Paul's standards of morality were the *same* as the Stoics'. For instance, Paul's extended treatment of the ethics of eating idol meat in 8:1–11:1, while incriminating for the Corinthian sub-Stoics as Christ followers, approaches the practice from quite a different perspective than a Stoic one. The σοφοί who claim to "have

---

44. Note also 1:30–31: it is ἐξ αὐτοῦ (from God) that they are "in Christ Jesus," a fact that rules out "boasting" (1:30–31).
45. See chapter 7, pp. 176–79.
46. Barclay, "Thessalonica and Corinth," 69n25.

knowledge" (8:1) claim, based on this knowledge, to know that "an idol is nothing" and that "there is no God but one" (8:4). To their thinking, those who remain averse to idol meat are in fact "weak" in mind, having failed to grasp the truth of this liberating "knowledge." The Corinthians' *intellectual* criteria for the ethics of eating were based, it seems, on a Stoic conception of intellectual misapprehension as "weakness" and a conception of nonintellectual matters as matters of "indifference."[47] From their perspective, then, the Corinthians remained very much in conformity with what was "right." On other matters, we find the Corinthians' behavior conflicting even with Stoic ethical standards. For instance, in contrast with the libertine attitude of their Cynic cousins, Stoics maintained strict sexual standards, generally agreeing that sex was permissible only within marriage and only for purposes of procreation (though they disagreed as to whether marriage itself was indifferent).[48] As 1 Cor 5:1–13 and 6:12–20 show, sexual immorality was an exceptional problem being committed by some in the church (quite possibly, but not definitely, by the σοφοί).

Comprehensive evaluation of the Corinthians' conformity/nonconformity with Stoic "virtue" (i.e., their "Stoic" morality) would require attention to each issue individually, along with more serious consideration of the doctrinal framework of Stoic ethics. Our more immediate focus precludes such attention. Let us suppose nevertheless that the standards of the Corinthian σοφοί were not in all ways consistent either with Paul's ethical standards or with those of the Stoics: on what grounds did the σοφοί justify deviation from Paul's norms, and from those of Stoicism, by which we have supposed that they were influenced?

John Barclay has proposed that a major impetus for the Corinthians' behavior was that they held to a religious ethos that did "*not entail significant social and moral realignment.*" According to Barclay, they were able to maintain this ethos because they considered their faith as being of "only limited significance" outside of their semi-private gatherings, where they embodied the most essential part of their identity as πνευματικοί by practic-

---

47. Brookins, *Corinthian Wisdom*, 165–68.
48. For example, Cicero, *Fin.* 4.17; Musonius Rufus, *Diatr.* 12–14; Epictetus, *Diatr.* 2.4; 2.23.12; 3.7.21; Stobaeus, *Anth.* 4.67.22; 4.67.24. Despite Zeno's preference that in the ideal city the wise would have "a community of wives with free choice of partners" (*SVF* 3:728 // Diogenes Laertius, *Vit. phil.* 7.131 [Hicks, LCL]), he did not allow adultery in established states (*SVF* 3:729). On the debate over marriage and indifference, see Will Deming, *Paul on Marriage and Celibacy: The Hellenistic Background of 1 Corinthians 7* (Grand Rapids: Eerdmans, 2004), 50–107.

ing "knowledgeable speech, tongues and prophecy."⁴⁹ "Beyond that socially (and temporally) confined context," Barclay suggests, "the πνευματικοί had authority to behave as they wished." In short, behavior as they saw it was not determined on grounds of ethics but on grounds of "'consciousness' and self-understanding."

I believe that Barclay's characterization of the Corinthian *habitus* is essentially correct, though I do not believe that the meeting context was determinative. I would like to add to Barclay's comments by inquiring further into the *rationale* through which the σοφοί arrived at their ethos. I suggest that their rationale was rooted in a classification of values that was structurally analogous to the ethical classification system adopted by the Stoics—but with a key difference.

The Stoics classified values into the categories of "good" (ἀγαθόν), "bad" (κακόν), and "indifferent" (ἀδιάφορον).⁵⁰ Virtue was the only good, vice the only evil. Everything intermediate was indifferent. In the latter category were included all external and bodily "goods" (so-called)—life, health, wealth, and the like and their opposites, death, disease, poverty, and things like these—things that people ordinarily consider either good or bad. What made the σοφός exceptional was that he assigned correct value to things based on his right use of reason. In particular, he was able to recognize *as indifferent* those things that people often mistake as good or bad. This meant that morality was fundamentally *cognitive* in nature. Seneca aptly summarizes the Stoic position: "What then is good? The knowledge [scientia] of things. What is evil? The lack of knowledge of things. Your wise man, who is also a craftsman, will reject or choose in each case as it suits the occasion" (*Ep.* 31.6 [Gummere, LCL]).

The system of evaluation assumed by the Corinthian σοφοί ran parallel with the Stoic one on several points. First, they considered to be "indifferent" things that others in their community, and Paul himself, would have considered "good" or "bad," and in particular, "bad." Second, these indifferents were matters that pertained primarily to the *body* (5:1–13; 6:12–20; 6:13; 8:1–11:1). Third, they reached these conclusions *reflectively*, claiming, as σοφοί, to have discerned what was indifferent by means of some kind of special "knowledge" or insight (γνῶσις, 8:1). Fourth, they identified the noetic state as the only consideration of evaluative importance. Their conviction on this point is concisely revealed in what others have definitively proven to be a Corin-

---

49. Barclay, "Thessalonica and Corinth," 70.
50. *SVF* 3:68–168.

thian slogan: "Every sin that a person commits is outside the body" (6:18).[51] Fifth, this noetic state was *absolutely* distinct from a state of ignorance. There was no variation of degree within states. The "immature" man (νήπιος), however he may have progressed, is *fully* not-wise. Sixth, the person who reached the highest state is the embodiment of "perfection" and is the "rule" against which all else or others must be measured (2:15).

There was something different, nevertheless, about the Corinthian viewpoint. Whereas the Stoics made *virtue* the only criterion of good, the Corinthian σοφοί substituted a different value—namely, *"the spiritual."* This modification resulted in a parallel system of classification, which was not now *good-bad*-indifferent, but *spiritual-unspiritual*-indifferent. It is most serendipitous for our thesis that this construal of the Corinthians' "ethical" framework finds concise confirmation in our analysis of the slogan in 2:15: "the spiritual man judges all things." As discussed, this slogan verbally and structurally, and in a word, precisely, parallels a Stoic doctrine that we have found encapsulated in the line treated earlier from Seneca, with *only* the substitution of "the spiritual man" (ὁ πνευματικός) for "virtue" (*virtus*). The "spiritual" thus functioned for the Corinthians as a structurally compatible replacement part and merely local modification within a larger configuration of systemically related Stoic ideas. Just as virtue (which the Stoic σοφός embodied) acts as the "rule" against which all else must be judged, so also does the Corinthian "spiritual man" (who also was a σοφός). This substitution introduces the key difference that explains the conflict between the acclaimed virtuousness of the Stoic σοφός on the one hand and the norm-violating immorality of the Corinthian σοφοί on the other. For these, it was not "virtue" that acted as the rule, but "the spiritual."

We cannot treat 1 Cor 12–14 in depth here, but I pose that these chapters fully support what the Corinthian slogan in 2:15 suggests. As Paul introduces the topic in 12:1, he refers in Corinthian-biased language to πνευματικά (12:1; 14:37; cf. 14:12), that is, to "spiritual things." The Corinthians' "spiritual things" included spiritual manifestations like tongues, interpretation of tongues, prophecy, discernment of spirits, and words of wisdom and knowledge (12:8–10). Apparently, the Corinthian πνευματικοί did not, however, think of "the spiritual" as spiritual "gifts." Rather, they understood the "spiritual"

---

51. Naselli, "Is Every Sin outside the Body except Immoral Sex?"; building on Jerome Murphy-O'Connor, "Corinthian Slogans in 1 Cor. 6:12–20," *CBQ* 40 (1978): 391–96; Jay E. Smith, "The Roots of a 'Libertine' Slogan in 1 Corinthians 6:18," *JTS* 59 (2008): 63–95; and others.

in terms of spiritual *manifestations* that "properly qualified" the spiritual man as spiritual. Consistent with their notion of self-sufficiency, the πνευματικοί failed to attribute their spiritual faculties to God. Constituted as πνευματικοί, at the highest level of pneumatic tension, they had "spiritual *powers*" (δυνάμεις) that they for all intents and purposes regarded as "their own." Against the Corinthian language of πνευματικά, then, Paul redefines "spiritual" phenomena as χαρίσματα, or "gifts" (12:4, 9, 28, 30, 31), things externally sourced and not proper qualities of God's human instruments or properties of humans themselves.

Our examination of the Corinthians' σοφία against the model of Stoicism, in sum, has yielded several insights. (1) A person's status as σοφός is made possible by the indwelling Spirit. (2) It is the immanence of the Spirit at high-level "tension" that produces higher-level faculties, and indeed human "perfection," and lower-level tension that limits the faculties of others to sub-πνευματικός status. In other words, differences in status are due to differences in tensive connection with connate Spirit. (3) This indwelling faculty becomes *proper* to the human qua human and is not, as a property, externally sourced; hence, the possessor may consider himself *self-sufficient*. (4) It is because the spiritual faculty is "their own" that they have full right to boast. (5) This "spiritual" state is the only true criterion of evaluation and perfection, matters of the body being relegated to the category of "indifference." At the same time, we found that (6) even the Corinthians' departure from the orthodox Stoic framework preserves a certain analogous structure: just as the Stoics classified things into the categories of *good-bad*-indifferent, the Corinthian σοφοί classified them into *spiritual-unspiritual*-indifferent. Hence, just as virtue constituted the absolute rule by which Stoics evaluated status, for the Corinthian σοφός, the absolute rule was "the spiritual": as they said, "the spiritual man judges all things."

Corinthian Wisdom in Summary

Our analysis has led to the conclusion that the Corinthian σοφοί did not just derive from Stoicism the title of "the wise man" and an assortment of descriptors found in the paradoxes. Rather, they adopted a self-understanding that mirrored a complex of Stoic ideas at a particular point where physics and ethics intersected: Stoic anthropology.

On the side of physics, the σοφοί not only viewed themselves as having the Spirit within; they also accepted a tiered view of God's creatures that, because of "tonic" differences in interaction with connate πνεῦμα, drew a distinct line between higher- (πνευματικοί) and lower-faculty (ψυχικοί) beings. They only substituted for Stoic "virtue" the concept of "the spiritual," and for the "virtuous man" the "spiritual man." They were wise (σοφοί), perfect (τέλειοι), and spiritual (πνευματικοί), able to "discern all things"; they were the standard against which others were measured and found to be immature (νήπιοι) and unspiritual (ψυχικοί). Their assessment of their peers need not imply that they considered them to be vacant of the Spirit entirely. Rather, like the Stoics, the Corinthian σοφοί merely understood σοφός status in all-or-nothing terms. Some may have made "progress," but everything short of perfection remained ignorance, a failure to reach the benchmark, like the man who continued to drown though he is but an inch beneath the surface. One could be a "Stoic" without being a "wise man."[52] One could also be a Christ person and still be a ψυχικός.

On the side of "ethics," the anthropology of the σοφοί entailed a doctrine of human self-sufficiency, or αὐτάρκεια. The σοφοί viewed their strength of Spirit as grounds for boasting, as if the Spirit were not "received" but were now "their own." To summarize the comparison:

Stoics	Corinthian σοφοί
λογικός tension	πνευματικός tension
reason	the Spirit
virtue/wise man as rule	the spiritual/wise man as rule
perfection	perfection
good, bad, and indifferent	spiritual, unspiritual, and indifferent

The Existence of the Wise Man

The question arises whether anyone in this milieu could have made claims like those we have attributed to the Corinthian σοφοί. Hans Betz remarked that the Corinthians' claims would have been perceived as problematic by most people at this stage in antiquity.[53] Indeed, skepticism about the existence of a wise man was widespread, and many doubted whether the ideal was attainable, especially as the Stoics articulated it.[54]

Bold claims of this purport, however, were not inconsistent with the categories of the culture. The wise man in the mold of the philosopher was

---

52. Seneca consistently denies that he was a *sapiens*; see n. 67 below.
53. Betz, "Problem of Rhetoric," 27–28n27.
54. See chapter 6, p. 143.

but one type in a broader class of persons that might be branded "divine men" (θεῖοι ἄνδρες). Though more a modern analytic term than an ancient technical one, the term θεῖος ἀνήρ helps us explain and classify a variety of character types that in their own ways fit the concept.[55] Biblical scholarship since the early twentieth century has applied the term primarily as a designation for a special type of ancient person known for miraculous feats or extraordinary exploits. Often included in this category are Alexander of Abonoteichus (Lucian's "false prophet"), Apollonius of Tyana, and, of course, Jesus of Nazareth. Scholarship has named as another type the philosophical wise man, whose status as a kind of θεῖος ἀνήρ derived from his exceptional wisdom and exemplary life.[56] Socrates was the paradigm of this type. In the Hellenistic philosophical schools, this type came to be epitomized in the portrait of the σοφός. Within Hellenistic Judaism, this model was applied to Moses.[57] Recently, biblical scholarship has compared Jesus against the philosophers' model.[58] Apart from θεῖοι ἄνδρες of these types are examples of individuals who claimed divine status for themselves, including both rulers and popular figures.[59]

One must confess that the bar to qualify as a Stoic wise man was especially high. In the opinion of F. Gerald Downing, this point proves that the Corinthians could not have been thinking in Stoic terms—the Stoic conception of the wise man being "an all but impossible ideal." This argument against a Stoic connection is quite invalid, however.[60] Downing's objection

---

55. For an assessment of the θεῖος ἀνήρ concept after its heyday in modern scholarship, see Aage Pilgaard, "The Hellenistic *Theios Aner*," in *The New Testament and Hellenistic Judaism*, ed. Peder Borgen and Soren Giversen (Peabody, MA: Hendrickson, 1995), 101–22. For a more recent look at the semantics of the associated word group, see David S. du Toit, *Theios Anthropos: Zur Verwendung von 'Theios Anthropos' und sinnverwandten Ausdrücken in der Literatur der Kaiserzeit*, WUNT 2/91 (Tübingen: Mohr Siebeck, 1997).

56. D. L. Tiede distinguishes two primary types—the philosophical type and the divine miracle worker—in *The Charismatic Figure as Miracle Worker* (Missoula: Scholars, 1972).

57. Philo, *Leg.* 3.140; *Abr.* 13; *Vit. Mos.* 1.1 and throughout. Grant ("Wisdom of the Corinthians," 51–55) notes that Philo, Josephus, and the Neoplatonist Porphyry portrayed the Essenes as ideal wise men (54).

58. Thorsteinsson, "Jesus Christ and the Wise Man," 73–87; Engberg-Pedersen, *John and Philosophy*.

59. Including Caesars (Caligula in Dio Cassius 59.11.12, 28.1–2; Domitian in Suetonius, *Dom.* 13; on Nero, cf. Tacitus, *Ann.* 13.8.1) and popular figures (note Lucian's *Alexander the False Prophet* and *Nigrinus*). On perceptions of Apollonius of Tyana, see Philostratus, *Vit. Apoll.* 3.50.1; 3.43; 7.20.1; 7.21.1; 7.32.1; 8.13.2; 8.5.1; etc. And see the survey in Pilgaard, "Hellenistic *Theios Aner*."

60. Downing, *Cynics, Paul, and the Pauline Churches*, 88.

The Sub-Stoic Wisdom of the Corinthians

is based on the claims not of the Stoics themselves, but of their critics. It was the Stoics' chiefly Academic and Middle Platonist opponents who criticized their doctrine of the wise man as an impossible ideal.[61] The very criticism implies that the Stoics themselves insisted that the goal was attainable. While Stoics like Seneca conceded that wise men have been, to be sure, scarce,[62] Seneca states unequivocally that the wise man is "not a fiction for us Stoics," that such can exist and have existed. He offers Marcus Cato as an exemplar who he "almost" thinks "surpasses" the wise man (*vereor ne supra nostrum exemplar sit*).[63] Stoics elsewhere admit Socrates and Diogenes of Sinope into this class.[64] Within the Hellenistic Jewish tradition, Philo consistently presents Moses as a wise man[65] and echoes Seneca's assertion that perhaps there have been but few wise men, but not none.[66]

If anything is an obstacle to the view that the Corinthians could have claimed σοφός status, it is that philosophers were loath to apply the designation to *themselves*. They did not claim to *be* wise men, but claimed that others had been such.[67] A key impetus for the Corinthians' boldness, however, may be found partly in the difference between philosophical teachers of the day and Paul himself. Seneca's note that Plato, Epicurus, and Zeno (the founders of the three most successful philosophical schools) told "not how they themselves were living, but how they ought to live" stands in stark contrast with Paul's refrain, "be my imitators."[68] With similar boldness, Paul exhorted his churches to imitate him *as he imitated Christ*.[69] As such, Paul did not just ask them to be like Christ, but claimed to have become a living paradigm of Christ—an *exemplum* or παράδειγμα—for them. If the Corinthians, then, were somewhat bolder than the philosophers of their times, they were in this respect much more like their own teacher.

---

61. E.g., Cicero, *Acad.* 2.145; *Tusc.* 2.51; Plutarch, *Mor.* 75b–76e; Sextus Empiricus, *Adv. prof.* 9.133–136 // LS 54D; Lucian, *Herm.* 76–77.

62. Seneca, *Ep.* 42.1; cf. Epictetus, *Diatr.* 2.19.20–28. See also comments on 3:18 in chapter 6.

63. Seneca, *Const.* 7.1; cf. 6.3–8.

64. Epictetus, *Ench.* 51.3 (Socrates); Epictetus, *Diatr.* 4.1.152 (Diogenes); Cicero, *Parad.* 2; and Seneca, *Const.* 7.1 (Cato).

65. σοφὸς τέλειος (*Leg. all.* 3.140); as πάνσοφος (*Abr.* 13); τελειότατος (*Vit. Mos.* 1.1).

66. *Alleg.* 1.102; *Prob.* 62–63, 73.

67. Seneca denies that he is one (*Ep.* 52.3; 57.3; 75.9–16; *Vit. Beat.* 11.1; 17.3–4; *Helv.* 5.2).

68. Seneca, *Vit. beat.* 18.1; versus 1 Cor 4:16; 11:1; Phil 3:17; cf. Phil 4:9; 1 Thess 1:6.

69. 1 Cor 11:1; 1 Thess 1:6; cf. Phil 2:5; 2 Cor 4:10–13.

Corinthian Sub-Stoicism and the Christ-Faith

If we can believe that Paul's converts proclaimed themselves σοφοί in the sense described, we are still left to explain how these people could have found this conception of themselves compatible with the Christ-faith that they espoused. Their conception of the Spirit as something properly "their own," their stance toward God as one effectively of self-sufficiency (αὐτάρκεια), their self-sufficiency as grounds for boasting, their distinguishing of tonic-spiritual status among members of the believing community, their relegation of "nonspiritual" things to the category of indifference—Paul opposes all of these things in some way. We may surmise that the Stoic connections began, minimally, from the common reference points of the indwelling Spirit (the immanent πνεῦμα), of Jesus as the paradigm of human excellence (as a "wise man"), and of the Spirit as the source (like Stoic "reason") of the faculties that enable humans to attain perfection. But from there they evidently exercised a degree of independent development of Paul's teaching, inspired by a fairly sophisticated matrix of Stoic ideas.

One could say that Paul's rebuke flowed largely from his theology of "grace."[70] First, the Stoic anthropology we have explored, with its notions of connate Spirit and innate *self-sufficiency*, clashes fundamentally with Paul's notion of "*efficacious*" grace. For Paul humanity could not rise to its highest level of fulfillment based on anything intrinsic in itself. As we noted in chapter 3, John Barclay aptly captures this aspect of Paul's thinking in terms of "ex-centric existence" in Christ. The new life of the believer is not sourced from within, but is sourced from something, or someone, outside of oneself.[71]

Paul's notion of ex-centric existence in Christ clashes fundamentally with the Stoic doctrine of human self-sufficiency. This is why Paul so persistently affirms the initiative and agency of God in 1 Corinthians: God has "enriched [them] in everything" (1:5) so that they "lack no *gift* [χάρισμα!]" (1:7); God has "established" them (1:8), "called them into participation with his Son" (1:9); all they have "received" comes from God (4:7), and Christ has "become righteousness, sanctification, and redemption *for* [them]" (1:29–31), leaving no room for "boasting" (1:29–31; 4:7); "all things are [theirs]" because they belong to Christ and Christ to God (3:21–23); they have not "the Spirit *of the world* [τοῦ κόσμου]" but "the Spirit *that is from* God [τὸ ἐκ τοῦ θεοῦ]" (2:12). This is

---

70. I borrow these terms from Barclay (*Paul and the Gift*), who refers to these as two "perfections" in Paul's theology of grace (referring to *efficacy* and *incongruity* on p. 69).

71. See chapter 3, p. 81; citing Barclay, *Paul and the Power of Grace*, 92.

also why Paul replaces the Corinthians' language of πνευματικά, "spiritual things," with χαρίσματα, or "spiritual *gifts*" (1:7; 12:4, 9, 28, 30, 31).

Just as efficacious grace grounds Paul's response to the Corinthians' anthropological claims, "*incongruous*" grace grounds his response to their acclaimed spiritual *status*. I have argued that 1:26–31 does not concern the agency of God versus the agency of the orator in producing salvation. Rather, it concerns the *incongruity* of election with the worth of the recipient. With regard to the σοφοί, Paul emphasizes that their status vis-à-vis God neither depended nor depends upon any qualities inherent in themselves. So far from electing the worthiest, God elected those whom humanity considers *least* worthy.

To return then to our question: How could the Corinthians have found their viewpoint compatible with the Christ-faith that Paul preached? I should like to address this question with reference to three analytical axes (*A1, A2, A3*).

A1. The first axis concerns the Corinthians' level of "reflectivity" toward the matter—reflectivity both with respect to their engagement with Stoicism/Paul's teaching and with respect to their approach to integrating the two. At the extremes, their orientation involved either reflective engagement or unreflective engagement. *Reflective engagement* concerns both the subject's awareness *that* they are thinking in a particular way and some level of reflection as to why they think in this way and how the pertinent material fits together. Conversely, *unreflective engagement* consists in low awareness of one's own thinking and a lack of reflection as to why they think as they do or how consistent their thinking is.

A2. The second axis concerns the nature of the cross-cultural "interactions" involved in their engagement with the relevant content. The points on this axis correlate with the seven different interaction types identified by Max Lee and introduced in chapter 2: eclecticism, refutation, competitive appropriation, irenic appropriation, concession, common ethical usage, and doctrinal reformulation.

A3. The third axis is oriented around the content itself. This axis addresses the possible "models" that might illustrate the integrative shape of the Corinthians' thinking. I want to propose three possible models, subdividing the third into three subtypes. Since our three axes interrelate, each model in *A3* correlates uniquely with points on the spectra of *A1* and *A2*.

1. *Stoic and Christian.* Here, with respect to Stoicism and the Christ-faith, a fundamental incompatibility or internal conflict remains in the thinking

of the Corinthian σοφοί, due to unreflective engagement (*A1*) with the matter, or at least *insufficiently reflective* engagement as to their doctrinal consistency. The resulting type of interaction (*A2*) could be considered that of eclecticism.

2. *Stoic over Christian.* The Corinthian σοφοί, as "philosophers," had so distorted Paul's teaching that it resembled Stoicism or a Greek "philosophy" more than it did Paul's gospel message. They made Stoicism the dominating framework, into which they worked Paul's teaching. This model entails a kind of reflective engagement (*A1*) in which either the Christ-faith concedes to Stoic σοφία or the Corinthians' Stoic σοφία irenically appropriates material from Paul's teaching (*A2*).

3. *Christian over Stoic.* This option admits of gradation. (a) On a "light Stoic" version of this model, the σοφοί viewed their encounter with Christ and reception of the Spirit on analogy with the instant and absolute transformation of the Stoic wise man (making them spiritual, self-sufficient, and the "perfect" standard), differing however from the Stoics in their belief that they did not possess their new faculties as "peculiarly their own," but as given by special external endowment. (b) On a "middle Stoic" version of this model, the σοφοί perhaps acknowledged that the Spirit was not inborn but given but believed that once given it became a peculiar quality of the human being per se and an inward source of self-sufficiency, perfection, and cognitive endowment sufficient to make them the "measure" of all evaluation. (c) On a "heavy Stoic" version of this model, the σοφοί shared the Stoic view that the Spirit indeed resided in *all* people by nature but believed that their encounter with Christ enlightened or enabled them to tap into its full resources.[72] In all variations, (a), (b), and (c), the Corinthians' orientation would entail reflective engagement (*A1*) as to the material, and their interactions something like irenic or competitive appropriation of Stoicism, or at the extreme, even some serious *concession* to Stoicism (*A2*). Still, the σοφοί believed that their views amounted simply to *doctrinal reformulation* of the teachings of Paul. For they still identified, emically, as Christ people.

---

72. This model might be compared with Engberg-Pedersen's model of Paul's own "ethics" (*Paul and the Stoics*, esp. 34–40).

A³ (content model)	A¹ (reflectivity)	A² (interaction type)
(1) Stoic and Christian	unreflective (or less reflective) engagement	eclecticism
(2) Stoic over Christian	reflective engagement	concession to Stoicism / irenic appropriation of Paul's teaching
(3) Christian over Stoic	reflective engagement	competitive or irenic appropriation of Stoicism + doctrinal reformulation of Paul's teaching

It is difficult to evaluate which model more fittingly captures the Corinthian *habitus* for at least two reasons. First, the question of reflectivity and integration can only be settled finally at a level of elaboration of their views that we do not have. Second, we must make allowance for a margin of incongruity between the Corinthians' views and Paul's characterization of them. It is even possible that Paul himself, being aware of his limitations as to their intentions, crafted a response that tempered *rebuke* with an admixture of *warning*. Put differently, Paul may not have known whether the Corinthian σοφοί tended more toward something like a "Stoic-over-Christian" model. Paul's partial ignorance could explain why he *addresses* the church (including the σοφοί) as if they are in fact *Christ's* church, while simultaneously *describing* a σοφία that belongs to the *world* (1:20, 21), a wisdom belonging to those who are "perishing" (1:18) and to those whom God has "shamed" (1:27–28) and will "destroy" (3:17). This message of warning would thus introduce a conditional element: *if* one embraces this model of wisdom fully, one is *in fact* a member of the "world."

Methodological hindrances notwithstanding, our purpose has been to construct as best we can a description of σοφία as the Corinthians conceived of it, that is to say, an *emic* description of their wisdom, mediated though it is through Paul. While the first model, (1) Stoic and Christian, does not seem altogether out of the question, the level of technicality with which I have tried to show the σοφοί appropriated Stoicism—at the intersection of Stoic physics and ethics—suggests to me that their acquaintance with Stoicism was probably direct and thus unlikely to be very unreflective. Against (2) Stoic over Christian, we must assume that from the Corinthians' emic standpoint they considered themselves to be Christ people. This we may deduce from the fact that their common faith in Christ is frequently Paul's rhetorical starting point (1:13; 12:12; 15:3–11, 12) and the fact that Paul believes he has any right to exhort them from a believing perspective at all (indeed, what business does he have judging those outside the church? Cf. 1 Cor 5:12).[73] As I shall argue in chapter 10, their commitment to the faith Paul preached is also assumed in their declaration of allegiance to him ("I am of Paul"). In sum, we may on the one hand justifiably suppose that the σοφοί would have considered themselves "Paulinists" before they considered themselves "Zenonians." On the other hand, the Corinthians' σοφία was in some sense consciously "Stoic." How, then, do we hold these two things together?

I anticipated our resolution in chapter 2. Stoicism dogmatically struggled to define itself in its early phases and it continued to evolve over time. As it dispersed throughout the wider culture, in some forms Stoic distinctness attenuated as Stoicism became assimilated in different cultural domains. While I thus acknowledged the problematic nature of "essentialist" definitions of cultural entities like Stoicism, we concluded that Stoicism could nevertheless be identified as an entity in its own right by means of "polythetic criteria" and resulting "family resemblances." I then posed as a possible description of the Corinthian σοφοί, "sub-Stoics." Although this is an etic term, it is appropriate as a description of the Corinthians' emic self-understanding. Constitutive of this label is the fact that the σοφοί not only appropriated the terminology of Stoicism in their self-description as "wise men"; they also appropriated a constellation of interrelating concepts indigenous to Stoic physics and ethics, centering around anthropology. By prefixing *sub-* however, I intended to qualify the Corinthians' "Stoicism" as being *subordinate* to their Christ-faith. This points to the conclusion that their *habitus* reflected something closest to (3) Christian over Stoic, though it is difficult to decide between variable degrees (a), (b), and (c). Ultimately, they believed that their *habitus* was rooted in Paul's teachings. Thus, their reflective interaction with Paul's teaching involved not a rejection of this teaching, but a *doctrinal reformulation* of it. In all, the *habitus* of the Corinthian σοφοί was the product of a tension between interaction type 7 (doctrinal reformulation), on the one hand, and type 3 (competitive appropriation)/type 4 (irenic appropriation), on the other. It was sub-Stoicism, or "sub(ordinated) Stoicism."

---

73. Hyldahl ("Paul and Hellenistic Judaism") is not sure that Apollos was a Christian (214) and thinks that Paul "in the end, does not consider these same people Christians at all" (215).

WISDOM AND STATUS IN 1 CORINTHIANS 1–4

Before concluding discussion of σοφία and its contribution to the divisions in Corinth, it is important to address the relationship between this σοφία as described and the orientation toward "status" that seems to have prevailed among its proponents.

Status is a nebulous term and for our purposes requires some differentiation of types. I would like to introduce two types in respect to the Corinthians. (1) Status in one sense describes what someone *is* in the absolute, disengaged from society. This kind of status considers the person, on philosophical grounds, in terms of ontology or *metaphysics*. In this sense, the Stoic σοφός is wise, rational, perfect, and so on not because these qualities are ascribed to him socially but because, being filled with the Divine Spirit/reason, that is what he *is*—a rational as opposed to an irrational creature. (2) In another sense, status is something socially ascribed. In this sense status refers to what one is by *social construct*. In short, the first kind of status refers to what one is absolutely, the second to what one is in society.

This distinction helps to clarify the relationship between the "Stoic" σοφία that the Corinthian σοφοί appropriated and the "social" disunity that came out of it. That the "wise man" was superior to the "inferior man" is, from the standpoint of Stoic physics, a philosophical claim, not a social one. Yet, within the Corinthian church our two types of status merge: (1) Stoic physics, with its *natural* distinctions of status, transferred to the Corinthian subjects (2) qualities that could be recognized at a *social* level. Thus, while the terms *wise, powerful, well-born, rich, kings*, and so on (1:26; 4:8–10) refer to "spiritual" qualities, this is not to say that these attributes were without "social" implications. On the contrary, within the domain of the church, "spiritual" status constituted the basis for "social" status, the latter being imputed on grounds of the former. From this merger, a second bifurcation of status types emerges, as (2′) conventional social status divides into (a) "ordinary social status" and (b) "transcendent social status." I have argued that the status of the Corinthian σοφοί as σοφοί depended not on "ordinary" criteria of status like education, rhetorical ability, or association with an established patron. Rather, it depended upon "transcendent" criteria like professed spiritual ability and intellectual acumen.

Our differentiation between status types (1) and (2) adds a needed qualification to our connection between the church's σοφία and the social conflict intertwined with it. Specifically, an identification of the Corinthians' σοφία with "Stoicism" must be qualified by the "sociology of σοφία," so to speak. Critically, it would not be true to say that Stoic physics per se *was* socially "elitist." Rather, the "sociology" of the Corinthians' unique *appropriation* of Stoicism constituted their (sub)Stoicism as such.

Conclusion

The purpose of this chapter has been to develop an analytic portrait of the Corinthians' σοφία against the comparative background of Stoic philosophy. This comparison began, at a more superficial level, with the Corinthians' self-definition as "wise men" and the long-noted consistency of Paul's characterization of them with the distinctive language of the Stoic paradoxes ("only the wise man is rich, king, well born, perfect," etc.; "all things belong to the wise man"). I argued, however, that the match between the Corinthians' self-understanding and the doctrines of Stoicism penetrated beneath the linguistic surface and to the heart of their anthropology. Specifically, I argued that the two pairs of terms that the σοφοί used to distinguish themselves from their lower-spiritual-status counterparts find their meaning within the framework of Stoic physics. This framework describes the indwelling πνεῦμα as inhabiting creatures at varying levels of "tension," or τόνος. Believing themselves to be inhabited with the Spirit at its highest level of potency (δύναμις), the Corinthian σοφοί viewed themselves as τέλειοι, against the more weakly constituted νήπιοι. While the Stoics did not employ the terms πνευματικός-ψυχικός, on the other hand, as a technical *pair*, I have shown that they did use ψυχικός as a technical term within this tonic framework and that the term πνευματικός fits this framework as a cognate term while also appearing as a name for the members of a unique, Stoic-influenced medical school datable to our period, namely, the Πνευματικοί. The Corinthians' slight innovation in their use of terminology (from λογικός to πνευματικός) reflects a definite substitution, but one that preserves a structural parallel between their anthropological assumptions and those of the Stoics. The key difference is that, whereas the Stoics presented their wise man as the embodiment of the standard of virtue, or "good," as determined by his right use of reason (λόγος), the Corinthians touted their wise, or πνευματικός, man as the embodiment and standard of the "spiritual." This structural similarity is not accidental, for as demonstrated, the Stoic idea of the virtue standard is paralleled exactly in the Corinthian slogan of 2:15 with only the substitution of this single term. Accordingly, while the Stoics maintained the threefold classification of values into "*good*," "*bad*," and "indifferent," the Corinthians substituted "*spiritual*," "*unspiritual*," and "indifferent."

From these observations it was concluded that the Corinthian σοφοί were "Stoic" at the point where physics intersected with ethics. As πνευματικοί they were self-sufficient, having as "their own" what Paul would remind them they had from God. At the same time, they identified as Christ people and probably would not have called themselves "Stoics." Thus, I have proposed describing the σοφία of the Corinthians as "sub-Stoicism," or "sub(ordinated) Stoicism." This complex consisted of substantial material *reflectively* appropriated from Stoicism, though the Corinthians ultimately viewed their outlook as a legitimate doctrinal reformulation of Paul's teaching.

PART III

Reconstructing the Occasion

10

1 Corinthians 1:10–17a: The Paul Faction as Philosophical School

What Paul says first I have decided to treat last (1:10–17). My reason for this is contextual. It is tempting to jump from the brief paragraph in 1:10–17a to the conclusion that the church's conflict was motivated most basically by "leadership preferences." This forward-reading approach, however, runs a risk of reading into the larger discussion of "wisdom" in 1:17b–3:23 a preformed conception of the divisions rather than allowing the body of the letter to gradually illuminate Paul's, here, unelaborated introduction of the divisions. Having made a case based on a full run through 1:17b–4:21 that the Corinthians' σοφία was distinctly "sub-Stoic," we now return to the letter's introduction to examine in this light the nature of the church's divisions.

Our discussion here shall have to address several questions: Were there distinct "parties" in the church? If so, how many? Can we determine anything about the nature of the parties based on the form of the slogans in 1:12? And most importantly, how does the matter of party allegiances dovetail with the explanation that we have given for the Corinthians' σοφία?

One could arrange the history of research by positioning viewpoints along several different axes, representing different, albeit overlapping, aspects of the overarching issues. These axes represent a spectrum of emphases relevant to each aspect. Views sometimes reflect a tension between extremes, and interpreters often view the two sides of an axis as complementary. At the same time, it is generally possible to position interpreters on one side more definitively than another. I pose the following four axes.

(1) The impetus for the Corinthians' conflict was related more to Corinthian wisdom or more to the Corinthians' relations with leaders.[1] (2) The divisions were more internally facing (internal rivalries) or more outwardly facing (leadership preferences).[2] (3) The conflict was more a matter of interparty conflict or more a matter of conflict between the church and Paul.[3] (4) The conflict involved distinct parties or it involved parties as rhetorical constructions of general dissension.[4]

Rather than structuring our discussion around the four axes, my approach will be to offer a progressive reconstruction of the situation, through which my position on the respective aspects of the question will emerge. The conception of the church's parties that I will develop shares some sim-

---

1. Wisdom: C. K. Barrett, "Christianity at Corinth," *BJRL* 46 (1964): 269–97; Lampe, "Theological Wisdom"; Barclay, "Thessalonica and Corinth," 61; and especially Inkelaar, *Conflict over Wisdom*, vii, 1–2, 20. Relations with leaders, including (a) mystical or spiritual connection: Funk, "Word and Word," 290; Meeks, *The First Urban Christians*, 117–21; (b) social or spiritual patronage: Hock, *Social Context of Paul's Ministry*, 52–65; Marshall, *Enmity in Corinth*, xii; Clarke, *Secular and Christian Leadership*, xiii; Chester, *Conversion at Corinth*, 240–45; (c) status association: Pogoloff, *Logos and Sophia*, 119; Chow, *Patronage and Power*, 12; Finney, *Honour and Conflict*, 79.

2. Internal rivalries: Welborn, "On the Discord in Corinth," 87 (though with elements of the counter tendency); Baird, "'One against the Other,'" 116; Martin, *Corinthian Body*, 15; Finney, *Honour and Conflict*, 79. Differing leadership preferences: Munck, "Menigheden uden Partier," 68; Horsley, "Wisdom of Words," 231–32; Davis, *Wisdom and Spirit*, 130; Litfin, *St. Paul's Theology of Proclamation*, 153; Pogoloff, *Logos and Sophia*, 177–79; Winter, *Philo and Paul among the Sophists*, 172–78; Welborn, "Μωρὸς γένεσθω," 432–33; Still, "Divisions over Leaders and Food," 20; Mihaila, *Paul-Apollos Relationship*, 1.

3. Interparty conflict: Welborn, "On the Discord in Corinth," 90–92; with elements of this in Winter, *Philo and Paul among the Sophists*. Between the church and Paul: Lütgert, *Freiheitspredigt und Schwarmgeister*; Dahl, "Paul and the Church at Corinth," 55; Pearson, *Pneumatikos-Psychikos Terminology*, 27; Fee, *First Epistle to the Corinthians*, 1st ed., 6; Barnett, *Corinthian Question*, 120; Bitner, *Paul's Political Strategy*, 262.

4. Those who distinguish distinct parties distinguish sometimes four: Barrett, "Christianity at Corinth," 269–97; sometimes three: Weiss, *Der erste Korintherbrief*, xxxvi–xxxviii; Marshall, *Enmity in Corinth*, 204; Lampe, "Theological Wisdom," 124; James B. Prothro, "Who Is 'of Christ'? A Grammatical and Theological Reconstruction of 1 Cor 1.12," *NTS* 60 (2014): 250–65; but most often, two main parties, sometimes with a third playing a minor role: Sellin, "Das 'Geheimnis' der Weisheit," 70–71; Meeks, *First Urban Christians*, 117; Fiore, "'Covert Allusion,'" 100; Litfin, *St. Paul's Theology of Proclamation*, 229; Pogoloff, *Logos and Sophia*, 177–78; Winter, *Philo and Paul among the Sophists*, 172–78. General dissension: Munck, "Menigheden uden Partier," 167; Clarke, *Secular and Christian Leadership*, 89; Helmut Koester, "The Silence of the Apostle," in *Urban Religion in Roman Corinth: Interdisciplinary Approaches*, ed. Daniel N. Schowalter and Steven J. Friesen, HTS (Cambridge, MA: Harvard Theological Studies, Harvard Divinity School, 2005), 339–50, esp. 342.

ilarities with a reconstruction offered recently by Thomas Schmeller. In a chapter in his monograph *Schulen im Neuen Testament*, Schmeller argues that the Corinthians' slogans in 1 Cor 1:12 reflect a conception of their ministers—Paul, Apollos, and Cephas—specifically as *philosophical* teachers, and of themselves as these teachers' students.[5] Thus the rivalries between parties paralleled the kinds of rivalries that raged between philosophical schools. According to Schmeller, it was primarily the more well-to-do members of the community who adopted the "school" conception of the community, though this conception also found favor among the majority. The source of the Corinthians' conception was missionaries who arrived in Corinth after Paul's departure, who taught that Christian teachers (i.e., Paul, Apollos, Cephas) imparted "wisdom" in the same manner as non-Christian teachers of philosophy.[6] Yet, there remained a key difference between the Christian teachers' message and that of non-Christian philosophers: the Christian emphasis on the Spirit.[7]

Despite sharing points of agreement with Schmeller, my understanding of the situation will differ on several particulars. First, Schmeller does not argue for connections between the Corinthians' σοφία and any philosophical school in particular, nor does he discuss similarities in regard to philosophical content. Second, my understanding of the factions also differs from his somewhat. Finally, Schmeller was not able in his short chapter to develop his argument at length. I attempt here to offer a modified and fuller reconstruction of the church's factionalism. It will be my contention that the σοφοί in the church viewed Paul as the founder of a philosophical "school" to whom they expressed "allegiance" in the manner of other philosophers of the day and that they took his teachings as the basis for the modified (or sub-Stoic) σοφία to which they adhered. This—the Paul party—was the first to form. Other parties formed in response.

The Slogans in 1:12

Following the proem in the letter's first nine verses, Paul wastes no time in revealing why he writes. In 1:10 he pleads with the church that there be no

---

5. Thomas Schmeller, *Schulen im neuen Testament? Zur Stellung des Urchristentums in der Bildungswelt seiner Zeit*, HbibS 30 (Freiburg: Herder, 2001).
6. Schmeller, *Schulen im neuen Testament?*, 117–19.
7. Schmeller, *Schulen im neuen Testament?*, 119–22.

"divisions" (σχίσματα) among them, and that they be "joined together in the same mind and in the same thought" (κατηρτισμένοι ἐν τῷ αὐτῷ νοῒ καὶ ἐν τῇ αὐτῇ γνώμῃ). He is not uninformed. He knows through "Chloe's people" that "dissensions" (ἔριδες) have broken out (1:11). He elaborates in 1:12 by attributing the following words to the church's members: "each of you says, 'I belong to Paul,' or 'I belong to Apollos,' or 'I belong to Cephas,' or 'I belong to Christ'" (NRSV).

In a 1987 article, Laurence Welborn observed that the "*form* [of the party slogans] has never been investigated." Taking this upon himself Welborn poses that "if one seeks the formal derivation of these expressions one is always led back to the realm of politics."[8] Beginning here, Welborn argues that the Corinthians' slogans reflect declarations of partisan support as for candidates for political office. In support Welborn draws attention in ancient sources to the formula στάσις or μερίς "with the genitive of the proper name" ("the party of *X*") and the formula οἱ περὶ τινά ("those around *X*"). He also mentions "nearly fifteen hundred specimens" of sponsorship of candidates in epigraphy and graffiti which contain slogans that consist typically of "the name of the candidate and his office, the sponsoring individual or group, and a verb of adherence or support," for example, "Vatiam aed(ilem) Verus Innoces facit," "Verus Innoces is making Vatia aedile."[9]

Shortly after Welborn's article, Margaret Mitchell pursued the question of form further. Mitchell objected that "Welborn has not produced one example of an ancient political slogan which has the same formula [as 1 Cor 1:12]."[10] In this regard, a declaration of partisan support of the form "I support Marius for aedile" is not the same as saying "I *belong* to Marius." Moreover, formulas like "the party of someone" (ἡ μερίς τινός) or "the people around someone" (οἱ περὶ τινά) are not distinctly political, for they occur in all kinds of ancient contexts.[11] Ranging outside the domain of politics, Mitchell locates one text that matches our text formally, though she observes that it does not constitute a *slogan* per se: "'Ἦσαν ... τινὲς μὲν Φιλίππου," "some belonged to Philipp" (Demosthenes, *Or.* 9.56). She notes that elsewhere one commonly finds in reference to factions or faction members the formula definite article + name of party leader in the genitive (e.g., Josephus, *J.W.* 1.142). Though similar to

---

8. Welborn, "On the Discord in Corinth," 90.
9. Welborn, "On the Discord in Corinth," 92.
10. Mitchell, *Paul and the Rhetoric of Reconciliation*, 84.
11. Mitchell, *Paul and the Rhetoric of Reconciliation*, 84, citing examples in BDAG; LSJ; Josephus, *J.W.* 2.440, 443; and other texts.

1 Corinthians 1:10–17a: The Paul Faction as Philosophical School

our formula, Mitchell cautions that this formula also is not identical with it, and in any case, the extant examples do not occur in context as slogans or first-person identifications. Finally, Mitchell observes that philosophical texts tend to refer to adherents of teachers as ἀκροατής/μαθητής + the genitive of the teacher (Diogenes Laertius, *Vit. phil.* 2.13), that is, "a hearer/student of *X*," and not simply as being "of *X*."

Mitchell concludes that the absence of any exact parallel in our "considerable corpus" of extant writings "casts doubt on the view that these [statements in 1 Cor 1:12] share a common *form* of political sloganeering."[12] She argues that the genitives in 1:12, rather, reflect a "genitive of possession or belonging," as sources commonly use in describing especially parent-child and master-slave relationships.[13] She offers as the "most exact formulaic parallel" the twice-repeated τοῦ θεοῦ εἰμι in LXX Isa 44:5 (also alluded to in Acts 27:23). Importantly, Mitchell adds that the statements in 1 Cor 1:12 are not the Corinthians' own formulations, but rather Paul's *impersonations* of the church: with the genitive of belonging, Paul characterizes the Corinthians in terms of "the language of slave ownership and childish dependence."[14]

Following Mitchell's article, Bruce Winter argued that the slogans in fact reflect declarations of allegiance to different *teachers*, despite Mitchell's objection that texts referring to students typically designate them as ἀκροατής/μαθητής + genitive. For Winter these teachers were, of course, rival sophists,[15] though Winter actually cites no examples involving student-teacher relationships. At the same time, Winter, like Mitchell, explains the genitive as describing "origin or relationship," citing the same section of BDF that Mitchell does, again offering the example of Acts 27:23 (τοῦ θεοῦ, οὗ εἰμι [ἐγώ], alluding to LXX Isa 44:5).[16]

Since Mitchell has provided the most robust form analysis of the slogans, further evaluation must address her conclusions. One must deal first with her factual observation that the expressions in 1 Cor 1:12 do not replicate any

---

12. Mitchell, *Paul and the Rhetoric of Reconciliation*, 85.

13. She cites (*Paul and the Rhetoric of Reconciliation*, 85) examples from Smyth: Διὸς Ἄρτεμις ("Artemis, daughter of Zeus," Sophocles, *Aj.* 172); Λυδὸς ὁ Φερεκλέους ("Ludus, the slave of Pherecles," Andoc. 1.17); examples from BDF 162; and LSJ's categorization of our text under this usage.

14. Mitchell, *Paul and the Rhetoric of Reconciliation*, 83.

15. Winter, *Philo and Paul among the Sophists*, 172–78.

16. Winter, *Philo and Paul among the Sophists*, 173; citing a parallel example in a nonbiblical text: τᾶς Ἀφροδίτας ἐμί (IKorinthKent 8.3.3; dating to late sixth or early fifth century BC).

common slogan formula known from extant sources. We need also address Mitchell's inference that the slogans in 1:12 reflect Paul's *own* formulations. Finally, we must address her judgment that Paul devised these slogans to depict the Corinthians *as childish* and *as slaves*.

Mitchell's analysis might lead one to conclude that we cannot justifiably establish a specific comparative-cultural description of the Corinthians' conception of the "parties" (if we decide to call them parties). I believe, however, that a more detailed cultural description is indeed justifiable. In the first place, even if the expressions in 1:12 cannot be shown to *exactly* replicate any *common* slogan formula, sources do witness to formally approximate expressions that function as typical designations of alignment or as declarations of self-identification and that involve the name of the one to whom allegiance is shown. Second, even if Mitchell is right in taking these expressions as Paul's own constructions, her understanding of the genitive as a description of "childish or slavish dependence" upon declared leaders is somewhat flexible and can arguably be extended to apply to more specific cultural domains. The background here, I suggest, is to be found in the concept of philosophical allegiance as shown by students toward the founders of their respective philosophical schools.

The Slogans and Other Formulae

Philosophers were loyal people. Students of philosophy almost invariably identified with one philosophical school only and with the teacher who founded it. Ancient sources employ a variety of formulas to describe partisans and their allegiances. Most of these involve the name of the one to whom allegiance is shown.

(1) Some formulas constitute *third-person* descriptions of partisans.

(a) Some of these designate the *group* as a whole. (i) The οἱ περί τινά formula ("those around *X*"), which applies sometimes to political parties, was also commonly used of philosophical sects, as for instance the school of Plato as "those around Plato" (οἱ περὶ Πλάτωνα).[17] This form of designation also appears in sources to describe the "Pneumatist" (Πνευματικοί) medical school of Athenaeus (οἱ περὶ Ἀθήναιον).[18] (ii) Common also was the similar formula οἱ ἀπ' *X*, as in the early designation of Stoics as "those around Zeno"

---

17. Diogenes Laertius, *Vit. phil.* 10.8. Οἱ περὶ Ἡράκλειτον in Plato, *Crat.* 440c.
18. Ps.-Galen, *Inst. log.* 9.9 (Petit, 21–22.17). On this formula and the medical sects, see Coughlin and Lewis, "What Was Pneumatist about the Pneumatist School?," 205.

1 Corinthians 1:10–17a: The Paul Faction as Philosophical School

(οἱ ἀπ' αὐτοῦ).[19] (iii) Partisans could be designated simply as "the students of X," as in "the students of Zeno" (μαθηταὶ Ζήνωνος).[20] (iv) The names of school founders were inevitably converted into adjectives, which were then used as either attributives or substantives to identify the allegiances of the group's members.[21] The students of the Stoic Zeno were known as "Zenonians" (Ζηνώνειοι) before they were called "Stoics" (Στωικοί). Philodemus indicates that they actually wanted to be called "Socratics" (Σωκρατικοί).[22] The students of Plato were "Platonists" (Πλατωνικοί), the students of Epicurus "Epicureans" (Ἐπικούρειοι), and so on even for branches within the schools.[23] This form of designation was also common among the medical sects (the "Hippocratics," after Hippocrates; the "Erasistrateans," after Erasistrates; the "Asclepiadeans," after Asclepiades).[24]

(b) One could refer to the *individual* partisan with similar eponymous expressions. (i) The partisan of Plato was a "Platonic philosopher" (φιλόσοφος Πλατωνικός),[25] the partisan of Epicurus an "Epicurean philosopher" (φιλόσοφος Ἐπικούρειος).[26] (ii) The formula "a student of X" (μαθητής + genitive) describes not only students who learned personally from the named teacher, but also individuals from later generations who adhered to that one's teachings: "a disciple of Plato" (Πλάτωνος μαθητής in Strabo, *Geogr.* 14.30), "a disciple of Socrates" (Σωκράτους μαθητής in Philodemus, *P.Herc.* 164), "a disciple of Zeno" (Ζήνωνος μαθητής in Lucian, *Macr.* 19.6). (iii) The formula ζηλωτής + genitive ("a zealous follower of X") appears abundantly in sources as a label for philosophers, as shown earlier (chapter 6). The ζηλωτής was in a sense not just a follower or in the ordinary sense a "rival," but a zealous "emulator" of the teacher. Strong allegiance is implied.

(2) Designations like these often do emphasize the individual's *emic* identification. (a) Even third-person descriptions could emphasize the element of the subject's "choice" of identification, especially by employing the verb

---

19. Diogenes Laertius, *Vit. phil.* 7.5.
20. Diogenes Laertius, *Vit. phil.* 7.36.
21. In addition to the other examples cited, note that the followers of the philosopher Apollonius of Tyana were called "Apollonians" (Ἀπολλωνιεῖοι) (Philostratus, *Vit. Apol.* 8.20.1).
22. Diogenes Laertius, *Vit. phil.* 7.5; Philodemus, *De Stoicis* 13.3–4.
23. Ἐπικούρειοι φιλόσοφοι in TAM II 910. A second-century CE source makes mention of rival Stoic clubs known under the names "Diogenists," "Antipatrists," and "Panaetiasts" (Sedley, "School, from Zeno to Arius Didymus," 29).
24. See Galen, *On Medical Experience* 135; *Outline of Empiricism* 1.
25. For instance, *IG* 2.8303; *IG* 7.3423; Smyrna 173; Ephesos 1511; TAM III.I 882.
26. For instance, Didyma 279; SEG 25.1138; 30.1627; 40.1362; *IG* 14.674.

αἱρέομαι ("choose"). Related was the noun cognate αἵρεσις, "choice," which became the standard term for a philosophical "sect." As Origen said, "one person *chooses to be* Stoic, another *chooses to be* a Platonist, etc." (αἱρεῖται ἤτοι Στωϊκὸς ἢ Πλατωνικὸς ἢ Περιπατητικὸς ἢ Ἐπικούρειος εἶναι).[27] (b) First-person declarations of philosophical commitment were commonplace, as when Cicero declares: "I have chosen particularly to follow that one [*potissimum consecuti sumus*] which I think agreeable to the practice of Socrates" (*Tusc.* 5.11), here referring to Cicero's Academic teacher Philo of Larissa (*Tusc.* 2.9). Apollonius of Tyana's declaration of commitment to the teachings of Pythagoras demonstrates that philosophical allegiance was not just theoretical, but a commitment of one's whole life: "I will live Pythagoras' way [ἐγὼ δὲ τὸν [τρόπον] Πυθαγόρου ζήσομαι]" (Philostratus, *Vit. Apoll.* 1.7.3; cf. 1.32.2; 4.16.1). Also worthy of consideration is the later, first-person declaration "I am a Christian," which defines the claimant's identity using an eponym (Χριστιανός) and indeed constitutes a "slogan," as shown by its recurrence in ancient sources beginning in the second century.[28]

This survey reveals some noteworthy similarities between the Corinthian slogans and the ways in which philosophers were identified and identified themselves. First, it shows that philosophers were standardly designated by a variety of eponymous expressions, generally being identified by the name of the teacher or founder, whether in nominal form ("those around Zeno," "student of Zeno") or adjectival form ("Zenonians"). Second, it shows that these designations were not merely incidental descriptions but defining designations of who or what one *was* ("he is a Platonist," "he is an Epicurean," "I am a Christian") and to whom they were strongly devoted ("a zealous follower of Zeno"). Third, it emphasizes that these identities were fundamentally a matter of emic identification since they were rooted in subjective sectarian choice (a αἵρεσις as a "choice"). Fourth, the sectarian nature of philosophical identity implied exclusive allegiance and resulted in strong rivalry between opposing sects. Finally, as we shall see, philosophical allegiance was often depicted by critics as a kind of "slavery" to the subjects' chosen masters—an important point if the genitive of belonging implies slavish dependence as Mitchell suggests. It is to the phenomenon of philosophical allegiance that we now turn.

---

27. Origen, *Cels.* 1.10.
28. Mart. Pol. 10.1 (cf. 12.1); Mart. Ign. 8.4.1; Mart. Lyons 1.19.3; 1.20.7; Acts of Justin and the Seven Martyrs 3.4.2; 4.1.2; 4.2.2; 4.3.2; etc.

1 Corinthians 1:10–17a: The Paul Faction as Philosophical School

Philosophical Allegiance

Mitchell's "genitive of belonging," with its depiction of adherents as children or slaves, suits well the dynamic of philosophical allegiance as ancient texts describe it. Christopher Gill remarks that during the Roman period "most philosophically committed thinkers saw themselves as having a determinate intellectual position and (unless someone was himself the founder of a new movement) maintained allegiance to a specific school together with its founder and conceptual framework."[29] In other words, most philosophers identified with one school only, and loyalty to one's school meant, above all, loyalty to the school's founder.[30]

That philosophical identity remained intrinsically tied to allegiance to particular teachers is illustrated in no better way than by the fact that attributive labels were etymologically derived from the names of the founders themselves ("Platonist," "Epicurean," etc.). David Sedley's remark that philosophical movements centered around a "virtually religious commitment to the authority of a founder figure," characterized by a "reverence" for the canon of texts they left behind,[31] may slightly exaggerate the truth in some cases,[32] but there is much in favor of the general description. The Epicureans regularly depicted Epicurus "as if a god."[33] Philodemus states that to disagree with Epicurus is "not at all far from parricide."[34] The Pythagoreans are said to have settled every doctrinal dispute with the peremptory mantra "He himself has spoken" (αὐτὸς ἔφα, or *ipse dixit*).[35] Boys-Stones aptly summarizes the perspective of Middle Platonists concerning the authority of Plato with the line "Plato is right."[36]

The main exception to this culture of allegiance was the Skeptics. Rather than defining themselves by allegiance to a single authority, their refusal to declare allegiance to an authority became virtually their single defining char-

---

29. Gill, "School in the Roman Imperial Period," 44.

30. Sedley, *Hellenistic Philosophers*, 1:5.

31. Sedley, "Philosophical Allegiance," 97, 117; cf. Gill, "School in the Roman Imperial Period," 36.

32. So Gregory H. Snyder, "'Not Subjects of a Despot': Stoics," in *Teachers and Texts in the Ancient World: Philosophers, Jews and Christians* (London: Routledge, 2000), 14–44.

33. Cicero, *Tusc.* 1.21.48; *Nat. d.* 1.16.43; Lucretius, *De rer. nat.* 3.1–30; 5.8–10.

34. *Rhetorica* A, col. VII 18–27 (Sudhaus, vol. 1, 12).

35. Diogenes Laertius, *Vit. phil.* 8.46; *ipse dixit* in Latin (Cicero, *Nat. d.* 1.10; Quintilian, *Inst.* 11.1.27).

36. Boys-Stones, *Platonist Philosophy*, 16, 24–30.

acteristic.[37] Skepticism thrived as a reaction to the dogmatic schools, particularly the schools of the Stoics and the Epicureans, from the beginning of the third century BCE on.[38] The Skeptics relentlessly ridiculed students of the dogmatic schools for being enslaved to the teachings they inherited from their founders without evaluating the probability of the doctrines for themselves.[39] In one of Cicero's dialogues, his spokesperson for the Skeptical Academy complains that the dogmatic schools "cease to employ their own judgment, and take what they perceive to be the verdict of their chosen master as settling the question" (Cicero, *Nat. d.* 1.5.10 [Rackham, LCL]). This Skeptical criticism is repeated relentlessly: members of the dogmatic schools "have assigned themselves to the authority of one [ad unius se auctoritatem]" (Cicero, *Acad.* 2.3.9); they defend whatever instructions their masters have "commanded" (*imperata*) (Cicero, *Acad.* 2.3.8); they "cling as to a rock" ("tamquam ad saxum adhaerescunt") to whatever master they first heard (Cicero, *Acad.* 2.3.8).[40]

A "puzzling exception,"[41] the Stoic Seneca proved reluctant to surrender his independence as a thinker and asserted his right to question Zeno and the other Stoic masters. With a defensiveness that betrays centuries of attacks from the Skeptics, Seneca declares that he does not "bind" (*alligo*) himself to "some particular one of the Stoic masters" (*Vit. beat.* 3.2.3). Yet, Seneca identifies openly as a "Stoic" ("we [Stoics]," *Const.* 2.1; cf. 3.1; *Ep.* 9.19–20; 117.2; *Ot.* 5.1), and his views remained consistently orthodox, with little divergence or innovation.[42] Ultimately, his defensiveness against a tendency toward slavish adherence is merely reflective of common perceptions and practices.

The Skeptics boasted that, unlike the sectarian philosophers, they were not "tied [*astricti*] to the laws of any single school of thought" (Cicero, *Tusc.* 4.4.7) or "restrained by bonds [*nulla vincula impediunt*] to any definite school" (Cicero, *Tusc.* 5.29.82). They were, rather, "more free" (*liberiores*) to judge which views were most probable (Cicero, *Acad.* 2.3.8).

Two qualifications must be added to this discussion of allegiance, which will prove relevant as we examine the divisions in Corinth. First, not every

---

37. These, as Galen says (*Outlines of Empiricism* 1), refused to take the name of a founder.

38. As leader of the Skeptical Academy, Carneades (214–129 BCE) was the chief opponent (Plutarch, *Mor.* 1036b). The later skeptic Sextus Empiricus wrote a multi-part treatise, *Against the Dogmatists.*

39. E.g., Cicero, *Nat. d.* 1.5.10; 1.24.66–67; 1.26.72; *Acad.* 2.3.8–9.

40. See also Cicero, *Nat. d.* 1.24.66–67; 1.26.72.

41. Sedley, "Philosophical Allegiance," 119.

42. On Seneca's orthodoxy see Rist, "Seneca and Stoic Orthodoxy," *ANRW* 2.36:1.

1 Corinthians 1:10–17a: The Paul Faction as Philosophical School

student of philosophy attached themselves to the first teacher they heard (though partisans were often accused of doing so).[43] One might "sample" the options for a time,[44] a practice well attested. In his youth, Cicero had studied with the heads of all three leading schools (Academic, Stoic, Epicurean) and years later spent six months more studying with two Epicureans and an Academic teacher in Athens. He then made the acquaintance of the esteemed Stoic teacher Posidonius in Rhodes before settling eventually on his identity as an Academic.[45] Galen sampled all the schools, and though he found his intellectual honesty an obstacle to declaring blind allegiance (*On the Passions of the Soul* 8), he himself remained firmly Platonist in his views.[46] Apollonius of Tyana is said to have sampled all the schools at age fifteen before committing to the teachings of Pythagoras (Philostratus, *Vit. Apoll.* 1.7.1–3). Justin Martyr relates that prior to his conversion to Christianity, he had studied with Stoic, Peripatetic, Pythagorean, and finally Platonist teachers in his quest for the truth (*Dial. Try.* 29.1, 3). Josephus describes a similar quest in his sampling of teachers among the Pharisees, Sadducees, and Essenes, which he presents as "sects" (αἱρέσεις) on analogy with the Greek philosophical schools (*Vita* 1.10). In all these examples, the subject's purpose was finally to find a home in the school that provided, for them, the most satisfactory answers. And this they did.

Second, the practice of sampling entailed the possibility that "disciple circles" could consist in something like two rings: one consisting of an inner circle of disciples and another consisting of listeners still searching for a home or for some reason holding looser affiliation.[47] As we shall consider, the parties in Corinth probably reflected something of the same dynamics.

School Rivalries

In this culture of dogmatic loyalty, rivalry between philosophical schools was constantly at the fore of philosophical activity. In chapter 6, I briefly

---

43. For accusations that sectarians acted so impetuously, see Cicero, *Nat. d.* 1.24.66; *Acad.* 2.3.8; Origen, *Cels.* 1.10.

44. Loveday Alexander, "Paul and the Hellenistic Schools: The Evidence of Galen," in *Paul in His Hellenistic Context*, ed. Troels Engberg-Pedersen (London: T&T Clark, 1995), 60–83, 76.

45. For his early teachers, see *Tusc.* 2.11.26; later, *Tusc.* 3.25.59; for a summary, *Nat. d.* 1.3.6–7. On his preference for the Academic viewpoint, see *Tusc.* 3.3.7; 5.4.11; *Nat. d.* 1.5.11.

46. Lee, *Moral Transformation*, 538–41.

47. Alexander, "Paul and the Hellenistic Schools," 76.

addressed Winter's proposal that the dissension among the Corinthians was analogous to rivalries that broke out over competing sophists.[48] I noted in turn that Winter provided no examples where the terms ζῆλος ("rivalry") or "strife" (ἔρις) (3:3) occurred in reference to such strife. I also noted that while one might be able to turn up examples, this language is far more prevalent in reference to the activity of the philosophical schools. I have more to add now.

One could hope for no clearer example of the potential for ἔρις ("dissension") to arise over philosophy than the occasion depicted in Lucian's *Symposium*, in which the opening lines announce exactly this as the theme of the work: "They say you had all kinds of sport yesterday, Lycinus, at the house of Aristaenetus, at dinner, and that several speeches on *philosophy* [λόγους φιλοσόφους] were made, out of which quite a *quarrel* [ἔριν] arose. Unless Charinus was lying, the affair even ended in wounds and the party was finally broken up by the shedding of blood" (*Symp.* 1 [Harmon, LCL]). The scene recounted involved a Stoic, a Peripatetic, an Epicurean, a Platonist, and a Cynic philosopher, along with one rhetorician (*Symp.* 6–7; 12). That the quarrel escalated due partly to adherents' reverence for their *teachers*—not just their doctrines—is perfectly illustrated in the response of Zenothemis the Stoic to a pair who criticized the school's first three scholarchs, Zeno, Cleanthes, and Chrysippus: "'What, do *you* dare to mention the name of Chrysippus?' said Zenothemis, rousing himself and shouting at the top of his voice. 'Dare you judge Cleanthes and Zeno, who were learned men?'" (*Symp.* 32 [Harmon, LCL]). As Zenothemis concludes his outburst, he flings upon his adversaries what remains in his goblet, this being about half full (*Symp.* 33). The narrator concludes his account by summarizing the dinner as "very like what the poets tell of *Discord*," that is, Ἔρις (*Symp.* 35 [Harmon, LCL]).

This (satirically depicted) dissension was not just a feature of the landscape during the Second Sophistic (second century CE) but was a perennial feature of the competitive philosophical culture that flourished during the period of the dogmatic schools, from about 300 BCE to 200 CE. In chapter 6, I referenced Luke Timothy Johnson's examination of the "conventional rhetoric of slander" in the Hellenistic world. As noted, Johnson catalogs several dozen examples that describe rivalries between rhetoricians and philosophers and between members of opposing philosophical schools; but he includes no examples of rivalry between sophists.[49] Debate between

---

48. Winter, *After Paul Left Corinth*, 32–36.
49. Johnson, "The New Testament's Anti-Jewish Slander," 430–34.

1 Corinthians 1:10–17a: The Paul Faction as Philosophical School

philosophical schools was so endemic to the culture of philosophical discourse that treatises of the type "against the X [Stoics, Epicureans, etc.]" actually emerged as a literary genre in its own right.[50] Partisans attributed the failure of their opponents to win others over to the latter's stupidity (Epictetus, *Diatr.* 1.5.9; 3.7.21). They depicted each other's views in parodies (Cicero, *Nat. d.* 1.24.67; Plutarch, *Mor.* 1100c). They attacked the hypocrisy of the opposing schools' founders (Plutarch, *Mor.* 1033b–1034c). Debates often descended to name-calling (Plutarch, *Mor.* 1086e; 1124c; Diogenes Laertius, *Vit. phil.* 10.8).

Fundamentally, this perennial conflict between philosophers owed to the inherently *dogmatic* and *sectarian* nature of the boundaries between philosophical "schools" and the generally unconditional allegiance required of students to the teachings of their founders and the succeeding heads of school. As Lucian's symposium illustrates, nothing roused the ire of partisans more than abuse of the teachers to whom they committed themselves, a fact attested both in Lucian's account and elsewhere (Lucian, *Symp.*; Plutarch, *Mor.* 1086e; 1124c).

Naturally, ancient education, in preparation for social advancement, was nothing if not competitive. Evidence that rhetorical education commonly involved rivalry *between students*, however,[51] must be allowed weaker significance than examples where students rival *on behalf of their teachers*. In view of the widespread dynamic of competition between philosophical schools and the very nature of philosophical schools as "sects" ("choices"), the evidence overwhelmingly favors the view that allegiances to diverse figures, as in Corinth, would have called to mind the commitment of students to opposing philosophical teachers before commitment of students to sophists.

Loveday Alexander provides an excellent summary of the dynamics of philosophical allegiance in discussing early outsider perspectives of Christian communities. In one of our earliest pagan descriptions of Christian communities (early second century CE), Galen compares Christians—whom he calls

---

50. E.g., Plutarch, *On Stoic Self-Contradictions*; *Against the Stoics on Common Conceptions*; *That Epicurus Makes a Pleasant Life Impossible*; *Reply to Colotes in Defense of Other Philosophers*; Galen, *Against Lycus*; Sextus Empiricus, *Against Dogmatists*; Alexander Lycopolis, *Against the Doctrines of the Manichees*; Augustine, *Against the Academics*. Disputes in the form of dialogues in Cicero, *Academica*; *On the Nature of the Gods*; etc. often rely on traditional arguments dating back to the third and second centuries BCE.

51. White, *Teacher of the Nations*, 102–6 (on p. 103 citing Munck, "Menigheden uden Partier," 153; Winter, *After Paul Left Corinth*, 41), 128–31 (on p. 129 citing Munck, "Menigheden uden Partier," 152–54).

"those from Moses and Christ" (τοὺς ἀπὸ Μωσοῦ καὶ Χριστοῦ)—to the philosophical schools, specifically on the charge that they accepted all their doctrines from their teacher on "faith."[52] Unsurprisingly, the comparison brings to Alexander's mind the divisions in 1 Cor 1–4. Yet, surprisingly, she does not describe the Corinthians as acting like partisans of competing philosophical teachers. Rather, she says, Paul would have been *happier* with this model, provided they viewed themselves as servants of the one master, Christ. Instead, they had become enamored as if "with the eristic teaching style of contemporary sophists, whose 'star' performances encouraged loyalty to individuals and whose adherents can be likened to the fans of a modern pop star."[53]

This is eloquently spoken, but one suspects that Alexander's inference reflects a perfunctory acknowledgment of Winter's recently released work, whom she cites on this point.[54] This outlying example in respect to the better-attested practice of philosophical allegiance comes somewhat offhandedly, in a note, and without evidence that this dynamic applied commonly to relationships between students and sophists. If examples of partisan predilection over sophist-teachers do occur in the sources,[55] as we have seen, this dynamic is attested far more abundantly in regard to philosophers, who were *named* after their teachers, and for whom boundaries that delineated αἱρέσεις naturally lent itself toward "choice," exclusion, and rivalry. Moreover, Alexander's momentary deviation from philosophical to sophistic allegiance is surprising in view of the fact that the factiousness reflected in the Corinthian slogans fits the framework of philosophical allegiance that she sketches. More importantly, Alexander's description of the Corinthians as being "fans" of their ministers as sophistic performers, as of "modern pop stars," fails to accord with Mitchell's findings about how the genitive constructions in 1:12 work—that is, to indicate "possession or belonging," with connotations of either childish dependence or slave ownership.[56] As we have seen (and as Alexander is aware), this kind of relationship in fact aptly

---

52. Galen, *Dig. puls.* 3.3; or "the school of Moses and Christ" (*Dig. puls.* 2.4). Similar is Lucian's description of Christians (*Peregr.* 13). Early Christian texts depict the philosophical schools in kind: Justin Martyr, *Dial. Tryph.* 1.2; Origen, *Cels.* 1.10.

53. Alexander, "IPSE DIXIT," 118.

54. Alexander, "IPSE DIXIT," 287n65; citing Winter, *Philo and Paul among the Sophists*, 126–44.

55. Regarding partisanship, Finney (*Honour and Conflict*, 82) cites one example that refers to the *secta* ("sect") of a certain sophist, but with no connotations of rivalry in context (Seneca, *Controv.* 10.pr.15).

56. See her citations in n. 13 above.

describes the orientations of philosophers toward their teachers. From the perspective of the subjects, belonging was a matter of strong, and usually exclusive, *allegiance* to the one *by whose name* they were called ("Platonist," "Zenonian," "Epicurean") and *on whose behalf* they stood ready to contend, retaliating against offenders with insult and (if we are to believe Lucian) even physical violence. From a negatively biased perspective, this kind of allegiance constituted, as the Skeptics relentlessly repeated, a kind of "slavery." Students of the dogmatic schools remained "tied" to their masters as if by "bonds," lacking the "freedom" that the Skeptics enjoyed to choose between the most probable views on each question.

All of this points to philosophical allegiance as a more fitting background than sophistry for the allegiances in Corinth: the σοφοί have derived from some Christian minister a σοφία that they regard, as it were, as a philosophy, with their teacher as its source. Only, the Corinthians' σοφία—derived, as they thought, from Paul—is not, Paul deplores, the σοφία that he had preached.

The Household and Philosophical Schools

The Analogy of Philosophical Schools

Among several analogies interpreters have explored to describe the "scholastic" qualities of Paul's communities,[57] perhaps the most comprehensively fitting has been that of the philosophical school.[58] In a seminal study, Meeks commented upon the resemblance of Paul's communities particularly to Pythagorean and Epicurean communities, noting their common concern for handing down traditional material (παραδόσεις) related to beliefs and norms, and their processes of admonition and exhortation.[59]

---

57. Hans Conzelmann described a "Schule des Paulus" after the pattern of Jewish schools of wisdom; Conzelmann, "Paulus und die Weisheit," *NTS* 12 (1965–1966): 231–44. E. A. Judge likened Paul to a "sophist" (which Judge admits is an etic evaluation) and described the circle that comprised his retinue as a "scholastic community." Judge, "Early Christians as a Scholastic Community: Part I," *JRH* 1 (1960): 4–15. Recently, Claire S. Smith has taken up Judge's description of early Christian communities. Smith, *Pauline Communities as 'Scholastic Communities': A Study of the Vocabulary of 'Teaching' in 1 Corinthians, 1 and 2 Timothy and Titus*, WUNT 2 (Tübingen: Mohr Siebeck, 2012).

58. In addition to the studies summarized below, see Schmeller, *Schulen im neuen Testament?*, esp. 15–27, 93–179.

59. Meeks, *First Urban Christians*, 82–84.

Since Meeks' study, Abraham Malherbe and others have extensively explored the comparison with the philosophical schools in regard specifically to methods of community admonition and growth.[60] As discussed, Loveday Alexander has explored the resemblance between Christian communities and the philosophical schools in regard to the dynamics of philosophical allegiance.[61] Stanley Stowers has undertaken a more comprehensive comparison, offering a list of seven "similar features" that Paul's communities and the philosophical schools shared at the level of "central practices."[62]

Ancient Perceptions of Christian ἐκλλησίαι

A perception of the earliest Christian communities as philosophical schools is in fact ancient. In a chapter essay on "Paul and the Hellenistic Schools," Loveday Alexander begins by observing that "to the casual pagan observer, the activities of the average synagogue or church would look more like the activities of a school than anything else."[63] She mentions the churches' practices of teaching, moral exhortation, and exegesis of canonical texts; the "whole idea of 'conversion' from one set of beliefs and way of life to another"; the demarcation of insiders from outsiders; nurturing practices and the holding of private meetings; and, as she discusses in the remainder of the article, the ideal of allegiance to the teachings of one's founder.[64] The article focuses on Galen's depiction of early Christian communities as analogous to the philosophical schools.[65]

Public versus Private Teaching

One aspect of the church-school comparison that has significant, and perhaps underappreciated, implications for explaining the background of 1 Corinthians is this: the practice of *private* meetings. The claim that Paul won his converts by standing on the platform in the forum proclaiming the gospel to

---

60. For example, Malherbe, *Paul and the Thessalonians*; Clarence Glad, *Paul and Philodemus: Adaptability in Epicurean and Early Christian Psychagogy*, NovTSup 81 (Leiden: Brill, 1995).

61. Alexander, "Paul and the Hellenistic Schools"; Alexander, "IPSE DIXIT."

62. Stanley Stowers, "Does Pauline Christianity Resemble a Hellenistic Philosophy?," in Engberg-Pedersen, *Paul beyond the Judaism-Hellenism Divide*, 81–102.

63. Alexander, "Paul and the Hellenistic Schools," 60.

64. Alexander, "Paul and the Hellenistic Schools," 62.

65. See n. 52 above.

large crowds of pagans or by imposing upon passersby and parties gathered on the street corners and the public markets, in the manner of the Cynic philosopher, was widespread in the past,[66] and it has been repeated by the many interpreters who see the church's conflict as one concerning Paul's (reputedly inferior) rhetorical skills. Litfin makes this kind of proclamation essential to Paul's self-understanding as a missionary, even claiming that Paul believed he "existed to function as a public speaker."[67]

In a masterful essay backed by a wealth of ancient evidence, however, Stanley Stowers has shown that Paul's "diatribe" style of teaching "suggests an audience of disciples, taught privately, and not occasional audiences of 'those who happened to be present.'"[68] The evidence marshalled by Stowers supports Acts' depiction of Paul as one who found audience primarily in the synagogues and, after being repeatedly rejected from this institution, in private homes. Stowers's evidence includes not only Acts' references to Paul's activity in private settings like the house of Titius Justus in Corinth (18:7), the "school" (σχολή) of Tyrannus in Ephesus (19:9), and his meetings "house to house" (20:20) but also evidence from Paul's personal social location. As Stowers observes, "Public speaking and often the use of public buildings required status, reputation, and recognized roles which Paul did not have." The private household, by contrast, "provided him with a platform where an audience could be obtained."[69]

Philosophical Schools and Households

Philosophical schools met in a variety of settings. Plato's Grove, Epicurus's Garden, and the Stoics' Porch in Hellenistic Athens offer examples of meeting places out in the open, albeit not (except for the Porch) easily accessible to the public. Lecture halls, the gymnasium, and other walled public spaces were also common meeting places.[70]

---

66. Dieter Georgi, "Forms of Religious Propaganda," in *Jesus in His Time*, ed. H. J. Schultz (Philadelphia: Fortress, 1971), 124–31, esp. 124; C. K. Barrett, *A Commentary on the Epistle to the Romans* (New York: Harper and Row, 1957), 43. Judge likens Paul to a "sophist." Judge, "Early Christians as a Scholastic Community: Part II," *JRH* 1 (1961): 125.

67. Litfin, *St. Paul's Theology of Proclamation*, 152.

68. Stanley Stowers, "Social Status, Public Speaking and Private Teaching: The Circumstances of Paul's Preaching Activity," *NovT* (1984): 59–82, esp. 63.

69. Stowers, "Social Status," 81.

70. E.g., in the Musaea: *RE* 16.797ff; *SIG* 900, f.17; *OGIS* 714n4. From Marcus N. Tod, "Sidelights on Greek Philosophers," *JHS* 77 (1957): 132–41, esp. 138. On gymnasia, see Brook-

Another common setting was the private household. Stowers lays out a wealth of evidence for the household setting. Philosophers might meet in homes to read philosophical literature or for occasional instruction. They might use homes as a school of "higher education" or as a philosophical center.[71] The teachers themselves could have varying levels of attachment to the households they used. When not using their own homes,[72] they might be enlisted as tutors of children in the households of the well-to-do; they might be guests afforded use of the household as a meeting place; and in some cases, they might be "salaried" members of the household.[73] After being consistently frustrated in the synagogues, Paul apparently found audience primarily in households. While he probably taught also in the less conventional—though not wholly uncommon—setting of the workshop,[74] workshops would have been physically attached in most cases to the households of those who worked there.[75]

While household meetings were less accessible to the public, such gatherings probably consisted in many cases of a more central core surrounded by an outer ring of inquisitive or less devoted members, these perhaps being social connections of the former group. Epictetus seems to refer to such figures in speaking of ἰδιῶται (*Diatr.* 2.12), a term meaning something like "the uninstructed," or "laymen"; Paul uses the same term in 1 Cor 14:16, 23, 24.

In sum, the extensive analogies existing between the philosophical schools and Paul's communities, together with second-century evidence that at least some outsiders viewed Christian groups as such, makes reasonable the supposition that some Christian groups were aware of the comparison, and that some may even have embraced it. In chapter 12, I shall argue that, as regards this Pauline community, the possibility that some had more-than-ordinary acquaintance with philosophy is quite realistic. If my primary thesis

---

ins, *Corinthian Wisdom*, 136–47; Dutch, *The Educated Elite*, 95–167; and J. T. Townsend, "Ancient Education in the Time of the Early Roman Empire," in *The Catacombs and the Colosseum*, ed. J. Benko and S. O'Rourke (Valley Forge, PA: Judson, 1971), 139–63.

71. Stowers, "Social Setting," 65–67.
72. Cornutus, *Life of Persis* 24–28.
73. The subject of Lucian's *On Salaried Posts in Great Houses*.
74. Hock, *Social Context*, 37–45; citing many examples in connection with Cynic philosophers, including among others: Diogenes Laertius, *Vit. phil.* 2.122; Teles, *fr.* IV[B]; Ps.-Socrates, *Epistle* 9, 4; and noting that Lucian associates Cynics with the artisan class in *Cat.* 14–29. I add Lucian, *Bis acc.* 6.
75. Based on the archeology of Pompeii: Peter Oakes, *Reading Romans in Pompeii* (Minneapolis: Fortress; London: SPCK, 2009), 25.

is correct, these individuals likely viewed the household where they met as a kind of philosophical school.

Paul as Teacher in Corinth

We now return to the thesis posed in our opening section: the Corinthian σοφοί viewed their group on analogy with the philosophical schools, seeing Paul as its founder, themselves as his students, and his teaching as their σοφία.

Paul's Rhetoric

The Corinthians' self-understanding as philosophers explains an aspect of Paul's rhetoric that interpreters have often commented upon—the prevalence of language common to the discourse of education. Two recent studies have examined this feature of 1 Corinthians at length.

A 2005 study by Robert Dutch examined Paul's use of education language that Dutch believes specifically evokes "gymnasium" education.[76] Common in Greek cities (though not unknown in Roman cities) and attended especially at the higher levels of education,[77] the gymnasium served as a sort of community center, equipped with a central space for exercise and athletics and outer, multipurpose rooms often used for lecturing and schooling. Dutch argues that the Corinthian church contained some among society's "elite" and that these had completed an education in the gymnasium in Corinth.[78] Paul thus appropriates the language of this institution in his response to them. Dutch considers as relevant language a possible reference to a gymnasium instructor (1:20), language of nursing and nature (3:1–4), certain agricultural metaphors (3:5–9), reference to early literate education (4:6), descriptions of Paul as "father" (4:14), references to corporal punishment (4:21) and removing the marks of circumcision (7:18–24), and boxing imagery (9:24–27).

A more recent study by Devin White (2017) has shown that the language that Dutch identifies has no *essential* connection with the gymnasium,

---

76. Dutch, *Educated Elite*.
77. For gymnasia in Roman cities, see Brookins, *Corinthian Wisdom*, 140n151.
78. Volume 23 in the Corinth series is dedicated to the finds from the gymnasium area in Roman Corinth excavated by James Wiseman between 1965 and 1972; the first fascicle is Mary C. Sturgeon, *The Gymnasium Area: Sculpture*, Corinth 23.1 (Athens: American School of Classical Studies at Athens, 2022).

even if some of the language offers plausible parallels.[79] Looking afresh at 1 Cor 1–4, White demonstrates that much of the same language, as well as other vocabulary, commonplaces, and images in these chapters, allude not to higher-level education such as one received in the gymnasium, but rather to the *early* stages of education, at the primary and secondary levels. White thus adds to Dutch's references, among other material, Paul's references to the philosopher, scribe, and sophist (1:20); his depiction of a teacher as mediator of revealed wisdom (2:10b–13); and in 4:14–21, his references to pedagogues (4:14–15), imitation (4:16), teaching in all the churches (4:17), memory (4:17), and the rod (4:21). White argues that when one catches the collective significance of this material across chapters 1–4, "it becomes clear that Paul described himself as a teacher, the Corinthians as his students, and his earliest message as a curriculum: that is, as the three most basic components of a school."[80] Thus, for White, 1 Cor 1:10–13 depicts the Corinthians' factions as competing schools, and Paul offers himself as a good teacher and the cross and wisdom as elements of his curriculum (1:18–25; 2:6–16).

I should like to add that 1 Cor 1–4 is saturated with allusions from the realm of education specific to *philosophical* education. In the preceding chapters I have frequently alluded to such aspects of Paul's rhetoric. Much of the relevant language constitutes what we have called "competitive appropriation" of Stoic discourse. That "the Spirit of God dwells in you" (3:16), that there is no wise man "in this age" (3:18), that "all things belong to [sc. you wise men]" (3:21), for instance—these all reflect competitive appropriations of Stoic language, redefined in the act of appropriation in terms of Paul's apocalyptic theology. Interpreters have often noted Stoic resonances in these chapters.[81] Here, we have discussed some less frequently noted texts (references to the "Spirit of the world" in 2:12; the "mind" of Christ in 2:16; the "power" of the Spirit in 2:4, 5; Paul's self-description as "architect" in 3:10; Paul's appeal to imitation in 4:16); and I have offered several novel interpretations, for instance, reading 4:4 as an allusion to the Stoic practice of self-examination, 4:6b as a possible reference to students' commitment to the philosophical teachings of their founder, 4:6c as a reference to boasting in what is "one's own," and 4:7 as a subversion of the Stoic concept of self-sufficiency. I also proposed reading

---

79. White, *Teacher of the Nations*, 12–14.
80. White, *Teacher of the Nations*, 25.
81. Lightfoot, *Notes on the Epistles*, 195, 200; Weiss, *Der erste Korintherbrief*, 89–91, 157–59; Grant, "Wisdom of the Corinthians," 51–55.

1 Corinthians 1:10–17a: The Paul Faction as Philosophical School

Paul's disjunction in 4:21 between the "rod" and "gentleness" as an allusion to the weaponized staff of the harsh (Cynic) philosopher versus the nurturing approach of the gentle (sometimes Cynic) philosopher.

That one could construe a few of the above references in connection with primary- or secondary-level education in addition to higher, gymnasium education demonstrates in some cases the overlapping resonances of the relevant language—for example, the teacher as "father" or the importance of "imitation." On the other hand, this mix of philosophical language and other allusions to education perhaps illustrates an important aspect of Paul's rhetorical strategy: although the σοφοί fancy themselves philosophers, Paul frequently addresses them in language appropriate to *lower*-level students. This treatment is clear for instance in his regretful statement that he had to treat them as "infants," feeding them milk rather than solid food (3:1–2); his statement that they had many "pedagogues" (4:15); and his description of them as his "children" and himself as their "father" (4:14).

Paul and His Interpreters

It is evident that some significant discrepancies existed between the respective views of the Corinthians and of Paul (chapter 9). If those who said "I am of Paul" viewed themselves as his students, in light of the usual attitude of philosophical allegiance, it must be asked how these discrepancies came to be.

These discrepancies may be explicable partly on the basis of differences of attitude traditionally shown toward *living* founders on the one hand and founders already *deceased* on the other, and partly on the basis of the kinds of qualifications that we have made with regard to the practice of philosophical allegiance. Consistently, the quality of "orthodoxy" within the philosophical schools emerged fully only after a founder's death.[82] While students' attachment to a teacher during his lifetime indicated overall a high level of commitment, a certain independence of thought was not deemed unacceptable. Sedley has remarked that there is "no reason to think that either Epicurus or Zeno was seen as above criticism in his own lifetime and within his own circle of philosophical friends and pupils."[83] Sedley eloquently rephrases:

---

82. Sedley, "Philosophical Allegiance," 98–99; "School, from Zeno to Arius Didymus," 13–15.

83. Sedley, "Philosophical Allegiance," 99.

"It is difficult at the best of times for a living philosopher to achieve the infallibility of a dead saint." Thus, during the lifetime of a school's founder, members of his circle could debate conflicting opinions on matters raised by his teachings. In the case of the Stoics, Aristo was a well-known dissenter from some of Zeno's views. Although he was an established member of Zeno's circle, Aristo's views on "indifferents" differed substantially enough from Zeno's that he came to be vilified, after the latter's death, as a Stoic "heretic." Sedley has demonstrated that the history of the other schools reflected the same dynamics.

Doctrinal development could still continue after the founder's authority became established,[84] though these developments were largely a matter of disagreement over the interpretation of the founder's writings.[85] In the case of the Stoics, sources offer some evidence that their devotion to their founder's writings was less than "religious."[86] Yet, in most cases development was a matter not of disagreement with the founder, but of intelligent innovation involving either modification or more sophisticated enlargement of less fully developed doctrines, whether to answer criticisms, to address deficiencies, or for pragmatic purposes.[87] With regard to the Stoics, this margin for disagreement explains in part why we have resorted to a definition of "Stoic" based on a criterion of "family resemblances" (chapter 2).

The kinds of developments initiated by the Corinthians, then, are in fact representative of the kinds of philosophical interactions that we find prevalently amid the philosophical schools. Specifically, the Corinthian sub-Stoics have engaged in traditional "doctrinal reformulation" (interaction type 7), in this case, of Paul's teaching. If their "sub(ordinated) Stoicism" deviated from the teachings of Paul, in their minds it was a legitimate appropriation of his thought.

---

84. For the representation of "authority" among later devotees of Plato, see the recent work Michael Erler, Jan Erik Heßler, and Federico M. Petrucci, *Authority and Authoritative Texts in the Platonist Tradition* (Cambridge: Cambridge University Press, 2021).

85. Sedley ("Philosophical Allegiance") cites examples on 98n2. For a treatment of Epicurean interpretations of Epicurus on participation in cultic rituals, see Max J. Lee, "Negotiating Piety: Epicureans, Corinthian Knowers, and Paul on Idols and Idol Food in 1 Cor 8–10," in Lee and Oropeza, *Practicing Intertextuality*, 148–66.

86. Snyder, "Not Subjects of a Despot"; in response to Sedley, "Philosophical Allegiance," 97.

87. For Neostoic innovations during the Roman period, see Lee's extensive treatment in *Moral Transformation*, 180–83, 271–374.

1 Corinthians 1:10–17a: The Paul Faction as Philosophical School

FORMATION OF THE PARTIES

Defining Parties

On grounds of common sense and expected complexities in social networks, it seems highly improbable that every member of the Corinthian church declared allegiance to someone. It also seems improbable that for everyone who did, they showed allegiance to one person exclusively. In this regard, there is validity to the thesis that "each one of you says" is an exaggeration.[88] It is more difficult to accept the conclusion that one, two, or even all of the named parties did not exist at all. The possibility that Paul would put into the Corinthians' mouths such *specific* and yet completely untrue assertions involving *named* allegiances strikes this interpreter as (to understate the point) an ineffective rhetorical strategy. Who would so greatly misrepresent the facts in the very opening of his argument?

With these qualifications in mind, I suggest that there were at least four loosely formed parties, consistent with Paul's representation of things. (1) I address the Paul party below. (2) That there were some who aligned themselves with Apollos is almost universally accepted based largely on Paul's discussion of their relationship in 3:4–4:6. Paul's special focus on the two of them, however, need not indicate that these two parties constituted the primary, much less the only, cliques that existed in the church. First Corinthians 3:4–4:6 is just as easily explained on the assumption that Apollos had a more significant role in ministering to Corinth than, say, Cephas did, and thus that the Paul-Apollos relationship offered a better illustration of Paul's point about unity. (3) In spite of growing doubts among interpreters about a visit to Corinth from Cephas, Witetschek has made a compelling case that arguments against a visit are based on comparatively more speculative readings of the evidence and, conversely, that Paul's references to Cephas are most easily explained on the supposition that Cephas had visited.[89] That Paul discusses Apollos's ministerial role but not Cephas's probably suggests only that Cephas's visit had been short or his role in ministry there more minor. (4) The question of a Christ party is ultimately inconsequential to our thesis, although I should state that I am not convinced by arguments

---

88. Mitchell, *Paul and the Rhetoric of Reconciliation*, 86.
89. Stephan Witetschek, "Peter in Corinth? A Review of the Evidence from 1 Corinthians," *JTS* 69 (2018): 66–82. First Corinthians references Peter in 1 Cor 1:12; 3:22; 9:5.

that this slogan reflects an interpolation, an error in transcription, or Paul's own response to the cries of the other three parties.[90] There is no evidence of textual problems in the manuscript tradition. Moreover, while a switch to the voice of Paul is not an impossible interpretation of the grammar,[91] the identical repetition of the formula with the formulas that precede (ἐγὼ μέν εἰμι... ἐγὼ δὲ... ἐγὼ δὲ Κηφᾶ, ἐγὼ δέ...) renders questionable the possibility that even the Greek-speaking Corinthians would have readily detected a switch in personal deixis.

The Paul Party

The preceding chapters have made the case that some in the Corinthian church viewed themselves as σοφοί in the mold of the Stoic wise man. I now propose, based on 1:10–17a, that the name to which the σοφοί group attached itself was none other than *Paul's*. I suggest, furthermore, that it was this party that formed first. Several factors point in this direction. First, Paul himself had founded the community (1 Cor 4:14–15; 2 Cor 10:13–14). Naturally, converts that he brought to faith will have (initially at least) looked to him as their founding figure and might be expected to maintain special allegiance to him against others. Second, Paul names himself *first* in citing the four party slogans in 1:12. Third, the Paul group is the only one of the four groups that Paul rebukes directly. His rhetorical questions in v. 13 passionately reject specifically the premise that *Paul* was crucified for them or that they were baptized into *his* name.

The Paul-Apollos theory suggests that things worked in reverse: some of the Corinthians found Apollos so charming a figure upon his visit to Corinth (Acts 18:27–28) that, wittingly or unwittingly, he drew a following and inspired a comparison between Paul and himself, which worked out unfavorably for the former.[92] Naturally, a schism cannot have existed before anyone broke away, and so it was the formation first of this party that made loyalists of Paul, in consequence, a "faction" in its own right. This order, however, has nothing in its favor except speculation. Apart from a preconceived recon-

---

90. See Baird's survey of interpretations in "'One against the Other,'" 116–36, esp. n. 102.
91. The argument of Prothro, "Who Is 'of Christ'?"
92. For example, Davis, *Wisdom and Spirit*, 133; Fee, *First Epistle to the Corinthians*, 1st ed., 8–9; Litfin, *St. Paul's Theology of Proclamation*, 160–62; 171; Welborn, "Μωρὸς γένεσθω," 432.

struction, one can be led to this sequence by nothing in the text where the divisions are actually discussed, that is, 1 Cor 1:10–17a.

I suggest, therefore, that the divisions—so far as σοφία contributed—began with the emergence of a Paul party. Its members viewed Paul as the founder, as it were, of a new philosophical "school." In this connection, the first slogan in 1:12, "I am of Paul," reflects a declaration of philosophical allegiance similar to declarations of allegiance in the philosophical schools.

Again, it is impossible to disentangle fully the Corinthians' self-understanding from the characterization of them that Paul constructs. Entailed in this point is the question whether the *form* of the slogans in 1:12 reflect verbatim formulations of the Corinthians or whether Paul has devised them in order to depict the Corinthians in a way consistent with their sectarian behavior. While the question is not of critical importance to our case, I suggest that the latter is more likely correct. For if Mitchell is right that the εἰμί + genitive construction was not a typical formula in antiquity, it would be surprising if all four parties happened to articulate their alignments using exactly the same formula.

The Boundaries of the Paul Party

The above comments regarding the nature of "disciple circles" and the practice of "sampling" in philosophical schools provide helpful context for filling out a picture of the likely boundaries of the Paul group. As noted, the philosophical schools often consisted of a central core of more committed members while remaining open to invited guests and those who might be called "seekers." The result was what Alexander has likened to two "rings" of participation, one inner and one outer.[93] Accordingly, even if the Paul party consisted of a "core" of confident "wise men," we need not conclude that everyone who aligned themselves with Paul, or with this group, was a dyed-in-the-wool advocate of the associated "wisdom" or that all affiliates of the group were card-carrying members. Surely the group consisted of some more dominant voices—these included chiefly the σοφοί. Their influence would have attracted particularly, though perhaps not exclusively, those with whom these individuals had special social ties, whether through friendship, socioeconomic standing, business, neighborhood, or household. Some would affiliate simply due to these ties. Others would be curious about their σοφία. Some would embrace it.

93. Alexander, "Paul and the Hellenistic Schools," 76.

Formation of the Other Parties

Thus formed a Paul party, defined most essentially by its σοφία. At least three parties formed in response. There may have been others. There were still others who chose not to affiliate.

Despite the reactive formation of the other parties, we need not assume that the Apollos, Cephas, and Christ groups viewed themselves as "rival philosophical schools."[94] I suggest, rather, that the other groups were reactionary as *factions* rather than as philosophical groups per se. The unique grounds for their choices cannot be known. Some may indeed have found Apollos a powerful orator. Cephas may have struck awe into many—he who had not only known Jesus personally but who also was among the Twelve. Some may have declared their allegiance to Christ in consternation or even disgust at these other human alignments. Still they were as sectarian as the others, perhaps even more elitist. One can only speculate.

Our conception of the three parties as reactive poses no problem for our interpretation of the slogans in 1:12. The slogans in general connote *allegiance*. The slogan "I am of Paul" need not imply an identical conception of their group as, say, "I am of Christ" implied for the other. Indeed, some shift of meaning is required also in Mitchell's interpretation of the slogans. As she suggests, the "genitive of belonging" connotes "slave ownership *and* childish dependence."[95] Both applications of course can be appropriately subsumed under the "belonging" label, but both do not apply equally appropriately when tested against each of the slogans: the Corinthians could consider themselves as being *either slaves or children* of Paul, Apollos, or Cephas, one supposes; but surely they cannot exactly have considered themselves *children* of Christ. This is more relevant given Mitchell's view that the final slogan, "I am of Christ," is not actually a quotation of the Corinthians, but an assertion of Paul.[96] Technically, *Paul* does not think of believers as Christ's *children* per se, but as Christ's brothers (Rom 8:15–17, 29). Mitchell's reading of the slogans, therefore, requires some variation of meaning depending upon the respective group. All the same, I find this shifting unproblematic. All will have conceived of their affiliations differently, depending on the grounds for their choice. As for the Paul group, they "belonged" to him as loyalists of his school.

---

94. A point on which I differ from Schmeller (*Schulen im neuen Testament?*, 115–19).
95. Mitchell, *Paul and the Rhetoric of Reconciliation*, 83n101, 85 (my italics).
96. Mitchell, *Paul and the Rhetoric of Reconciliation*, 83n101.

1 Corinthians 1:10–17a: The Paul Faction as Philosophical School

The Question of Multiple House Churches

It has long been suggested that the divisions in Corinth were fostered by the existence of multiple house churches.[97] We know from 1 Cor 16:15 that there was at least one house church in Corinth, that associated with Stephanas. Paul's letter to the Romans suggests that there may have been several house churches in Rome (16:5, 10, 11, 14, 15). In the same letter is Paul's reference to Gaius as "my host and the host of"—intriguingly—"the *whole* [ὅλης] church" (16:23). The reference is to the "whole" church in Corinth, whence Paul writes. ὅλη ἡ ἐκκλησία is found elsewhere in Paul's letters only in 1 Cor 14:23 (cf. 11:20), where it also refers to the Corinthian church.[98] The oddity of this expression in reference to a local assembly, next to the slightly more common *church in the house of X* and the much more common *church*, suggests that the attributive ὅλη may indicate a larger aggregate. This aggregate would have consisted of multiple house churches from the region, which perhaps met together less periodically.[99]

For this and other reasons, it seems plausible that multiple house churches existed in Corinth. It seems unlikely, however, that the party lines that separated partisans of different ministers were essentially coextensive with fractures between different house churches. For if this were true, then the strategy that Paul uses to address the divisions would surely have served to exacerbate the problem, not heal it. Paul urges unity by pointing the church back to the leadership of a specific household, that of Stephanas (16:15). But if this household constituted the basis of the Paul party, why does he begin the letter by rebuking them (1:13)? Conversely, if this household supported Apollos or Peter, how will his recommendation of it not further weaken the household (of Stephanas) that supported *him*?[100] In any case, it is surely unlikely that each minister founded an independent church, rather than hooking into the already-existing community.

I would like to suggest a scenario that is more consistent with Paul's rhetorical strategy in 1 Corinthians and that also comports with Acts' account of Paul's operations in Corinth. According to Acts, after being forced out

---

97. Meeks, *First Urban Christians*, 76; Edward Adams, "First-Century Models for Paul's Churches: Selected Scholarly Developments Since Meeks," in *After the First Urban Christians*, ed. Todd Still and David Horrell (Edinburgh: T&T Clark, 2009), 65.

98. Elsewhere in the NT only in Acts 5:11 and 15:22; in the latter it clearly indicates the whole church and not just the apostles and elders.

99. Ἡ κατ' οἶκον ἐκκλησία in Rom 16:5; 1 Cor 16:19; Col 4:15; Phlm 2.

100. A point suggested to me in an email exchange with Richard Fellows.

of the synagogue, Paul stationed himself in the house of "a certain Titius Justus" (18:7). This testimony should not be dismissed just because Acts is its source. It is consistent with what is the most plausible scenario for Paul's local operations. We discussed above Stowers's compelling thesis that, in lieu of the synagogue, the household provided Paul with the most accessible and most convenient space for regular teaching. In Corinth, the house of Titius Justus supplied this space. Though his intention could have been merely to offer patronage through the provision of a meeting space, as a "God-fearer" (σεβομένου τὸν θεόν) turned sympathetic ally, Titius Justus had likely become a Christian.

These data open up a conceivable scenario in which the house of Titius Justus operated as something like a "school," perhaps not unlike the σχολή of Tyrannus in Ephesus (Acts 19:9). This house offered a space for regular instruction and might have drawn participants from multiple house churches. The school setting would further reinforce for attendees the impression that their community was like a philosophical school, with their teacher Paul as its founder.

Whether or not the household of Titius Justus functioned as a house church proper (in which were hosted weekly meetings of *worship*), Paul's exclusive endorsement of the household of Stephanas would serve to undermine the legitimacy of the former's operations and their misguided conception of their teacher and "wise community."

The Question of Baptism

Paul's immediate response to the slogans in 1:12 is short and to the point: "Is Christ divided?" (v. 13a). From there the discourse takes a somewhat surprising turn, as Paul makes a passing reference to crucifixion (v. 13b) before dwelling on baptism from vv. 13c–16.

The function of this section has long perplexed interpreters. Possible explanations can essentially be reduced to two. Either (1) baptism contributed to the church's divisions in some fashion, or (2) baptism per se played little or no role and this section functions as a reductio ad absurdum argument, the conclusion to which is that the church's divisions are illogical.

The first option has multiple variants. These cannot all be treated here, nor can they be examined in detail. (a) Many interpreters maintain that the Corinthians viewed baptism as an initiation into the world to come, with which came wisdom and charismatic power. They attributed importance to

1 Corinthians 1:10–17a: The Paul Faction as Philosophical School

the particular person who had brought this boon upon them.[101] (b) Other interpreters emphasize the human bond, suggesting that baptism established the baptizer as "patron" of the baptized.[102] (c) Still others identify baptism and wisdom (understood in terms of oratory) as two apparently independent causes of the divisions.[103]

Out of the options under (1), I believe that (a) has the most in its favor both in terms of the social-religious context and coherent integration of the Corinthian conflict. On balance, however, I believe that view (2), the "reductio ad absurdum" argument, reflects the better reading. In the first place, ancient sources offer no links specifically with the use of washing as a religious entry ritual that endued initiates with the kind of charismatic powers practiced in the Corinthian church (esp. 1 Cor 12–14). Second, Paul does not here oppose the premise that he is responsible for *bestowing the Spirit* but rather the premise that anyone was baptized into his *"name."* Third, it is problematic to establish baptism as the grounds for allegiance since Paul claims that he baptized "no one except Crispus and Gaius" (v. 14) and, he adds, the household of Stephanas (v. 16). Fourth, we must not overlook the fact that Paul asks, first, whether he had been "crucified" for them (v. 13b), before asking the parallel question about whether they were baptized "into his name." Surely it cannot be that the Corinthians' views on "crucifixion" were also related to the allegiances. Rather, the two rhetorical questions are asked in parallel form and both serve the same point: that the Corinthians' identity is not defined in reference to Paul. In vv. 13–16, Paul's purpose is to emphasize that, just as Christ's *crucifixion* was efficacious for *all*, *all* also were *baptized* into Christ's name. Paul later reiterates this point in terms that clearly present baptism as a common community experience and source of unity: "For in one Spirit we were all baptized into one body—Jews or Greeks, slaves or free—and all were made to drink of one Spirit" (12:13). In vv. 13c–16, then, Paul's references both to crucifixion and baptism make sufficient sense strictly as theological assertions of *Paul*, which he here applies to the Corinthians' common, though perhaps forgotten, experience. We need not assume

---

101. Meeks, *First Urban Christians*, 117–19, 121; Wire, *Corinthian Women Prophets*, 68; Patterson, "The Baptists of Corinth."

102. As secular patron: Clarke, *Secular and Christian Leadership*, 92; or as human and spiritual patron: Chester, *Conversion at Corinth*, 292, 295, 302; Prothro, "Who Is 'of Christ'?," 252–53.

103. Barnett, *Corinthian Question*, 89.

that *they* believed that they were baptized into Paul's name any more than they believed that Paul was crucified for them.

On these grounds, I conclude that vv. 13c–16 constitutes rather a reductio ad absurdum argument, the point of which is the absurdity of the church's divisions. Paul's full argument, in sum, runs as follows: "Christ is the basis of your common spiritual state; he was crucified for *all of you* and you were *all* baptized into his name. And since I know you affirm this, you must also see that it would be absurd for you to declare some kind of sectarian allegiance to Paul (or anyone else). Now, if I had baptized *everyone* in the community, I can see, hypothetically, how one might declare that there is unity in me. Since, however, I have baptized nearly no one, this is not a reasonable conclusion. So I am grateful that I baptized but a few." The argument succeeds because it works out a premise on which Paul and his audience in fact agree: their common state as Christ people. Against this common ground, Paul demonstrates that their current behavior as divided people is inconsistent with spiritual reality and its cause.

Conclusion

Any reconstruction of 1 Cor 1–4 remains plausible only to the extent that it offers a coherent explanation for the connection between Paul's discourse on σοφία in the opening of the letter's body (1:17b–4:21) and the problem of divisions broached in the letter's introduction (1:10–17a). Such an explanation has been offered here.

This reconstruction began with Mitchell's observation that the slogan formulas in 1:12 do not assimilate to any *typical* formula known from ancient sources and with her conclusion that the genitive construction likely indicates "belonging," as is typical in descriptions of childish dependence and slave ownership. Mitchell's understanding of the genitive, however, remains functionally consistent with standard ways in which philosophers were identified and ways they identified themselves with regard to the following: the use of designations that incorporated the name of the teacher; the nature of the slogans as declarations of personal identity, sectarian choice, and exclusive allegiance; and the feature of students' commonly "slavish" allegiance to their founders' teachings. Declarations of philosophical allegiance, moreover, represent verbal manifestations of the rivalry between schools that the nature of these philosophies as "choices" (αἱρέσεις) entailed. At the

1 Corinthians 1:10–17a: The Paul Faction as Philosophical School

same time evidence shows that philosophical schools sometimes consisted of a more dedicated core of students, augmented by a ring of more loosely affiliated guests, outsiders, or seekers.

Due to a variety of essential similarities, interpreters have often viewed the philosophical schools as an appropriate analog to early Christ groups. The legitimacy of this comparison is confirmed by ancient observers. It has been proposed here that the σοφοί in Corinth in fact viewed themselves as such, or more specifically as students of their founder Paul, as if constituting a new philosophical school. The boundaries of this group, however, remained somewhat permeable, not unlike other localized schools, with their inner and outer rings. As students were sometimes wont to do, the σοφοί also adapted Paul's teaching (a type of interaction that Lee has called "doctrinal reformulation"), in this case resulting in a unique brand of "sub(ordinated)-Stoicism." Being apprised of their conception of his teaching, Paul embraced his role as "teacher" for rhetorical purposes and admonished them in language that appropriated the discourse of their philosophy.

Paul's party was the first to form, and at least three others formed in response—the parties of Apollos, Cephas, and Christ. By aligning themselves with other leaders (or with Christ), they emulated the factious behavior of the first party, although without necessarily connecting their alignments with rival "wisdoms." The boundaries of these parties, too, were permeable. Some declined to declare allegiance to anyone. The phenomenon of baptism (vv. 13c–16) probably did not relate situationally to the divisions and σοφία. Rather, vv. 13c–16 function as a reductio ad absurdum argument intent on exposing the Corinthians' divisive practices as illogical.

We can now summarize how this reconstruction correlates with the four axes introduced at the opening of the chapter. The divisions involved distinguishable *parties*, though these were not sharply defined and did not represent the church exhaustively (axis 4). The Corinthians' predilection for *wisdom* was a more basic impetus for the divisions than the leadership preferences themselves (axis 1). The divisions were more *internally oriented* than they were oriented toward opposing leaders (axis 2). The dissension concerned the attitudes of various parties toward *each other* more than of the whole church toward Paul (axis 3).

A number of important questions remain. We have not yet addressed the plausibility of Stoic influence on the Corinthian church itself or the question of membership in the σοφός group. Also to be considered are questions of a more speculative nature, such as concern the sequence of events reaching from Paul's visit until his dispatch of 1 Corinthians: Had the Paul party as such emerged after his departure or were the members of the group already consolidating and mulling over their notions of σοφία while he was still present? If the group took shape after his departure, were these converts his own or had they come to the faith second-hand? Such matters will be the subject of our next two chapters.

11

Philosophy in the Roman Empire and Roman Corinth

In his 2003 monograph *Conversion at Corinth*, Stephen Chester declares rejection of the gnostic and the Hellenistic-Jewish hypotheses on grounds that they are not able "to demonstrate that these influences were present in the local environment."[1] Though Chester offers a different explanation than the one we have pursued here, his statement conveys a truism that applies equally to any attempt to reconstruct the church's problems: the interpreter must be able to demonstrate that the *specific* influences proposed were likely present in the Corinthians' immediate environment.

By similar reasoning to Chester, Bruce Winter dismisses the likelihood of philosophical wisdom in the church. Or rather, he suggests that philosophy's influence in first-century culture was slight in comparison with the enormously popular "wisdom" of rhetoric. Winter asserts: "Parents and 'the People' had voted with their feet and were only too anxious to enroll their sons in the sophists' schools. Alas, for the philosophers of his day, they no longer held centre stage in the public's estimation."[2] It is to Winter's credit that in arguing for the sophistic background, his strategy relies largely on an attempt to demonstrate the influence of the sophistic movement in Corinth near the time of Paul. I do not say *at* the time of Paul, but *near* to it. In fact the relationship between the Corinthian correspondence and Winter's other sources is not as close as he implies. Winter adduces several examples of

---

1. Chester, *Conversion at Corinth*, 225.
2. Winter, *Philo and Paul among the Sophists*, 219; and this also is the implication of his overview of philosophy and rhetoric in Alexandria (44–58).

sophists active in Corinth during the Second Sophistic period.³ While Winter acknowledges that, in order to prove that the sophistic movement constitutes the background for 1 Cor 1–4, one would need to demonstrate this "from a discussion of the text," Winter appears also to want his external evidence to count as background for the period during which Paul wrote, for as he says in the same sentence and in preface to his treatment of 1 Corinthians, "We have at least shown" that "sophists were a major force in first-century Corinth."⁴ Unfortunately, Winter's survey of sophists in Corinth does not serve his argument that the sophistic movement constituted such a force, for his evidence all dates between 100 and 180 CE (making this evidence hardly more useful than second-century gnostic sources). Consequently, 1 Corinthians *is* his evidence for the sophistic movement in mid-first-century Corinth.⁵ Ultimately, Winter exploits the evidence in circular fashion.

Another issue that has figured into the discussion of background is the question of the general culture of "Roman Corinth." In a second monograph on the Corinthian letters (*After Paul Left Corinth*), Winter grounds his explanation for the Corinthians' conflict in the claim that Roman Corinth was a "*thoroughly* Roman colony" which "*invariably* took its cue from Roman and *not* Greek culture" and that "whether rich or poor, bond or free, the cultural milieu which impacted life in the city of Corinth was *Romanitas*."⁶ Beginning from this characterization, Winter protests that "it would be *inappropriate* to search for ethics, customs, etc. in ancient classical Greek or Hellenistic eras rather than the late Republic and early Roman period." Winter's statements about Roman Corinth are meant to establish his firm exclusion of "Greek" influences in favor of "Roman" ones, which, as he says, "played *the* role in shaping life in Corinth for more than a century."⁷

The purpose of the present chapter is to demonstrate from ancient sources that philosophy did in fact have perceptible and significant direct influence on an extensive population within the Roman Empire, not just in the most thriving intellectual centers in the Greek east but also in Roman colonies and in Rome itself, and not just among the highest elites but also among lower-level magistrates, the "middle classes," and more marginalized groups

---

3. Winter, *Philo and Paul among the Sophists*, 111–40.

4. Winter, *Philo and Paul among the Sophists*, 140.

5. Litfin (*St. Paul's Theology of Proclamation*, 143–45) cites Favorinus (ca. 80–160 CE) as evidence of the popularity of rhetoric in Corinth.

6. Winter (*After Paul Left Corinth*; italics added): a "*thoroughly* Roman colony" (11), "*invariably* took its cue" (12; emphasis added), "whether rich or poor" (22).

7. Winter, *After Paul Left Corinth*, 20.

like freedmen, women, and slaves. In this way, the present chapter also accomplishes two subordinate goals. First, it calls into question the legitimacy of the move away from explanations of the Corinthian conflict related to Greek religion or philosophy on the ostensible grounds that Roman Corinth was, as many put it, a "Roman, not Greek" city. Second, it demonstrates that, despite the popularity of rhetoric and its importance in the ancient school curriculum, the impact of other intellectual influences on contemporary culture, not least Stoic philosophy, has been seriously underestimated in recent discussion of 1 Corinthians.

Roman Corinth

The history of ancient Corinth has been recited repeatedly in Corinthians scholarship, and we will not retrace it in detail here.[8] The short history is that the Greek city of Corinth in the region of Achaia was destroyed by Roman invasion in 146 BCE and reestablished by Julius Caesar a century later (44 BCE) as a Roman colony. The expanded version of this story narrated frequently in biblical scholarship emphasizes that the new city introduced a distinctive cultural shift, from "Greek" to "Roman." Summaries of this shift emphasize that the original city's destruction was complete, that the city lay desolate and unpopulated for the next one hundred years, that the city was reestablished as a Roman colony and repopulated with Roman citizens and veterans, and consequently that the culture of the new Corinth was "Roman, not Greek."[9]

While evidence offers partial support for this narrative, the final conclusion lacks nuance in ways that critically impact recent discussions of 1 Co-

---

8. For two recent histories, see James R. Harrison and L. L. Welborn, eds., *The First Urban Churches*, vol. 2, *Roman Corinth*, Writings from the Greco-Roman World Supplement 8 (Atlanta: Society of Biblical Literature, 2016), 1–46; and a briefer version in David W. J. Gill, "Early Christianity in Its Colonial Contexts in the Provinces of the Eastern Empire," in *The Urban World and the First Christians*, ed. Steve Walton, Paul R. Trebilco, and David W. J. Gill (Grand Rapids: Eerdmans, 2017), 68–85, esp. 70–73.

9. See the language in Thiselton, *First Epistle to the Corinthians*, 3–4 (but cf. p. 6); and Garland, *1 Corinthians*, 3; cf. David W. J. Gill, "Corinth: A Roman Colony in Achaea," *BZ* 37 (1993): 259–64, esp. 264; David W. J. Gill, "In Search of the Social Elite in Corinth," *TynBul* 44 (1993): 323–37, esp. 328; Adams and Horrell, *Christianity at Corinth*, 6; V. H. T. Nguyen, *Christian Identity in Corinth: A Comparative Study of 2 Corinthians, Epictetus, and Valerius Maximus* (Tübingen: Mohr Siebeck, 2008), 122–23; and Robert M. Grant, *Paul in the Roman World: The Conflict at Corinth* (Louisville: Westminster John Knox, 2001), 19.

rinthians. Two recent collections of essays have examined various cultural facets of Roman Corinth more closely.[10] On the whole these essays support the conclusion that Roman Corinth, though indeed established as a Roman colony, maintained strong continuities with its Greek past. In the first place, the notion that Corinth was left devoid of a (Greek) population in the period between its destruction and refounding is now known to be an exaggeration;[11] and in the city's refounding, most of the colonizers were freedmen from Rome and themselves Greeks.[12] While most official inscriptions were indeed written in Latin (as is often remarked), a vast majority of extant non-official markings are in Greek, suggesting that Greek remained the primary spoken language of the population.[13] The architecture displayed Greek styles with an admixture of Roman ideology, but the styles themselves could not determine completely what resonances would be felt by the people.[14] Local religion incorporated traditional Roman cults, but fused them with traditional elements from Greek religion.[15] Of course, the values of the population varied according to social and economic class. Even still, it is not possible to separate class preferences into neat "Roman" and "Greek" options. As expected, given the ambitions of elites, Roman values were stronger among the upper classes, though, as Benjamin Millis observes, even elites tended to "straddle the cultural divide." The remainder of the population remained "more solidly Greek in outlook."[16] As one might expect from this summary, the essays in these volumes abound with terms like *hybrid*, *complex*, and *multilayered* in their descriptions of Corinth's culture.

---

10. Steven J. Friesen, Daniel N. Schowalter, and James C. Walters, eds., *Corinth in Context: Comparative Studies on Religion and Society* (Leiden: Brill, 2010); Steven J. Friesen, Sarah James, and Daniel N. Schowalter, eds., *Corinth in Contrast* (Leiden: Brill, 2013).

11. For a discussion of the primary sources, see James Wiseman, "Corinth and Rome I: 228 BC–AD 267," *ANRW* 7.1:438–548, esp. 493–96.

12. Benjamin Millis argues that they were freedmen and "entirely Greek in origin." "The Social and Ethnic Origins of the Colonists in Early Roman Corinth," in Friesen, Schowalter, and Walters, *Corinth in Context*, 30. The group did not, as has sometimes been said (e.g., J. Walters, "Civic Identity in Roman Corinth and Its Impact on Early Christians," in Schowalter and Friesen, *Urban Religion in Roman Corinth*, 402), consist of both freedmen *and* veterans.

13. Millis, "Social and Ethnic Origins," 23–30.

14. Laird, "Emperor in a Roman Town," 67–116, esp. 110.

15. B. L. Wickkiser, "Asklepios in Greek and Roman Corinth," in Friesen, Schowalter, and Walters, *Corinth in Context*, 37–66; Jorunn Økland, "Ceres, Κόρη, and Cultural Complexity," in Friesen, Schowalter, and Walters, *Corinth in Context*, esp. 229.

16. Millis, "Social and Ethnic Origins," 32.

One might ask how these conclusions weaken studies in recent decades that underscore the role of "distinctly Roman" values in the church's divisions.[17] For our purposes, these conclusions point already to the likelihood that St. Paul's Corinth, "Roman" though it was, would surely not have been devoid of the influence of "Greek philosophy."

THE ROMANS AND PHILOSOPHY

The tradition cited by Cicero about the origin of philosophy is surely not true (*Tusc.* 4.1.2–3; 5.3.10). According to Cicero, philosophy traced back originally to an ancestor of the Romans—none other than Pythagoras. The first man to call himself a "philosopher" (*philosophus*), Pythagoras is alleged to have had Trojan descent (being therefore an ancestor of the Romans) and to have migrated to Italy around 700 BCE, where he introduced philosophy to Rome's second king, Numa Pompilius.

In truth, philosophy originated in the sixth century BCE with Greek-speaking men around Sicily, Ionia, and the Aegean islands, and the Romans were much later in joining the pursuit.[18] Until the early first century BCE, the Roman attitude toward philosophy could be described as somewhere between ambivalent and distrustful. The first breakthrough occurred in 155 BCE, when an Athenian embassy consisting of representatives of various philosophical schools made a visit to Rome. Reportedly, the philosophers spent days lecturing and inspired amazement in the city's youths, much to the consternation of traditional-minded Romans.[19] Nearly a century later (86 BCE), Rome's invasion of Athens in the Mithridatic Wars precipitated the disbandment of the centralized philosophical schools and dispersion of the philosophers overseas. The happy result of this disaster was the establishment of small local philosophical schools in Rome, Alexandria, Tarsus, Rhodes, and elsewhere.[20]

It was only then that Romans began to warm to philosophy. In the mid-first century BCE, a tradition of "Latin philosophy" began to emerge,[21] as best represented in the voluminous philosophical writings of Cicero. Roman

17. For such language, see works cited in nn. 6 and 9 above.
18. Cicero, *Tusc.* 1.1.1–1.2.5.
19. Plutarch, *Cato Maj.* 22.2–3; Aulus Gellius, *Noct. Att.* 6.14.
20. Sedley, "School, from Zeno to Arius Didymus," 28.
21. Gareth D. Williams and Katharina Volk, eds., *Roman Reflections: Studies in Latin Philosophy* (New York: Oxford University Press, 2016).

philosophical writers had proclivities, respectively, toward all the major schools.[22] Yet it was Stoicism that dominated the upper-class outlook.[23] Stoicism entered into a kind of marriage with Roman political philosophy. The empire had become preeminent through divine providence and represented a political embodiment of the Stoic idea of the cosmos: a single world city, united under a universal code of law (Vergil, *Aen.* 7.98–101). The value system of the Roman patrician class—with its emphases on austerity (*severitas*), courage (*fortitudo*), benevolence (*benevolentia*), and reciprocity (*reditio*)—dovetailed naturally with Stoic ideals. A number of eminent figures from this period were both Roman statesmen and Stoics: the younger Cato and younger Seneca, as well as Helvidius Priscus, Arulenus Rusticus, and, later, the emperor Marcus Aurelius.[24] Augustus elevated the Greek Stoics Athenodorus and Arius Didymus to high positions on his staff. These played a kind of advisory role, as Seneca would later for Nero.[25] The marks of Stoicism are also visible in Roman poetry, both epic and satire.[26]

We find nonetheless a hesitancy among Roman elites to adopt "philosopher" (*philosophus*) as a term of identity. Even after the rise of Latin philosophy, Rome continued to have troubled relations with philosophers.[27] That we do not find Latin writers appropriating the term *philosophus* as an identity until Apuleius in the second century CE (though the term appears infrequently in epigraphy)[28] demonstrates that for Roman elites a certain stigma, lingering from earlier times, still attached to the label.[29] This point, however, is not as telling as it at first appears. Roman writers were indeed willing to describe their involvement with philosophy using cognate terms,

---

22. See Sedley's table ("School, from Zeno to Arius Didymus," 187–91) of seventeen names and their respective allegiances.

23. Long, "Roman Philosophy," 207; Gill, "School in the Roman Imperial Period," 34.

24. P. A. Brunt, "Stoicism and the Principate," *Papers of the British School at Rome* 43 (1975): 7–35.

25. On Stoic Roman statesmen, see Sedley, "School, from Zeno to Arius Didymus," esp. 30–31.

26. See Gill, "School in the Roman Imperial Period," esp. 56–57.

27. See for example Dio Chrysostom's reference to the philosophers' troubles under Domitian (*Or.* 3.13).

28. Note application of *philosophus* to a Roman man in *CIL* 6.09785 (late first century CE); *CIL* 6.9784 (30–70 CE).

29. Harry Hine, "Philosophy and *philosophi*: From Cicero to Apuleius," in Williams and Volk, *Roman Reflections*, 13–29, esp. 14–21.

like the verb "philosophize" (*philosophari*), or with antonomastic labels like "one devoted to philosophy." Moreover, when one turns to epigraphy, "most people in the corpus who are called 'philosophers' appear to be people with Roman citizenship" (even though examples come primarily from the Greek east).[30]

It was their involvement in politics that made Roman elites more reticent to identify as *philosophi*. In a recent graduate thesis, Tuuli Ahlholm has observed that "despite the plethora of high-born Romans known as having philosophical pretensions from literary sources, almost no one among them was portrayed as a philosopher in extant public epigraphy."[31] The clear explanation for this reticence is that most Roman philosophers were statesmen rather than teachers.[32] Because the professional pursuit of philosophy required "leisure" (*otium*), philosophy could divert attention from civic duty. Hence, the "politically active Roman citizen" would not readily advertise as a "philosopher" in public.[33] In addition, the dogmas of the philosophical schools could sometimes be perceived as discouraging participation in politics (for example, the Epicurean rejection of providence as a deterrent to taking on a priesthood). Yet, abundant evidence suggests that those with philosophical pretensions who did serve in public office (including Epicureans with priesthoods) routinely adapted their doctrines "to fit the social expectations of the context," and the dogmas of the schools "probably evolved towards more tolerant views of religious and civic participation."[34]

Despite their hesitancies, by the first century BCE Romans were doing "Latin philosophy." We have abundant evidence of Roman citizens (many of them ethnically Greek) who declared *philosophus* as an identity and of Roman elites who embraced the pursuit of philosophy despite the partial deterrent of public service. Actually, as we shall now see, philosophy was ubiquitous among all social classes in the empire, and it was present in first-century "Roman Corinth."

---

30. Tuuli Ahlholm, "Philosophers in Stone: Philosophy and Self-Representation in Epigraphy of the Roman Empire" (MPhil thesis, Oxford University, 2017), 38, 39–40.
31. "Philosophers in Stone," 42.
32. Long, "Roman Philosophy," 193.
33. Ahlholm, "Philosophers in Stone," 8.
34. Ahlholm, "Philosophers in Stone," 87.

Sources of Philosophy

Literate Education

According to the testimony of sources, ancient education was essentially education in rhetoric.[35] The early stages of education seem to have included a limited emphasis on philosophy at most, though on this point there is some discrepancy between literary sources and school exercises preserved in the papyri. Literary sources from the Roman period regularly advocate for exposure to philosophy even from the early stages.[36] The dominant Roman rhetorical tradition emphasized that the orator should also be virtuous, making philosophy indispensable and an essential complement to rhetorical training.[37] Theon (first century CE) preferred that students acquire a grasp of philosophy even *before* undertaking rhetorical education (*Prog. pr.*). On the other hand, when we turn to actual school exercises, we are missing the kind of interaction with philosophical literature that we might expect given the preferences of elite sources. Among the authors most frequently cited, philosophers are poorly represented.[38] The evidence shows that what little exposure non-elite students had to philosophy came primarily via gnomic sayings (*sententiae*, γνωμαί), especially sayings of Diogenes the Cynic.

Intense formal study of philosophy therefore came, for most people, not in the primary through tertiary stages of education (the rhetorical stages), but after this.[39] For the self-identifying "philosopher," the earlier stages of education were preparatory.[40] This was not always the pattern, however. Apart from the indications of elite literature, we have considerable epigraphical testimony of people who studied philosophy as children or teens.[41] If this exposure did not come as part of the child's literate or rhetorical education,

---

35. This (*ars bene dicendi*) is Quintilian's definition of "rhetoric" (*rhetoricē*) (Quintilian, *Inst.* 2.17.37); also, the "science of speaking well [bene dicendi scientia]" (Quintilian, *Inst.* 2.16.11; 2.18.38).

36. E.g., literary tractates frequently recommend the study of philosophy as part of students' training: Quintilian, *Inst.* 10.1.35–36, 81–84, 131; Cicero, *De or.* 1.52–57; and see those cited below.

37. Cicero, *Inv.* 1.1; Ps.-Plutarch, *Lib. ed.* 7d–e; Ps.-Cicero, *Rhet. Her.* 1.1.1; 4.55.69; Quintilian, *Inst.* 1.pr.9–20.

38. See Morgan's tabulation of authors in *Literate Education*, 122–23; and see table 15 on p. 313.

39. On Cicero's post-rhetorical, philosophical education, see *Tusc.* 2.26, 61; 3.59; 5.113.

40. As Philo says, *Congr.* 1.79; so also Alcinous, *Handbook of Platonism* 28.4.

41. Ahlholm, "Philosophers in Stone," citing *CIL* 2.01434; *CIL* 11.6435; Tod ("Sidelights," 140) cites *IG* 6.3226; *IBM* 925b, 14; *IG* 2.10046a; *IG* 7.3425; *IG* 5.1.1186.7–8.

Philosophy in the Roman Empire and Roman Corinth

it likely came through homeschooling overseen by the child's parents or else philosophically educated slaves.

Philosophical Schools

Although some children obtained formal exposure to philosophy in their early years, for most people significant exposure came through other channels. Formal training in a philosophical school, after completion of rhetorical education, would require both leisure and means and would for many people require travel to cities where such schools existed. Still, one could access philosophical instruction in schools in ways that did not require formal membership. A "school" in those days did not require a building, only an instructor and a circle of students.[42] In addition to using households, schools might meet out in the open (in places like Plato's Grove, Zeno's painted Porch, Epicurus's Garden in Athens) or in manifold types of public meeting spaces,[43] including temples, club rooms, gymnasia, multipurpose rooms attached to shops, and even shops themselves.

Instructors were entitled to fees, though many philosophers objected to fees in principle.[44] The existence of public and pro bono options meant access potentially for a much broader audience than elites who had completed rhetorical education. Listeners need not have been dedicated members or "professional" philosophers with ample leisure for study. As discussed in chapter 10, schools often consisted of a core group of students, with an outer ring of seekers or samplers not yet prepared or able to commit.[45]

Popular Philosophy

Philosophy came to most people in a form known today as *popular philosophy*.[46] In one sense of the term, popular philosophy consisted in a loose set of ethical principles associated most recognizably with the Stoic and Cynic

---

42. Raffaella Cribiore, *Gymnastics of the Mind: Greek Education in Hellenistic and Roman Egypt* (Princeton: Princeton University Press, 2001), 17–20.

43. Cribiore, *Gymnastics of the Mind*, 21–22.

44. While some argued that this was a legitimate means of livelihood (said of Socrates, Zeno, Cleanthes, and Chrysippus in Quintilian, *Inst.* 12.7.9; of Epicurus in Diogenes Laertius, *Vit. phil.* 10.120), others considered this to be the very definition of sophistry (cf. Aristotle, *Eth. nic.* 9.1.7; Philo, *Mos.* 1.24; Diogenes Laertius, *Vit. phil.* 7.188; Arius Didymus, *Epit.* 11m).

45. Alexander, "Paul and the Hellenistic Schools," 76.

46. See p. 33 n. 28 above.

traditions but belonging to no philosophical system in particular and finding representation in a variety of public forms of discourse. Popular philosophy in this sense disseminated itself through many channels. (1) "Epitomes" of the schools' doctrines could be found in circulation, offering memorable maxims and basic summaries of views in place of the primary-source authors, making sectarian doctrine in some form accessible to those at least who were literate and had some opportunity for leisurely reading and discussion.[47] (2) Philosophers sometimes made efforts to promote philosophy publicly through inscriptions. A second-century inscription carved under the patronage of Diogenes of Oenoanda, for instance, promulgates the core teachings of Epicureanism. (3) Many tombstones bore inscriptions that display "philosophical attitudes," which are not always possible to associate with a distinctive philosophical school.[48]

On the other hand, philosophy was disseminated more broadly through nonliterary channels. (4) The accessibility of schools that met in public spaces might, for the "inquirer" or less devoted student, tend to foster only a thin understanding of the schools' doctrines.[49] (5) Display rhetoricians who took up philosophical subjects in the forum, street-corner preachers intent on reforming the masses, and wandering charlatans who peddled philosophy for a living all served as conduits of philosophy to the public. Typically these were of a Stoic-Cynic stamp and indeed often called themselves "philosophers."[50] (6) Since cities took charge of entertainment and leisure, public spaces and civic events became special occasions for the intermingling of social classes. All kinds of people frequented the forum, the baths, and other public spaces. Public performances of the arts also served as occasions for transmitting ideas. Seneca tells us that tragedy, drama, mime, and the stage—art forms exceedingly popular among the people—conveyed the "same ideas" as philosophy.[51] (7) Roman social structures allowed for the free exchange of ideas across its varied social strata. In the patron-client system, social strata related not as castes but as interlacing levels between which

---

47. *Ep.* 33.4–8; 39.1. Extant examples include those of Arius Didymus, Stobaeus, and Diogenes Laertius.

48. Cf. Ahlholm, "Philosophers in Stone," 20–24.

49. Long and Sedley, *Hellenistic Philosophers*, 1:2–3.

50. On such figures, see Dio, *Or.* 32.9; 72.4; Lucian, *Fug.* 3–4; Philo, *de Plant.* 151; Lucian, *Bis acc.* 6; Origen, *Cels.* 3.50; Stoics: Epictetus, *Diatr.* 2.12.17; Horace, *Sat.* 2.3. For discussion in the secondary literature, see Malherbe, *Paul and the Popular Philosophers*, 38–39.

51. Seneca, *Ep.* 8.8.

cultural exchange flowed bidirectionally.[52] Indirect influence was possible at any level of society, whether through patrons or clients, friends, slaves, pedagogues, or institutional functionaries.[53]

Ahlholm uses the term *popular* in a different sense. In speaking of "philosophy as a 'popular' phenomenon," she refers rather to the *reach* of philosophy in the public rather than specifically its level of *purity*.[54] As we shall see, philosophy per se could be an important part of identity construction for people of all social classes. Though largely hidden in the literary sources, this population comes into clearer view in the epigraphic record.

Attestation of Philosophers

Having looked at the place of philosophy in Roman culture and possible contexts for its acquisition, we now examine the wealth of literary, epigraphical, and other sources that attest to actual proponents of philosophy during the imperial era.

Philosophers in the Roman Empire

For the Roman era, the list of elite writers whose writings survive, and who either identified as philosophers or were clearly educated in philosophy, is fairly short. Most of these identified with Stoicism, and most were Roman citizens. Among such writers were Seneca (first century CE); the Stoic-leaning Marcus Aurelius (second century CE); Cornutus (first century CE); Stoic teachers like Musonius Rufus (first century CE) and Epictetus (late first and early second century CE), whose students preserved their teachings; and a number of philosophers whose writings survive in fragments preserved in later compendia (Hierocles, Cornutus, Arius Didymus). To this list we can add philosophers of whom literary sources make mention, as for instance the first-century Stoics Q. Paconius Agrippinus (Tacitus, *Ann.* 16.28; cf. Epictetus, *Diatr.* 1.1.28; 1.2.12; *fr.* 21; 22), Thrasea (Tacitus, *Ann.* 13.49; 16.12), Helvidius

---

52. Downing (*Cynics and Christian Origins*, 107–8) mentions transference of information through eavesdropping slaves, nurses, teachers, and pedagogues.

53. See discussions of philosophical influence on the public also in Downing and Thorsteinsson. On public Cynic influence: Downing, *Cynics and Christian Origins*, 96–112; on public Stoic influence: Runar M. Thorsteinsson, *Roman Christianity and Roman Stoicism: A Comparative Study of Ancient Morality* (Oxford: Oxford University Press, 2010), 80–86.

54. Ahlholm, "Philosophers in Stone," 13, cf. 38, 65.

Priscus (Suetonius, *Vesp.* 15; Tacitus, *Ann.* 16.28), Euphrates (Apollonius of Tyana, *Ep.* 1–8; Pliny, *Ep.* 1.10; Epictetus, *Diatr.* 3.15.8; 4.8.17–20), and Bassus (Apollonius of Tyana, *Ep.* 36; 37; 74; Philostratus, *Vit. Apoll.* 4.24, 26).

We get a better sense of the size of the philosopher population from literary references that refer to philosophers as a *class*. Though surely exaggerated, the satires of Lucian in particular suggest (not without disdain) that philosophers thronged the public places in his day.[55] We find similar comments in other sources.[56]

Nonliterary records disclose a vastly larger crowd of self-identifying philosophers and individuals whose attitudes were consciously shaped by philosophy. Thousands of inscriptions, epitaphs, letters, and school exercises attest to such individuals, in addition to the plethora of coins, busts, herms, statues, mosaics, and other artistic media that bear the images or opinions of philosophers. A number of important studies have begun gathering this data together. In 1957 Marcus Tod collected some "Sidelights on Greek Philosophers" from the Hellenistic and Roman eras, with a prospective interest in the question of "how deeply and in what directions philosophic teachings affected the thought and speech and life of the common people of the Greek and Greco-Roman world."[57] Tod includes a wealth of references to Platonic, Pythagorean, Epicurean, and Stoic philosophers, or others identified simply as "philosophers," from both the epigraphic and archeological records. Provenances range across the Mediterranean.

To limit our focus, many of Tod's inscriptions identify individuals as Stoics (Sarapion in *IG* 2.3796; Theoxenus in *IG* 2.3631; T. Avianius Bassus Polyaenus of Hadriani in *BCH* 33.409–10; Lucius Peticius Propas in *IOlympia* 453; an unnamed Athenian in *IG* 12.9.40; Ti. Claudius Alexander and C. Tutilius Hostilianus in *CIL* 6.9784, 9785). The famously long inscription sponsored by the Epicurean Diogenes of Oenoanda criticizes several Stoic doctrines.[58] Two Athenian inscriptions refer to individuals as διάδοχοι ("successors") of Zeno, the founding Stoic (*IG* 2.3801, 11551).[59] A group of Athenian decrees celebrate the comprehensive philosophical studies completed by the ephebes in the

---

55. In one dialogue Zeus asks (*Bis. acc.* 6): "Do not you see how many short cloaks and staves and wallets there are? On all sides there are long beards ... the public walks are full of people ... there is nobody who does not ... ," etc. (Harmon, LCL); cf. *Fug.* 3–4.

56. Dio Chrysostom, *Or.* 32.9; 72.4.

57. Tod, "Sidelights," 141.

58. Tod, "Sidelights," 135.

59. As Ahlholm notes ("Philosophers in Stone," 19), this term could be used in the Roman era of heads of local schools.

gymnasium; one inscription mentioning the Stoic Zenodotus, referring apparently to the successor to the one-time head of school Diogenes of Babylon (240–152 BCE).[60] Tod's examples of decrees, honorary inscriptions, statue bases, and epitaphs witnessing to philosophers could be multiplied.

In a much more recent study, Tuuli Ahlholm has emphasized that even now (2017) "philosophy as a 'popular' phenomenon in imperial Roman society has largely been neglected."[61] Focusing on epigraphical evidence, she gleans a corpus consisting not only of inscriptions that identify subjects as "philosophers" but also inscriptions that include "philosophical phrases or attitudes."[62] This more inclusive approach reveals a much larger, and much more socially varied, population of philosophers. Notably, Ahlholm's inventory does not include every instance where sources describe individuals as "philosophers" (for this could include "lovers of wisdom" in general terms) but rather confines itself to instances where the subjects use the title of "philosopher" or philosophical phrases, in a more limited sense, "as part of their identity construction."[63]

Ahlholm's study is especially valuable for what it reveals about the demographic representation of philosophers.[64]

(1) *Roman citizens in Rome.* Inscriptions dating to the first or second century CE attest to Stoic philosophers who were Roman citizens and who resided in Rome. These inscriptions come in both Latin (*CIL* 6.9784; *CIL* 6.9785) and Greek (*IGUR* 2.371). Interestingly, Ahlholm's epigraphical inventory attests to almost none of the philosophers known to us from literary sources. This feature of the record is consistent with the fact that, as already noted, the public duties of elites who served at the highest levels of Roman administration prevented, or discouraged, intense public commitment to philosophy. Thus even those who identified as philosophers remained moderately restrained in declaring this identity publicly.

(2) *Roman citizens in the Greek east.* What we find widely attested are many Roman citizens who served in local administration in Greek *poleis* in the east. One Greek inscription identifying a local magistrate as a "philosopher" comes from Corinth in the mid-second century CE (*SEG* 31.285). A group of inscriptions dating between 90 and 160 CE name several individuals as "successors" (διάδοχοι) of the Athenian scholarchs; these do not all have Athenian citizen-

---

60. *IG* 2.1006. On Zenodotus, see Diogenes Laertius, *Vit. phil.* 7.30.
61. Ahlholm, "Philosophers in Stone," 13.
62. Ahlholm, "Philosophers in Stone," 13.
63. Ahlholm, "Philosophers in Stone," 38.
64. Her database includes many of the inscriptions that Tod's study includes.

ship, but they do all have Roman citizenship.[65] In an Athenian inscription apparently dating to the late first century CE (*IG* 2.3571), a certain T. Coponius Maximus is named a "Stoic successor" (διάδοχος Στω[ικός]). Two inscriptions from Athens dating to the second century CE refer to youths (members of the Athenian ephebate) who have Roman names and are called "successors of Zeno" (διάδοχον τῶν ἀπὸ Ζήνωνο[ς]/λόγων), *Zeno* here referring presumably to the founder of the Stoic school (*IG* 2.3801, 11551).[66] In several inscriptions from the first through the third centuries CE, other philosophers from the Greek east with Roman names appear (*IOlympia* 453; *SEG* 27.798; *IPrusaOlymp* 18).

(3) *Women and lower social orders.* A much larger portion of inscriptions attest to individuals who neither held positions of significant power nor had the social potential to obtain them. In addition to elites of the Greek *poleis* were many "*peregrini*, members of the 'middle classes,' freedmen, . . . and even marginalized groups such as women and slaves."[67] Ahlholm includes a lengthy discussion of female philosophers,[68] some of whom are identifiable as Stoic.[69] Like the famous Epictetus, slaves sometimes enjoyed the freedom to study philosophy. A litany of inscriptions assign to slaves and freedmen sentiments that Ahlholm argues ties them to specific philosophical schools,[70] including Stoicism.[71]

(4) *Children and youths.* Ahlholm includes a few examples where inscriptions point to philosophical instruction received by children and teens,[72] adding to the examples already cited by Tod.[73]

---

65. James H. Oliver, "The *Diadochē* at Athens under the Humanistic Emperors," *The American Journal of Philology* 98 (1977): 160–78.

66. In the latter inscription, the subject (Iulius Zosimianus) has Roman but apparently not Athenian citizenship.

67. Ahholm, "Philosophers in Stone," 13.

68. Ahlholm, "Philosophers in Stone," 46–56; including among other examples: *IG* 2.1099; *SEG* 4.661; *CIL* 6.33898; *CLE* 1965; *IG* 12.7.418; *IDidyma* 491; many inscriptions containing the Epicurean "*non sum*" formula; and in literary sources, the empress Julia Domna, Philostratus, *Vit. soph.* 622; Dio Chrysostom, *Or.* 76.15.7; 78 (Ahlholm's citations appear to be incorrect).

69. From Rome and dating to the second or third century CE: *IGUR* 3.1221; *IG* 14.1618; Kaibel 603; a husband and wife included in Ahlholm, "Philosophers in Stone," appendix 3, #5.

70. Ahlholm, "Philosophers in Stone," 56–64; e.g., *CIL* 5.01939 (1); *SEG* 47.1757; a female slave in *CIL* 6.33898; *CLE* 1965; freedmen in *ISardBR* 1355; *CIL* 11.04485 (1); *CIL* 6.38506 (1); *CIL* 9.04840.

71. The freedman featured in *SEG* 47.1757.

72. Ahlholm, "Philosophers in Stone," citing *CIL* 2.01434 (appendix 2, #29); *CIL* 11.6435 (appendix 3, #6).

73. Tod ("Sidelights," 140) also gives examples: *IG* 7.3226; *IBM* 925b, 4; *IG* 2.1.10046a; *IG* 7.3425; *IG* 5.1.1186.7–8.

Augmenting Ahlholm's epigraphic collection is the extensive but not yet complete Hairesis project, an online database that collects philosopher inscriptions dating between the sixth century BCE and the fourth century CE.[74] The database contains the names of 326 philosophers known from nonliterary sources. Among these are a good number of figures identifiable as Stoics and datable to around the time of Paul. These include, from Rome, (1) Q. Paconius Agrippinus (*IGR* I 980, 1013), (2) Ti. Claudius Alexander (*CIL* 6.9784), (3) Arria Maior (*CIL* 10.5920), (4) Graecinus Iulius (*AE* 1946, no. 94), (5) C. Tutilius Hostilianus (*CIL* 6.9785), and (6) Aibulius Liberanus (*CIL* 3, Supp. 9973); from Athens, (7) Musonius Rufus (*IG* 2.2472); from Ephesus, (8) Ti. Claudius Balbillus (*Ephesos* 3041; 3042); from Silicia, (9) Meleagre of Seleuca; and from Corinth, (10) Lucius Peticius Propas (*IOlympia* 453). All ten of these individuals date to the first century CE.

We have to thank another project for putting together the most comprehensive repository of ancient philosophers available. The monumental seven-volume *Dictionnaire des philosophes antiques* (1989–2018), a product of the collective efforts of some two hundred specialists, and edited by Richard Goulet, includes a list of nearly 3,000 philosophers attested between the sixth century BCE and the sixth century CE in inscriptions, papyri, and literary sources.[75] In a later article, Goulet has done a most useful service by distilling this material into an array of statistical charts and graphs.[76] Excluding some attestations from the original list, Goulet begins with a list of 2,463 "historical persons" identifiable as philosophers.[77] As he aptly notes, this population hardly represents a fraction of history's total representatives, since "the average teacher of philosophy and the crowd of their students in the ancient world had probably a very slight chance to escape complete obscurity."[78]

I note several highlights from Goulet's statistics. (1) Only eighty-five of the 2,463 (or 3 percent) are women.[79] (2) Of 202 philosophers dating to the first century CE, sixty-three (or 31 percent) are Stoics, making Stoics by far

---

74. Hairesis, https://hairesis.msh-lse.fr/?menuIndex=0&submenuIndex=-1.

75. Richard Goulet, *Dictionnaire des Philosophes Anciennes*, 7 vols. (Paris: CNRS Editions, 1994–2018).

76. Richard Goulet, "Ancient Philosophers: A First Statistical Survey," in *Philosophy as a Way of Life: Ancients and Moderns; Essays in Honor of Pierre Hadot*, ed. Michael Chase, Stephen R. L. Clark, and Michael McGhee (Oxford: Wiley Blackwell, 2013), 10–39.

77. Goulet, "Ancient Philosophers," 12.

78. Goulet, "Ancient Philosophers," 11.

79. Goulet, "Ancient Philosophers," 17, graph 2.1.

the most represented group among philosophers at that time.[80] (3) In the first century, geographical representation puts the most philosophers in Italy (35 individuals), followed by Greece (32) and Asia Minor (28), though philosophers are most prevalent in Greece when moving from philosophers' *origins* to their place of *activity*.[81] (4) Providing more extensive support for Ahlholm's survey of philosophers and social status, Goulet's study reveals that 405 philosophers were also associated with other intellectual pursuits and that many practiced non-elite occupations. Included are cart drivers, tanners, painters, sculptors, pantomimes, wrestlers, boxers, shoemakers, and barbers, among others.[82]

Philosophers in Corinth

Clearly the epigraphical evidence from the late Republic and early Roman era brings to light a substantial population of otherwise hidden "philosophers" from all across the Mediterranean basin. It is therefore not surprising that evidence also survives for philosophers in Roman Corinth.

In searching for Corinthian Stoics, at least three inscriptions are of interest. (1) One inscription, dating to ca. 145/146 CE, honors a Roman citizen and "philosopher" (φιλόσοφον), from an unidentified school, named Αὖλον Φλάβιον Ἀρριανόν (*SEG* 31.285).

Of greater interest are two individuals whom sources identify explicitly as Stoic philosophers and who can be dated precisely to the middle of the first century CE. (2) Three letters attributed to Apollonius of Tyana (*Ep.* 36; 37; 74; cf. 60; 77) refer to a certain Βάσσος, whom the sources identify as a Stoic (*Ep.* 37).[83] Both Apollonius's historical interactions with Bassus (datable to 61 CE) and Bassus's identity as a Stoic philosopher are corroborated in Philostratus's *Vit. Apoll.* (4.24; 26). (3) Another inscription, dating between 1

---

80. Goulet, "Ancient Philosophers," 23, graph 2.2.
81. Goulet, "Ancient Philosophers," 29, graph 2.8; 30, chart 2.5; 34, chart 2.7.
82. Goulet, "Ancient Philosophers," 38.
83. Not to be confused with the second-century Stoic T. Avianius Bassus Polyaenus (*BCH* 303.409–10). The three letters of Apollonius are not among those that can be proven spurious. Moreover, both Apollonius's historical interactions with Bassus (datable to 61 CE) and Bassus's pretensions as a Stoic philosopher are corroborated by Philostratus's *Vit. Apoll.* (4.24; 26). See commentary on Apollonius's letters in Robert Penella, *The Letters of Apollonius of Tyana* (Leiden: Brill, 1979), 109, 128–9; and on the question of their authenticity, 23–29.

and 67 CE,[84] refers to a "Corinthian Stoic philosopher" (φιλόσοφον Στωϊκὸν Κορίνθιον) and Roman citizen named Λούκιον Πετίκιον Πρόπαντα (*IOlympia* 453). The base of the statue indicates that the inscription was dedicated by his mother, Occia Prisca, "because of his virtue and wisdom" (ἀρετῆς ἕνεκα καὶ σοφίας).

Both first-century Stoics were of high status. Bassus is described as coming from an affluent family (Apollonius, *Ep.* 74), and Lucius is identifiable as a Roman citizen.

That we have clear testimony of at least two Stoic philosophers from Corinth active in the middle of the first century CE is significant given the expectation that only the tiniest fraction of philosophers will have been inscribed into the public record and given the assurance that only the smallest percentage of the public record has survived.

Testing the Numbers

While we know of several thousand philosophers from antiquity, apart from some kind of comparative data it is difficult to assess how significant that number is. With regard to possible metrics, a search through the *LGPN* reveals a curious and potentially significant statistic about the sum total of *philosophers* in comparison with *rhetoricians and sophists* attested in the ancient record.[85] The results of a search through the *LGPN* by "profession" includes forty-two individuals who are identifiable as "philosophers" (plus one instance of a philosopher/doctor) but only twenty-three total individuals who are identifiable as either "rhetors" (seven, plus one called a rhetor/Asiarch) or "sophists" (sixteen). When limited to the period between the first century BCE and the second century CE, the results include twelve individuals whom sources identify as philosophers versus ten individuals identified as either rhetors (three) or sophists (seven). While only one or two of the philosophers within this range date to the first century CE, not one of the rhetors or sophists does. All seven sophists date to the second century CE. It would be interesting to pursue further why the statistics skew unevenly

---

84. A. D. Rizakis and S. Zoumbaki list the inscription as "second half of 1st c. A.D." *Roman Peloponnese I. Roman Personal Names in Their Social Context* [*Achaia, Arcadia, Argolis, Corinthia and Eleia*], Meletemata 31 (Athens: Research Centre for Greek and Roman Antiquity, 2001), 512.

85. The online *Lexicon of Greek Personal Names* (www.lgpn.ox.ac.uk) contains the aggregated data of the eight printed volumes in the Lexicon of Greek Personal Names series.

toward philosophers (are some of them "lovers of wisdom" in a more generic sense?), but these preliminary results surely give grounds for questioning the assumption that, as regards the Corinthian conflict, the immense popularity of rhetoric in the first century compared, supposedly, with philosophy makes the former de facto a more likely background than the latter.[86]

Conclusion

The purpose of this chapter has been to investigate the plausibility of a Stoic background for the Corinthians' conflict based on evidence for the pervasiveness of philosophy in the Roman Empire during and around the first century CE. We first examined the complicated history of the relationship between "Roman" and "Greek" culture in Roman Corinth and the way in which this sort of relationship advises against any hard separation between the two. We also traced Roman attitudes toward the influx of "Greek" philosophy and how the Romans, at first uneasy toward philosophy, became increasingly relaxed toward it, taking up the pursuit of "Latin philosophy" and ultimately admitting the label of "philosopher" as an acceptable marker of identity. We looked next at the various conduits through which people absorbed philosophical teachings, from literate education, to homeschooling, to participation (at some level) in philosophical schools, to various forms of transfer in popular culture and public life.

In the final part of the chapter, we looked at prosopographic evidence attesting to self-identifying philosophers, or people who consciously incorporated philosophy into their identity construction. This survey established several points of importance for our study. First, it became evident that the population of individuals in the Roman Era who advertised themselves as "philosophers" was exponentially larger than the group of representatives known to us from literary sources. Second, the epigraphical record includes a great many philosophers who were Roman citizens and residents of Rome. We found, moreover, that the number of results surviving for philosophers of this profile is deflated due to the traditional Roman unease about claiming *philosophus* as a public identity. Third, the record contains a large number of philosophers who were Roman citizens and served as local magistrates in the Greek east. Fourth, the record contains extensive evidence for philosophers who were from more marginalized demographic groups; these include

---

86. See pp. 271–72 and n. 2 above.

women, freedmen, and slaves. Finally, the record reveals that, not unlike Rome itself, Roman Corinth was also home to self-identifying philosophers, at least two of whom we can identify as Stoics and can date to the middle of the first century CE.

What remains for our investigation is to examine whether any of the Corinthian church's members had the sort of social profile that would put them within the ambit of direct Stoic influence. This question is the subject of our next, and final, chapter.

12

CHURCH PROSOPOGRAPHY AND THE SUB-STOIC SCHOOL IN CORINTH

Among Paul's churches, we know more about the Corinthian church than perhaps any other. First Corinthians, together with the final salutations in Paul's letter to the Romans and the narrative of Acts, identify more than a dozen individuals who belonged among this church's members. In many cases, data accompanying the names proves useful for extrapolating something about their ethnic, social, and economic profiles. Even the names may convey information of use.

This data puts us in the fortunate position of being able to test the thesis we have been pursuing against the profile of the church's members. In the previous chapter it was shown that Stoic influence—and indeed, identifiably Stoic philosophers—were present within the Corinthians' immediate contemporary environment. We will now explore whether Stoicism can have directly reached the kinds of people contained in the Corinthian church.

PROFILING THE GROUP OF AGITATORS

Although 1 Corinthians is patently addressed to the whole "church of God in Corinth" (1:2), most interpreters maintain that the agitators targeted in 1:17b–4:21 constitute a smaller group of individuals. (a) Some interpreters identify the culpable party as the church's wealthier members, especially wealthy "patrons."[1] (b) Others view the culprits as being indeed wealthy but emphasize

---

1. See pp. 8–9 n. 19 above and further discussion below.

their status as "educated" elites.[2] (c) Wire identifies the culprits as certain wise, or rather charismatic, women.[3] (d) Throughout the last century and a half, the predominant view has been that the culpable party consisted of the "wise" partisans either of Peter or Apollos and, more recently, of the latter.[4]

It is worth pointing out that differences in judgment as to the part/whole scope of Paul's target group owe largely to the interpreter's main theme of interest. With regard to partisanship (or if one prefers, "leadership"), the participation of the whole church, or a large portion of it (1:10–13), indeed supports the point that Paul targets the church as a whole. Over the course of Paul's discourse, however, 1:17b–4:21 explicitly puts σοφία at the center. Unless one takes the improbable, and generally rejected, view that each party had its own theology of "wisdom,"[5] one must assume that those whom Paul accuses of espousing the "wisdom of the world" constituted a smaller group. I have identified this group as the Paul party. I should now like to consider a more specific profile of this group.

The Size and Structure of the Church

We can extrapolate a reasonable estimate of the church's size from various pieces of data. If one begins with the individuals that Paul identifies by name, we can identify as members some sixteen individuals, give or take: Prisc(ill)a and Aquila (Acts 18:2), Titius Justus (Acts 18:7), Crispus (Acts 18:8; 1 Cor 1:14), Sosthenes (Acts 18:17), Gaius (1 Cor 1:14; Rom 16:23), Stephanas (1 Cor 1:16; 16:17), Fortunatus (1 Cor 16:17), Achaicus (1 Cor 16:17), Lucius, Jason, Sosipater, Tertius, Erastus (Rom 16:21–24), Quartus (Rom 16:21–24), and, from nearby Cenchrea, Phoebe (Rom 16:1–2). One could perhaps add "Chloe's people" (1 Cor 1:11) or subtract Lucius, Sosipater, or Sosthenes, whose community of origin cannot be definitively determined from the references.[6]

---

2. Dutch (*Educated Elite*) refers to them as "the educated elite." Similarly Paige ("Stoicism, *Eleutheria*, and Community," 182) suggests that they learned philosophy at the secondary or tertiary level of schooling, if not in the ephebic college.

3. Wire, *Corinthian Women Prophets*, 48, 65.

4. For example, of Peter: Goulder, "Σοφία in Corinthians"; of Apollos: Horsley, "Wisdom of Words."

5. Barrett, "Christianity at Corinth."

6. It is uncertain whether Chloe was a Corinthian or even a Christian. Against Friesen's hypothesis that Erastus was not a Christian ("The Wrong Erastus: Ideology, Archaeology, and Exegesis," in Friesen, Schowalter, and Walters, *Corinth in Context*, 249–55), I find the usual view, which has been ably defended by John Goodrich, to be far more convincing.

Jerome Murphy-O'Connor adds that, besides the husband-wife pair of Prisca and Aquila, the other fourteen individuals probably also had spouses and that the households of Crispus and Stephanas, containing no doubt children, servants, and other relations, may have been baptized along with the householders. Thus Murphy-O'Connor calculates a "base figure" for the church's size of "around 50 persons."[7]

Attempts to delimit the church's size more precisely have relied primarily on two considerations: (1) the archeology of available meeting spaces and (2) Paul's reference to Gaius as the host of the "whole [ὅλης] church" (Rom 16:23). Based on the remains of several houses from the Roman period, Murphy-O'Connor extrapolated that the church cannot have exceeded his proposed base figure of "around 50," since a "typical" home (Murphy-O'Connor asks us to suppose), like that owned by Gaius (if his house was "typical"), could "barely" have accommodated so many individuals. If, moreover, Paul's reference to the "whole church" implies that the church regularly met in cell groups that assembled in smaller spaces than Gaius's home, and if this reference implies that they only occasionally "crowded" into Gaius's home, we must assume that there was no larger space available than the slightly undersized space that Gaius provided.[8]

Since Murphy-O'Connor's essay in 1983, several studies have explored alternative meeting spaces. Apart from homes, the church might have met in a variety of semiprivate or public spaces, like multipurpose club rooms, workshop areas, warehouses, small apartment blocks, the kinds of rooms found in and above a variety of buildings that remain in Corinth's East Theatre Street area, and even open spaces.[9] These studies have concluded, however, that the closed spaces known to us from Corinth's archeological record, like Murphy-O'Connor's "average" house, could probably not have accommodated more than forty or fifty people comfortably.[10]

Goodrich, "Erastus of Corinth (Romans 16.23): Responding to Recent Proposals on His Rank, Status, and Faith," *NTS* 57 (2011): 589–90.

7. Murphy-O'Connor, *St. Paul's Corinth*, 157–58.

8. Murphy-O'Connor, *St. Paul's Corinth*, 155–58.

9. David L. Balch, "Rich Pompeiian Houses, Shops for Rent, and the Huge Apartment Building in Herculaneum as Typical Spaces for Pauline House Churches," *JSNT* 27 (2004): 27–46; David Horrell, "Domestic Space and Christian Meetings at Corinth: Imagining New Contexts and the Buildings East of the Theatre," *NTS* 50 (2004): 349–69; Edward Adams, "First-Century Models for Paul's Churches: Selected Scholarly Developments Since Meeks," in Still and Horrell, *After the First Urban Christians*, 60–78; Bradly S. Billings, "From House Church to Tenement Church: Domestic Space and the Development of Early Urban Christianity—the Example of Ephesus," *JTS* 62 (2011): 541–69.

10. Balch, "Rich Pompeiian Houses," 41; Horrell, "Domestic Space," 367.

Several counter points must be considered. (1) Archeological remains offer us only a partial glimpse into the architectural landscape of first-century Corinth, for much has surely not survived. (2) Murphy-O'Connor's characterization of Gaius's home as "average" in size is merely imaginative. We have no way of knowing whether his house was larger (it cannot have been smaller) than Murphy-O'Connor supposes. (3) We need not assume that Gaius necessarily hosted the "whole church" in his *home*. As others have suggested, he may have "hosted" merely as the patron responsible for procuring some other space,[11] including an open space. (4) We might also consider rented spaces available in the towns of Cenchrea and Lechaion,[12] about five miles down the road—a trek hardly too laborious to undertake for these rarer occasions.

Furthermore, several pieces of data lead one to suspect that an estimate of forty or fifty persons is too low. First, one gets the impression of exceptional success in Paul's Corinthian ministry from several points: (a) according to Acts, God told Paul that he "has many people in this city" (18:10); (b) Paul's ministry there lasted eighteen months (Acts 18:11); (c) the church there did not experience persecution (Acts 18:9–10 and all indications in 1 Corinthians); and (d) its members remained well connected with outsiders;[13] outsiders—or "seekers"—apparently even participated in their worship services (the ἰδιῶται of 14:16, 23–24). Second, if the church contained four parties (1:12), or more, and not everyone attached themselves to one of them, we may easily imagine a church larger than fifty. Additionally, while Paul's non-identification of the agitators may simply suggest reluctance, per habit, to identify an "opponent," this silence could equally be explained on the premise that he did not know who they were, which would be increasingly likely the larger the church was. Finally, and I think most compellingly, it seems incredible that Paul would happen to have named at least one member from *every* married couple in the church—the tally of which Murphy-O'Connor uses for his "base figure" of forty or fifty. One can hardly doubt that there were other individuals besides and therefore additional household units.

For these reasons, those who estimate a church membership of some one hundred or more individuals are likely closer to the mark.[14] Admittedly, the impression is subjective, and the estimate somewhat arbitrary, but on

---

11. De Vos, *Church and Community Conflicts*, 203.
12. Finney, *Honour and Conflict*, 68n133.
13. Barclay, "Thessalonica and Corinth," 57–60.
14. Hays proposes 150–200 (*1 Corinthians*, 7); Finney (*Honour and Conflict*, 66) is "inclined to concur" with Hays.

balance it seems more probable than estimates determined by our limited archeological record and guesses about Gaius's facilities.

Religious and Ethnic Profile

The Corinthian church consisted predominantly of gentiles. The list of known names offers ambiguous, and potentially misleading, evidence. While nine known individuals have distinctively Greek (Stephanas, Erastus, Phoebe) or Roman names (Achaicus, Fortunatus, Gaius, Tertius, Quartus, Titius Justus) and are not identifiable as Jews, almost as many can be identified as Jews (Aquila, Prisca, Crispus, Sosthenes, Lucius, Jason, Sosipater). This relative balance, however, cannot have represented the church at large. Apart from the fact that Paul himself targeted gentiles in his ministry (Rom 11:13; Gal 2:7), in 1 Corinthians he generalizes his audience as "gentiles" who were once led astray by "dumb idols" (1 Cor 12:2). Participation by some of them in the eating of "idol meat" (8:1–13; 10:1–11:1) is self-evidently a "gentile" problem. Paul explicitly identifies "wisdom" as a "Greek" pursuit, in distinction from the Jewish desire for "signs" (1:22). Fee has astutely remarked: "nothing in the letter *cannot* be explained in light of its Greco-Roman origins."[15]

Social and Economic Profile

The Corinthian church seems to have remained well integrated in pagan society. They apparently experienced no persecution.[16] Some members had unbelieving spouses (7:12–16). Some continued to receive invitations to participate in pagan religious meals and apparently continued to eat idol meat (8:1–13; 10:14–22), as they were accustomed (8:7). The ἰδιῶται who participated in the church's worship services (14:16, 23–24) were likely to have been friends, partners, and neighbors with whom members had prior connections. Even unbelievers (ἄπιστοι) made appearances at their gatherings (14:23–24).

More disputed is the socioeconomic spectrum represented. This question became a subject of special interest in the late 1970s and early '80s with the work of Gerd Theissen, Abraham Malherbe, and Wayne Meeks. Following a growing consensus after the seminal work of E. A. Judge nearly two decades

---

15. Fee, *First Epistle to the Corinthians*, 1st ed., 14.
16. Barclay ("Thessalonica and Corinth") has demonstrated this in a comparison between the Thessalonian and Corinthian churches.

earlier,[17] Theissen and the others characterized the early church as representing an economic cross section of society, missing only the extreme top and bottom echelons, but including some among the sub-elite well-to-do.[18] They observed that significant social stratification was possible within that range of economic levels. This observation led Theissen to the thesis that social stratification may have been a major contributor to the problems that occasioned 1 Corinthians.[19] Specifically, Theissen proposed that the church contained "a few influential members" who came from "the upper classes" and that this created tension with other members in the church, tensions that become salient in the situation around idol meat treated in chapters 8–10 and in the divisions at the Lord's Supper addressed in 11:17–34.[20] Through the 1980s and '90s, several studies extended Theissen's thesis in offering other areas where social stratification may have played a role, for example, in the church's leadership allegiances (1:12; 4:6), their non-judgment of norm-breakers due to patronage relationships (5:1–13), and litigation of rich over poor (6:1–11).[21]

A common premise in studies of this kind was that the greater responsibility for the divisions fell upon the higher-class members of the community. Even though the whole church was complicit, it was this group whose behavior Paul primarily targets in connection with many of the letter's topics, including his discussion of σοφία in chapters 1–4. This viewpoint has remained widely accepted in Corinthians scholarship since.[22]

While it is difficult to say whether the σοφοί can be definitively identified with the "wealthier" members of the community, it seems to me that this

---

17. Judge, *Social Pattern*.

18. Theissen, *Social Setting*, 69, 106; Malherbe, *Social Aspects*, 87; Meeks, *First Urban Christians*, 73.

19. The view that a small, prosperous minority wielded disproportionate influence is widely shared: e.g., Malherbe, *Social Aspects*, 72; Theissen, *Social Setting*, 69, 73, 95–96; Theissen, "Social Conflicts in the Corinthian Correspondence: Further Remarks on J. J. Meggitt, *Paul, Poverty and Survival*," *JSNT* (2003): 371–91, esp. 377; Murphy-O'Connor, *Paul*, 271; and see n. 22 below.

20. Theissen, *Social Setting*, 121–43, 145–74.

21. Patronage: Hock, *Social Context*, 52–65; Marshall, *Enmity in Corinth*; Clarke, *Secular and Christian Leadership*, xiii; Chow, *Patronage and Power*, 130–40; litigation: Alan Mitchell, "Rich and Poor in the Courts of Corinth: Litigiousness and Status in 1 Cor 6:1–11," *NTS* 39 (1993): 562–86.

22. In addition to those cited in n. 19, see Paige, "Stoicism, *Eleutheria*, and Community," 182; Martin, *Corinthian Body*, xvii, 72–73; Horrell, *Social Ethos*, 115–36; Tomlin, "Christians and Epicureans," 55n17; Holloway, "Religious 'Slogans' in 1 Corinthians."

is more likely correct than not.[23] On the one hand, neither the presence of wealthy members nor the contribution of social stratification in other issues proves that it was the wealthy who incited the divisions or advocated for the church's problematic σοφία.[24] Yet, the thesis for which I have been arguing, together with the level of substance and relative technicality with which the σοφοί drew from Stoicism, suggests that the σοφοί were more likely to have come from the educated classes than not. As discussed, philosophy had a limited role in the curriculum of literate and rhetorical education. The traditional curricular sequence usually put any extensive formal training in philosophy after rhetorical training, even if some elite theorists advocated for philosophy as preparation for the latter. Furthermore, literary and inscriptional evidence demonstrates that most people who explicitly self-advertised as "philosophers" were Roman citizens, if not elites, and that these were commonly municipal magistrates.

Still, I hesitate in limiting the wise group to the church's wealthier members only. For we have seen that many people from less privileged groups, though perhaps not identifying as "philosophers," consciously had philosophical pretensions—including women, children, freedmen, and slaves—and some received formal training in philosophy in less traditional ways (for example, through homeschooling).[25] We know that the Corinthian church contained both slaves and freemen, if not also freed-men (7:20–23).[26] Even apart from the possibility of training, it is conceivable that one or more individuals from the wealthier, and more formally trained, group became a conduit of their σοφία to members who represented the less educated classes. Thus, I leave open the possibility that some among the latter were included.

A final word should be said regarding the implications of the wise group's profile for weighing "ideological" versus "social" factors as causes of the divisions. We need not view σοφία as being an economically loaded term in order to view social stratification as a factor in the church's divisions. Put differ-

---

23. Though, as indicated in our exegetical chapters, I do not read 1:26 or 4:8 as referring to the economic level of the Corinthians.

24. At least 8:1–11:1 seems to me to point in this direction. The higher-status members are those who claim to "have knowledge" (γνῶσις). The contrast between "weak" and "knowledgeable" is paralled in Stoicism, as shown in Brookins, *Corinthian Wisdom*, 165–69.

25. See chapter 11, p. 284, notes 71 and 72.

26. Benjamin Schliesser, "Striefzüge durch die strassen von korinth: Wer waren die ersten christusgläubigen der stadt und wo trafen sie sich," in *Paulus und die christliche Gemeinde in Korinth: Historisch-kulturelle und theologische Aspekte*, ed. Jacob Thiessen and Christian Stettler (Göttingen: Vandenhoeck & Ruprecht, 2020), 9–53.

ently, if σοφία in Corinth had as its semantic content something more akin to φιλοσοφία than to παιδεία (i.e., "education" as the cultural refinement characteristic of the upper classes), it may be nevertheless that those of higher social status were the ones attracted to it. Other "social" dynamics would certainly have contributed to the formation of the group. What attracted some to this φιλοσοφία would surely attract those who associated with them. If these were the wealthy, it would also attract their business partners, friends, neighbors, clients, or patrons. Thus, the reciprocal dynamics of ideology and social pressures would work together to attract a like-minded, and perhaps roughly homogeneous, group.

Gender Profile

The Corinthian church contained both males and females. Of females we know only the names Prisca and, in nearby Cenchrea, Phoebe. On the other hand, we must assume that most if not all of the men had wives. Paul explicitly discusses husband-wife relations in 7:1–16.

In an important study, Antoinette Wire argued that the "wise" and "spiritual" in the church consisted of a group of charismatic women. Yet, the evidence of 1 Corinthians strongly undermines this thesis. Paul is willing to address women directly where he finds the behaviors of women problematic (11:2–16). Likewise, Greek writers were willing to use the grammatically feminine forms when referring to "wise" women.[27] Moreover, all the attributes that Paul assigns to the problematic individuals in chapters 1–4 are grammatically masculine—σοφός, πνευματικός, τέλειος, δυνατοί, σάρκινοι, κεκορεσμένοι, φρόνιμοι, and so on. It is true that Paul's letters are largely androcentric in address and that they use masculine language even when addressing both genders (ἀδελφοί rather than ἀδελφοὶ καὶ ἀδελφαί, etc.). But use of the inclusive masculine is not the same as using the masculine when the referent is actually exclusively feminine. Thus, the group of σοφοί in Corinth surely consisted of men in the main. Only, given the possibility of an inclusive masculine—and some ancient evidence for female philosophers—we cannot rule out the inclusion of a small female minority.

---

27. E.g., γυναῖκα σοφήν in Plutarch, *Mor.* 262d, though sources very rarely use the feminine *philosopha* for the female "philosopher"; Ahlholm cites an example in *CIL* 6.33898. Thus, Plutarch describes the goddess Isis as σοφὴν καὶ φιλόσοφον, using both the feminine and masculine forms (*Mor.* 351e).

Summary

In sum, while 1 Corinthians unequivocally addresses the whole church as complicit in the body's divisions, it is apparent that portions of 1 Corinthians target a narrower group, and chapters 1–4 suggest that this group almost certainly consisted primarily of those who espoused the problematic σοφία. These were predominantly gentile males who represented the more privileged classes.

IDENTIFYING INDIVIDUAL AGITATORS

It remains to consider whether we can determine *which* of the church's members belonged to this σοφοί group. In this regard the first matter is to decide whether the relevant individuals are among those whom the letter specifically references.

(1) If Paul does name the culprits in 1 Corinthians, these may, on the one hand, (a) have been individuals that he had known while in Corinth. Furthermore, he (i) may be aware that they are the culprits, or (ii) he may not know that they specifically are the culprits. On the other hand, (b) he may not have met these individuals while in Corinth. (i) He may still be unacquainted with them, or (ii) he may since have become acquainted with them, whether in person or by letter. In the instance of either (i) or (ii), he (α) may know (at least by report) that these are the culprits, or (β) he may not know that they specifically are the culprits.

(2) If the culprits are *not* explicitly named in the letter, the same subordinate questions arise: Paul (a) may or (b) may not have known them while in Corinth, and so on.

Interpreters often note that Paul never names an "opponent."[28] Frequently, he refers to his targets of criticism with pronominal substitutes like τις (1 Cor 3:12, 17, 18; 6:1; etc.), τίνες (4:18; 8:7; etc.), and τοιοῦτος (5:5). Paul's general practice of non-naming, however, does not rule out as antagonists individuals named in the letter; for the rule is to avoid naming them *as* opponents, not to avoid naming them at all. We may initially keep as candidates, then, not only (1) individuals unknown to us from the NT and (2) individu-

---

28. De Vos (*Church and Community Conflicts*, 202) calls this a "standard Greco-Roman rhetorical convention," perhaps borrowing this observation from Marshall (*Enmity in Corinth*, 342–43).

als not named in 1 Corinthians but known from other NT sources, but also (3) individuals known to us from 1 Corinthians.

Socioeconomic Characteristics

If we begin from the assumption that the group consisted largely of wealthier members of the church, we can begin to narrow down a list of candidates based on prosopographic analysis of known members. We need not make a definite guess as to the specific individuals who belonged to this group. It will be sufficient if we are able to determine that this church (of perhaps one hundred or more members) contained individuals who fit the *profile*. These may or may not have belonged to the σοφοί group.

Based on several criteria (references to offices, references to houses, references to services rendered, references to travel),[29] Theissen identified nine individuals in the Corinthian church as belonging to the "upper classes": Aquila, Priscilla, Stephanas (houses, service, travel); Erastus, Sosthenes (offices, travel); Crispus (offices, house); Phoebe (services, travel); Gaius, and Titius Justus (services).[30] A separate analysis by Meeks identified probable evidence of wealth for the same individuals. Meeks also noted several suggestive indicators of higher status for others: Fortunatus, Quartus, and Lucius may have been Roman citizens, and Achaicus a freedman; Tertius had a Latin name and was a trained scribe.[31]

Friesen's more recent analysis has offered more precise descriptions of individuals by placing them on a seven-tiered "Poverty Scale" (PS1–7).[32] Friesen confined the category of "elites" strictly to the upper Roman "orders" of the decuriones, equestrians, and senators, which he calculated constituted less than 3 percent of urban society (PS1–3). Based on evidence from Paul's letters, Friesen found no Corinthians at the elite level, though he found several at the "middling" level, constituting the next 7 percent (PS4): Gaius, Chloe, and potentially Erastus, Priscilla and Aquila, and Phoebe.[33] Not long after, Bruce Longenecker offered a slightly revised seven-tiered scale ("Economy Scale"), placing at the middling level (now 15 percent) Erastus, Gaius, Phoebe,

29. Theissen, *Social Setting*, 73–94.
30. Theissen, *Social Setting*, 94–95.
31. Meeks, *First Urban Christians*, 56–63.
32. Steven Friesen, "Poverty in Pauline Studies: Beyond the So-Called New Consensus," *JSNT* (2004): 323–61, esp. 348.
33. Friesen, "Poverty in Pauline Studies," 357.

and, with less certainty, Priscilla and Aquila, Stephanus, and Crispus.[34] Erastus he assigned to the upper middling level (ES4a), and proposed that Gaius plausibly fit there as well.

Two points about prosopographic analyses deserve further comment. First, subsequent evaluation of these and other recently proposed scales has pointed to the conclusion that the middling group in *urban* environments—as opposed to the empire-wide average—was probably about double of Friesen's and Longenecker's estimates, thus constituting more like 15–25 percent of the urban population.[35] This figure makes it scarcely implausible that one of Paul's earliest churches could have contained at least a small population at this level. Second, Friesen and Longenecker excluded from evaluation individuals identified only in Acts—Titius Justus (Acts 18:7) and Sosthenes (Acts 18:17)—as well as those about whom we have more limited data—Fortunatus (1 Cor 16:17), Achaicus (16:17), Lucius, Jason, Sosipater, Tertius, and Quartus (Rom 16:21–24).[36] Yet, some of these are strong candidates for the middling level. As noted, Theissen placed Titius Justus and Sosthenes in the "upper classes."

It would be redundant, and not very productive, to reexamine the evidence for each Corinthian figure.[37] The evidence is slight for all of them, and almost entirely lacking for several of them. Subjective biases can come into play in use of the evidence, and inevitably one is faced with the choice between a "minimalist" and "maximalist" use of the data. It seems reasonable to proceed, however, based on the general consensus of those who have undertaken prior analyses. Comparing the lists of Theissen and Meeks, and of Friesen and Longenecker, we find seven individuals who at least three of the four scholars agree possibly, probably, or most likely fell within the wealthy-but-sub-elite (Theissen and Meeks) or middling-sub-elite levels

---

34. A first revision in Bruce W. Longenecker, "Exposing the Economic Middle: A Revised Economy Scale for the Study of Early Christianity," *JSNT* 31 (2009): 243–78; and a second, with prosopographic analysis, in *Remember the Poor: Paul, Poverty, and the Greco-Roman World* (Grand Rapids: Eerdmans, 2010), 220–58.

35. For a more comprehensive history of economic scales, see Timothy A. Brookins, "Economic Profiling of Early Christian Communities," in *Paul and Economics*, ed. Thomas Blanton and Ray Pickett (Philadelphia: Fortress Press, 2017), 57–87, esp. 71–80. Brookins demonstrates that the higher percentages in urban areas are mathematically plausible when considering the distribution of classes in urban versus nonurban areas. The higher percentage in urban areas would be due to the economic opportunities afforded by cities.

36. Friesen, "Poverty in Pauline Studies," 348n79; Longenecker, *Remember the Poor*, 249–51.

37. See also Brookins, *Corinthian Wisdom*, 108–19.

(Friesen and Longenecker): Priscilla, Aquila, Stephanas, Erastus, Crispus, Phoebe, and Gaius. Not subjected to analysis by Friesen and Longenecker, but identified as being among the wealthy by both Theissen and Meeks, is the additional figure of Titius Justus. While we do not have enough information to make informed judgments about other named individuals, it seems somewhat more reasonable (given the nature of social networks) to suppose that someone among them qualified for middling or upper-middling status than that all of them did not.

Erastus merits further comment because indicators of his economic status suggest that he was more exceptional than Longenecker and, especially, Friesen supposed. Several issues around the evidence continue to be debated.[38] The essential matter is the long-debated meaning of the title Paul uses to describe him: οἰκονόμος τῆς πόλεως (Rom 16:23).[39] The most recent discussion of this title is also the most comprehensive. Alexander Weiss has shown that the title in fact does identify Erastus as Corinth's *aedile* (= οἰκονόμος).[40] Since this position required Roman citizenship and constituted one of the four highest magisterial positions in the Roman colony of Corinth, Erastus would indeed have been among the city's highest municipal elites. Thus, Erastus would have qualified within the range that Friesen and Longenecker consider "elite" (PS3/ES3). Erastus's profile in this regard is consistent with that of the many subjects referenced explicitly in inscriptions as "philosophers" in the eastern provinces.

It should be added that both Longenecker and Friesen place another individual just below elite level (PS/ES4a), namely, Gaius. Hesitancy about Gaius owes only to the unknown factor of his house size. If we are wrong to impose a limit based on comparison to other houses that survive in our limited archeological evidence (see above), we have no evidential basis for excluding him from PS/ES4a (or even higher). Finally, what was said in chapter 10 bears repeating: that *self-identifying* philosophers are more likely to

---

38. See recent discussion of the dating in Friesen, "The Wrong Erastus," in Friesen, Schowalter, and Walters, *Corinth in Context*, 231–56; and discussion of the frequency of the name Ἔραστος in Timothy A. Brookins, "The (In)frequency of the Name 'Erastus' in Antiquity: A Literary, Papyrological, and Epigraphical Catalog," *NTS* 59 (2013): 496–516.

39. John Goodrich, "Erastus, Quaestor of Corinth: The Administrative Rank of ὁ οἰκονόμος τῆς πόλεως (Rom 16:23) in an Achaean Colony," *NTS* 56 (2010): 90–115; Goodrich, *Paul as an Administrator of God*, 27–102.

40. Alexander Weiss, *Soziale Elite und Christentum: Studien zu ordo-Angehörigen unter den frühen Christen*, Millennium-Studien/Millennium Studies 52 (Berlin: de Gruyter, 2015), esp. 145–47.

have come from the highest classes, but often they did not. Those from the lower classes cannot be ruled out.

Other Characteristics

We can narrow our list of candidates further based on other features of the profile we have identified. First, since the Corinthian agitators are of gentile origin ("Greeks seek wisdom," 1:22), of either Greek or Roman descent, we may eliminate from the group's core those members known to be of Jewish origin: Aquila, Prisca, Crispus, Sosthenes, Lucius, Jason, and Sosipater. Second, the group consisted of men, or at least mostly of men. Unless the masculine forms are "inclusive," this rules out Phoebe and again Prisca. Third, the agitating group surely excluded Stephanas, for reasons widely agreed upon and already discussed in chapter 10.[41]

Conclusions

Through process of elimination, this leaves Erastus, Gaius, and based on the testimony of Acts, Titius Justus as those best fitting our profile. Tertius cannot be left out of consideration.[42] It is a curious point that two of these (or three, if we add Tertius) not only fit the profile we have identified but also are not named in 1 Corinthians (Erastus, Titius Justus, Tertius). Paul's practice of avoiding the names of opponents, on balance, could possibly weigh further in favor of their candidacy.

I do not suggest that because these men fit the profile, they *were* among the σοφοί. Other named figures could have belonged to this group, not to mention individuals entirely unknown to us—in this church of some one hundred or more members. Our purpose has only been to examine evidence that the church plausibly contained members whose social profile was consistent with the typical profile of the self-identifying "philosopher" or person who completed higher levels of philosophical education. We have found that it did.

An Imagined Sequence of Events

Were one to indulge in speculation, one might offer a fuller reconstruction of the sequence of events, from the founding of the church to the composi-

---

41. See p. 265.
42. Bitner (*Paul's Political Strategy*, 268–69) includes as the best candidates Erastus, Titius Justus, and Crispus, finally identifying Crispus as the most likely candidate.

tion of 1 Corinthians, that includes a guess as to the personal origins of the σοφοί group and a timeline of the group's growth and development relative to Paul's time in Corinth. The following scenario is consistent with the broader reconstruction that I have offered in this and earlier chapters.

Sometime between 50 and 51 CE, Paul visited Corinth and founded its first church.[43] Naturally, he first established connections with the city's Jews (Priscilla and Aquila in 18:1–3) and with the synagogue,[44] where he tried to persuade the Jews that Jesus was the messiah (18:4–6). While he was successful in making some converts, his relationship with the synagogue soon ruptured, and as was his habit, he moved operations from the synagogue to the household.

It was a certain gentile—a well-to-do man named Titius Justus—who offered him a space. Linking into the network of Titius Justus, Paul began to draw gentile converts. Meanwhile the house of Titius Justus became their center of instruction. Paul continued to find success in Corinth, primarily among gentiles, and encountered no trouble with the locals (18:9–10) for a period of eighteen months (18:11), until at last dissension with the city's Jews brought him before the city's authorities and forced him from the city.

While Paul was still in Corinth, a certain conception of the household instructional center as a sort of "philosophical school" was already beginning to take shape. Imperceptible to Paul or regarded as mostly innocuous at the time, this conception developed more fully in his absence. The central characters were Titius Justus and his acquaintances. One or more of them had formal acquaintance with the doctrines of Stoic philosophy. They even had a direct source. As privileged men (within the top 3–10 percent in socioeconomic status) in a mid-sized city (of 30,000–50,000), they had social connections with some of the more prominent men in the city, who made up a fairly narrow sector of the population (maybe 1,000 or 2,000 men),[45] among which the larger part of the city's "philosophers" were found. The latter group included individuals like Bassus and Lucius Peticius Propas—two Corinthian Stoics who were active in the city at the time. If Titius Justus and

---

43. The dating can be determined from the Gallio inscription in *IG* 7.1676; cf. Acts 18:12–17.

44. The Jewish population was his most natural connection to a new city. See Timothy A. Brookins, "From Analogy to Identity: Did an Association of Leather-Workers 'Turn' into the Thessalonian Church?," in *Associations, Deities, and Early Christianity*, ed. Bruce W. Longenecker (Waco, TX: Baylor University Press, 2022), 271–87, esp. 277–79.

45. On the population, see the synthesis of studies in Rinse Willet, "Whirlwind of Numbers: Demographic Experiments for Roman Corinth," *Ancient Society* 42 (2012): 127–58.

his colleagues were not connected with Bassus or Lucius Peticius personally, they were surely connected with members of their philosophical circles.

The sub-Stoic wisdom born from this group did not come to its fullness immediately, for at least two years separated Paul's departure from Corinth and his composition of 1 Corinthians (cf. 1 Cor 16:8; Acts 19:10). The development of his converts' perspective came about probably as a gradual drift in his absence, potentially driven along further by some figure(s) later introduced into the community. What the members of the emerging σοφοί group at first viewed merely as intriguing "parallels" between Paul's teaching and Stoic philosophy began to grow into a Stoicizing "doctrinal reformulation" of Paul's message (interaction type 7). A new identity began to crystallize: Paul had taught a new philosophy; the household of Titius Justus was a center of "school" instruction; they were Paul's students; their σοφία embodied the school's doctrines; they themselves were σοφοί.

Conclusion

As to the question whether the Corinthian church contained individuals who could have been directly influenced by Stoic philosophy, the answer is almost certainly yes. Stoicism, as we saw in chapter 11, had a very strong presence across the first-century Roman world. We have found evidence of Stoic presence even in mid-first-century Corinth. As the present chapter has shown, we can identify several individuals in the Corinthian church whose profiles make plausible a certain level of formal philosophical instruction. Our purpose here was not to pinpoint the individuals who must have composed this group, but to demonstrate that the church contained hypothetical candidates even among the small percentage of individuals known to us.

The group of sub-Stoic σοφοί represented a minority in the church and consisted primarily of gentile men of higher socioeconomic standing. I have added several qualifications to this profile, however. First, one must leave open the possibility that the group contained a minority constituency of women. Second, though a higher-class constituency is more likely on grounds of the evidence treated in chapter 11, our survey of philosophers there allows for the possibility of members from other social classes. Third, as previously argued, philosophical "schools" (circles of disciples) did not consist exclusively of card-carrying members, but usually of a core of committed students and an outer circle of looser affiliates.

More speculatively, I suggested that the self-conception of the σοφοί could have originated from the instructional activity that took place in the house of Titius Justus—and still more speculatively, from this group's ties with Bassus or Lucius Peticius or their circles. The viewpoint of the σοφοί had not fully developed during Paul's time in Corinth, though the seeds of possibility had already been planted. Having noticed "parallels" between Stoicism and Paul's message, this group gradually drifted in a more Stoicizing direction in his absence and adapted, second-hand, what they learned from him in the direction of sub(ordinated)-Stoicism.

Conclusion

This book has been an exercise in rediscovery. In one sense, I mean a rediscovery of older insights on 1 Cor 1–4 that for the last four decades or so have been downplayed, dismissed, and in some ways ignored. In particular, I refer to insights that attach some kind of "religious" meaning (whether theological or philosophical) to the Corinthians' conception of σοφία. As we have seen, apart from the classic gnostic thesis, scholarship in the more recent era has not engaged critically with prior theses or, more importantly, argued for the *comparative* value of their conclusions where the interpretive options are not supplementary, but indeed, mutually exclusive.[1] Overviews of scholarship frequently omit mention entirely of the thesis that Corinthian σοφία found its closest cultural parallel in some kind of ancient philosophy. With the jump from religious to "social" explanations for σοφία (as *paideia* or rhetoric), there has also been a move from a comparative-religious to a more sociological approach to interpretation. As noted, a sociological approach, however, does not rule out religious explanations, only religion understood as theological abstraction.

On the other hand, I mean *rediscovery* in the sense of *new* discovery. I have not presented my thesis as a "return" to any specific thesis of earlier times. More critically, I have questioned some of the key "discoveries" of recent scholarship on 1 Cor 1–4 and have made it my purpose to help readers "discover" the meaning of this text *again*, or rather, to discover it *differently*. I have tried to offer a reading that demonstrates maximal global

---

1. Though see pp. 13–14.

coherence—a reading that is internally coherent as to a running exegesis of the text, externally coherent as to a reconstruction of the occasion, and mutually coherent vis-à-vis our internal reading and occasional reconstruction. My primary thesis was that Corinthian σοφία is best characterized in terms of what I have called "sub-Stoicism," or "sub(ordinated)-Stoicism"; the Corinthian σοφοί themselves were "sub-Stoics." The σοφία of this group shared with Stoicism a similar configuration of systemically related ideas located, specifically, at a cross-section where Stoic physics and anthropology intersected with Stoic ethics. On the side of physics, the σοφοί adopted the view that πνεῦμα inhabited things at different levels of pneumatic tension (τόνος). Creatively appropriating this doctrine, the σοφοί developed a two-tiered view of those within the church, with status varying according to the strength of one's respective union with connate s/Spirit. Constituted at the highest level of tension, the σοφοί were πνευματικοί and τέλειοι; the others in the church were ψυχικοί and νήπιοι. On the side of ethics, the σοφοί viewed the immanent πνεῦμα, now, as a peculiar property of themselves as human beings, resulting in the possibility of αὐτάρκεια, or human self-sufficiency, and conferring a right to boast in what was "their own." Consequently, the Corinthian σοφός or πνευματικός, like the Stoic σοφός, became the standard by which all others should be measured.

To the pertinent Stoic doctrines, the Corinthians, however, made a local systemic modification, substituting "Spirit/the spiritual" as a replacement part for "virtue/the rational." Thus, whereas for the Stoics the σοφός was *virtuous*, and *virtue* was the ideal measure of value, for the Corinthian σοφοί, the wise man was *spiritual*, and *spiritual manifestations* were the ideal measure of value. This substitution amounted to a slight modification of the Stoic ethical classification *good, bad*, and indifferent into the parallel classification *spiritual, unspiritual*, and indifferent.

This modification prevented our identifying the Corinthians' σοφία as "Stoicism" per se. This σοφία, however, had sufficient family resemblance with Stoicism for the two to be associated under a common family name. Max Lee's typology of the dynamics of interaction between opposing philosophical schools allowed us to identify the Corinthians' σοφία as the product of a tension between *doctrinal redevelopment* of Paul's teaching (interaction type 7) and *competitive or irenic appropriation* of Stoicism (types 3 and 4). Thus, the σοφοί on the one hand identified as Christ people, loyal to the teachings of Paul; on the other hand, they had been influenced by Stoicism—probably directly and probably consciously—at a certain level of substance, technicality, and interrelation of parts. In their final personal analysis, they subordinated their Stoicism to their Christ-faith and, from an emic standpoint, identified as Christ people. Hence, they were *sub*-Stoics, and their sub-Stoicism a *sub(ordinated)* Stoicism.

This sort of σοφία was intimately related to the church's factions (1:10–17a). There was indeed a Paul faction within the church, and it was constituted at its core by none other than the σοφοί. These viewed Paul as a founder of a philosophical school, his teaching as their σοφία, and themselves as his "loyal" students. Their cry of allegiance ("I am of Paul") mimicked the standard practice of philosophical allegiance reflected in the competing philosophical schools of the day. Yet, while the σοφοί were committed to Paul's teachings, they engaged in creative doctrinal reformulation of his teaching under the influence of the teachings of Stoicism.

While the sub-Stoic σοφοί formed the core of the Paul faction, an outer ring may have affiliated more loosely or for different reasons. Other parties formed in response to or in imitation of this one, gathering around different leaders for reasons that may have had nothing to do with a rival σοφία. Not all aligned with a faction.

An examination of the Corinthians' immediate environment and their own prosopographic profile demonstrates high plausibility for the thesis that the σοφοί could have been influenced by Stoicism directly. Based largely on inscriptional evidence, chapter 11 demonstrated that philosophers and other people for whom philosophy was an essential part of their identity construction made up a much larger population in antiquity than is often appreciated. During the Roman Era these people were concentrated especially in Greece, Asia Minor, and Rome and represented Stoicism far more heavily than any other philosophical school. While most self-identifying "philosophers" (*philosophi*, φιλοσοφοί) were elites in municipal administration in the Greek provinces, we found extensive evidence of conscious philosophical pretensions also among less privileged groups, including the working classes, slaves, and freedmen. While women philosophers also were attested, these made up a very small minority. Importantly, we have found evidence of at least two identifiably Stoic philosophers whom we can place in Corinth in the middle of the first century CE.

In an attempt to develop a more comprehensive reconstruction of the occasion, we pursued in chapter 12 further elaboration of the situation by pressing some details, posing some possibilities that were admittedly more speculative, though not essential to our overall thesis. It was suggested that the Paul faction began in the house of a well-to-do man named Titius Justus, whose house became an instructional center where Paul instructed primarily gentile converts after his relationship severed with the synagogue. Titius Justus and some of his connections had some level of formal training in Stoic philosophy and were connected with local Stoics. If they did not know the Corinthian Stoics Bassus and Lucius personally, they probably had some acquaintance with their circles. The sub-Stoicism of Titius Justus's group did not formalize immediately but developed gradually as they interacted with Paul's teachings and mulled over perceived similarities with the doctrines of Stoicism. Paul was not aware of this group's activity until he received reports from Chloe's people, the letter from the Corinthians, or the report of its carriers.

The thesis about the Corinthians' σοφία presented here, together with the larger reconstruction of the situation offered, represents a marked change of perspective from some of the dominant trends in scholarship over the last three or four decades. I hope to have succeeded in convincing readers that it offers, on the whole, a better alternative. While I share fully with contemporary scholarship the view that the Corinthians' divisions were not exclusively rooted in "theological" differences and that a deep understanding of the occasion must take into account the contemporary "social" world, I have found some other essential aspects of recent reconstructions problematic. In my perusal of both the scholarly literature and the text of 1 Corinthians in researching this project, I found that the predominant views—chiefly those that associate the conflict with either (1) rhetoric/sophistry or (2) patronage/financial practices—have not adequately been tested at an *exegetical* level, and that when one does test them, they often fail at both the finer points of exegesis and in regard to coherence at several levels. My purpose in chapters 3–8 was both to critically evaluate this scholarship and to test my own thesis by means of painstaking, and admittedly prolonged, exegesis.

It would be regrettable if, after this detailed exegetical analysis and critical examination of the scholarship, the interpreter drew back to a kind of both-and objection—"well, why couldn't it be both rhetoric *and* philosophy?" or "why not both philosophy *and* patronage practices"—for such a response would show that the reader has not taken seriously (or, I daresay, fully engaged with) the exegetical demonstrations that occupied a large portion of this book. Whatever the merits of my arguments for the Stoic thesis, I have tried to show that *both-and* viewpoints frequently cannot be sustained when tested within the cohesive flow of the discourse, for depending on which background one tries, the meaning of the text changes at the level of the propositions and of the logic that holds them together. The meaning of the text or the possibility of integration, for this reason, cannot just be declared at the thematic level of the paragraph or the sentence but must be demonstrated at the level of the finely woven texture of the discourse.

In regard to the finer points of exegesis, I have pointed out that interpreters repeatedly omit consideration of the logical connectives in the discourse (so often γάρ!) and that when one considers them, the emergent train of thought often belies the proposed readings. Another tendency found repeatedly in the literature has been a tendency to rely upon what one might call a surplus of meaning in order to fit the interpretive reconstruction. I do not mean a surplus in regard to word semantics (Paul actually exhibits a marked tendency toward word play and multivalence). Rather, I mean this in regard to syntax, application, and propositions: a single preposition requires two distinct syntactical functions (2:4–5; 4:6d); the same words apply to multiple specific people or things resulting in two distinct propositions at the level of thought (1:20–21, 27–29; 3:21b; 4:18); the correlation of actions and actors becomes ambiguous or confused (who is boasting, whose eloquence is meant, who is preaching, esp. in 1:26–31; 2:6–3:4; 4:18–19).

My analysis has shown that these tendencies appear to emerge from a kind of big-idea approach in which the interpreter asserts the general idea of the passage—with summary statements, elaborate paraphrases of the text, or from prolix discussion of the social world—but neglects to demonstrate their reading exegetically. At the largest level of interpretation, this kind of reconstruction represents, I have posed, a *background* of the text rather than a background of the *text*.

Bibliography

Adams, Edward. "First-Century Models for Paul's Churches: Selected Scholarly Developments Since Meeks." In *After the First Urban Christians*, edited by Todd Still and David Horrell, 60–78. Edinburgh: T&T Clark, 2009.

Adams, Edward, and David Horrell, eds. *Christianity at Corinth: The Quest for the Pauline Church*. Louisville: Westminster John Knox, 2004.

Adkins, A. W. H. "Review of Burkhard Gladigow's *Sophia und Kosmos: Untersuchungen zur Frühgeschichte von σοφός und σοφία*." *The Classical Review*, New Series 21 (1971): 391–93.

Ahlholm, Tuuli. "Philosophers in Stone: Philosophy and Self-Representation in Epigraphy of the Roman Empire." MPhil thesis, Oxford University, 2017.

Alexander, Loveday. "IPSE DIXIT: Citation of Authority in Paul and in the Jewish and Hellenistic Schools." In *Paul beyond the Judaism/Hellenism Divide*, edited by Troels Engberg-Pedersen, 103–27. Louisville: Westminster John Knox, 2001.

——. "Paul and the Hellenistic Schools: The Evidence of Galen." In *Paul in His Hellenistic Context*, edited by Troels Engberg-Pedersen, 60–83. London: T&T Clark, 1995.

Allo, E. B. *St. Paul Première épître aux Corinthiens*. 2nd ed. Paris: Gabalda, 1956.

Anderson, R. Dean. *Ancient Rhetorical Theory and Paul*. Contributions to Biblical Exegesis and Theology 18. Leuven: Peeters, 1999.

Baird, William. "'One against the Other': Intra-Church Conflict in 1 Corinthians." In *The Conversation Continues: Studies in Paul and John in Honor of J. Louis Martyn*, edited by Robert T. Fortna and Beverly R. Gaventa, 116–36. Nashville: Abingdon, 1990.

Balch, David L. "Rich Pompeiian Houses, Shops for Rent, and the Huge Apartment Building in Herculaneum as Typical Spaces for Pauline House Churches." *JSNT* 27 (2004): 27–46.

Barclay, John M. G. "Crucifixion as Wisdom: Exploring the Ideology of a Disreputable Social Movement." In *The Wisdom and Foolishness of God: First Corinthians 1–4 in Theological Exploration*, edited by Christophe Chalamet and Hans-Christoph Askani, 1–20. Minneapolis: Fortress, 2017.

———. "Mirror-Reading a Polemical Letter: Galatians as a Test Case." *JSNT* 31 (1987): 73–93.

———. *Paul and the Gift*. Grand Rapids: Eerdmans, 2015.

———. *Paul and the Power of Grace*. Grand Rapids: Eerdmans, 2020.

———. "Thessalonica and Corinth: Social Contrasts in Pauline Christianity." *JSNT* 47 (1992): 49–74.

Barclay, John M. G., and B. G. White, eds. *The New Testament in Comparison: Validity, Method, and Purpose in Comparing Traditions*. London: T&T Clark, 2020.

Barnett, Paul W. *The Corinthian Question: Why Did the Church Oppose Paul?* Nottingham: Apollos, 2011.

Barrett, C. K. "Christianity at Corinth." *BJRL* 46 (1964): 269–97.

———. *A Commentary on the Epistle to the Romans*. New York: Harper & Bros., 1957.

———. *A Commentary on the First Epistle to the Corinthians*. London: Adam and Charles Black, 1971.

Baur, F. C. "Die Christusparti in der korinthischen Gemeinde, der Gegensatz des paulinischen und petrinischen Christentums in der altesten Kirche, der Apostel Petrus in Rom." *Tübinger Zeitschrift für Theologie* 4 (1831): 61–206.

Berger, Peter L., and Thomas Luckmann. *The Social Construction of Reality: A Treatise in the Sociology of Knowledge*. Garden City, NY: Doubleday, 1966.

Betz, Hans Dieter. "The Problem of Rhetoric and Theology according to the Apostle Paul." In *L'Apôtre Paul: Personalité, style et conception du ministère*, edited by A. Vanhoye, 16–48. BETL 73. Leuven: Leuven University Press, 1986.

Biber, D., and S. Conrad. *Register, Genre, and Style*. CTL. Cambridge: Cambridge University Press, 2009.

Billings, Bradly S. "From House Church to Tenement Church: Domestic Space and the Development of Early Urban Christianity—the Example of Ephesus." *Journal of Theological Studies* 62 (2011): 541–69.

Bitner, Bradley J. *Paul's Political Strategy in 1 Corinthians 1–4: Constitution and Covenant*. SNTSMS 163. Cambridge: Cambridge University Press, 2015.

Bonazzi, Mauro. "Antiochus' Ethics and the Subordination of Stoicism." In *The*

Origins of the Platonic System: Platonisms of the Early Empire and Their Philosophical Contexts, edited by Mauro Bonazzi and Jan Opsomer, 33–54. Collection d'Études classiques 23. Leuven: Peeters, 2009.

Boyarin, Daniel. "Nominalist 'Judaism' and the Late-Ancient Invention of Religion." In *Religion, Theory, Critique: Classic and Contemporary Approaches and Methodologies*, edited by Richard King, 23–40. New York: Columbia University Press, 2017.

Boys-Stones, G. R. *Platonist Philosophy 80 BC to AD 250: An Introduction and Collection of Sources in Translation*. Cambridge Source Books in Post-Hellenistic Philosophy. Cambridge: Cambridge University Press, 2018.

Branick, V. P. "Source and Redaction Analysis of 1 Corinthians 1–3." *JBL* 101 (1982): 251–69.

Brookins, Timothy A. *Ancient Rhetoric and the Style of Paul's Letters*. Eugene, OR: Cascade, 2022.

———. "An Apology for Exegesis of 1 Thess 2,1–12." *Bib* 103 (2022): 89–113.

———. *Corinthian Wisdom, Stoic Philosophy, and the Ancient Economy*. SNTSMS 159. Cambridge: Cambridge University Press, 2014.

———. "Economic Profiling of Early Christian Communities." In *Paul and Economics*, edited by Thomas Blanton and Ray Pickett, 57–87. Philadelphia: Fortress, 2017.

———. "From Analogy to Identity: Did an Association of Leather-Workers 'Turn' into the Thessalonian Church?" In *Associations, Deities, and Early Christianity*, edited by Bruce W. Longenecker, 271–87. Waco, TX: Baylor University Press, 2022.

———. "The (In)frequency of the Name 'Erastus' in Antiquity: A Literary, Papyrological, and Epigraphical Catalog." *NTS* 59 (2013): 496–516.

———. "Rhetoric and Philosophy in the First Century: Their Relation with Respect to 1 Corinthians 1–4." *Neot* 44 (2010): 233–52.

———. "The Wise Corinthians: Their Stoic Education and Outlook." *Journal of Theological Studies* 62 (2011): 51–76.

Brunschwig, Jacques, and David Sedley. "Hellenistic Philosophy." In *The Cambridge Companion to Greek and Roman Philosophy*, edited by David N. Sedley, 151–83. Cambridge: Cambridge University Press, 2003.

Brunt, P. A. "Stoicism and the Principate." *Papers of the British School at Rome* 43 (1975): 7–35.

Bullinger, E. W. *Figures of Speech Used in the Bible*. London: Eyre & Spottiswoode, 1898. Reprint, Grand Rapids: Baker, 1968.

Bullmore, Michael. *St. Paul's Theology of Rhetorical Style: An Examination of*

1 Corinthians 2:1–5 in the Light of First-Century Rhetorical Criticism. San Francisco: International Scholars Publications, 1995.

Burkert, Walter. "Platon oder Pythagoras? Zum Ursprung des Wortes 'Philosophie.'" *Hermes* 88 (1969): 159–77.

Butts, James R. "The Progymnasmata of Theon: A New Text with Translation and Commentary." PhD diss., Claremont Graduate School, 1986.

Byron, John. "Slave of Christ or Willing Servant? Paul's Self-Description in 1 Corinthians 4:1–2 and 9:16–18." *Neot* 37 (2003): 179–98.

Castelli, Elizabeth Anne. *Imitating Paul: A Discourse of Power*. Louisville: Westminster John Knox Press, 1991.

Chester, Stephen J. *Conversion at Corinth: Perspectives on Conversion in Paul's Theology and the Corinthian Church*. Studies of the New Testament and Its World. London: T&T Clark, 2003.

Chow, John. *Patronage and Power*. JSNTSup 75. Sheffield: JSOT Press, 1992.

Ciampa, Roy E., and Brian S. Rosner. *The First Letter to the Corinthians*. PNTC. Grand Rapids: Eerdmans, 2010.

Clarke, Andrew. *Secular and Christian Leadership in Corinth: A Socio-historical and Exegetical Study of 1 Corinthians 1–6*. Leiden: Brill, 1993.

Collins, Raymond. *First Corinthians*. SP 7. Collegeville, MN: Liturgical, 1999.

Conzelmann, Hans. *1 Corinthians: A Commentary on the First Epistle to the Corinthians*. Hermeneia. Philadelphia: Fortress, 1975.

———. "Paulus und die Weisheit." *NTS* 12 (1965–66): 231–44.

Coughlin, Sean, and Orley Lewis. "What Was Pneumatist about the Pneumatists School?" In *The Concept of Pneuma After Aristotle*, edited by Sean Coughlin, David Leith, and Orley Lewis, 203–36. Berlin: Freie Universität Berlin, 2020.

Cribiore, Raffaella. *Gymnastics of the Mind: Greek Education in Hellenistic and Roman Egypt*. Princeton: Princeton University Press, 2001.

Dahl, Nils. "Paul and the Church at Corinth according to 1 Corinthians 1:10–4:21." In *Studies in Paul: Theology for the Early Christian Mission*, 40–61. Minneapolis: Augsburg, 1977.

Davis, James A. *Wisdom and Spirit: An Investigation of 1 Cor 1:18–3:20 against the Background of Jewish Sapiential Traditions in the Greco-Roman Period*. Lanham, MD: University Press of America, 1984.

Deming, Will. *Paul on Marriage and Celibacy: The Hellenistic Background of 1 Corinthians 7*. Grand Rapids: Eerdmans, 2004.

De Witt, Norman Wentworth. *St. Paul and Epicurus*. Minneapolis: University of Minnesota Press, 1954.

Dingeldein, Laura B. "'Ὅτι πνευματικῶς ἀνακρίνεται': Examining Translations of 1 Corinthians 2:14." *NovT* 55 (2013): 31–44.

Divjanović, Kristin. *Paulus als Philosoph: Das Ethos des Apostels vor dem Hintergrund antiker Populärphilosophie.* Münster: Aschendorff, 2015.

Dodson, Joseph R., and Andrew W. Pitts, eds. *Paul and the Greco-Roman Philosophical Tradition.* LNTS 527. London: T&T Clark, 2017.

Dodson, Joseph R., and David E. Briones. *Paul and Seneca in Dialogue.* Ancient Philosophy and Religion 2. Leiden: Brill, 2017.

Doughty, Darrell. "The Presence and Future of Salvation in Corinth." *ZNW* 66 (1975): 61–90.

Downing, F. Gerald. *Cynics and Christian Origins.* Edinburgh: T&T Clark, 1992.

———. *Cynics, Paul, and the Pauline Churches.* London: Routledge, 1998.

Dunn, James D. G. *1 Corinthians.* New Testament Guides. Sheffield: Sheffield Academic, 1995. Reprint, London: T&T Clark, 2004.

———. "Reconstructions of Corinthian Christianity." In *Christianity at Corinth: The Quest for the Pauline Church,* edited by Edward Adams and David Horrell, 295–310. Louisville: Westminster John Knox, 2004.

Dutch, Robert S. *The Educated Elite in 1 Corinthians: Education and Community Conflict in Graeco-Roman Context.* JSNTSup 271. New York: T&T Clark, 2005.

Edwards, Catherine. "Self-Scrutiny and Self-Transformation in Seneca's Letters." In *Seneca,* edited by J. G. Fitch, 84–101. Oxford Readings in Classical Studies. Oxford: Oxford University Press, 2008.

Engberg-Pedersen, Troels. *Cosmology and the Self in the Apostle Paul: The Material Spirit.* Oxford: Oxford University Press, 2010.

———, ed. *From Stoicism to Platonism: The Development of Philosophy, 100 BCE–100 CE.* Cambridge: Cambridge University Press, 2017.

———. *John and Philosophy: A New Reading of the Fourth Gospel.* Oxford: Oxford University Press, 2017.

———. *Paul and the Stoics.* Louisville: Westminster John Knox, 2000.

———. "Setting the Scene: Stoicism and Platonism in the Transitional Period in Ancient Philosophy." In *Stoicism in Early Christianity,* edited by Tuomas Rasimus, Troels Engberg-Pedersen, and Ismo Dunderberg, 1–14. Grand Rapids: Baker Academic, 2010.

———. "Stoicism in Early Christianity." In *Routledge Handbook of the Stoic Tradition,* edited by John Sellars, 19–43. Routledge Handbooks in Philosophy. London: Routledge, 2016.

Erler, Michael, Jan Erik Heßler, and Federico M. Petrucci. *Authority and Authoritative Texts in the Platonist Tradition.* Cambridge: Cambridge University Press, 2021.

Fee, Gordon. *First Epistle to the Corinthians.* NICNT. Grand Rapids: Eerdmans, 1987; 2nd ed., 2014.

Ferguson, Everett. *Backgrounds of Early Christianity*. 3rd ed. Grand Rapids: Eerdmans, 2003.

Finney, Mark T. *Honour and Conflict in the Ancient World: 1 Corinthians in Its Greco-Roman Social Setting*. LNTS 460. London: T&T Clark, 2011.

Fiore, Benjamin. "'Covert Allusion' in 1 Cor 1–4." *CBQ* 47 (1985): 85–102.

———. *The Function of Personal Example in the Socratic and Pastoral Epistles*. AnBib 105. Rome: Biblical Institute Press, 1986.

———. "The Sage in Select Hellenistic and Roman Literary Genres." In *The Sage in Israel and Ancient Near East*, edited by John G. Gammie and Leo G. Perdue, 329–42. Winona Lake: Eisenbrauns, 1990.

Fitzgerald, John T. *Cracks in an Earthen Vessel: An Examination of the Catalogues of Hardships in the Corinthian Correspondence*. SBLDS 99. Atlanta: Scholars, 1988.

Fitzgerald, John T., and L. Michael White. "*Quod est comparandum*: The Problem of Parallels." In *Early Christianity and Classical Culture*, edited by John T. Fitzgerald, T. H. Olbricht, and L. Michael White, 13–39. Leiden: Brill, 2003.

Fitzmyer, Joseph. *First Corinthians: A New Translation with Introduction and Commentary*. AYBC 32. New Haven: Yale University Press, 2008.

Francis, James M. M. "'As Babes in Christ': Some Proposals regarding 1 Corinthians 3:1–3." *JSNT* 7 (1980): 41–60.

Frid, Bo. "The Enigmatic AΛΛA in 1 Corinthians 2:9." *NTS* 31 (1985): 603–11.

Friesen, Courtney J. P. "Paulus Tragicus: Staging Apostolic Adversity in First Corinthians." *JBL* 134 (2015): 813–32.

Friesen, Steven J. "Poverty in Pauline Studies: Beyond the So-Called New Consensus." *JSNT* (2004): 323–61.

———. "The Wrong Erastus: Ideology, Archaeology, and Exegesis." In *Corinth in Context: Comparative Studies on Religion and Society*, edited by Steven J. Friesen, Daniel N. Schowalter, and James C. Walters, 231–56. Leiden: Brill, 2010.

Friesen, Steven J., Sarah James, and Daniel N. Schowalter, eds. *Corinth in Contrast*. Leiden: Brill, 2013.

Friesen, Steven J., and Walter Scheidel, eds. "The Size of the Economy and the Distribution of Income in the Roman Empire." *Journal of Roman Studies* 99 (2009): 61–91.

Friesen, Steven J., Daniel N. Schowalter, and James C. Walters, eds. *Corinth in Context: Comparative Studies on Religion and Society*. Leiden: Brill, 2010.

Funk, Robert. "Word and Word in 1 Cor 2:6–16." In *Language, Hermeneutic, and Word of God*, 275–303. New York: Harper & Row, 1966.

Bibliography

Garcilazo, Albert V. *The Corinthian Dissenters and the Stoics*. New York: Peter Lang, 2007.

Garland, David E. *1 Corinthians*. Baker Exegetical Commentary on the New Testament. Grand Rapids: Baker Academic, 2003.

Georgi, Dieter. "Forms of Religious Propaganda." In *Jesus in His Time*, edited by H. J. Schultz, 124–31. Philadelphia: Fortress, 1971.

———. *The Opponents of Paul in Second Corinthians: A Study of Religious Propaganda in Late Antiquity*. Philadelphia: Fortress, 1986.

Gerring, John. "What Makes a Concept Good? A Criterial Framework for Understanding Concept Formation in the Social Sciences." *Polity* 31 (1999): 357–93.

Gill, Christopher. "The School in the Roman Imperial Period." In *Cambridge Companion to the Stoics*, edited by Brad Inwood, 33–53. Cambridge: Cambridge University Press, 2002.

Gill, David W. J. "Corinth: A Roman Colony in Achaea." *Biblische Zeitschrift* 37 (1993): 259–64.

———. "Early Christianity in Its Colonial Contexts in the Provinces of the Eastern Empire." In *The Urban World and the First Christians*, edited by Steve Walton, Paul R. Trebilco, and David W. J. Gill, 68–85. Grand Rapids: Eerdmans, 2017.

———. "In Search of the Social Elite in Corinth." *TynBul* 44 (1993): 323–37.

Given, Mark. "Paul and Rhetoric: A *Sophos* in the Kingdom of God." In *Paul Unbound: Other Perspectives on the Apostle*, edited by Mark D. Given, 175–200. Grand Rapids: Baker Academic, 2010; 2nd ed., 2021.

Glad, Clarence. *Paul and Philodemus: Adaptability in Epicurean and Early Christian Psychagogy*. Leiden: Brill, 1995.

Goodrich, John K. "Erastus of Corinth (Romans 16.23): Responding to Recent Proposals on His Rank, Status, and Faith." *NTS* 57 (2011): 583–93.

———. "Erastus, Quaestor of Corinth: The Administrative Rank of ὁ οἰκονόμος τῆς πόλεως (Rom 16:23) in an Achaean Colony." *NTS* 56 (2010): 90–115.

———. *Paul as an Administrator of God in 1 Corinthians*. SNTSMS 152. Cambridge: Cambridge University Press, 2012.

Goulder, Michael. "Σοφία in Corinthians." *NTS* 37 (1991): 516–34.

Goulet, Richard. "Ancient Philosophers: A First Statistical Survey." In *Philosophy as a Way of Life: Ancients and Moderns; Essays in Honor of Pierre Hadot*, edited by Michael Chase, Stephen R. L. Clark, and Michael McGhee, 10–39. Oxford: Wiley Blackwell, 2013.

———. *Dictionnaire des Philosophes Anciennes*. 7 vols. Paris: CNRS Editions, 1994–2018.

Goulet-Caze, Marie-Odile. *Cynicism and Christianity in Antiquity*. Grand Rapids: Eerdmans, 2019.

Grant, Robert M. *Paul in the Roman World: The Conflict at Corinth*. Louisville: Westminster John Knox, 2001.

———. "The Wisdom of the Corinthians." In *The Joy of Study*, edited by S. E. Johnson, 51–55. New York: Macmillan, 1951.

Grindheim, Sigurd. "Wisdom for the Perfect: Paul's Challenge for the Corinthian Church (2:6–16)." *JBL* 121 (2002): 689–709.

Grosheide, Frederick. *Commentary on the First Epistle to the Corinthians*. Grand Rapids: Eerdmans, 1953.

Hall, David R. "A Disguise for the Wise: Μετασχηματισμός in 1 Corinthians 4.6." *NTS* 40 (1994): 143–49.

———. *The Unity of the Corinthian Correspondence*. London: T&T Clark, 2003.

Halliday, M. A. K., and Ruqaiya Hasan. *Language, Context, and Text: Aspects of Language in a Social-Semiotic Perspective*. Oxford: Oxford University Press, 1989.

Hanges, James C. "1 Corinthians 4:6 and the Possibility of Written Bylaws in the Corinthian Church." *JBL* 117 (1998): 275–98.

Harich-Schwarzbauer, H. "Women Philosophers." In *Der neue Pauly: Enzyklopädie der Antike*, edited by H. Cancik and H. Schneider. Stuttgart: Metzler Verlag, 1996–. https://referenceworks.brillonline.com/browse/der-neue-pauly.

Harrill, J. Albert. *Paul the Apostle: His Life and Legacy in Their Roman Context*. Cambridge: Cambridge University Press, 2012.

Harrison, James R. *Paul and the Ancient Celebrity Circuit: The Cross and Moral Transformation*. Louisville: Mohr Siebeck, 2019.

Harrison, James R., and L. L. Welborn, eds. *The First Urban Churches 2: Roman Corinth*. Writings from the Greco-Roman World Supplement 8. Atlanta: Society of Biblical Literature, 2016.

Hays, Richard B. "The Conversion of the Imagination." *NTS* 45 (1999): 391–412.

———. *1 Corinthians*. Louisville: John Knox, 1997.

Hiigel, John. *Leadership in 1 Corinthians: A Case Study in Paul's Ecclesiology*. Studies in the Bible and Early Christianity 57. Lewiston, NY: E. Mellen, 2003.

Hine, Harry. "Philosophy and *philosophi*: From Cicero to Apuleius." In *Roman Reflections: Studies in Latin Philosophy*, edited by Gareth D. Williams and Katharina Volk, 13–29. New York: Oxford University Press, 2016.

Hock, Ronald F. *The Social Context of Paul's Ministry: Tentmaking and Apostleship*. Philadelphia: Fortress, 1980.

Holloway, Paul. "Religious 'Slogans' in 1 Corinthians: Wit, Wisdom, and the Quest

Bibliography

for Status in a Roman Colony." *Journal of Theological Studies* 72 (2021): 125–54.

Holmberg, Bengt. "Methods of Historical Reconstruction." In *Christianity at Corinth: The Quest for the Pauline Church*, edited by Edward Adams and David Horrell, 255–71. Louisville: Westminster John Knox, 2004.

———. *Sociology and the New Testament: An Appraisal*. Minneapolis: Fortress, 1990.

Hooker, Morna D. "'Beyond the Things Which Are Written': An Examination of I Cor. IV. 6." *NTS* 10 (1963): 127–32.

Horrell, David. "Domestic Space and Christian Meetings at Corinth: Imagining New Contexts and the Buildings East of the Theatre." *NTS* 50 (2004): 349–69.

———. *The Social Ethos of the Corinthian Correspondence: Interests and Ideology from 1 Corinthians to 1 Clement*. Studies of the New Testament and Its World. Edinburgh: T&T Clark, 1996.

Horsley, Richard. *1 Corinthians*. Nashville: Abingdon, 1998.

———. "Pneumatikos vs. Psychikos: Distinctions of Spiritual Status among the Corinthians." *HTR* 69 (1976): 269–88.

———. "Wisdom of Words and Words of Wisdom in Corinth." *CBQ* 39 (1977): 224–39.

Hughes, Frank W., and Robert Jewett. *The Corinthian Correspondence: Redaction, Rhetoric, and History*. Minneapolis: Fortress Academic; Lanham, MD: Lexington Books, 2021.

Hurd, J. C. *The Origin of 1 Corinthians*. New York: Seabury, 1965.

Hyldahl, Niels. "Paul and Hellenistic Judaism in Corinth." In *The New Testament and Hellenistic Judaism*, edited by Peder Borgen and Soren Giversen, 204–16. Peabody, MA: Hendrickson, 1995.

Ijsseling, Samuel. *Rhetoric and Philosophy in Conflict: An Historical Survey*. Hague: M. Nijhoff, 1976.

Inkelaar, Harm-Jan. *Conflict over Wisdom: The Theme of 1 Corinthians 1–4 Rooted in Scripture*. Leuven: Peeters, 2011.

Inwood, Brad, and Lloyd P. Gerson, eds. *The Stoics Reader: Selected Writings and Testimonia*. Indianapolis: Hackett, 2008.

Johnson, Luke Timothy. "The New Testament's Anti-Jewish Slander and the Conventions of Ancient Polemic." *JBL* 108 (1989): 419–41.

Judge, E. A. "Early Christians as a Scholastic Community: Part I." *JRH* 1 (1960): 4–15.

———. "Early Christians as a Scholastic Community: Part II." *JRH* 1 (1961): 125–37.

———. *The Social Pattern of Christian Groups in the First Century*. London: Tyndale, 1960.

Kammler, H.-C. *Kreuz und Weisheit: Eine exegetische Untersuchung zu 1 Kor 1,10–3,4*. WUNT 159. Tübingen: Mohr, 2003.

Kennedy, George. *Classical Rhetoric and Its Christian and Secular Tradition from Ancient to Modern Times*. 2nd ed. Chapel Hill: University of North Carolina Press, 1999.

Ker, Donald P. "Paul and Apollos—Colleagues or Rivals?" *JSNT* 77 (2000): 75–97.

Kerferd, George B. "The Sage in Hellenistic Philosophical Literature." In *The Sage in Israel and Ancient Near East*, edited by John G. Gammie and Leo G. Perdue, 320–28. Winona Lake: Eisenbrauns, 1990.

Kloppenborg, John S. "Disciplined Exaggeration: The Heuristics of Comparison in Biblical Studies." *NovT* 59 (2017): 390–414.

Klutz, Todd E. "Re-reading 1 Corinthians after *Rethinking 'Gnosticism.'*" *JSNT* 26 (2003): 193–216.

Koester, Helmut. "The Silence of the Apostle." In *Urban Religion in Roman Corinth: Interdisciplinary Approaches*, edited by Daniel N. Schowalter and Steven J. Friesen, 339–50. HTS. Cambridge, MA: Harvard Theological Studies, Harvard Divinity School, 2005.

Kremer, Jacob. *Der erste Brief an die Korinther*. Regensburg: F. Pustet, 1997.

Krentz, Edgar. "Logos or Sophia: The Pauline Use of the Ancient Dispute between Rhetoric and Philosophy." In *Early Christianity and Classical Culture: Comparative Studies in Honor of Abraham J. Malherbe*, edited by John T. Fitzgerald, Thomas H. Olbricht, and L. Michael White, 277–90. Leiden: Brill, 2003.

Kuck, D. W. *Judgment and Community Conflict: Paul's Use of Apocalyptic Judgment Language in 1 Corinthians 3:5–4:5*. NovTSup 66. Leiden: Brill, 1992.

Kudlien, F. "Pneumatische Ärtzte." In *Real-Encyclopädie der classischen Altertumswissenschaft, Supplement 11*. Edited by A. F. von Pauly and G. Wissowa, 1097–1108. Stuttgart: Metzler, 1968.

———. "Poseidonios und die Ärtzeschule der Pneumatiker." *Hermes* 90 (1962): 419–29.

Kwon, Oh-Young. "A Critical Review of Recent Scholarship on the Pauline Opposition and the Nature of Its Wisdom (σοφία) in 1 Corinthians 1–4." *CurBR* 8 (2010): 386–427.

Lampe, Peter. Review of *The Routledge Handbook of the Stoic Tradition*, ed. John Sellars. *Bryn Mawr Classical Review*. https://bmcr.brynmawr.edu/2017/2017.06.30/.

———. "Theological Wisdom and the 'Word about the Cross': The Rhetorical Scheme in 1 Corinthians 1–4." *Int* 44 (1990): 117–31.

Lang, Friedrich. *Die Briefe an die Korinther*. Göttingen: Vandenhoeck & Ruprecht, 1994.

Lang, T. J. "We Speak in a Mystery: Neglected Greek Evidence for the Syntax and Sense of 1 Corinthians 2:7." *CBQ* 78 (2016): 68–89.

Lautenschlager, Markus. "Abschied vom Disputierer: Zur Bedeutung von συζητητής in 1 Kor 1,20." *ZNW* 83 (1992): 276–85.

Lee, Max J. *Moral Transformation in Greco-Roman Philosophy of Mind*. WUNT 2/515. Tübingen: Mohr Siebeck, 2020.

———. "Negotiating Piety: Epicureans, Corinthian Knowers, and Paul on Idols and Idol Food in 1 Cor 8–10." In *Practicing Intertextuality*, edited by Max J. Lee and B. J. Oropeza, 148–66. Eugene, OR: Cascade, 2021.

———. "A Taxonomy of Intertextual Interactions Practiced by NT Authors: An Introduction." In *Practicing Intertextuality*, edited by Max J. Lee and B. J. Oropeza, 3–16. Eugene, OR: Cascade, 2021.

Levison, John R. "Did the Spirit Inspire Rhetoric?" In *Persuasive Artistry*, edited by Duane F. Watson, 25–40. Sheffield: Sheffield Academic, 1991.

Lightfoot, J. B. *Notes on the Epistles of St. Paul*. Edited by J. R. Harmer. London: Macmillan, 1895. Reprint, Grand Rapids: Baker, 1980.

Lim, Timothy. "Not in Persuasive Words of Wisdom, but in the Demonstration of the Spirit and Power (1 Cor 2:4)." *NovT* 29 (1987): 137–49.

Lindemann, Andreas. *Der erste Korintherbrief*. Handbuch zum Neuen Testament. Tübingen: Mohr Siebeck, 2000.

Litfin, Duane. *St. Paul's Theology of Proclamation: 1 Corinthians 1–4 and Greco-Roman Rhetoric*. SNTSMS 79. Cambridge: Cambridge University Press, 1994.

Long, A. A. "Roman Philosophy." In *The Cambridge Companion to Greek and Roman Philosophy*, edited by David N. Sedley, 184–210. Cambridge: Cambridge University Press, 2003.

Long, A. A., and D. N. Sedley. *The Hellenistic Philosophers*. 2 vols. London: Cambridge University Press, 1987.

Long, A. G. *Plato and the Stoics*. Cambridge: Cambridge University Press, 2013.

Longenecker, Bruce. "Exposing the Economic Middle: A Revised Economy Scale for the Study of Early Christianity." *JSNT* 31 (2009): 243–78.

———. *Remember the Poor: Paul, Poverty, and the Greco-Roman World*. Grand Rapids: Eerdmans, 2010.

Lüdemann, Gerd. *Paulus der Heidenapostle, II: Antipaulinismus im frühen Christentum*. Göttingen: Vandenhoeck & Ruprecht, 1983.

Lütgert, W. *Freiheitspredigt und Schwarmgeister in Korinth.* Göttingen: C. Bertelsman, 1908.

Lutz, Cora E. *Musonius Rufus, the Roman Socrates.* Yale Classical Studies 10. New Haven: Yale University Press, 1947.

Lyons, George. *Pauline Autobiography.* SBLDS 73. Atlanta: Scholars, 1985.

Malherbe, Abraham J., ed. *The Cynic Epistles: A Study Edition.* Missoula, MT: Scholars, 1977.

———. "Exhortation in First Thessalonians." *NovT* 25 (1983): 238–56.

———. "'Gentle as a Nurse': The Cynic Background to 1 Thess II." *NovT* 12 (1970): 203–17.

———. "Hellenistic Moralists and the New Testament." *ANRW* 26.1:267–333.

———. *The Letters to the Thessalonians: A New Translation with Introduction and Commentary.* New Haven: Yale University Press, 2004.

———. *Paul and the Popular Philosophers.* Minneapolis: Fortress, 1989.

———. *Paul and the Thessalonians: The Philosophic Tradition of Pastoral Care.* Philadelphia: Fortress, 1987.

———. *Social Aspects of Early Christianity.* Philadelphia: Fortress, 1983.

Markovich, Daniel. *Promoting a New Kind of Education: Greek and Roman Philosophical Protreptic.* International Studies in the History of Rhetoric 16. Leiden: Brill, 2021.

Marshall, Peter. *Enmity in Corinth: Social Conventions in Paul's Relations with the Corinthians.* WUNT 2/23. Tübingen: Mohr Siebeck, 1987.

Martin, Dale B. *Corinthian Body.* New Haven: Yale University Press, 1995.

———. "Paul and the Judaism/Hellenism Dichotomy." In *Paul beyond the Judaism/Hellenism Divide*, edited by Troels Engberg-Pedersen, 29–62. Louisville: Westminster John Knox, 2001.

———. *Slavery as Salvation: The Metaphor of Slavery in Pauline Christianity.* New Haven: Yale University Press, 1990.

Meeks, Wayne. *The First Urban Christians.* New Haven: Yale University Press, 1983.

Mihaila, Corin. *The Paul-Apollos Relationship and Paul's Stance Toward Greco-Roman Rhetoric.* LNTS 402. New York: T&T Clark, 2009.

Miller, Anna C. "Not with Eloquent Wisdom: Democratic *Ekklēsia* Discourse in 1 Corinthians 1–4." *JSNT* 35 (2013): 323–54.

Miller, Gene. "Archontōn Tou Aiōnos Toutou: A New Look at 1 Corinthians 2:6–8." *JBL* 91 (1972): 522–8.

Millis, Benjamin. "The Social and Ethnic Origins of the Colonists in Early Roman Corinth." In *Corinth in Context: Comparative Studies on Religion and Society*, edited by Steven J. Friesen, Daniel N. Schowalter, and James C. Walters, 13–36. Leiden: Brill, 2010.

Bibliography

Mitchell, Alan. "Rich and Poor in the Courts of Corinth: Litigiousness and Status in 1 Cor 6:1–11." *NTS* 39 (1993): 562–86.

Mitchell, Margaret M. *Paul and the Rhetoric of Reconciliation.* Louisville: Westminster John Knox, 1993.

Moffatt, J. *The First Epistle of Paul to the Corinthians.* London: Hodder & Stoughton, 1938.

Morgan, Teresa. *Literate Education in the Hellenistic and Roman World.* Cambridge: Cambridge University Press, 1999.

Moses, Robert Ewusie. *Practices of Power: Revisiting the Principalities and Powers in the Pauline Letters.* Minneapolis: Fortress, 2014.

Moule, C. F. D. *An Idiom Book of New Testament Greek.* Cambridge: Cambridge University Press, 1959.

Munck, Johannes. "Menigheden uden Partier." *Dansk Teologisk Tidsskrift* 15 (1952): 215–33. ET: "The Church without Factions: Studies in 1 Corinthians 1–4." In *Paul and the Salvation of Mankind*, 135–67. London: SCM, 1959.

———. *Paulus und die Heilsgeschichte.* Copenhagen: E. Muncksgard, 1954. ET: *Paul and the Salvation of Mankind.* London: SCM, 1959.

Murphy-O'Connor, Jerome. "Co-authorship in the Corinthian Correspondence." *RB* 100 (1993): 562–79.

———. "Corinthian Slogans in 1 Cor. 6:12–20." *CBQ* 40 (1978): 391–96.

———. *Paul: A Critical Life.* Oxford: Oxford University Press, 1996.

———. *St. Paul's Corinth: Texts and Archaeology.* Collegeville, MN: Liturgical, 2002.

Naselli, Andrew David. "Is Every Sin outside the Body except Immoral Sex? Weighing whether 1 Corinthians 6:18b Is Paul's Statement or a Corinthian Slogan." *JBL* 136 (2017): 969–87.

Needham, Rodney. "Polythetic Classification: Convergence and Consequences." *Man* 10 (1975): 349–69.

Nguyen, V. H. T. *Christian Identity in Corinth: A Comparative Study of 2 Corinthians, Epictetus, and Valerius Maximus.* Tübingen: Mohr Siebeck, 2008.

Oakes, Peter. *Reading Romans in Pompeii.* Minneapolis: Fortress; London: SPCK, 2009.

O'Day, Gail R. "Jeremiah 9:22–23 and 1 Corinthians 1:26–31: A Study in Intertextuality." *JBL* 109 (1990): 259–67.

Økland, Jorunn. "Ceres, κόρη, and Cultural Complexity." In *Corinth in Context: Comparative Studies on Religion and Society*, edited by Steven J. Friesen, Daniel N. Schowalter, and James C. Walters, 199–229. Leiden: Brill, 2010.

Oliver, James H. "The *Diadochē* at Athens under the Humanistic Emperors." *The American Journal of Philology* 98 (1977): 160–78.

Omanson, Roger L. "Acknowledging Paul's Quotations." *BT* 43 (1992): 201–13.
O'Neil, Edward. *Teles (The Cynic Teacher)*. Missoula, MT: Scholars, 1977.
Paige, Terrence. "Stoicism, *Eleutheria*, and Community at Corinth." In *Worship, Theology and Ministry in the Early Church*, edited by Michael J. Wilkins and Terrence Paige, 180–93. Sheffield: JSOT Press, 1992.
Parsons, Mikeal C. "Sarkinos, Sarkikos in Codices F and G: A Text-Critical Note." *NTS* 34 (1988): 151–55.
Pascuzzi, Maria. "Baptism-Based Allegiance and the Divisions in Corinth: A Reexamination of 1 Corinthians 1:13–17." *CBQ* 71 (2009): 813–29.
Patterson, Stephen J. "The Baptists of Corinth: Paul, the Partisans of Apollos, and the History of Baptism in Nascent Christianity." In *Stones, Bones and the Sacred: Essays on Material Culture and Religion in Honor of Dennis E. Smith*, edited by Alan H. Cadwallader, 315–27. Early Christianity and Its Literature 21. Atlanta: SBL Press, 2016.
Pearson, B. A. *Pneumatikos-Psychikos Terminology in 1 Corinthians*. Missoula: Society of Biblical Literature for the Nag Hammadi Seminar, 1973.
Penella, Robert. *The Letters of Apollonius of Tyana*. Leiden: Brill, 1979.
Perelman, Chaim, and L. Olbrechts-Tyteca. *The New Rhetoric: A Treatise on Argumentation*. Translated by J. Wilkinson and P. Weaver. Notre Dame: University of Notre Dame Press, 1969; paperback ed., 1971.
Petit, Caroline. *Galien. Le médecin. Introduction*. Collection des Universités de France. Paris: Les Belles Lettres, 2009.
Pike, Kenneth L. *Language in Relation to a Unified Theory of Human Behavior*. 2nd ed. University of Illinois, Summer Institute of Linguistics, 1954.
Pilgaard, Aage. "The Hellenistic *Theios Aner*." In *The New Testament and Hellenistic Judaism*, edited by Peder Borgen and Soren Giversen, 101–22. Peabody, MA: Hendrickson, 1995.
Plessis, Johannes du. *Teleios: The Idea of Perfection in the New Testament*. Kampen: J. H. Kock, 1959.
Pogoloff, Stephen M. *Logos and Sophia: The Rhetorical Situation of 1 Corinthians*. SBLDS 134. Atlanta: Scholars, 1992.
Prothro, James B. "Who Is 'of Christ'? A Grammatical and Theological Reconstruction of 1 Cor 1.12." *NTS* 60 (2014): 250–65.
Reichel, G. *Quaestiones Progymnasmaticae*. PhD diss., University of Leipzig, 1909.
Reitzenstein, R. *Die Hellenistischen Mysterienreligionen: Ihre Grundgedanken und Wirkungen*. Berlin: Teubner, 1927.
Reydams-Schils, Gretchen. *The Roman Stoics: Self-Responsibility, and Affection*. Chicago: University of Chicago, 2005.
Rist, J. M. "Seneca and Stoic Orthodoxy." *ANRW* 2.36:1993–2012.

Bibliography

Rizakis, A. D., and S. Zoumbaki. *Roman Peloponnese I. Roman Personal Names in Their Social Context [Achaia, Arcadia, Argolis, Corinthia and Eleia]*. Meletemata 31. Athens: Research Centre for Greek and Roman Antiquity, 2001.

Robertson, Archibald, and Alfred Plummer. *A Critical and Exegetical Commentary on the First Epistle of St. Paul to the Corinthians*. ICC. Edinburgh: T&T Clark, 1914.

Robinson, James M. "Kerygma and History in the New Testament." In *Trajectories through Early Christianity*, edited by Helmut Koester, 20–70. Philadelphia: Fortress, 1971.

Robinson, James M., and Helmut Koester. *Trajectories through Early Christianity*. Philadelphia: Fortress, 1971.

Sandmel, Samuel. "Parallelomania." *JBL* 81 (1962): 1–13.

Schliesser, Benjamin. "Striefzüge durch die strassen von korinth: Wer waren die ersten christusgläubigen der stadt und wo trafen sie sich." In *Paulus und die christliche Gemeinde in Korinth: Historisch-kulturelle und theologische Aspekte*, edited by Jacob Thiessen and Christian Stettler, 9–53. Göttingen: Vandenhoeck & Ruprecht, 2020.

Schmeller, Thomas. "Dissimulatio artis? Paulus und die antike Rhetorik." *NTS* 66 (2020): 500–520.

———. *Schulen im neuen Testament? Zur Stellung des Urchristentums in der Bildungswelt seiner Zeit*. HbibS 30. Freiburg: Herder, 2001.

Schmidt, J. E. C. *Bibliothek für Kritik und Exegese des Neuen Testaments und älteste Christengeschicthe*. Vol. 2.3. n.p.: Hadamar, 1801.

Schmithals, Walter. *Die Gnosis in Korinth: Eine Untersuchung zu den Korintherbriefen*. Göttingen: Vandenhoeck & Ruprecht, 1969. ET: *Gnosticism in Corinth: An Investigation of the Letters to the Corinthians*. Nashville: Abingdon, 1971.

Schmitz, Philip. *"Cato Peripateticus"—stoicische und peripatetische Ethik im Dialog: Cic. fin. 3 und der Aristotelismus des ersten Jh. v. Chr [Xenarchos, Boethos und 'Areios Didymos']*. Untersuchungen zur antiken Literatur und Geschichte 113. Berlin: de Gruyter, 2014.

Schrage, Wolfgang. *Der erste Brief an die Korinther*. 4 vols. EKKNT 7. Zürich: Benziger Verlag, 1991–2001.

Sedley, David N. Introduction to *The Cambridge Companion to Greek and Roman Philosophy*, edited by David N. Sedley, 1–19. Cambridge: Cambridge University Press, 2003.

———. "Philosophical Allegiance in the Greco-Roman World." In *Philosophia Togata*, edited by Mirian Griffin and J. Barnes, 97–119. Oxford: Clarendon, 1989.

———. "The School, from Zeno to Arius Didymus." In *Cambridge Companion to the Stoics*, edited by Brad Inwood, 7–32. Cambridge: Cambridge University Press, 2002.

———. "Self-Sufficiency as a Divine Attribute in Greek Philosophy." In *Ecology and Theology in the Ancient World: Cross-Disciplinary Perspectives*, edited by A. Hunt and H. Marlow, 41–47. London: Bloomsbury, 2019.

Sellars, John. *The Art of Living: The Stoics on the Nature and Function of Philosophy*. Ashgate New Critical Thinking in Philosophy. Aldershot/Burlington: Ashgate, 2003.

———. Introduction to *The Routledge Handbook of the Stoic Tradition*, edited by John Sellars, 1–13. Routledge Handbooks in Philosophy. London: Routledge, 2016.

Sellin, Gerhard. "Das 'Geheimnis' der Weisheit und das Rätsel der 'Christuspartei' (au 1 Kor 1–4)." *ZNW* 73 (1982): 69–96.

Senft, C. *La Première épître de Saint Paul aux Corinthiens*. Commentaire du Nouveau Testament. 2nd ed. Geneva: Labor et Fides, 1990.

Smit, Joop F. M. "Epideictic Rhetoric in Paul's First Letter to the Corinthians 1–4." *Bib* 84 (2003): 184–201.

———. "'What Is Apollos? What Is Paul?' In Search for the Coherence of First Corinthians 1:10–4:21." *NovT* 44 (2002): 231–51.

Smith, Claire S. *Pauline Communities as 'Scholastic Communities': A Study of the Vocabulary of 'Teaching' in 1 Corinthians, 1 and 2 Timothy and Titus*. WUNT 2. Reihe 335. Tübingen: Mohr Siebeck, 2012.

Smith, Jay E. "1 Corinthians 6:13–14: Isolating Slogans, Rethinking Soma, 'Correcting' Translations." Paper presented at the annual meeting of the Southwest Commission on Religious Studies, Irving, TX, March 10, 2012.

———. "The Roots of a 'Libertine' Slogan in 1 Corinthians 6:18." *Journal of Theological Studies* 59 (2008): 63–95.

———. "Slogans in 1 Corinthians." *BSac* 167 (2010): 74–86.

Smith, Jonathan Z. *Drudgery Divine: On the Comparison of Early Christianities and the Religions of Late Antiquity*. Chicago: University of Chicago Press, 1990.

———. *Map Is Not Territory: Studies in the History of Religions*. Chicago: University of Chicago Press, 1982.

———. "Re: Corinthians." In *Redescribing Paul and the Corinthians*, edited by R. Cameron and M. P. Miller, 17–34. Atlanta: Society of Biblical Literature, 2011.

Smith, Richard Upsher. *A Glossary of Terms in Grammar, Rhetoric, and Prosody for Readers of Greek and Latin: A Vade Mecum*. Mundelein, IL: Bolchazy-Carducci Publishers, 2011.

Bibliography

Smyth, Herbert W. *Greek Grammar*. Cambridge, MA: Harvard University Press, 1956.

Snyder, Gregory H. "'Not Subjects of a Despot': Stoics." In *Teachers and Texts in the Ancient World: Philosophers, Jews and Christians*, 14–44. London: Routledge, 2000.

Spengel, Leonardus, ed. *Rhetores Graeci*. Vol. 2. Leipzig: Teubner, 1854.

Stanley, Christopher D. *Paul and the Language of Scripture: Citation Technique in the Pauline Epistles and Contemporary Literature*. Cambridge: Cambridge University Press, 1992.

Sterling, Gregory E. "The Love of Wisdom: Middle Platonism and Stoicism in the Wisdom of Solomon." In *From Stoicism to Platonism: The Development of Philosophy, 100 BCE–100 CE*, edited by Troels Engberg-Pedersen, 198–213. Cambridge: Cambridge University Press, 2017.

Still, E. Coye, III. "Divisions over Leaders and Food Offered to Idols: The Parallel Thematic Structures of 1 Corinthians 4:6–21 and 8:1–11:1." *TynBul* 55 (2004): 17–41.

Stowers, Stanley. "Does Pauline Christianity Resemble a Hellenistic Philosophy?" In *Paul beyond the Judaism/Hellenism Divide*, edited by Troels Engberg-Pedersen, 81–102. Louisville: Westminster John Knox, 2001.

———. "Social Status, Public Speaking and Private Teaching: The Circumstances of Paul's Preaching Activity." *NovT* (1984): 59–82.

Sturgeon, Mary C. *The Gymnasium Area: Sculpture*. Corinth 23.1. Athens: American School of Classical Studies at Athens, 2022.

Sudhaus, Siegfried, ed. *Philodemi Volumina Rhetorica*. Vol. 1. Leipzig, Teubner, 1892.

Sumney, Jerry. *Identifying Paul's Opponents: The Question of Method in 2 Corinthians*. Sheffield: JSOT Press, 1990.

Talbert, Charles. *Reading Corinthians: A Literary and Theological Commentary*. Macon, GA: Smyth & Helwys, 2002.

Theissen, Gerd. "Social Conflicts in the Corinthian Correspondence: Further Remarks on J. J. Meggitt, *Paul, Poverty and Survival*." *JSNT* (2003): 371–91.

———. "Social Integration and Sacramental Activity: An Analysis of 1 Cor. 11:17–34." In *The Social Setting of Pauline Christianity*, 145–74. Philadelphia: Fortress, 1982.

———. *Studien zur Soziologie des Urchristentums*. ET: *The Social Setting of Pauline Christianity*. Philadelphia: Fortress, 1982.

Thiselton, Anthony C. *The First Epistle to the Corinthians*. NIGTC. Grand Rapids: Eerdmans, 2000.

———. "Realized Eschatology at Corinth." *NTS* 24 (1978): 510–26.

Thorsteinsson, Runar. "Jesus Christ and the Wise Man: Paul and Seneca on Moral Sages." In *Paul and Seneca in Dialogue*, edited by Joseph R. Dodson and David E. Briones, 73–87. Leiden: Brill, 2017.

———. *Roman Christianity and Roman Stoicism: A Comparative Study of Ancient Morality*. Oxford: Oxford University Press, 2010.

Tiede, D. L. *The Charismatic Figure as Miracle Worker*. Missoula, MT: Scholars, 1972.

Tod, Marcus N. "Sidelights on Greek Philosophers." *The Journal of Hellenic Studies* 77 (1957): 132–41.

Toit, David S. du. *Theios Anthropos: Zur Verwendung von 'Theios Anthropos' und sinnverwandten Ausdrücken in der Literatur der Kaiserzeit*. WUNT 2/91. Tübingen: Mohr Siebeck, 1997.

Tomlin, Graham. "Christians and Epicureans in 1 Corinthians." *JSNT* 68 (1997): 51–72.

Townsend, J. T. "Ancient Education in the Time of the Early Roman Empire." In *The Catacombs and the Colosseum*, edited by J. Benko and S. O'Rourke, 139–63. Valley Forge, PA: Judson, 1971.

Tyler, Ronald L. "First Corinthians 4:6 and Hellenistic Pedagogy." *CBQ* 60 (1998): 97–103.

———. "The History of the Interpretation of τὸ μὴ ὑπὲρ ἃ γέγραπται in 1 Corinthians 4:6." *RQ* 43 (2001): 243–52.

Vos, Craig Steven de. *Church and Community Conflicts: The Relationships of the Thessalonian, Corinthian, and Philippian Churches with Their Wider Civic Communities*. SBLDS 168. Atlanta: Scholars, 1999.

Walters, J. "Civic Identity in Roman Corinth and Its Impact on Early Christians." In *Urban Religion in Roman Corinth: Interdisciplinary Approaches*, edited by Daniel N. Schowalter and Steven J. Friesen, 339–50. HTS. Cambridge, MA: Harvard Theological Studies, Harvard Divinity School, 2005.

Watson, Edward W., and Martin M. Culy. *Quoting Corinthians: Identifying Slogans and Quotations in 1 Corinthians*. Eugene, OR: Pickwick, 2018.

Weiss, Alexander. "Keine Quästoren in Korinth: Zu Goodrichs (und Theissens) These über das Amt des Erastos (Röm 16.23)." *NTS* 56 (2010): 576–81.

———. *Soziale Elite und Christentum: Studien zu ordo-Angehörigen unter den frühen Christen*. Millennium-Studien/Millennium Studies 52. Berlin: de Gruyter, 2015.

Weiss, Johannes. *Der erste Korintherbrief*. Göttingen: Vandenhoeck & Ruprecht, 1910.

Welborn, L. L. *End to Enmity: Paul and the 'Wrongdoer' of 2 Corinthians*. Berlin: de Gruyter, 2011.

———. "Μωρὸς γενέσθω: Paul's Appropriation of the Role of the Fool in 1 Corinthians 1–4." *BibInt* 10 (2002): 420–35.

———. "On the Discord in Corinth: 1 Corinthians 1–4 and Ancient Politics." *JBL* 106 (1987): 85–111.

———. *Paul, the Fool of Christ: 1 Cor 1–4 in the Comic-Philosophic Tradition*. London: T&T Clark, 2005.

———. *Politics and Rhetoric in the Corinthian Epistles*. Macon, GA: Mercer University Press, 1997.

White, Devin L. *Teacher of the Nations: Ancient Educational Traditions and Paul's Argument in 1 Corinthians 1–4*. BZNW 227. Berlin: de Gruyter, 2017.

Wickkiser, B. L. "Asklepios in Greek and Roman Corinth." In *Corinth in Context: Comparative Studies on Religion and Society*, edited by Steven J. Friesen, Daniel N. Schowalter, and James C. Walters, 37–66. Leiden: Brill, 2010.

Wilckens, Ulrich. *Weisheit und Torheit*. BHT 26. Tübingen: Mohr, 1959.

Willet, Rinse. "Whirlwind of Numbers: Demographic Experiments for Roman Corinth." *Ancient Society* 42 (2012): 127–58.

Williams, Demetrius K. "Paul's Anti-imperial 'Discourse of the Cross': The Cross and Power in 1 Corinthians 1–4." *Society of Biblical Literature Seminar Papers* 39 (2000): 796–823.

Williams, Gareth D., and Katharina Volk, eds. *Roman Reflections: Studies in Latin Philosophy*. New York: Oxford University Press, 2016.

Willis, Wendel. "Corinthusne deletus est?" *BZ* 35 (1991): 233–41.

Winter, Bruce W. *After Paul Left Corinth: The Influence of Secular Ethics and Social Change*. Grand Rapids: Eerdmans, 2001.

———. "Philo and Paul among the Sophists: A Hellenistic Jewish and a Christian Response." PhD diss., Macquarie University, 1988.

———. *Philo and Paul among the Sophists: A Hellenistic and a Christian Response*. Cambridge: Cambridge University Press, 1997.

———. *Philo and Paul among the Sophists: Alexandrian and Corinthian Responses to a Julio-Claudian Movement*. 2nd ed. Grand Rapids: Eerdmans, 2002.

———. "Rhetoric." In *The Dictionary of Paul and His Letters*, edited by Gerald F. Hawthorne and Ralph P. Martin, 820–22. Downers Grove, IL: InterVarsity, 1993.

Wire, Antoinette Clark. *The Corinthian Women Prophets: A Reconstruction through Paul's Rhetoric*. Philadelphia: Fortress, 1990.

Wiseman, James. "Corinth and Rome I: 228 BC–AD 267." *ANRW* 7.1:438–548.

Witetschek, Stephan. "Peter in Corinth? A Review of the Evidence from 1 Corinthians." *Journal of Theological Studies* 69 (2018): 66–82.

Witherington, Ben. *Conflict and Community in Corinth: A Socio-rhetorical Commentary on 1 and 2 Corinthians*. Grand Rapids: Eerdmans, 1995.

Wolff, Christian. *Der erste Brief des Paulus an die Korinther*. Leipzig: Evangelische Verlagsanstalt, 1996.

Wuellner, Wilhelm. "Haggadic Homily Genre in 1 Corinthians 1–3." *JSNT* 89 (1970): 199–204.

Yamauchi, Edwin M. *Pre-Christian Gnosticism*. Grand Rapids: Eerdmans, 1973.

———. "Pre-Christian Gnosticism Reconsidered a Decade Later." In *Pre-Christian Gnosticism: A Survey of the Proposed Evidences*, 187–249. Grand Rapids: Baker Book House, 1983.

Young, Norman. "Paidagogos: The Social Setting of a Pauline Metaphor." *NovT* 29 (1987): 150–76.

Index of Authors

Adams, Edward, 6, 13, 191, 265, 273, 292
Ahlholm, Tuuli, 277, 278, 280, 281, 282, 283–86, 297
Alexander, Loveday, 37, 249, 251–52, 254, 263, 279
Allo, E. B., 99
Anderson, R. Dean, 57, 90, 99, 138, 164

Baird, William, 5, 118, 169, 240, 262
Balch, David L., 292
Barclay, John M. G., 8, 20, 21, 41, 70, 76, 80, 81, 208, 220, 221–22, 228, 240, 293, 294
Barnett, Paul W., 4, 5, 54, 68, 150, 240, 267
Barrett, C. K., 4, 99, 239, 240, 255, 291
Baur, F. C., 6, 131
Berger, Peter L., 64
Betz, Hans Dieter, 84, 208, 225
Biber, D., 18
Billings, Bradly S., 292
Bitner, Bradley J., 8, 17, 137, 139, 163, 166, 167, 240, 302
Bonazzi, Mauro, 37
Boyarin, Daniel, 35
Boys-Stones, G. R., 35, 247
Branick, V. P., 4, 5, 21, 133, 142
Brookins, Timothy A., 7, 21, 22, 23–24, 25, 51, 57, 86, 89, 142, 156, 211, 213, 221, 257, 296, 300, 301, 303
Brunschwig, Jacques, 30

Brunt, P. A., 276
Bullinger, E. W., 154
Bullmore, Michael, 10, 14, 15, 58, 83, 84, 99, 102
Butts, James R., 72
Byron, John, 151

Castelli, Elizabeth Anne, 191
Chester, Stephen J., 7, 13, 22, 183, 240, 267, 271
Chow, John, 8, 10, 13, 137, 240, 295
Ciampa, Roy E., 13, 68, 97, 98
Clarke, Andrew, 8, 13, 17, 169, 179, 240, 267, 295
Collins, Raymond, 58, 84, 88, 97, 154
Conrad, S., 18
Conzelmann, Hans, 5, 6, 42, 99, 107, 151, 152, 208, 253
Coughlin, Sean, 213–15, 254
Cribiore, Raffaella, 279
Culy, Martin M., 23, 117

Dahl, Nils, 150, 191, 195, 197, 201, 240
Davis, James A., 5, 6, 7, 10, 69, 84, 114, 118, 121, 208, 209, 216, 240, 262
Deming, Will, 221
De Witt, Normann Wentworth, 7, 110
Dingeldein, Laura B., 124
Divjanović, Kristin, 33

INDEX OF AUTHORS

Dodson, Joseph R., 16, 62
Doughty, Darrell, 183
Downing, F. Gerald, 7, 33, 36, 37, 176, 203, 226, 281
Dunn, James D. G., 13
Dutch, Robert S., 8, 202, 203, 256, 257, 258, 291

Edwards, Catherine, 157
Engberg-Pedersen, Troels, 16, 20, 32, 33, 34–35, 36, 37, 39, 41, 43, 226, 230, 249, 254
Erler, Michael, 260

Fee, Gordon, 5, 21, 58, 97, 121, 149, 151, 152, 153, 169, 172, 196, 197, 199, 216, 240, 262, 294
Ferguson, Everett, 34
Finney, Mark T., 8, 10, 13, 20, 22, 69, 70, 76, 93, 146, 169, 240, 252
Fiore, Benjamin, 136, 167, 176, 240
Fitzgerald, John T., 11, 53, 186
Fitzmyer, Joseph, 22
Francis, James M. M., 133
Frid, Bo, 109, 110
Friesen, Courtney J. P., 186
Friesen, Steven J., 240, 274, 291, 299, 300, 301
Funk, Robert, 5, 22, 77, 88, 119, 240

Garcilazo, Albert V., 23
Garland, David E., 97, 152, 153, 273
Georgi, Dieter, 255
Gerring, John, 35
Gerson, Lloyd P., 28, 62
Gill, Christopher, 31, 32, 38, 247, 276
Gill, David W. J., 273
Given, Mark, 92
Glad, Clarence, 254
Goodrich, John K., 151, 291, 292, 301
Goulder, Michael, 6, 131, 291
Goulet, Richard, 285–86
Goulet-Caze, Marie-Odile, 203
Grant, Robert M., 7, 71, 176, 226, 258, 273
Grosheide, Frederick, 153, 154

Hall, David R., 22, 164
Halliday, M. A. K., 17
Hanges, James C., 166, 167

Harich-Schwarzbauer, H., 62
Harrill, J. Albert, 35
Harrison, James R., 193, 273
Hasan, Ruqaiya, 17
Hays, Richard B., 7, 157, 176, 183, 293
Hessler, Jan Erik, 260
Hiigel, John, 13, 15, 179, 180, 194
Hine, Harry, 276
Hock, Ronald F., 8, 10, 184, 240, 256, 295
Holloway, Paul, 191, 295
Holmberg, Bengt, 13
Hooker, Morna D., 163–64, 165, 166
Horrell, David, 6, 8, 15, 273, 292, 295
Horsley, Richard, 6, 10, 13, 22, 56, 69, 117, 119, 120, 180, 185, 208, 210–11, 217, 218, 240, 291
Hughes, Frank W., 4
Hurd, J. C., 4, 7
Hyldahl, Niels, 10, 180, 209, 232

Inkelaar, Harm-Jan, 4, 5, 21, 61, 62, 107, 113, 139, 160, 209, 240
Inwood, Brad, 28, 62

Jewett, Robert, 4
Johnson, Luke Timothy, 135, 250
Judge, E. A., 12, 253, 255, 294, 295

Kammler, H.-C., 107
Kennedy, George, 14, 83, 84
Ker, Donald P., 10, 139
Kerferd, George B., 62
Kloppenborg, John S., 40, 41
Klutz, Todd E., 6, 14
Koester, Helmut, 35, 240
Kremer, Jacob, 22
Krentz, Edgar, 52, 53, 83, 84, 90, 106
Kuck, D. W., 5, 6, 7, 64, 141–42, 146, 150, 176, 183
Kudlien, F., 214
Kwon, Oh-Young, 6, 14, 16, 57, 90

Lampe, Peter, 34, 66, 84, 240
Lang, Friedrich, 154
Lang, T. J., 108, 109
Lautenschlager, Markus, 61
Lee, Max J., 16, 31, 43, 44, 47, 120, 122, 127, 157, 158, 209, 229, 249, 260, 269, 308
Levison, John R., 84, 102

Index of Authors

Lewis, Orley, 213–14
Lightfoot, J. B., 83, 88, 146, 147–48, 157, 176, 181, 258
Lim, Timothy, 15, 84, 87, 102
Lindemann, Andreas, 83
Litfin, Duane, 9, 10, 14, 15, 16, 24, 53, 54, 57, 58, 65, 66, 67, 72, 77, 78, 79, 83, 84, 85, 88, 89, 90, 92, 96, 97, 102, 104, 105, 114, 144, 174, 196, 199, 240, 255, 262, 272
Long, A. A., 29, 32, 46, 62, 212, 276, 277, 280
Long, A. G., 28
Longenecker, Bruce W., 299, 300, 301, 303
Luckman, Thomas, 64
Lüdemann, Gerd, 131
Lütgert, W., 6, 18, 131, 240
Lyons, George, 21

Malherbe, Abraham J., 12, 13, 19, 33, 86, 115, 133, 168, 192, 193, 202, 203, 254, 280, 294, 295
Markovich, Daniel, 168
Marshall, Peter, 8, 10, 13, 15, 20, 84, 105, 150, 169, 174, 179–80, 181, 184, 195, 196, 240, 295, 298
Martin, Dale B., 7, 8, 17, 35, 55–56, 70, 72, 84, 89, 102, 115, 117, 151, 169, 200, 208, 213, 240, 295
Meeks, Wayne, 8, 12, 240, 253, 254, 265, 267, 294, 295, 299, 300, 301
Mihaila, Corin, 10, 14, 57, 76, 77, 83, 84, 92, 97, 102, 127, 128, 131, 163, 240
Miller, Anna C., 11, 181
Miller, Gene, 110
Millis, Benjamin, 274
Mitchell, Alan, 295
Mitchell, Margaret M., 4, 11, 37, 138, 144, 145, 150, 151, 152, 242–44, 246, 247, 252, 261, 263, 264, 268, 295
Morgan, Teresa, 72, 278
Moses, Robert Ewusie, 110
Moule, C. F. D., 98
Munck, Johannes, 14, 69, 139, 191, 240, 251
Murphy-O'Connor, Jerome, 6, 68, 107, 180, 223, 292, 293, 295

Naselli, Andrew David, 22, 223
Needham, Rodney, 36
Nguyen, V. H. T., 273

Oakes, Peter, 256
O'Day, Gail R., 80
Økland, Jorunn, 274
Olbrechts-Tyteca, L., 38
Oliver, James H., 284
Omanson, Roger L., 117

Paige, Terrence, 7, 176, 291, 295
Parsons, Mikeal C., 118, 119
Pascuzzi, Maria, 10
Patterson, Stephen J., 5, 267
Pearson, B. A., 7, 10, 13, 21, 69, 113, 207, 208, 209, 210, 211, 240
Penella, Robert, 286
Perelman, Chaim, 38
Petit, Caroline, 244
Petrucci, Federico M., 260
Pike, Kenneth L., 36
Pilgaard, Aage, 226
Pitts, Andrew W., 16
Plessis, Johannes du, 107, 127
Plummer, Alfred, 4, 154, 157
Pogoloff, Stephen M., 5, 8, 9, 10, 13, 19, 24, 53, 54, 55, 57, 70, 72, 87, 88, 89, 94–96, 102, 105, 110, 115, 144, 169, 179, 182, 240
Prothro, James B., 240, 262, 267

Reitzenstein, R., 111
Reydams-Schils, Gretchen, 158
Rist, J. M., 31, 248
Rizakis, A. D., 287
Robinson, James M., 35
Rosner, Brian S., 13, 68, 97, 98

Sandmel, Samuel, 11
Schliesser, Benjamin, 296
Schmeller, Thomas, 92, 241, 253, 264
Schmidt, J. E. C., 6, 131
Schmithals, Walter, 6, 18, 19, 21, 131, 207
Schmitz, Philip, 33
Schowalter, Daniel N., 274
Schrage, Wolfgang, 22
Sedley, David N., 28, 29, 30, 32, 38, 39, 46,

115, 168, 212, 219, 245, 247, 248, 259, 260, 275, 276, 280
Sellars, John, 34, 158
Sellin, Gerhard, 4, 131, 240
Smit, Joop F. M., 10, 58, 61, 102, 136, 137, 139
Smith, Claire S., 258
Smith, Jay E., 22, 223
Smith, Jonathan Z., 40
Smith, Richard Upsher, 88
Smyth, Herbert W., 154, 233
Snyder, Gregory H., 247, 260
Spengel, Leonardus, 204
Stanley, Christopher D., 143
Sterling, Gregory E., 43
Still, E. Coye, III, 165, 174, 240
Stowers, Stanley, 254, 255, 256, 266
Sturgeon, Mary C., 257
Sudhaus, Siegfried, 247

Talbert, Charles, 22, 117, 126
Theissen, Gerd, 8, 12, 13, 18, 19, 68, 294, 295, 299, 300, 301
Thiselton, Anthony C., 4, 6, 7, 22, 88, 97, 117, 163, 169, 183, 273
Thorsteinsson, Runar, 62, 226, 281
Tiede, D. L., 226
Tod, Marcus N., 255, 278, 282–83, 284
Toit, David S. du, 226
Tomlin, Graham, 7, 295
Townsend, J. T., 256
Tyler, Ronald L., 166, 167

Volk, Katharina, 275, 276
Vos, Craig Steven de, 8, 293, 298

Walters, James C., 274
Watson, Edward W., 22, 117
Weiss, Alexander, 301
Weiss, Johannes, 4, 14, 83, 119, 139, 146, 176, 181, 240, 258
Welborn, L. L., 8, 10, 11, 13, 14, 75, 90, 104, 120, 167, 240, 242, 262, 273
White, Benjamin G., 41
White, Devin L., 11, 167, 190, 192, 202, 203, 251, 257–58
White, L. Michael, 11
Wickkiser, B. L., 274
Wilckens, Ulrich, 6, 14, 18, 83, 131, 207
Willet, Rinse, 303
Williams, Demetrius K., 69, 96, 110, 191–92
Williams, Gareth D., 275
Winter, Bruce W., 5, 8, 9, 10, 14, 20, 53, 58, 60, 61, 69–70, 72, 73, 74, 76–77, 83, 84, 86–87, 88, 89, 90, 92, 93, 105, 133, 134, 135, 144, 173, 181, 182, 196, 199–200, 240, 243, 250, 251, 252, 271–72
Wire, Antoinette Clark, 22, 38, 107, 117, 125, 139, 185, 267, 291, 297
Wiseman, James, 257, 274
Witetschek, Stephan, 261
Witherington, Ben, III, 13
Wolff, Christian, 22, 83, 84
Wuellner, Wilhelm, 21

Yamauchi, Edwin M., 207
Young, Norman, 190

Zoumbaki, S., 287

Index of Subjects

Academics, Academy, Academia, 32, 33, 39, 62, 227, 246, 249, 251. *See also* Skeptics, Skepticism
agitators, 290–91, 293, 298–302
anthropology. *See* Stoic, Stoicism
Apollos, 9–10, 78, 130–32, 135–42, 148, 150–52, 160–61, 163–66, 169–75, 189–91, 196–97, 199, 261, 262, 264
appropriation. *See* interaction, philosophical
architect, wise architect, 138–39, 258
Aristotle, Aristotelianism, 28, 30, 32, 39, 57
αὐτάρκεια. *See* self-sufficiency (αὐτάρκεια)

background, of 1 Corinthians 1–4, 5–16
baptism, 266–68
Bassus, 282, 286, 287, 303–4, 305, 310
boasting, 76–81, 144–46, 149, 162, 165, 168–69, 171–79, 219, 220, 224, 225, 228, 258, 308; puffed up, 165–69, 195–98

Cephas, 142, 145, 148, 149, 191, 241, 242, 261, 264, 269
Christ crucified. *See* cruciformity, cruciform
Chrysippus, 28–29, 30, 31, 36, 39, 41, 44, 46, 47, 214, 250, 279
church profile (Corinthian), 290–98; gender profile, 297–98; religious and ethnic profile, 294; size of church, 291–94; socioeconomic profile, 294–97
client, clients. *See* patron-client system, patronage
comparison, genealogical and illustrative, 39–42
cruciformity, cruciform, 92, 103, 126, 183, 185, 188, 192, 194; Christ crucified, 65–67, 92–93, 100–101, 106, 126, 151, 201; mind(set) of Christ, 124–26
Cynic, Cynicism, 7, 28, 33, 34, 36, 37, 115, 147, 176, 181, 202–4, 250, 255, 256, 259, 278, 279, 280

deixis, deictic perspective. *See* emic; etic
deliberative rhetoric, 138, 151
divine man (θεῖος ἀνήρ), 226–27
δύναμις. *See* power (δύναμις)

eclectic, eclecticism. *See* interaction, philosophical
education: as background, 8, 52, 104, 175, 233; in 1 Corinthians 1–4, 167–68, 192–95, 202–4, 256–59; gymnasium, 255, 257–59, 283; philosophy, philosophical, 167–68, 278–79, 202; primary and secondary, 278–79; rhetoric of, 167–68
efficacy, efficacious, 80–81, 183, 228–29

337

INDEX OF SUBJECTS

eloquence (as instrument), 56, 65, 76–78, 94, 97–98, 127, 128, 199, 229
emic, 36, 37, 41, 230–32, 245, 246, 309
enthusiasm (spiritual), 6, 7
Epicurean, Epicureanism, 7, 27, 32, 39, 62, 110, 115, 168, 245, 246, 248, 249, 250, 251, 253, 260, 277, 280, 282, 284
eschatology (over-realized), 6–7, 13–14, 118, 183
essentialism, essentialist, 27, 34–35, 44, 47–48, 232
etic, 36, 38, 232, 253
evaluation. *See* judging, evaluation
ex-centric existence, 81, 228
exempla, exemplum, 138, 160–61, 167, 193–94, 227. *See also* imitation, imitators

factions, partisanship, parties: baptism and, 266–68; boundaries of, 263; formation of, 264; house churches and, 265–66; number of, 261–62; wisdom and, 257–60. *See also* Paul faction, the; philosophical allegiance
family resemblance, 34–36, 38, 47, 232, 260, 308; polythetic taxonomy, 35–36, 47, 323; versus essentialism, 35–36, 47
follower (ζηλώτης), emulator, 134–35, 245
form analysis, formulas. *See* paradoxes (Stoic)

genealogical comparison. *See* comparison, genealogical and illustrative
γνῶσις. *See* knowledge (γνῶσις)
Gnosticism, gnostic, 6, 12, 13, 14, 18, 19, 27, 69, 105, 179, 180, 207, 271, 272
goods (bodily, external, intellectual), 70–71, 222

habitus, 20, 21, 23, 26, 44, 45, 126, 201, 222, 231, 232
hardship catalog, 186
Hellenistic Judaism, 7, 10, 12, 13, 15, 69, 105, 131, 176, 179, 208, 209, 210–11, 217, 226, 227, 271
hierarchy (spiritual), 82, 118–26, 148, 152, 159–60, 210–13, 216–18, 224, 233–34

illustrative comparison. *See* comparison, genealogical and illustrative
imitation, imitators, 93, 126, 132, 138, 148, 150, 185, 186, 187, 192–94, 195, 201, 202, 205, 227, 258, 259. See also *exempla, exemplum*
immature (νήπιος). *See* perfect (τέλειος) versus immature (νήπιος)
incongruity, congruity, worth, 60, 65, 67–68, 76–80, 183, 229
indifferents: good, bad, indifferent, 22, 24, 25, 29, 186, 194, 207, 219, 221, 223–25, 235, 308; spiritual, unspiritual, indifferent, 220–24, 225, 228, 235, 308
interaction, philosophical, 37–39, 43–48, 229–32, 260, 308; common ethical usage, 43; competitive appropriation, 43; concession, 43, 230, 231; doctrinal reformulation, 43, 45, 230, 232, 260, 269, 304, 308; eclecticism, 37, 230; irenic appropriation, 43, 45, 230, 231, 232, 308; refutation, 43; subordinating or polemical appropriation, 45, 46, 230, 231, 232, 308
intertextuality, intertext, citation adaptation, 61, 79–80
irenic appropriation, subordinating or polemical. *See* interaction, philosophical

judging, evaluation, 121–23, 140, 142, 157–60, 172–74, 216–17, 223–24

knowledge (γνῶσις), 6, 22, 24, 64, 140, 142, 217, 221, 222, 223, 296; self-knowledge, 154–60, 174

Lucius Peticius Propas, 282, 285, 287, 303–4, 305, 310

paradoxes (Stoic), 72–73, 80, 120, 179, 181–83, 186–87, 206–7, 209, 224, 234
parenesis, parenetic, 168, 193–94, 201, 202, 205
parties (Corinthian). *See* factions, partisanship, parties
patron-client system, patronage, 8, 10, 13,

Index of Subjects

15, 16, 20, 41, 82, 105, 131, 163, 175, 179, 181, 184, 195, 267, 281, 290, 295, 297, 310

Paul faction, the, 10, 25, 26, 101, 131, 163, 241, 257–60, 262–66, 269, 270, 291, 309

perfect (τέλειος) versus immature (νήπιος), 207–10, 225

peristasis catalog. *See* hardship catalog

philosophers, philosophy: attestation of philosophers, 281–88; education, 167–68, 202, 258, 278–79; identity, 35, 36–37, 38, 135, 244–49, 268, 276–77, 281, 283, 288, 309; popular philosophy, 279–81; pseudo-philosopher, 199–200; in Roman Corinth, 286–87; the Romans and, 275–77, 283; social class and, 278–79, 283–84, 288–89

philosophical allegiance, 126, 131, 244–54, 268, 309; dogmatic schools, 247–53; founders, 247, 250, 259–60, 262–63; rivalry, 249–53; schools, 247–53; Skepticism, Skeptics, 247–48

philosophical schools: as analogy for Christ groups, 253–54; disciple circles, 249, 260, 263, 279, 304; houses as instructional space, private meetings, 254–57; the Paul faction as, 259–60, 262–63; sects, *haireseis*, 135, 168, 244–53; seekers, sampling, 248–49, 263, 269, 279, 293. *See also* parenesis, parenetic

Plato, Platonism, 28, 30, 34, 39, 57, 115, 154, 155, 157, 193, 218, 244, 245, 246, 247, 249, 250, 253, 282; Middle Platonism, 32–33, 227

pneumatic people (πνευματικοί [σοφοί]), 21, 22, 100, 117–18, 119, 120, 121–24, 127, 128, 142, 152, 159, 207, 210–13, 216–18, 222, 223–25, 234, 235, 308

Pneumatists (Πνευματικοί), 213–15, 217, 244

politics, political partisanship, 8, 120, 167, 192, 242, 243, 244

polythetic taxonomy. *See* family resemblance

popular philosophy. *See* philosophers, philosophy

power (δύναμις), 22, 60, 84, 90, 91, 94, 100, 111, 199–201, 211–15, 217, 218, 224, 234

reason, Reason, 29, 112, 113, 147, 148, 159–60, 177–78, 211–13, 219, 220, 222, 225, 228, 233, 234

reflective, 25, 32, 222, 229–31, 232, 235; unreflective engagement, 229–31

rivalry. *See* philosophical allegiance

self-evaluation, self-examination, 153, 157–60, 161–72, 258; as spiritual exercise, 157–59

self-sufficiency (αὐτάρκεια), 25, 81, 176–79, 183, 187, 207, 218–20, 224, 225, 228, 230, 235, 258, 308

Skeptics, Skepticism. *See* Academics, Academy, Academia; philosophical allegiance

slogans: Corinthian, 21, 22, 24, 125–26; in 1 Corinthians 2:14–15, 121–24, 125–26, 216–17, 223, 234; party slogans in 1 Corinthians 1:12, 9, 133, 148, 167, 195, 239, 241–46, 252, 262–64, 266, 268

socioeconomic status, 8, 15, 68–69, 75, 184, 263, 294–97, 299–302, 303, 304; economy scales, 299–302

Socrates, 61, 70, 134, 143, 226, 227

sophists, sophistry, 20, 52, 69, 73–74, 76–77, 80, 86–87, 89–90, 92, 134–35, 162, 181–82, 196–97, 199–200, 243, 250–53, 258, 271–72, 287, 310

σοφοί (πνευματικοί), the (pneumatic people), 21, 24, 25, 26, 44, 45, 47, 63, 74, 82, 104, 108, 110, 119, 123, 128, 132, 139, 147, 148, 159, 176, 182, 185, 198, 206–7, 210, 212, 215–18, 220–25, 229–35, 241, 253, 257, 259, 262–63, 295–305, 308–9

spirit, Spirit (πνεῦμα) (Stoic), 111–13, 210–18, 220, 224, 258, 308. *See also* spiritual

spiritual: power (πνευματικὴ δύναμις), 91, 111, 211; as rule or standard, 122–23, 216, 223; the spiritual, the unspiritual, 220–25, 235, 308; spiritual gifts, 75, 118, 144–45, 223–24, 229; spiritual man, unspiritual man, 121–25, 216–18, 223–25. *See also* virtue, as rule or standard

status, ordinary (social) versus transcendent (spiritual), 76, 82, 185–86, 233–34

Stoic, Stoicism: anthropology, 25, 207–20, 225, 232, 234, 308; sources, 46–47; system (physics, logic, ethics), 28–29. *See also* Chrysippus; indifferents; paradoxes (Stoic); tension, tonic theory; wise man (Stoic); Zeno

sub(ordinated) Stoicism, sub-Stoic(s), 25, 26, 45, 48, 206–35, 260

τέλειος. *See* perfect (τέλειος) versus immature (νήπιος)

tension, tonic theory, 211–18, 220, 224–25, 234, 308; ψύχικος and λόγικος, 211–13; ψύχικος and πνευματικός, 210–13, 216–18, 224–25, 234, 308. *See also* perfect (τέλειος) versus immature (νήπιος)

θεῖος ἀνήρ. *See* divine man (θεῖος ἀνήρ)

Titius Justus, 255, 266, 291, 294, 299, 300, 301, 302, 303–4, 305, 309–10

virtue, as rule or standard, 122–23, 216, 223

wisdom: as an "account," 56–59, 63, 81; form versus content, 51–56, 60, 61, 66, 67, 81–82, 83–84, 88, 89–92, 93, 97, 99, 100, 101, 103, 104, 106–7, 109, 114, 116; human, 115–16, 135, 145–46; rhetoric versus philosophy, 41–42, 57, 106–7, 310; "wisdom of word," 52–56; wisdom of the world (human wisdom) versus wisdom of the cross, 52–65; "wisdom or word," 88–92

wise man (Stoic), 69–73, 181–83, 206–7; as architect, 138–39, 258. *See also* σοφοί (πνευματικοί), the (pneumatic people); paradoxes (Stoic)

words and deeds, 97, 98, 199–201

ζηλώτης. *See* follower (ζηλώτης), emulator

Zeno, 19, 28–30, 31, 32, 34, 36, 39, 44, 47, 227, 232, 244, 245, 246, 248, 250, 253, 259–60, 282, 284

Index of Scripture and Other Ancient Sources

Old Testament

Genesis
2:7	210

Job
5:13	143
27:6	155, 156

Psalms
8:4	146
82:6–7	146
93:11	143
144:3	146

Proverbs
20:27	112, 120, 218

Ecclesiastes
6:10	146

Isaiah
3:3	62
3:12	62
19:11	62
19:11–12	61, 62
19:12	62
24:16	61
29:13	61
29:14	61, 62
29:14–16	61
29:15	160
31:2	62
33:18	61
40:13	113, 120, 124, 218
44:5	243
64:4	110
65:16e	110

Jeremiah
9:22	80
9:22–23	79, 80
9:23	79, 80, 146

Ezekiel
37:26	140

Daniel
2:18–19	109
2:27–28	109

Zechariah
13:9	140

Deutero-canonical Books

Wisdom of Solomon
3:6	140

Sirach
1	67
2:1	192
3:1	192
3:17	192
6:23	192
18:1–10	146
24	67
44:4	149
44:21	149

1 Maccabees
2:50–68	66
9:21	66

INDEX OF SCRIPTURE AND OTHER ANCIENT SOURCES

2 Maccabees
5:21	146
9:8	146
12	146

4 Maccabees
1:16	115

Pseudepigrapha

2 Baruch
14:13	149
40:1–4	66
70:9	66
72:2	66
81:4	109

4 Ezra
6:55–59	149
7:10–11	149
13:1–13	66

Jubilees
22:14	149
47:9	192

Psalms of Solomon
2:28–32	146

Sibylline Oracles
3:767–769	149

Testament of Moses
1:12	149

Ancient Jewish Writers

Josephus

Antiquitates judaicae
9.346–50	146
17.269	66
17.273–777	66
18.11	134
20.97–98	66
20.169–172	66

Bellum judaicum
1.142	242
2.119	134
2.261–263	66
2.440	242
2.443	242

Vita
1.10	249
1.10–12	135
7–9	192

Philo

De Abrahamo
13	226, 227
119–121	67

De aeternitate mundi
76–77	31

De agricultura
1.157–162	209
1.165	209
9	120, 208

De congressu eruditionis gratia
1.79	115, 278

De fuga et inventione
1.195	115

De gigantibus
1.147	115

De migratione Abrahami
1.29	120, 208
1.33	120, 208
29	208
197	176

De mutatione nominum
1.30	139

De opificio mundi
1.24	139

De plantatione
151	280

De posteritate Caini
1.138	115
43	121, 209
111	121, 209

De sobrietate
9–10	120, 208
56–57	187
57	183

De somniis
2.10	120, 208
2.234–236	209
2.244	182

De specialibus legibus
1.81	67
2.228	192

De vita Mosis
1.1	226, 227
1.24	279
1.156	147
1.158	182
1.158–159	193

Legum allegoriae
1.93–94	120, 209
1.102	227
3.140	226, 227
3.159	209
3.210	120

Quis rerum divinarum heres sit
1.117	115
1.129	115
1.160	120

Quod omnis probus liber sit
1.160	208, 209
62–63	227
73	227

Index of Scripture and Other Ancient Sources

New Testament

Matthew
6:24	169
10:10	203
24:42	198
24:42–51	198
24:43	198
24:44	198
24:46	198

Mark
1:15	101
6:8	203

Luke
9:3	203
12:41–48	198
12:43	198
12:45	198
17:34	169
18:10	169
23:14	121

John
3:15	101

Acts
2:2	151
2:7	151
4:9	121
5:11	265
5:33–39	66
12:19	121
12:21–23	146
15:22	265
17:11	121
17:18–21	86
18:1–3	303
18:2	291
18:4–6	303
18:7	255, 266, 291, 300
18:8	291
18:9–10	293, 303
18:10	293
18:11	293, 303
18:12–17	303
18:17	300
18:24	131
18:27–28	262
19:9	255, 266
19:10	304
20:20	255
21:38	66
24:8	121
27:23	243
28:18	121

Romans
2:8	88
4:13	149
5:3	101
6:2–11	149
6:16	140
7:11	124
8:9	100, 108
8:15–17	264
8:29	264
8:32	149
9:17	113
10:15	113
11:13	294
12:19	166
13:9	166
13:13	88
14:11	166
14:17	98
15:1–2	170
16:1–2	291
16:5	265
16:10	265
16:11	265
16:14	265
16:15	265
16:21–24	291, 300
16:23	265, 291, 292, 301
16:26	92, 109

1 Corinthians
1–2	92, 108, 115, 135, 142, 146, 147
1–3	150
1–4	3, 4, 10, 11, 12, 16, 17, 19, 20, 21, 23, 25, 27, 45, 58, 63, 75, 90, 93, 105, 109, 132, 150, 167, 189, 197, 201, 204, 233, 252, 258, 268, 272, 295, 297, 298, 307
1:2	290
1:5	51, 228
1:7	228
1:8	228
1:9	228
1:10	138, 241
1:10–13	258, 291
1:10–17	150, 239
1:10–17a	4, 26, 51, 239, 262, 263, 268, 309
1:10–4:21	46, 51, 142, 167
1:11	242, 291
1:12	3, 9, 25, 105, 133, 139, 148, 150, 167, 195, 241, 242, 243, 244, 261, 262, 263, 264, 266, 268, 293, 295
1:13	139, 232, 262, 265
1:13–16	5, 150, 267
1:13–17	137
1:13a	266
1:13b	266, 267
1:13c–16	266, 267, 268, 269
1:14	267, 291
1:16	267, 291
1:17	53, 54, 56, 57, 59, 64, 83, 88, 91, 94, 96, 99, 106, 107, 113, 152, 165, 199, 229
1:17–18	59, 91
1:17–31	91, 100, 127
1:17–2:5	92, 106, 133
1:17–2:10	102

343

INDEX OF SCRIPTURE AND OTHER ANCIENT SOURCES

1:17–2:16	91, 106, 132, 135, 162	1:25	67, 107, 109, 133, 152, 159, 220	2:4–5	94, 96, 101, 106, 205, 311
1:17–3:20	145	1:26	13, 22, 45, 46, 67, 68, 69, 70, 71, 72, 73, 74, 75, 76, 78, 80, 90, 121, 152, 159, 182, 186, 206, 209, 233, 296	2:5	22, 45, 84, 87, 90, 101, 106, 107, 109, 133, 199, 220, 258
1:17–3:23	148			2:6	21, 45, 46, 104, 106, 107, 108, 114, 118, 119, 151, 207, 211
1:17–4:5	165, 166				
1:17b	51, 52, 55, 58, 89, 108, 133				
1:17b–c	56				
1:17b–25	52, 81	1:26–27	73, 78	2:6–12	104, 114
1:17b–31	51, 52, 72, 81, 84, 93, 103, 105, 119, 161	1:26–28	69, 73, 79	2:6–13	117
		1:26–29	78, 199	2:6–15	124
		1:26–30	3, 79	2:6–16	56, 75, 76, 100, 103, 104, 105, 106, 107, 114, 118, 119, 120, 126, 127, 128, 129, 132, 133, 148, 159, 169, 258
1:17b–2:5	53, 65, 128	1:26–31	51, 65, 67, 68, 69, 75, 77, 79, 80, 82, 85, 197, 205, 220, 229, 311		
1:17b–2:16	119, 126, 133				
1:17b–3:3	4				
1:17b–3:23	51, 148, 149, 239				
1:17b–4:21	26, 47, 189, 207, 218, 220, 239, 268, 290, 291	1:27	63, 72, 143		
		1:27–28	73, 76, 77, 78, 231	2:6–3:4	127, 128, 311
		1:27–29	79, 311	2:6–3:23	151
1:18	22, 56, 59, 60, 61, 75, 90, 91, 107, 127, 188, 199, 231	1:28b	76	2:7	91, 108, 109, 110, 114
		1:29	3, 69, 73, 74, 77, 78	2:7–12	91, 108
		1:29–31	73, 77, 146, 169, 171, 228	2:8	109, 110, 124
1:18–25	51, 58, 85, 107, 258			2:9	110
1:18–31	55, 56, 58, 169, 186	1:30	60, 73, 78, 79, 80, 146	2:10	110, 124, 128
1:18–2:5	104, 108	1:30–31	220	2:10–12	111, 114, 140
1:18–2:16	141	1:31	3, 69, 79, 80, 145, 146	2:10–13	120
1:18–3:23	142, 183	1:31–3:21	145	2:10b–13	258
1:18a	56	2	100	2:11	110
1:19	61, 63, 152, 159, 166, 206	2:1	51, 57, 64, 83, 84, 85, 86, 87, 89, 90, 91, 93, 94, 96, 106, 113, 132, 133, 152, 199	2:12	112, 128, 133, 228, 258
				2:13	51, 64, 94, 104, 110, 114, 116, 133, 199, 220
1:20	3, 61, 62, 63, 64, 107, 109, 152, 159, 206, 231, 257, 258			2:14	22, 104, 117, 118, 121, 123, 124
		2:1–2	83		
1:20–21	64, 311	2:1–5	15, 83, 84, 85, 86, 87, 88, 90, 91, 93, 94, 96, 100, 103, 104, 105, 106, 107, 142, 149, 205	2:14–15	21, 46, 119, 124
1:21	63, 64, 65, 75, 78, 107, 152, 231			2:14–16	110, 152
				2:14a	125
1:21–25	68			2:15	3, 22, 45, 104, 117, 118, 121, 122, 123, 124, 125, 159, 185, 216, 218, 223, 234
1:21b	146	2:2	93, 126, 139, 201		
1:22	152, 217, 294, 302	2:3	88, 90, 93		
1:22–24	65	2:3–4	83	2:16	46, 113, 124, 125, 133, 258
1:22–28	205	2:4	22, 45, 51, 57, 64, 83, 84, 87, 89, 90, 94, 96, 97, 98, 99, 100, 101, 106, 199, 201, 258		
1:23	59, 65, 100, 106, 126, 139				
				2:16–3:3	118
1:23–24	60, 77, 107			2:16a	125
1:24	22, 67, 90, 100, 101, 152, 199, 201			2:16b	125, 126
				3	164

344

Index of Scripture and Other Ancient Sources

3–4	142	3:12	139, 140, 298	4:5	160
3:1	21, 45, 116, 118, 119, 133, 140, 207	3:12–18	205	4:6	3, 14, 46, 69, 74, 163, 165, 167, 169, 170, 172, 176, 187, 189, 196, 198, 257, 295
3:1–2	161, 259	3:13	124, 139		
3:1–3	127, 130, 133	3:13–17	140		
3:1–4	130, 167, 257	3:14	139		
3:1–10b	132	3:15	127, 139, 140	4:6–7	172, 173, 174
3:1–17	141, 142	3:16	46, 108, 140, 142, 161, 258	4:6–8	3, 13, 162, 175, 189
3:1–4:5	130, 160			4:6–9	170
3:3	107, 109, 116, 119, 133, 134, 135, 211, 220, 250	3:17	139, 142, 231, 298	4:6–10	176, 205
		3:18	3, 21, 45, 46, 63, 140, 142, 143, 152, 159, 161, 227, 258, 298	4:6–13	162, 179, 185, 187, 189, 191
				4:6–21	4
3:3–5	139	3:18–23	4, 105, 130, 141, 142, 161, 162	4:6a	164, 165, 175
3:4	107, 109, 133, 135, 148, 165, 220			4:6a–c	168
		3:19	3, 63, 113, 143, 152, 161, 206	4:6b	165, 166, 168, 258
3:4–9	163			4:6c	165, 167, 168, 187, 258
3:4–4:5	4, 130, 131	3:20	63, 143, 152, 161, 206		
3:4–4:6	261			4:6d	165, 168, 170, 172, 173, 174, 175, 187, 311
3:5	136, 140, 151, 160, 161, 191, 201	3:21	3, 45, 46, 69, 74, 101, 107, 109, 144, 145, 147, 149, 169, 171, 198, 207, 258		
				4:6d–7	187
3:5–9	137, 191, 257			4:7	46, 69, 74, 124, 165, 172, 173, 174, 175, 177, 178, 179, 181, 185, 187, 228, 258
3:5–10b	130, 132, 135, 138, 161				
		3:21–23	146, 148, 173, 175, 228		
3:5–4:5	137, 163, 165, 187				
3:5d	136, 137	3:21b	311	4:7–8	75, 77, 187, 198, 220
3:6	136, 137, 140	3:21b–23	146	4:7a	172, 173
3:6–7	191	3:22	145, 148, 160, 161, 261	4:7a–c	173
3:6–9	138			4:7b	173
3:6–10	136, 205	3:23	188	4:7c	173
3:6–10b	161	4	105, 180	4:8	13, 14, 22, 45, 46, 74, 149, 176, 180, 181, 182, 183, 185, 186, 187, 198, 201, 206, 296
3:7	136	4:1	151, 161, 191, 201		
3:7b–c	172	4:1–5	130, 150, 151, 159, 160, 163, 168, 192		
3:8	137, 138				
3:9	137, 139	4:1–13	205		
3:9b	138	4:2	152, 153, 154, 160	4:8–10	72, 73, 165, 176, 179, 233
3:9c	138	4:2–3b	153		
3:10	45, 63, 139, 166, 258	4:2–5	150, 161	4:8–13	162
3:10–17	163	4:3	121, 123, 152, 159	4:9	184, 190
3:10–18	191	4:3–5	160	4:9–13	184, 185, 186, 188, 189, 192, 201
3:10a	138	4:3b	153		
3:10b	138	4:3c	153, 156, 160	4:10	22, 45, 46, 162, 179, 184, 185, 186, 187, 198, 207
3:10c–17	130, 138, 141, 161	4:4	46, 121, 123, 155, 156, 159, 258		
3:10c–21a	132				
3:10d–17	142	4:4–5	153, 159	4:11–13	184
3:11	139, 187, 198	4:4a	153, 156, 160	4:14	189, 190, 257, 259
3:11–17	142	4:4c	153, 160	4:14–15	167, 258, 262

345

INDEX OF SCRIPTURE AND OTHER ANCIENT SOURCES

4:14–16	194	7:1–16	297	11:17–34	295		
4:14–21	189, 192, 193, 201, 202, 205, 258	7:1a–b	22	11:20	265		
4:15	190, 192, 202, 205, 259	7:3	124	12–14	75, 76, 118, 170, 183, 223, 267		
4:16	93, 150, 167, 192, 193, 202, 227, 258	7:4	46	12:1	223		
		7:7	138	12:2	294		
		7:8	138	12:3–14:40	108		
4:16–17	138, 201, 205	7:12–16	294	12:4	224, 229		
4:17	138, 167, 192, 193, 202, 258	7:18–24	257	12:4–6	46		
		7:19	46	12:4–11	118		
4:18	3, 69, 74, 195, 196, 198, 298, 311	7:20–23	296	12:7	46		
		7:21	72	12:8	51		
4:18–19	195, 205, 311	7:29–34	46	12:8–10	223		
4:18–21	150, 205	7:37	46	12:9	224, 229		
4:19	3, 22, 69, 74, 90, 195, 196, 198, 199	8–10	75	12:12	137, 232		
		8:1	22, 45, 64, 69, 121, 140, 171, 221, 222	12:12–26	118, 138		
4:19–21	198	8:1–13	294	12:12–27	46		
4:20	22, 90, 97, 199, 200	8:1–11:1	220, 222, 296	12:13	267		
4:21	167, 192, 203, 257, 258, 259	8:1a	22	12:20	137		
4:22	151	8:2	142	12:28	224, 229		
5–16	4, 191	8:4	22, 45, 121, 221	12:30	224, 229		
5:1–11	138	8:5–6	22	12:31	224, 229		
5:1–13	221, 222, 295	8:6	46	13:3	69		
5:2	69, 74	8:7	294, 298	13:4	69, 171		
5:5	298	8:8	22, 45, 121	13:4–7	138		
5:6	69, 74	8:13	138	13:5	170		
5:8	88	9:1–23	195	13:10	45		
5:12	232	9:1–27	138	13:10–11	21, 119		
6–8	22	9:3	121	13:11	45, 211		
6:1	298	9:5	261	13:12	64		
6:1–11	295	9:7	46	14–15	45		
6:5	3, 21, 45, 46, 63, 124, 159, 206	9:8–10	46	14:1	170		
		9:15–16	69	14:1–5	118		
6:7	46	9:17	138	14:4	118, 170		
6:11	108	9:18	46	14:6–25	118		
6:12	22, 45, 46, 121	9:24–27	46, 257	14:12	21, 118, 223, 256, 293, 294		
6:12–20	221, 222	10:1–13	138				
6:12a	22	10:1–11:1	294	14:18–19	138		
6:12c	22	10:14–22	294	14:20	21, 45, 119, 211		
6:13	22, 45, 121, 125, 222	10:23	22	14:21	113		
6:13a	22, 125, 126	10:24	46, 170	14:23	256, 265		
6:13b	125, 126	10:25	121	14:23–24	293, 294		
6:13c	125, 126	10:27	121	14:24	121, 256		
6:14	125, 126	10:33–11:1	138	14:26–33	118		
6:18	22, 45, 121, 223	11:1	138, 193, 227	14:37	21, 118, 142, 223		
6:18b	22	11:2–16	297	15:3–11	232		
6:19	46, 108	11:14–15	46	15:12	22, 121, 183, 232		

Index of Scripture and Other Ancient Sources

15:24	88	1:28	61	**EARLY CHRISTIAN**	
15:28	46	2:4	170	**WRITINGS**	
15:31	46	2:5	126, 227		
15:33	46	2:5–10	126	Acts of Justin and	
15:39–41	46	2:7	126	the Seven Martyrs	
15:42–49	46	2:8	60, 126	3.4.2	246
15:47–49	211	3:17	227	4.1.2	246
15:54	113	3:18	60	4.2.2	246
15:55	113	3:19	61	4.3.2	246
16:8	304	4:9	227		
16:9	265			Augustine	
16:12	142	**Colossians**			
16:15	265	1:4	101	*De civitate Dei*	
16:17	291, 300	1:16	88	8.4	219
		1:26–27	92, 109		
2 Corinthians		2:2	109	Eusebius	
2:15	61	4:3	92, 109	*Praeparatio evangelica*	
3:17	100	4:15	265	9.3.6	219
4:10–13	227				
5:12	101	**1 Thessalonians**		Hippolytus	
10:13–14	262	1:6	227		
10:15	101	2:1	86	*Refutatio*	
11:12	101			1.18.2	219
		2 Thessalonians			
Galatians		1:11	100	Ignatius	
1:6–7	137	2:13	100	*To the Philadelphians*	
2:7	294			5.2	101
2:19–20	149	**2 Timothy**			
3:3	100	4:1	88	John Chrysostom	
3:10	166			*Homilies on 1 Corinthians*	
3:13	66	**Titus**		3.4	176
3:26	101	2:13	88	6.3	84
4:22	166			12.1	176
4:27	166	**Philemon**			
5:11	59	2	265	Justin Martyr	
5:14	166			*Dialogue with Trypho*	
6:1	108, 118	**James**		1.2	252
6:12	59	3:15	118	29.1	249
6:14	59			29.3	249
		1 Peter			
Ephesians		1:7	140	Martyrdom of Ignatius	
1:15	101			8.4.1	246
5:9	98	**Jude**			
		19	118		
Philippians					
1:19	100				

347

INDEX OF SCRIPTURE AND OTHER ANCIENT SOURCES

Martyrdom of Polycarp

10.1	246
12.1	246

Martyrs of Lyons

1.19.3	246
1.20.7	246

Origen

Contra Celsum

1.10	246, 249, 252
3.48	68
3.50	280

De principiis

4.1.7	84

Shepherd of Hermas

Visions

24.4	140

GRECO-ROMAN LITERATURE

Alcinous

Handbook of Platonism

28.4	278

Apollonius of Tyana

Epistles

1–8	282
36	282, 286
37	282, 286, 287
60	286
74	282, 286
77	286

Apuleius

De dogma Platonis

1.3	219

Aristotle

Ethica nichomachea

1.8.2	70
9.1.7	279
1152b	138

Politica

1260a	138

Arius Didymus

Epitome of Stoic Ethics

11m	279

Aulus Gellius

Noctes Atticae

6.14	275

Cicero

Academicae quaestiones

1.19	219
2.3.8	248, 249
2.3.8–9	248
2.3.9	248
2.26	98
2.47.145	71
2.66–67	62
2.136	147
2.145	227

De finibus

3.10.34	209
3.34	209
3.48	209, 210
3.75	73, 176, 182, 206
4.17	221

De inventione rhetorica

1.1	278

De natura deorum

1.3.6–7	249
1.5.11	249
1.7	193
1.10	247
1.15.10	248
1.16	33
1.16.43	247
1.24.66	249
1.24.66–67	248
1.24.67	251
1.26.72	248
2.36	148
2.37–39	112
2.118	31
2.153	148

De officiis

1.153	115
2.5	66

De oratore

1.52–57	278
3.65	72

Paradoxa Stoicorum

2	227

Rhetorica ad Herennium

1.1.1	278
4.55.69	278

Tusculanae disputationes

1.1	66
1.1.1–1.2.5	275
1.21.48	247
2.4.11–13	193
2.9	246
2.11.26	249
2.22.51	71
2.26	278
2.51	121, 206, 209, 227
2.61	278
3.1.2–3	70, 194
3.1.3	71
3.3.7	249
3.25.59	249
3.59	278
4.1.2–3	275
4.3.5	66
4.4.7	248
5.2.5	194

Index of Scripture and Other Ancient Sources

5.3.10	275	2.113	134	1.1.28	281
5.4.11	249	2.122	256	1.2.12	281
5.11	246	3.56	219	1.2.21	281
5.11.32	33	4.59	134	1.2.22	281
5.23.69–72	28	6.2	203	1.5.9	251
5.29.82	248	6.4	203, 204	1.9.31–32	158, 177
5.41.120	33	6.13	203	1.14.6–17	141
5.113	278	6.21	203, 204	1.14.11–14	112
		6.32	203, 204	1.14.13–14	158
Crates		6.37	147	1.29.4	158, 177, 178, 179
		6.72	147	1.30.1–2	158
Epistle 27		6.102	203	2.4	221
15–17	147	7.5	28, 245	2.8.9–17	112
		7.30	283	2.8.9–29	141
Demosthenes		7.36	245	2.9.12–14	194
Orations		7.39–40	219	2.12	256
9.56	242	7.40	219	2.12.17	280
		7.44	98	2.14.11	158
Dio Cassius		7.52	98	2.16.39	120, 209
		7.79	98	2.19.20–28	71, 228
Roman History		7.89	210	2.23.12	221
59.11.12	226	7.117–124	62	3.1.24	203
59.28.1–2	226	7.122	72	3.3.34	193
		7.124	182	3.7.2	70
Dio Chrysostom		7.125–126	209	3.7.21	221, 251
		7.127	209	3.7.34	134
Orations		7.131	221	3.15.8	282
3.13	276	7.188	279	3.22.45–49	186
8.9	134	7.189–202	28	3.24.9	120, 209
8.16	186	8.46	247	3.24.40	134
13.11	200	8.55	134	4.1.51	158, 177
18.17	200	9.38	134	4.1.152	227
31.121	184	9.64	134	4.8.17–20	282
32.9	280, 282	10.2	134	4.9.17	177
47	90	10.8	244, 251	4.12.15–21	158
55.1–5	134	10.11	147		
55.6	134	10.22	134	*Enchiridion*	
72.4	280, 282	10.117–120	62	1.5	158
76.15.7	284	10.120	279	46.2	143
78	284	143	111	48	177, 178
				48.2–3	158
Diogenes Laertius		**Epictetus**		51.3	227
Vitae philosophorum		*Diatribai*			
2.13	243	1.1	91		

INDEX OF SCRIPTURE AND OTHER ANCIENT SOURCES

Euripides

Orestes
396 — 155

Galen

De causis contentivis
1.1–2.4 — 214

De dignoscendis pulsibus
2.4 — 252
3.3 — 252
3.641–642 — 214

De propriorum animi cuiuslibet affectuum et peccatorum dignotione et curatione
10.41.5–11 — 193

Institutio logica
9.9 — 244

Horace

Epistulae
1.1.61 — 155, 156

Satirae
2.3 — 280

Lucian

Bis accusatus
6 — 256, 280, 282

Cataplus
14–29 — 256

Demonax
10 — 204
13 — 203
48.6 — 135

De morte peregrini
13 — 252
15 — 135, 203
36 — 203

Eunuchus
13 — 98

Fugitivi
3–4 — 280, 282

Hermotimus
14.7 — 135
76–77 — 71, 227

Macrobius
19.6 — 245

Philopseudes
7 — 203

Piscator
24 — 203, 204

Symposium
1 — 135, 250
6–7 — 250
12 — 250
16 — 204
19 — 204
32 — 250
33 — 250
35 — 250

Lucretius

De rerum natura
1.635–644 — 66
3.1–30 — 247
5.7–12 — 66
5.8–10 — 247

Marcus Aurelius

Meditations
2.13 — 141
2.17 — 141
3.5 — 141
3.12 — 141
3.16 — 141
4.24 — 158
5.10 — 141
5.11 — 158
5.32 — 212

7.59 — 177
8.2 — 158
8.36 — 158
8.45 — 141
8.50 — 219
10.13 — 158
11.2 — 158

Musonius Rufus

Diatribes
1 — 200
4 — 193
5 — 59, 200
6 — 70, 194, 200
8 — 200
11 — 184
12–14 — 221
17.14–16 — 200

Ovid

Metamorphoses
3.329 — 164
13.896–897 — 164

Tristia
2.63–64 — 164

Philodemus

De Stoicis
13.3–4 — 245

Herculaneum Papyri (P.Herc.)
164 — 245

Philostratus

Vita Apollonii
1.7.1–3 — 249
1.7.3 — 246
1.32.2 — 246
3.43 — 226
3.50.1 — 226
4.16.1 — 246

Index of Scripture and Other Ancient Sources

4.24	282, 285	*Respublica*		17–21	203
4.26	282, 286	331a.2	155, 156	20	203
7.20.1	226	354c	143	*Epistle 10*	
7.32.1	226	485d	200	5–6	147
8.5.1	226				
8.13.2	226	**Pliny the Younger**		*Epistle 30*	
8.20.1	245	*Epistulae*		4	204
Vitae sophistarum		1.10	282	25–34	203
208	134			30	203
479–492	42	**Plutarch**		**Ps.-Socrates**	
490–491	134	*Cato maior*		*Epistle 9*	
622	284	20.1–4	192	4	256
		22.2–3	275		
Plato		*De liberis educandis*		**Quintilian**	
Alcibiades maior		7d–e	278	*Institutio oratoria*	
129a	157	*Moralia*		1.pr.9–20	278
Apologia		58e	69, 72	1.pr.14	66
21b.4	155	75b–76e	227	2.2.5	192
22d.1	154	119d	167	2.5.1	152
23a.8–9	115	262d	297	2.9.1	192
34b	155	351e	297	2.16.11	278
Charmides		439a–440c	115	2.17.37	278
164d–165b	157	472a	70, 72	2.18.38	278
175a–b	143	476e	155	10.1.35–36	278
Cratylus		485a	70, 72	10.1.81–84	278
440c	244	485d	70, 72	11.1.27	247
		780e–781a	193	12.2.8	66
Leges		1033a	59	12.7.9	279
11.923a	157	1033b–1034c	251		
		1036b	248	**Seneca**	
Lysis		1086e	251	*Ad Helviam*	
222d–e	143	1100c	251	5.2	227
Phaedrus		1124c	251	*De beneficiis*	
229e	157	**Ps.-Crates**		2.29.3	148
235c.7	155	*Epistle 26*		6.38.5	158
279c	146	10–11	147	7.2.2	148
Philebus				7.2.5	147
48c	157	**Ps.-Diogenes**		7.3.2–3	147
Protagoras		*Epistle 7*		7.12.2	182
316a–b	143	3	203	7.16.5–7.19.6	31
343b	157				

351

INDEX OF SCRIPTURE AND OTHER ANCIENT SOURCES

De clementia
1.7.1 — 193

De Constantia
2.1 — 248
2.3 — 186
3.1 — 248
6.3–8 — 227
7.1 — 143, 227
15.1 — 186
19.3 — 186

De ira
1.20.3 — 155
2.28.1 — 158
2.28.1–8 — 158
3.36.1–3 — 158
3.36.1–4 — 158

De Otio
3.5 — 152
5.1 — 248

De tranquillitate animi
6.1–2 — 158
7.4–5 — 71

De vita beata
3.2.3 — 248
11.1 — 227
17.3–4 — 227
18.1 — 227
24.4 — 66

Epistulae morales
2.28.6–8 — 159
5.1 — 159
6.5 — 167, 193
6.5–6 — 193
7.2–5 — 184
8.8 — 280
9.3 — 219
9.19–20 — 248
11.9 — 158
16.2 — 158, 159
20.2 — 200
24.28 — 31
25.4 — 194
25.4–7 — 158
25.5–6 — 167
27.1 — 159
28.9 — 157
28.10 — 158
30.7 — 194
30.15 — 194
31.5 — 138, 177
31.6 — 222
31.9 — 112
31.11 — 159
32.1 — 158
33.5 — 219
33.7 — 133
34.4 — 200
35.2 — 159
35.4 — 159
41 — 159, 178
41.1 — 112, 141
41.1–2 — 177
41.2 — 159
41.4–9 — 159
41.6 — 178, 219
41.8–9 — 212
42.1 — 71, 143, 227
43.5 — 158
49.12 — 112
52.3 — 227
52.7–8 — 167
52.8 — 193
53.8 — 194
53.11 — 148, 159
57.3 — 227
66.12 — 112, 159
66.39 — 193
68.6–7 — 158
68.8 — 159
71.20 — 121, 122, 216, 218
71.34 — 31
71.36 — 155
72.6 — 31
73.13 — 148
73.16 — 159
75.9–16 — 227
76.9 — 148
76.9–10 — 212
83.1 — 159
83.2 — 158
84.8 — 193
85.1 — 219
85.5 — 159
89 — 28
89.1–2 — 219
89.4 — 66
89.6 — 66
92.7 — 148
92.27–28 — 212
92.27–31 — 159
92.28 — 148
92.30 — 141
94.21 — 194
94.48 — 194
94.50 — 133
94.55 — 194
95.50 — 193
104.20–33 — 167, 193
109.1 — 159
109.10 — 31
113.2 — 123
113.17 — 148
115.11 — 70, 194
117.2 — 248
118.2–3 — 159
120.14 — 148, 159
123.6–9 — 194
124.7 — 112
124.10 — 113
124.14 — 148

Naturales quaestiones
4.5.1–2 — 219

Seneca Maior

Controversiae
2.3.7 — 152
10.pr.15 — 252

Sextus Empiricus

Adversus mathematicos
7.16 — 219
9.133–136 — 71, 227

Index of Scripture and Other Ancient Sources

Pyrrhoniae hypotyposes
2.135–143 — 98

Sophocles

Ajax
172 — 243

Stobaeus

Anthology
3.24.7 — 155
4.67.22 — 212, 221
4.67.24 — 221

Stoicorum Veterum Fragmenta
1:85 — 212
1:87 — 212
1:158 — 211, 212
1:161 — 212
1:216 — 186, 187
1:495 — 111
1:532 — 111
1:566 — 120
2:35–36 — 115
2:35–40 — 28, 219
2:37 — 28
2:75 — 29
2:459 — 211
2:460 — 211
2:566 — 209
2:633–45 — 112
2:879 — 212
3:68–168 — 222
3:197–213 — 122
3:272 — 176, 219
3:276 — 176, 219
3:295–304 — 122, 147
3:305–7 — 123
3:351 — 147
3:359 — 183
3:364 — 73, 206
3:512 — 120, 209
3:519 — 120, 209
3:522 — 121, 206, 209
3:539 — 209, 210
3:544–656 — 73
3:548 — 120, 206, 209
3:548–56 — 206
3:557–66 — 147, 206
3:567 — 71, 186, 187
3:582–88 — 206
3:589–603 — 206
3:590 — 147, 206
3:591 — 147
3:593 — 71, 182
3:594 — 71, 72, 73, 206
3:597 — 147, 206
3:598 — 71, 182
3:599 — 147, 206
3:603 — 71, 72, 182, 183, 187
3:609 — 121, 206, 209
3:615 — 71, 176, 182
3:617 — 71, 176, 182
3:618 — 71, 176, 182
3:619 — 71., 176, 182
3:622 — 72
3:631 — 147
3:654 — 72
3:655 — 71, 72, 176, 182, 186
3:657–70 — 71
3:657–84 — 209
3:728 — 221
3:729 — 221
3:754 — 120, 209

Strabo

Geographica
2.3.5 — 98
14.30 — 245

Suetonius

Divus Claudius
34.1–2 — 184

Domitianus
13 — 226

Vespasianus
15 — 282

Tacitus

Agricola
4 — 66

Annales
13.8.1 — 226
13.49 — 281
16.12 — 281
16.28 — 281, 282

Dialogus de oratoribus
20.5 — 152

Vergil

Aeneid
7.98–101 — 276

Inscriptions

CIL
3, Supp. 9973 — 285
2.01434 — 278, 284
5.01939 — 284
6.09785 — 276
6.33898 — 284, 297
6.38506 — 284
6.9784 — 276, 282, 285
6.9785 — 282, 283, 285
9.04840 — 284
10.5920 — 285
11.04485 — 284
11.6435 — 278, 284

Ephesos
1511 — 245
3041 — 285
3042 — 285

IDidyma
279 — 245
491 — 284

IG II²
1006 — 283

1099	284	**IG XII⁹**		**OGIS**	
1368	168	40	282	714	255
1369	168				
2472	285	**IG XIV**		**SEG**	
3571	284	674	245	4.661	284
3631	282	1618	284	25.1138	245
3796	282			27.798	284
3801	282, 284	**IGR I**		30.1627	245
8303	245	980	285	31.285	283, 286
10046a	278, 284	1013	285	40.1362	245
11551	282, 284			47.1757	284
		IGUR			
IG V		2.371	283		
1186.7–8	278, 284	3.1221	284	**SIG**	
				900 f.17	255
IG VI		**IKorinthKent**		985	168
3226	278	8.3.3	243		
				Smyrna	
IG VII		**IOlympia**		173	245
1676	303	453	282, 284, 285, 287		
3226	284				
3423	245	**IPrusaOlymp**		**TAM II**	
3425	278, 284	18	284	910	245
IG XII⁷		**ISardBR**		**TAM III**	
418	284	1355	284	882	245